THE AMERICAN STYLE

AMERICAN PROJECT SERIES
Center for International Studies
MASSACHUSETTS INSTITUTE OF TECHNOLOGY

THE AMERICAN STYLE ☆ Essays in Value and Performance

A REPORT ON THE DEDHAM CONFERENCE OF MAY 23–27, 1957

ELTING E. MORISON • *Editor*

Harper & Brothers, Publishers
New York

CONTENTS

PREFACE — vii
Max F. Millikan

PART I

AMERICAN ETHICS AND PUBLIC POLICY — 3
Abraham Kaplan

THEORY VERSUS PRACTICE IN AMERICAN VALUES
AND PERFORMANCE — 111
J. Robert Oppenheimer

AMERICA'S ADMINISTRATIVE RESPONSE TO ITS
WORLD PROBLEMS — 124
George F. Kennan

HAVE THERE BEEN DISCERNIBLE SHIFTS IN
AMERICAN VALUES DURING THE PAST GENERATION? — 145
Clyde Kluckhohn

INDIVIDUALITY — 218
Henry A. Murray

THE NATIONAL STYLE — 246
W. W. Rostow

PART II

LIST OF PARTICIPANTS

COMMENTARIES:

Elting E. Morison — 319
David M. Potter — 327
Richard M. Bissell, Jr. — 334
Richard Hofstadter — 353
David Riesman — 358

SELECTIONS OF TRANSCRIBED DISCUSSION — 369
THE COURSE OF DISCUSSION — 395
Elting E. Morison

INDEX — 417

v

Books From the Center for International Studies

PUBLISHED BY HARPER & BROTHERS

A PROPOSAL: *Key to an Effective Foreign Policy*
 by M. F. Millikan and W. W. Rostow

FORGING A NEW SWORD: *A Study of the Department of Defense*
 by William R. Kintner, with Joseph I. Coffey and Raymond J. Albright

THE AMERICAN STYLE: *Essays in Value and Performance*
 edited by Elting E. Morison

OTHER BOOKS FROM THE CENTER FOR INTERNATIONAL STUDIES

THE DYNAMICS OF SOVIET SOCIETY
 by W. W. Rostow, Alfred Levin, and Others, Norton, 1953; Mentor Books, 1954

THE PROSPECTS FOR COMMUNIST CHINA
 by W. W. Rostow and Others, Technology Press of MIT and John Wiley, 1954

NINE SOVIET PORTRAITS
 by Raymond A. Bauer and Edward Wasiolek, Technology Press of MIT and John Wiley, 1955

AN AMERICAN POLICY IN ASIA
 by W. W. Rostow and Richard W. Hatch, Technology Press of MIT and John Wiley, 1955

MOSCOW AND THE COMMUNIST PARTY OF INDIA
 by John H. Kautsky, Technology Press of MIT and John Wiley, 1956

FRANCE DEFEATS EDC
 by Daniel Lerner and Raymond Aron, Praeger, 1957. (Published as *La Querelle de la C.E.D.*, Armand Colin, Paris, 1956.)

THE ECONOMICS OF COMMUNIST EASTERN EUROPE
 by Nicolas Spulber, Technology Press of MIT and John Wiley, 1957

SOVIET EDUCATION FOR SCIENCE AND TECHNOLOGY
 by Alexander G. Korol, Technology Press of MIT and John Wiley, 1957

INDONESIA'S ECONOMIC STABILIZATION AND DEVELOPMENT
 by Benjamin Higgins, Institute of Pacific Relations, 1957

HANDBOOK FOR INDUSTRY STUDIES
 by Everett E. Hagen, Free Press, 1958

THE JAPANESE FACTORY: *Aspects of Its Social Organization*
 by James C. Abegglen, Free Press, 1958

SCRATCHES ON OUR MINDS: *American Images of China and India*
 by Harold R. Isaacs, John Day, 1958

CHANGING IMAGES OF AMERICA: *A Study of Indian Students' Perceptions*
 by George V. Coelho, Free Press, 1958

THE INFLATIONARY SPIRAL: *The Experience in China, 1939–1950*
 by Chang Kia Ngau, Technology Press of MIT and John Wiley, 1958

INDUSTRIAL CHANGE IN INDIA: *Industrial Growth, Capital Requirements, and Technological Change, 1937–1955*
 by George Rosen, Free Press, 1958

THE PASSING OF TRADITIONAL SOCIETY: *Modernizing the Middle East*
 by Daniel Lerner, with Lucille W. Pevsner, Free Press, 1958. (Co-sponsored by The Bureau of Applied Social Research, Columbia University.)

COMMUNIST CHINA'S GROSS NATIONAL PRODUCT, 1950–1957
 by William W. Hollister, Free Press, 1958

INDUSTRIAL GROWTH IN SOUTH INDIA: *Case Studies in Economic Development*
 by George B. Baldwin, Free Press, forthcoming

MARKETING IN AN UNDERDEVELOPED ECONOMY: *The North Indian Sugar Industry*
 by Leon Hirsch, Free Press, forthcoming

PREFACE

For the past seven years the Center for International Studies at M.I.T. has been conducting research on foreign areas designed to throw light on the more pressing foreign policy problems confronting the United States. Underlying these studies has been the implicit premise widely held in this country that the difficulties with which we are confronted in our international relations spring primarily from the nature and evolution of the foreign countries with which we deal—from the special characteristics of the Soviet system, from the revolutionary changes in China, from the political and economic upheavals in the underdeveloped countries, from the altered position and prospects of Europe.

As we have pursued studies in each of these fields we have been impressed anew with the fact that the characteristics of our own society are as important as developments abroad in determining the shape of our foreign relations. Again and again we have been forced to the conclusion that a more imaginative and constructive international performance by the United States is inhibited not so much by the intransigent forces outside our borders as by our values, by the way our government functions, by the American image of the world we live in, by our historically determined national style.

We therefore decided three years ago to launch a project explicitly focused on a fundamental re-examination of American society and institutions. We were fortunate enough to persuade W. W. Rostow to direct this study, and the Carnegie Corporation generously provided the necessary financial support. As one element in this project, officers of the Carnegie Corporation suggested that we hold a conference of persons with intimate knowledge of one or another aspect of the American scene

vii

in the hope that such a gathering might suggest new approaches to the analysis of contemporary America. The conference was held at Endicott House, Dedham, Massachusetts, May 23–27, 1957. This book contains the record of that conference.

The conference was planned by a committee consisting of McGeorge Bundy, Clyde Kluckhohn, Elting Morison, David Potter, W. W. Rostow, and Arthur Schlesinger, Sr. The themes which the conference was to take up were ones which Mr. Rostow had formulated at an early stage of his work as central to the project's task. The following issues were suggested to the participants and served to guide those who were asked to write background papers:

Theory versus practice in American values and performance. What are the origins of the acutely pragmatic national style and its consequences for American military and diplomatic performance and for the pattern of domestic life? How does this pragmatism relate to the American difficulty in dealing with foreign policy problems until they become full-blown crises? More generally, how does it relate to the costs and advantages of the traditional national premium on operations rather than staff functions, on engineering rather than basic science? To what extent has there been a significant change in the classical American pragmatic bias in the past twenty years?

American concepts of administration. Is the United States peculiarly committed to heavy, overmanned bureaucratic structures which reduce the potential values of individual talents and lead to greater inertia and a lesser rate of innovation than is required to deal successfully with the nation's domestic and foreign policy problems? How do Americans organize themselves when they face a problem of innovation and change? Is the American commitment to large-scale bureaucracy, with functions excessively specialized, in fact different from that of other modern societies?

The meaning and content of individuality in an increasingly bureaucratized and specialized society. To what extent is the maintenance of traditional American values compromised by current trends? What is the significance of the apparent obsession of American writers in recent years with the problem of the individual's relation to bureaucracy?

The manner in which the problem of good and evil is handled by

American society and its culture. What is the relation of ideology to power both in the articulation of foreign policy objectives and in actual American performance? How are ideal goals and special interests reconciled on the domestic scene? In what ways does the American method for dealing with this universal human problem differ from the methods of other societies and cultures?

The evolution of effective values within American society in the past twenty years. On balance, have Americans shifted their priorities away from the pursuit of material gain and personal power toward more private values, e.g., suburban living, more children, security, leisure? If so, what are the consequences of this shift for the American economy, the domestic political process, foreign policy?

These themes were expected to do no more than establish the framework for writing and debate. Each of the authors was, of course, left entirely free to deal with his subject in any way he saw fit. As is evident from the text, no effort was made to discipline the papers with respect to length, style, or interconnection. It was Mr. Rostow's task to write a paper interrelating these themes; his concept of the American national style emerged from that assignment.

In Part II an attempt is made to give some sense of the kind of conference discussion that grew out of the formal papers. The remarks made at any conference are probably never as good in retrospect as they appeared to be at the time to the people who made or listened to them. But enough of more than passing interest seems to us to have emerged in the conversation of these men to merit the effort to record a portion of the discussion for the benefit of those who may wish to probe beyond the papers. This summary includes replies to the formal papers, prepared in advance by certain members of the conference, excerpts taken from the transcribed discussion, and a brief summarizing description of the course of the whole three-day conversation.

June 1958   Max F. Millikan

PART I

AMERICAN ETHICS AND PUBLIC POLICY

by Abraham Kaplan

as freedom is a breakfast food
or truth can live with right and wrong
or molehills are from mountains made
—long enough and just so long
will being pay the rent of seem
e. e. cummings

INTRODUCTION

Nowadays a writer must begin by showing his credentials, especially if he is writing on such things as morality and politics. The reader's psyche, its integrity threatened by an unceasing flow of news, news behind the news, analysis, interpretation, admonition, and appeal, has come to a system of security regulations for its own defense: no ideas admitted without appropriate clearance. It does not matter that the credentials will receive only a cursory glance or that, if scrutinized, they can be distinguished from the counterfeit only with the greatest difficulty. The important thing is to have the talisman. A writer who begins by announcing his viewpoint not only disarms suspicion, but may even find that he is taken at his own word. And if the announcement includes his presuppositions, frames of reference, and (holy name!) methodology, scarcely anything more need be said; success with the reader is assured. Americans love frankness, and a freely admitted fault is almost better than unvarying virtue. Academically, remission of sin needs only confession, not penance.

But there *is* an academic sin which cannot be forgiven, the sin against specialization. Every writer must be an expert, and every expert must write only on his own specialty—unless, to be sure, there has been ritual expiation by communion in an interdisciplinary project. Each expert thereby partakes mystically of the expertness of all the rest, and the failings of each become the virtues of all. But setting out alone, as I am, I approach the reader burdened with a presumption of guilt. Is this

3

an essay in the history of ideas? I am not a historian. Does it purport to
delineate American culture or to categorize American politics? I am
neither sociologist nor political scientist. If the essay deals with matters
of fact at all, where are my surveys, polls, and interviews, my tables and
graphs, clinical observations, and experimental results? And if it presents
only relations of ideas, where are my postulates, definitions, demonstrations? If it does neither, must it not be committed to Humean flames
as sophistry and illusion?

Alas, it does neither—and both; responsive, I hope, to fact, and contributing, as I hope again, to a clearer conceptualization of fact. Yet
not limited to these, but setting out also what I prize and condemn—
judgments of value where I have succeeded, and caprice or crotchet
masquerading as judgment where I have failed. And more too: what is
praised or censured is so presented as to invite like-mindedness; and perhaps even fragments of a metaphysics of man and nature strategically
placed to hide the nakedness of personal valuation. How each sentence
in what follows is to be classed in these categories—or perhaps in categories more felicitous though less commendable—I leave to others. If I
must bear the responsibility for such bastard discourse, why then, I
suppose I must. A man cannot moralize for others and expect to go
scot free himself.

Here is a reason for demanding credentials of a writer on morals
and politics. There can be today no moral ventriloquism, no speaking
for a pretended consensus or with a mock authority that deceives no one.
The reader wants to know, and rightly, whom he can hold responsible;
the critic wants the address of next of kin. The fact is that there are
specialists in morality, too; the American division of labor is detailed and
thorough. There are priests, social workers, and psychiatrists. There are
administrators of moral codes for industries and professions. There are
even associations organized to promote and defend the moral decencies.
There are, indeed, so many experts of this breed that their very number
makes identification all the more imperative. Morality is relative to the
person of the moralizer. Relativity is the great Boyg around which
contemporary ethics cannot go, subjectivity the Mountain King.

To theorize about values—so runs the tale—is scarcely more than
to rationalize the moralities (or lack of them) that we have bound to
our Gyntish selves, and the sovereignties to which we have vowed alle-

giance by submitting to a nick of the eyeball. If thereafter, we squint, we can all the more easily share with Rousseau the joy of discovering in our researches on government new reasons for loving that of our own country, with Kant the awe at the grandeur of the moral law which we ourselves have given to ourselves, and with Hegel the confidence that our state is the highest embodiment of universal reason that history has as yet unfolded.

But theorizing is not to be trusted; in the perversity of too much cleverness, what if we were to find reasons for skepticism? Cotton Mather records in his diary that "the employing of so much time upon Ethics in our colleges" is not only "very unwise," but indeed, "a vile 'Piece of Paganism,'"[1] and Charles Peirce, closer by half to our day than to Mather's, observes that "nothing makes a man so much of a scoundrel as a prolonged study of ethics." To be sure, writers on America have not distinguished themselves for dwelling on whatever things are lovely and of good report—with the occasional exceptions of some "intellectuals" who have wished to dissociate themselves from that dissociated class. We must look on the good as well as on the bad, neither in self-justification nor as sitting in judgment on others, but because the good is the only resource by which the bad can be transformed.

But "good" and "bad"—is this not still to say, my good and bad? There is no help for it, I must identify myself: by training a positivist, by inclination a pragmatist, in temperament a mystic, in practice a Democrat; my faith Jewish, educated by the Catholics, an habitual protestant; born in Europe, raised in the Midwest, hardened in the East, and softened once more in California; psychoanalyzed, naturalized, denatured—in short, an American academician.

Most American, perhaps, in the respects in which I am most aberrant; for America is so multiple, so varied and vast, that only the deviant is truly representative. On the morals of politics there are not two parties but hundreds, differing in region and religion, caste and class, ethnic origin and personal destination. If we were to blur these differences by appealing to a "national character," that would but be, as Max Weber warned, "a mere confession of ignorance."[2] Yet the mind must have its universals, subsuming the many under an abstract unity. "Of course the one American I speak of," Santayana confesses, "is mythical; but to speak in parables is inevitable in such a subject, and it is perhaps as well to do so frankly." [3] In such a subject, perhaps the speaker himself is inevitably something of a parable.

I ask, then, of this mythical American, what is his way of good and evil? what he does, his morals; what he says or thinks he does, his moral code; the theories and principles with which he justifies or rationalizes both, his ethics; and, of course, what he *should* do and why he should do it, *my* code and ethics but also, in intention at least, my judgment of a truth that lies outside me.

But in such questions to link morals with politics might be thought to be yoking together an ox and an ass—morality is one thing, political action another. Not so. Morality covers the area of prizing of the human personality, in the self and in others, and its province is as wide as all action bearing on man's worth—which is to say, as wide as all man does. Political morality is not a matter only of bribery and corruption, fraud and venality, or their absence. It is not a private possession making from time to time a public appearance when the private citizen holds public office. It is intrinsic to all policy whose decisions significantly affect the value placed on things human. Public morality is the morality of public policy.

In what follows I try to sketch an experimental basis for this morality. While insisting on the historical importance for American democracy of religious doctrines and the metaphysics of "natural rights," I reject the widespread assumptions that without such transcendent faiths the belief in democracy is untenable, and that the future of democracy therefore rests on a "spiritual" revival. On the contrary, I am persuaded that the divorce of the spirit from the matter of daily experience itself endangers moral values. It is in this dualism of transcendent ideals and earthly expediences that I localize the degradation of our political life. What is needed is not more idealism, but more realistic ideals; not exhortations to an abstract virtue, but support of concrete measures for the betterment of specific situations.

In this perspective I also criticize moral absolutism, the pretense that the right and the good are unequivocal and certain, and that they are realizable in every case by unswerving adherence to high principle. Yet the rejection of absolutism still allows, as I hope, a place for principled action, and even for moral heroism. Only, I have urged that it is not principles themselves on which morality requires a firm stand, but rather the concrete values to which moral principles are instrumental. Our democracy has assumed too defensive a posture. Because we are determined not to take the offensive in a military sense, we tend to withdraw from the ideological offensive as well.[4] We underplay the positive content of democratic values; national defense becomes the substance of national ideals. The Oxford don who was asked during the First World War what he was contributing to the war effort replied, "Sir, I represent the civilization you are fighting to preserve." Events may have proved him mistaken; but only in his identification of the ends sought, not in his insistence that for a democracy military superiority cannot be an end in itself. I want to redirect attention from the communist threat to the democratic values that are threatened.

The moral failings with which I charge our political life are, I suppose, somewhat less in actuality than I may make them out to be, in defense of my own emotional investments. I must rely on the reader to introduce whatever corrections seem to him to yield a more balanced assessment. Undoubtedly the cultural lag from which philosophy inevitably suffers will have made my account somewhat anachronistic—less true of America today than it might have been a few years ago. Certainly a recent series of decisions in the federal courts, as well as various acts of Congress and Executive orders, mark a significant revitalization of our political morality. Were I to enlarge the frame in which I am here picturing American life so as to include other patterns than the narrowly political, my somber coloring would surely need to be brightened; the politics of conformism, for example, by no means implies a corresponding conformity in all the details of personal life, at any rate in the perspectives of a Californian!

Yet the passion for accuracy in every detail might properly be forced to yield to other passions. However comforting it might be, I cannot find it in myself to believe in a pre-established harmony between the true and the good. Discords between what values project as facts and what facts hold up as values recur over and over again, and must be resolved over and over again. Such resolutions are the very stuff of the moral life, and how to achieve them provides the terms in which every moral problem is posed. I make no claim that my account of American public policy is wholly true or that my ideal for American ethics is wholly good. But I am convinced that even a fragmentary truth may find its uses for a greater good.

METAPHYSICAL FOUNDATIONS OF AMERICAN VALUES

An interconnection of morals and politics has characterized ethical theory from the outset: whether because, as in Plato, the state is the individual writ large; or because, as with Aquinas, it has a moral aim; whether it is the source of morality, as for Hobbes; guided by a moral principle, as in the utilitarians' conception; or serves as the instrumentality for morals, as the pragmatists have it. In one way or another, theorists have persistently linked public and private morality.

Even more, they have urged that some ethical theory or other lies at the basis of political practice. They have looked into politics and, being philosophers, have found therein—a philosophy. On the political arena they have traced the outlines of their own shadows. So today there is much pretentious talk to the effect that the issues we face are at bottom metaphysical issues, that our political uncertainties reflect epistemological confusion, that world peace is attainable only through a world philosophy. In this respect, at any rate, American hard-headedness and practicality is largely a myth. There is widespread veneration for abstract "principles," philosophical foundations, some bedrock on which social policy can be firmly grounded. In a culture where values are not experienced as "given," there is a felt need for philosophical justifications. Armed with a philosophy, a man can feel doubly secure. The incantation has its own efficacy; should it fail, the pundits will provide him with more powerful wizardry. It is comforting to know that such assistance is available for the asking; being a sage is also a specialty at the service of the public.

But the claims that each philosophy makes for itself are significantly weakened by the counterclaims made by conflicting philosophies. For Walter Lippmann, liberal democracy is "unworkable" save by adherence to the philosophy of natural law in which it was conceived and founded. But Croce, being an idealist, finds that it is idealism "which is one with the liberal concept of life," and to be contrasted with "naturalism, positivism, and scientific principles, all associated with the authoritarian concepts or leading to them." On the other hand, Dewey is convinced of "the undoubted historic fact that the whole modern liberal social and

political movement has allied itself with philosophic empiricism."
Maritain is certain that only Catholic Christianity can justify a belief
in the democratic charter; and a recent European analyst of the psychology of democracy and dictatorship finds in some type of neo-
Kantianism "one of the most adequate expressions, at the philosophical
level, of the cultural climate of democracy." [5] Can it be that only some
happy few stand firm in their democratic convictions, while the rest
have built on sand?

That there is *some* connection between underlying philosophies and
political practice need not be doubted—philosophies *do* matter. The
question now is whether the connection is a logical one. Can we speak
here of "basic premises"? Is the truth of the philosophy a necessary or
even sufficient condition for the truth or rightness of the politics which
appeals to it? No. The so-called "premises" serve instead as idols of the
theater or, in the current idiom, as defense mechanisms, deflecting responsibility from the citizen to a system, rationalizing personal choice as
the logical outcome of shared principles. Concrete policy can be deduced from abstract philosophy only if the latter is rich in normative
ambiguity, so that it can be taken in one reading as a truth of man and
nature, and in another as formulating a norm of good and evil. With
such equivocation in the premises, questions of policy can be gracefully
begged.

Charles Stevenson has described the technique of "persuasive definition" so often applied to this end.[6] If Hegelian principles define "freedom" as obedience to the state, lovers of freedom can be given reasons
for such obedience; and what is distressing, such reasons may be most
effective. What *leads* to belief, and thereby action, is a very different
thing from what *entails* belief. The range of policies to which a principle may lead and which it is believed to justify is limited in practice
only by the skills of the ideologue and by the predispositions of his
audience. Dostoevski's Grand Inquisitor was able to "prove" that he
was acting entirely on the principles of his Prisoner; if we remain un-
convinced, it is not because we reject the premises or because we detect
a *non sequitur*, but because we are no longer mediaevals.

If abstract principles are not logically sufficient, for concrete policy,
neither are they politically necessary. The United Nations Universal
Declaration of Human Rights was subscribed to by representatives of

Vedanta and positivism, Buddhism and pragmatism, Christianity and neo-Confucianism. Was only one, at most, consistent? In his introduction to the UNESCO volume on *Human Rights*, Maritain writes: "If both believed in the democratic charter, a Christian and a rationalist would still give mutually incompatible justifications for their belief. . . . And God forbid that I should say that it does not matter to know which of the two is right! It matters essentially. The fact remains that, on the practical expression of this charter they are in agreement and can formulate together common principles of action." [7] It is this fact which is of the first importance: that there can be agreement on policy without agreement on what is called "the underlying philosophy." But if such agreement extends throughout the entire range of policy affected by the philosophies, if the two are at one in all their "practical expressions," I find it hard to see why the difference makes any difference at all, to say nothing of an "essential" one.

As a matter of political and psychological fact, it is absurd to argue that values cannot be preserved if their "metaphysical basis" is repudiated. And as a matter of logic, the argument is trivial, for the "basis" can be nothing other than a statement of the values themselves transposed into a metaphysical key. Confusion here, as Sidney Hook has often pointed out, incurs the penalty of putting ideological obstacles in the way of agreement on the plane of action. And in some quarters it may provide a rationale for thought control on behalf of that ultimate absurdity: an "official" philosophy of democracy.

Has philosophy, then, come to this, that those who profess it do so only to proclaim its futility? Not at all! Futile only as a body of ultimate truths from which values are to be deduced; indispensable as a loosely knit texture of perspectives within which action finds meaning, both as significance and as worth. What matters is the philosophy lived by, commitment as well as conceptualization. And that philosophy, what makes for each man his experience intelligible and his life worth while, is not an abstract doctrine but a part of all that he has met. It is a product of the whole of culture and character—all the institutions which shape his actions, all the habits which canalize them, all the impulses which give them substance: in science, religion, art, industry, and in politics as well. The search for a philosophy of politics is a search, not just for ultimate premises, but for conclusions, too. And perhaps most

of all, it is for those inferential links by which each man can fasten together all he knows and loves and bind it to the fabric of his life among
other men. Such a search no man can carry out for another, and what is
found answers only to his own seeking. In America, three main paths
have been followed: through a social religion, through moral intuition,
and through empirical science. I shall consider them in turn.

It is not to be forgotten that the liberty in which this nation was
conceived was in important measure a religious liberty. To be sure, the
Thanksgiving ritual is not altogether a paradigm of Colonial history;
but the airy fancies of the folk myth are no more fanciful than the stony
mythology of economic determinism. Economic, political, social forces
—what you will; but the religious impulse, too, played its part, and it
was more than an off-stage voice. The liberty sought, it is true, was often
for a single sect, and that one's own; the victim of Old World intolerance sometimes, alas, avenged himself in the New. Yet toleration spread,
and though sectarian faith, as the orthodox had feared, was thereby
weakened, in the aggregate it waxed great. The number of denominations in America today is to be counted, not in the dozens, but in the
hundreds.

Church membership, however, may owe more to the fact that we are
a nation of joiners than to our being a fellowship of the devout. Yet on
the American political scene religion is prominent far beyond any
measure of churched and unchurched citizens. Particularly is this true
of political symbolism, Merriam's "miranda" of politics.[8] Within the
last decade our oath of allegiance proclaimed us to be one nation "under
God"; our coinage has long reposed its trust in the treasures laid up in
Heaven as well as in the Federal Reserve; our Congress enters upon its
deliberations only after assurance that its proceedings will be viewed
with interest from heights even above the press galleries. And a recent
distinguished statesman is perhaps less likely to be remembered for his
legislative wisdom than because, known to have had presidential aspirations, he died speaking the words: "I had rather be a servant in the
house of the Lord than sit in the seats of the mighty."

To suppose that in politics all this is no more than rhetoric is to
forget that in government by discussion politics is a manner of speaking.
If a candidate for office cannot risk publicly dissociating himself from
religion, something of political importance is involved. Even if candi-

date and electorate alike are pretending to a concern neither feels, a genuine force is at work to maintain the pretence. How great this force is has been attested to innumerably: Bryce and Myrdal, separated by more than half a century, are able to agree in the flat assessment that religion is probably more influential in America than in any other country.[9]

And its influence is not a matter of symbols only, however important these may be, but a matter of practices as well. American religion is not mystic and monastic, but follows the social gospel. It may recoil from humanism in its faith, but its works are frankly humanitarian. Unlike what has happened in many theocentric or transcendental religions of Europe and Asia, here moral values have become at least as significant for the church as distinctively spiritual ones. Perhaps this marks the substitution of a moral faith for a religious one. At any rate, the consequence is that for many Americans religion is indeed something to live by. In the last century, three of the major churches split on the issue of slavery; today, integration marks another area of religious relevance.[10] Yet it is not merely an easy cynicism which notes the disparity between creed and performance.

Not just action, but the perspectives in which action acquires significance, what I called the working philosophies, bear in America the unmistakable marks of religious patterns. Bryce goes so far as to say that "the prevalence of evangelical Protestantism has been quite as important a factor in the intellectual life of the nation as its form of government." [11] Certainly the dominant American philosophies, idealism and pragmatism, are both indeed evangels, bearers of glad tidings, holding out the promise of salvation by resolute loyalty to ideal purposes. The story is that when Emerson Hall was built at Harvard to house the philosophy department, James proposed for it the inscription, "Man is the measure of all things"; but he was overruled by his colleague, Royce, who countered with, "What is man that Thou art mindful of him?" Both agreed, however, in seeing man as the locus of vast potentialities, and the world as limitless in its possibilities for good. These are the perspectives of American religion, and of American politics as well.

In such perspectives, political values are put on a spiritual basis, political morality is objectified as a product of divine will. Liberty is God-given, equality is the leveling of man in the eyes of God, fraternity is God's injunction to love our neighbor. "Can the liberties of a nation be thought to be secure when we have removed their only firm basis, a conviction in the minds of the people that their liberties are the gift of God?" This question was asked, not by a minister of the church, but by Thomas Jefferson. Statesmen join with the ministry in deriving social legislation from the words of Job: "If I did despise the cause of my man-servant, or of my maid-servant, when they contended with me— what then shall I do when God rises up? . . . Did not He that made me make him? And did not one God fashion us both?" [12] The brotherhood of man is annually deduced in every pulpit from the common fatherhood of God.

Such deductions signify more than homiletic embellishment. The classic postulates of democratic theory affirm the existence of an objective difference between good and evil, and the capacity of every citizen to distinguish them and to choose freely between them. The religious philosophies account for the difference by reference to a divine order, and for the capacity to distinguish and choose by reference to conscience and free will. The dependence of democracy on religion in America is not, as is sometimes argued, that democracy lives only by the faith in it of its citizens, and faith is all of a piece. Such talk, equivocating on "faith," establishes connections of fact only by obscuring distinctions of meaning. Only verbal trickery can identify the weakening of a faith in God with a loss of that faith in man that democracy calls for. The point is that religion in America, or the dominant Protestantism at any rate, insists that man is in no need of humanly authoritative guidance and help to find the truth and thereby to attain the good. It is this insistence that constitutes the democratic faith: that men are not so depraved, so ignorant, or so helpless as not to be trusted with the making of their own lives. The reliance that each individual may put in his own conscience in matters of religion is easily generalized to a political individualism. The inviolability of each man's firmness in the right as God gives him to see the right finds its counterpart in the dignity of the free citizen as the source and not just the subject of state authority.

Thus a religious man, committed to democratic values, can interpret them in religious terms, and in America has usually done so. But religious beliefs alone cannot compel him to such values. That men are equal in the eyes of God does not of itself entail that they must be so in the eyes of the state: earthly inequalities may be among those things which the faithful must render unto Caesar. The church which prizes the dignity of each man's soul may call upon the secular arm to destroy his body for the sake of his soul. In human history deprivation of life and liberty, to say nothing of interference with the pursuit of happiness, has been justified rather more often by appeal to divine law than by reference solely to a civil order.[13] The relation between political morality and religious faith is not that either can be deduced from the other, but that, in man's urge toward coherent and comprehensive perspectives of action, both political aspirations and religious ideals are shaped and strengthened by the realms of value disclosed in the other.

I do not see, therefore, that democratic conclusions can be denied, as a matter either of logic or of psychology, to those who reject the religious premises from which some persons mistakenly suppose such conclusions to be derived. It is said that Bertrand Russell, in a public lecture at Cooper Union, was once asked, "Lord Russell, how do you account for the fact that, though all men were created equal, there is so much injustice in the world?" To which he promptly replied, "Well, you see, I don't believe that men were created at all!" The religious premise carries with it only a religious conclusion, not a political one; and a morality is entailed by it only when the morality has been presupposed.

But such a presupposition can as easily be secular as sacred. If we must first believe men to be created equal in order to justify the ideal of political equality, can we not just as well believe to start with that men are equal in their own nature, and thus base our political ethics on a natural rather than a supernatural order? In American thought this alternative has been an even more influential conception of the ground of value, for both man and the state, than the purely religious one. Explicitly formulated, it constitutes the theory of natural rights and natural law.

Some such theory has played a part in many of the world's great religious philosophies. By it, religion is naturalized, and the supernatural projected onto the face of nature as a principle of cosmic order. The Law of Heaven reaches down into life on earth as the injunction to maintain this order. The tao of Chinese philosophy, dharma in Indian thought, the torah of the Hebrews, and ananke of the Greeks are from this point of view variations on a single theme. In all, moral obligation and natural necessity are fused into a conception of a system of nature which accommodates both facts and values. Fundamentally, the principle of value lies in the orderliness of the facts: when all is in place, the outcome is a cosmic equilibrium reflected in man's mind as the idea of justice. Wrongdoing is an upsetting of the balance, a departure from the path on which alone righteousness lies.

Such a system of nature may find its political counterpart in a fixed social order, a hierarchy of positions each of which carries a determinate set of rights and duties. Crime and sin coincide as *hubris*, not knowing one's place. Natural law here becomes the ideology of conservatism and absolutism, as in Aquinas and Hobbes. The violation of the natural order, so conceived, was the basis of Greek tragedy. But as the fixities of the social order are dissolved, such violations may become the matter of comedy. The tragic victim of fate in Sophocles gives way in Shaw to the comic hero who disregards social roles.

For the system of nature may be thought to be reflected, not in society as such, but in the microcosm of the individual mind. In this perspective, shared rationality binds men together in universal brotherhood, while endowing each individual with inviolable rights grounded in his own rational nature. Such a philosophy lends itself to a liberal society where obligations are freely contracted by each individual, not deduced from a preassigned status. This is the conception of natural law running through the Stoics, Spinoza, Locke, and thence to the founders of the American republic.

The objective difference between good and evil called for by the religionist is here provided in a more economical metaphysics by the natural order. Governments exist to secure the rights which by nature belong to the governed; political morality consists in the scrupulous acknowledgment of these rights. The Declaration of Independence demands for the American people only "the separate and equal station to which the Laws of Nature and of Nature's God entitle them." In the same vein, though not so explicitly, the preamble of the Universal Declaration of Human Rights adopted by the General Assembly of the United Nations affirms that "recognition of the inherent [sic] dignity and of the equal and inalienable [sic] rights of all members of the human family is the foundation of freedom, justice and peace in the world." And Article One lays it down that "all human beings are born [sic] free and equal in dignity and rights." Natural law, though not a premise for the deduction of political rights, is in America and throughout the contemporary world an acknowledged platform of political aspiration to such rights.[14]

The theory of natural rights, in its modern setting, can be understood as an extension of the religious right of emancipation from institutional authority. "Every man his own priest" leads easily to the principle of "every man a king." The primacy of the individual conscience, read out into nature as an objectified system of norms, accounts for the distinctive traits of the law of nature. Natural law is self-evident as a deliverance of moral intuition, irrevocable as sharing in the binding force of a self-imposed moral obligation, universal as the moral standard which is applied to the self only as holding for all men everywhere. Natural law is not the ground of political morality but its projective expression.

For the "nature" of the theory is not the nature disclosed to empirical inquiry, but what is identified as "natural" in the sense of conforming to a norm externally imposed. Is it "natural" for a mother to deprive her children, or a ruler his loyal subjects, of their lives and liberties? Such things *have* been done. Nature as the totality of observed and observable fact includes the violation of every "natural right" and "natural law" that political theorists have laid down. The "nature" of the theory is only what answers to the norms of the theorizer; it is these norms, not nature herself, from which the political rights are derived. "A great multitude of people are continually talking of the Law of Nature," Bentham observes, "and then they go on giving you their sentiments about what is right and wrong; and these sentiments, you are to understand, are so many chapters and sections of the Law of Nature." [15] We who condemn despotism and injustice must ourselves assume the responsibility for the code of political morality by which we judge them to be damnable.

The whole apparatus of natural law adds nothing to the moral content of our politics, but only changes its form of expression. Beginning with whatever code of political rights and duties our needs and knowledge, traditions and experience have produced, we covertly construct from it a system of natural law, present this as objective in origin and universal in application, then triumphantly derive from it the rights and duties with which we started. The futility of such logic was clearly seen by Hume: ". . . How fruitless it is to . . . seek in the laws of nature a stronger foundation for our political duties than interest and human conventions, while these laws (the laws of nature) themselves are built on the very same foundation." We walk this circle only because, if it be sufficiently great, we can return convinced that we stand at the still point of the turning world. Rights to be defended as our ideals and secured through our efforts can then be seen as antecedently guaranteed, absolute and fixed in the nature of things. Such a conviction may indeed produce a show of courage: with a stacked deck a man will stake everything. But when we are challenged by competing absolutes, the courage called for must have deeper roots, or it will vanish.

Of itself, then, natural law has no definite content; the morality it proclaims is the product of moral intuition, not of metaphysical deduction. Now the fact is that intuitions differ. However much we may insist that what is intuited is a law outside the self, as fixed in its own character as are the principles of science and mathematics discerned by sense and reason, the question still remains which of several conflicting moralities has properly intuited its object. And this question intuition alone cannot answer, but can only beg. If conscience speaks to each man the word of the one God, what a pity she speaks in so many different tongues! Indeed, when it comes to conscience, a man may fail to understand even his native accents. The oracle must perforce speak in riddles when the God within is himself of two minds.

Moreover, the law of nature claims to rest on what is innate in man, not on what is imposed or withheld by merely human institutions. But habit becomes second nature, and natural law must inevitably change as men become habituated to changed institutions. Moral sensibility is notoriously capable of being blunted: vice, we have been warned, may be first endured, then pitied, then embraced. An all-powerful state need not fear the moral intuitions of its citizenry; it can shape these intuitions to its own ends, as a succession of modern novelists have pictured with fearful realism. It is easy to see how natural law may be made matter for indoctrination; not so easy to conceive of a process of education of the faculty on which its recognition depends, without presupposing the infallibility of the educator.

In sum, we need not wonder that in American history natural rights and natural law have been argued on behalf of the most diverse policies: by Federalists and anti-Federalists, slaveholders and abolitionists, reformers and reactionaries. For the "nature" appealed to was not given in experience, but imposed on experience to accord with pre-determined values. "The views held regarding human nature," John Dewey has observed, "were those appropriate to the purposes and policies a given group wanted to carry through. . . . What passed as psychology was a branch of political doctrine." [16] And the same is true of what passed as the metaphysics of political morality.

EMPIRICAL FOUNDATIONS OF AMERICAN VALUES

The theory of natural law has content only in association with some specific political doctrine, a set of values determining, in a concrete situation, a concrete social policy. But if the theory does not give these values a metaphysical ground, it does put them in a special class. In calling rights "natural" it makes for them a claim quite out of the ordinary. Can we interpret this claim in empirical rather than metaphysical terms? Can natural rights be truly naturalized, made all of a piece with the stuff of concrete experience? I believe they can; and what is more, I believe that in American history the theory has largely been used in this empirical sense. Perhaps we should say that we have here, not one conception of political ethics, but two, finding expression in the same words. It is an axiom of practical semantics that not words but uses determine meanings. Talk of "natural" rights does not of itself commit politics to a transcendent metaphysics, just as talk of "experience" does not make politics genuinely empirical.

What, then, might be meant, in terms of everyday experience, by calling a right "natural"? Surely, that it is in some sense a fundamental right, of prime importance, basic to other rights. This would not be true of a right resulting from some special agreement—I mean a real agreement, not the myth of a social contract. Such a right would be enjoyed only by the parties to the agreement and would be subject to the conditions set by the terms of the agreement. To call a right "natural" is to characterize it as presupposed by agreements, like the right to expect agreements to be kept. It is to characterize it as not dependent on any voluntary act of the claimant to the right or indeed of any person whatever. There is a legend that at the moment of birth there is revealed to

each soul its fate on earth, and the soul is offered a final choice of remaining in its heavenly home. In sober fact there is no such choice; as
the wag has it, it is much better never to have been born at all. But not
one man in ten thousand has such luck. A right is "natural," not as
literally innate, a concomitant of birth, but as not acquired by subsequent choice. Man, if he is free at all, must be born free, for he could
not choose freedom unless first he were free to choose.

But could not freedom be conferred on him from without? This, too,
is just what is denied in placing freedom among the natural rights. A
right is "natural" rather than "conventional" in the sense of belonging
to a man in his own capacity and not as related to other men. But this
need not mean that natural law is outside of and antecedent to society,
as Hobbes argued; outside some human relatedness there are no men at
all. It may mean, rather, in the spirit of Locke, that such law is basic to
social living, that it is the fundamental law, that it provides, in a word,
what Americans call the Constitution for the society. The metaphysical
interpretation stands the logic of experience on its head. Natural rights
are not specified in a constitution because they are natural; they are
natural because a constitution specifies them.

Of course, it is not a written constitution that is in question here.
Americans put altogether too much weight on the written word. What
matters is the complex of predispositions and practices that are expressed
in and sustained by constitutional formulae. And these patterns of valuation and action come to this: that politics is subordinate to morals.
Political enactments are subject to moral appraisal, not the other way
about. The appeal to natural law is a reminder that politics is not
autonomous: human law must justify itself before the bar of natural
justice. What is important is not that this standard is "natural" in some
metaphysical sense, but that it is not political in the plain everyday
sense. One of the cartoons of this century shows a helpless citizen being
beaten by a thug in a storm trooper's uniform; the caption reads: "Yuh
want da police? I'm da police!" The theory of natural law, in its experiential meaning, amounts to the insistence, not that there *is*, in a
world of pure idea, but that there *ought* to be, on this bloody earth,
another court of appeal. The metaphysics of "nature" ontologizes ideals,
and takes "ought" for "is" to escape a painful "should."

The rights of nature are inalienable because in calling them "natural" we express our determination not to *allow* their alienation. The belief in natural law is a tissue of commitment to other men, but even more to our moral selves. The "nature" appealed to is not the object of a cognition from which a valuation is deduced, but is itself made up of what is valued. The "laws of nature" have always been closely linked with "nature's God," and in the religious idiom, to know God is not other than to love Him, and those who deny Him live in a hell of their own making, for they deny themselves.

As I read Spinoza and the Stoics, this is the great insight in their appeal to nature. Freedom is of man's essence, for only one who is already sunk in human bondage can agree not to be his own master. You may put my body in prison, but not me, says Epictetus; he did not conceive of the power of the modern totalitarian state to imprison men's minds as well. Yet somehow he was right: God made men upright even though they have sought out many inventions. It is this truth of man's own makeup that the theory of natural rights obliquely expresses. One who is truly free owes his freedom to no man.

But he *does* owe to others something of the self which, in its maturity, achieves such freedom. Here, I think, is the root error of romantic individualism. Rousseau proclaims, in the opening words of his *Social Contract*, that "man is born free yet he is everywhere in chains." But man is individuated only in society. What is born is a cluster of potentialities, and societies allow now some, now others, to reach actuality. If we are to speak of birth literally, Aristotle is more consistent in holding some men born to be masters and others slaves. We say in America that freedom is an "inalienable" right in the insistence that it is *this* potentiality in all men which is to become actual. But the insistence is ours, not nature's, and it acquires meaning in experience only as we have the courage and wisdom to imitate "nature" in our social arts. The Declaration which begins with an appeal to the law of nature ends with a pledge of lives, fortunes, and sacred honor.

Natural rights, then, are an achievement, not a heritage. It is the blunting of this point in the attempt to justify these values by referring them to a basis in "nature" which is a danger to democratic values. But once it is recognized that endless vigilance and courage are needed to secure these rights, the question of how they are to be justified is of no great moment. It gives way, instead, to the question of how they are to be known: their truth will appear in their verification. And the fact is that, whatever their source, they are known only in experience. Correspondingly, it is by reference to their outcome, not to their origins, that we judge them.

The founders of the American republic, sons of the Enlightenment, spoke the language of their century, and that was the language of "nature." But the doctrine they spoke in that language was in significant degree an empirical one. "Experienec is the oracle of truth; and where its responses are unequivocal, they ought to be conclusive and sacred." These are the words, not of a doctrinaire empiricist, but of Hamilton and Madison, in No. XX of the *Federalist Papers*. Jefferson over and over again speaks of this government as "an experiment." And the Declaration of Independence, having laid against British rule the charge of an absolute tyranny, concludes its opening paragraphs with the sentence, "To prove this, let Facts be submitted to a candid world"— facts, not dialectical reasonings or deliverances of intuition. And, indeed, it continues with twenty-seven paragraphs detailing specific wrongs and injuries which justify the declared separation. The natural right of the people is a right to institute a government founded "on such principles . . . as to them shall seem most likely to effect their Safety and Happiness." Such a likelihood can ultimately be grounded only in experience.

But does this say anything more than that experience dictates the choice of means for given ends? Experience may show that separation is necessary to the "safety and happiness" of the American colonies; can it show that the colonists have a right to these things? It will not do to argue, as the utilitarians did, that "right" and "good" mean nothing more than this. To argue in this way is to be guilty of what G. E. Moore called the "naturalistic fallacy." Unless words like "happiness" are so construed as to be completely empty (and they often are!), we can always ask, but is the pursuit of that *particular* happiness morally right? For democracy makes a particular claim: it defines the aim of the state, not as the welfare of a race, nation, or class, but as the happiness of its individual citizens. And *this* end cannot in turn be justified by a definition.

An empirical theory of value must hold that ends as well as means are empirically judged. This is the position expounded in American life most influentially by John Dewey.[17] Every valuation is grounded in an evaluation; we are justified in prizing only what emerges as worthy from an empirical appraisal. The injunctions of morality cannot be divided, as Kant assumed, into hypothetical imperatives and categorical imperatives. At bottom they are all hypothetical, and only experience can warrant the presumed connection between hypothetical antecedent and enjoined consequent.

On this view, moral imperatives can be intelligently arrived at and maintained only after full exposure—directly, or mediated by transmitted knowledge—to facts concerning the conditions and consequences of the values involved. To be sure, such imperatives, serving as norms of action, are not propositional in form, and so cannot be certified as true, whether on an experiential basis or on any other. But American philosophy today avails itself of a technique known as the *method of coordination*. To each imperative there is coordinated a set of declarative propositions, and it is the truth of these propositions that provides the basis for the imperative. It cannot be denied that on the contemporary philosophic scene so-called "cognitivists" and "emotivists" differ from one another on the question whether the coordination exhausts the content of the norm. Does the imperative also have a noncognitive "emotive meaning," or does its cognitive content leave a residue only of a normative use? But more and more it is coming to be felt that the significance of this difference has been exaggerated by academic debate, a fruitless polemic in the name of labels and schools. There is widespread agreement that, whether in the last analysis or only penultimately, facts are of overriding relevance to values.

What truth attaches to a moral norm? By what coordination can it be given cognitive meaning? There is first its *reflexive* sense, that those who enjoin the imperative are themselves committed to the values it holds out. The values of a propagandist are false because they are insincere, insincere not as a matter of individual psychology but of political commitment. A master morality is false because it serves only to create a population of docile slaves: *thou* shalt, but not *I* will. And whether a morality is reflexively true is a question of fact, though the fact be hard to come by when minds are corrupted and the incorruptible are silenced.

There is second the *derived* cognitive meaning of implicit hypotheticals, that adequacy of means to ends which justifies the normative use of the categorical. We make one choice rather than another because of the consequences experience has led us to expect—consequences on character and personality, to be sure, as well as on the material world, but consequences rooted in experience nevertheless. The necessity of the moral law is at bottom the ineluctability of fact. We must, because, the world being what it is, we have no choice. Nature, to be commanded, must be obeyed, and obedience to the moral law is the condition of power over such values as life affords.

And there is third the *extended* cognitive meaning of a moral imperative which consists in the fittingness to its object of the attitude and emotion expressed by it. To value something is to take up a certain attitude toward it, but attitudes are not compartmentalized from beliefs. Our emotions are not withdrawn into themselves, but reach out into the world and are rational only as the world goes out to meet them in turn. Joy and sorrow, love and fear, all the substance of our moral life, may be groundless in particular circumstances, as ignorance, error, prejudice, and confusion seal us off from the world as it truly is. Whether they are well grounded in given circumstances is again a question of fact.

In short, an empirical theory of value judges by the fruit not the seed. From Locke through Hume and Russell, British empiricism has validated knowledge by reference to its mode of origination; the pragmatic epistemology of American thought looks instead to the consequences of the idea, just as in American life (or in its ideology, at any rate) a man is judged by the fulfillment in his future, not by the promise in his antecedents. Not their source in God or Nature but their destination in man certifies human values.

This is to say that there are no value properties as such. There are no simple traits whose possession or lack is the mark of good and evil. A thing becomes of value by virtue of its status and function in ongoing behavior. Values are thought to be transcendental because every empirical property is just what it is, a brute fact, and its value is then imagined to extend into another dimension outside experience, religious or metaphysical. But its capacity to satisfy human desires, its delicacy in answering to human emotion, its readiness to respond to human volition—all this is also matter of fact and can be uncovered in experience.

Not that morality consists simply in the immediate satisfaction of desire! Such satisfactions are a necessary condition of value but not themselves sufficient. No act could be right which added only pain and suffering to the world, and which could not reasonably have been expected to do anything else. This morality belongs to the Devil. But an immediate experience of satisfaction cannot itself certify to morality, for life extends beyond the fleeting moment, and in the pursuit of any one value we must perforce put all our values at stake. Only long-range and comprehensive satisfactions suffice for moral judgment.

Science, too, must distinguish between reality and the momentary appearance to sense; yet it must relate all its truths to the world as sense, while recognizing that what always and everywhere appears in a particular way really *is* as it appears to be. The proper contrast is not between appearance and reality, satisfaction and the good, but between a momentary appearance or a fleeting and passing satisfaction, and the enduring and comprehensive ones. In its own status every appearance is real, just as every felt good is genuinely good; the fool's paradise is just as heavenly—while it lasts. Our troubles come only when we move, as move we must, from what is here and now to what lies elsewhere. It is in this movement that we may find ourselves misguided; and only experience can be our guide.

Here, then, is a truly naturalistic ethics, one which bases values in the nature that flows through the channels of human sensibility. It is because of what we are, not what man is, that we are mindful of him; it is enough for human action that it attain a human good. Naturalism is the position that there is no other good; as C. I. Lewis put it, man's own experience is ultimately the only touchstone we have for what is good.[18] And it will serve.

On this theory, it is easy to see the importance for policy of a thoroughgoing knowledge of man's ways and works. But it is not the only theory which gives knowledge this place: the *philosophes* of the Enlightenment, the English utilitarians and French positivists, the "scientific" socialists of several varieties—all agreed in relying on experience to choose public policy. Given this agreement, differences in theory become secondary. There is a naturalistic core in every ethics which relies on experience for the recognition of what is good, even if it is not experience that *makes* it good. Even a religious ethic, if it is no longer involved with heavenly reward and punishment, must turn to naturalistic sanctions for its morality: the direct experience of good and bad consequences in this earthly life. We are all "empiricists" today, just as we are all "liberals"! But when there are differences on the level of moral practice, not just of ethical theory, the case is altered. Sooner or later the problem of relativism must be faced. Does naturalism bring us at last to the admission that the Russians are right in dismissing human rights as bourgeois values, as well as the knowledge on which their espousal rests as class science?

The centrality of man in modern political theory has raised the specter of relativism. "The fundamental difference between even ancient republican and modern democratic governments," Dewey has pointed out, "has its source in the substitution of human nature for cosmic nature as the foundation of politics." [19] While cosmic nature is single and constant, human nature is multiple and varied. It is one world, to be sure, but it is inhabited by many men, and they are not all alike. Class and culture do affect values, and within these large differences are the countless variations of lesser groupings and individual idiosyncrasies. When values become humanized, the way is opened for each man to play God, and the first act of infantile omnipotence is not to create but to destroy. Hence the moral nihilism of sophomoric rebellion, or the nihilism of the larger political rebellion expressed in that "critique of ideology" which dismisses as "propaganda" all political ideals—save the rebel's own.

But in the end these, too, must give way. If *I* must do God's work, it will after all remain undone. If my values are only in my think-so, they are no values at all. When a man mistakes himself for God he denies what is godly within him: the capacity to know and love the good in God's world—the world as it really is—and not just in the madhouse of his own mind. The sin is not in eating of the fruit of the tree of knowledge of good and evil, but in taking so little, and that from another's hand. It is the little learning, and that little once removed from our own direct experience of value, which is the dangerous thing.

The simple fact of moral experience is that *what* we judge is distinct from the fact of our judging it. Our judging, like all else we do, is conditioned by all that makes us what we are; but whether we have judged well or ill is not determined by those conditions. Science as a process of inquiry is as conditioned by society as are all other social practices and institutions. But this affects only what we believe, not what is true. We ask the questions in the language of our culture and prompted by our

individual desires to know; but the answers are nature's. What is good
for one man may not be so for another; this fact, however, is indifferent
to what either man may think to be good, whether for himself or for the
other. The principle of one man's meat holds true, but it does not undermine the objectivity of a dietetics grounded in physiology and a knowledge of the individual case. In short, relativism does not condemn us to
subjectivity but frees us from it, for only when we have relativized the
value judgment to the needs and circumstances of the human beings
whose values are in question can the judgment become truly objective.
We live each of us, not as we wish, but as we must, in the circumtances
in which we find ourselves. Morality may impose upon us the duty to
change these circumstances; it cannot become, nor would we have it
become, any the less circumstantial.

This *objective relativism* contrasts markedly with the cultural relativism of a few decades ago. The comparative ethnology of the last century, in disclosing the astonishing variety in patterns of culture, was
taken by many as providing a scientific warrant for moral subjectivism.
Of course, it does no such thing; we cannot rationalize our failure to assume responsibility for our values by pointing out that they are not
shared by the Kwakiutl. As a matter of fact, there is a wider commonalty
of values than was at first supposed: all cultures impose taboos on
murder and incest, for example, regulating in some fashion libidinal and
aggressive impulses. More to the point is the recognition that each culture inhabits, in a very real sense, a world of its own—different in fact,
and even more markedly different in what is taken to be fact. What is
sound political morality in Massachusetts may not be so in Madagascar—
and why should it! If it were, ignorance and error, in the one locale as in
the other, would produce a show of disagreement without an underlying
difference.

Conversely, there may be differences in value without disagreement,
differences in taste which can be allowed for without invoking a margin
for error. The Victorian ladies watching a tempestuous performance of
Antony and Cleopatra were overheard to remark, "How different, how
very different, from the home life of our own dear queen!" We need not
fear that the awareness of other patterns forces upon us at once the burden of defending our own. Not every disagreement rests on a real difference, and not every difference involves a real conflict. As the world

really becomes one, in fact and in the perspectives on it of the world's peoples, values also may be expected to be increasingly shared. And where they diverge, a larger value may lie in the divergence itself.

THE DUALISTIC CODE

I turn now from ethical theories to moral codes, from the foundations of moral judgment to its content. Ethics and morals are only loosely linked: the same values may be prized whether their warrant be from God, nature, or man; and the pursuit of different values may seek justification by appeal to the same ethics. Regardless of whether America bases its values on religion, on a metaphysics of natural rights, or on an empirical naturalism, what are its values?

At the very outset, we must face the stale charge of American "materialism," which over and over again has been pictured as excluding that life of the spirit in which religious, moral, esthetic, and intellectual values have their being. For some curious reason, classical imagery is usually invoked here: America is a new Carthage, sunk in barbaric sensuality; at the same time, it is a coarse and unfeeling Sparta, confronting the Athenian temper of a mellow European culture; or else it is another Rome, substituting engineering and military prowess for the glorious heritage of Greek civilization.

Whatever the metaphor, it is literalized in the platitudes describing America as an acquisitive society in which success is pursued at any price, worth measured by the dollar, and wealth made the basis of invidious distinction by expenditure for conspicuous consumption and waste. The indictment continues by charging that in America goods are thought to define the Good. All values are reduced to sales value, and even good will has a price put upon it. America is materialistic because above all else it prizes material objects; though its cars, refrigerators, and bathtubs are all that one could wish, Americans are incapable of genuine and deep satisfaction with them or with anything else. In short, in the course of the last half century Europe's image of America as "liberty lighting the world" has given way to the Hollywood stereotype of the poor little rich girl who owns everything and can enjoy nothing.

What is dangerous about this image is not merely the effect it has on the attitudes of other nations to us; it is even more dangerous because of the effect it has on our own self-image. Americans are pathetically prone to act out their fantasies. Nature imitates art—executives posture like men of distinction, lovers counterfeit the movie manner, statesmen groom themselves for television appearances and the covers of national weeklies. The danger in the myth of American materialism is that we will accept with enthusiasm—and naïveté—the role in which it casts us of the world's plumbers and policemen.

Properly understood, no myth is wholly mythical. The wildest dream fulfills some real wish, and plausibility demands a core of fact for every fantasy. We can recognize something of ourselves in the image Europeans project of us, which is no less ours because we can also see it so readily, if we choose, in those who are projecting it. In matters of religion, we must admit that the American Christmas is as much the concern of the chamber of commerce as of the church. As for morality, to the commandment "Honor thy father and mother" we have added the codicil "Say it with Flowers." The career of the fabulous Duveen makes it difficult to deny that art in America is a commodity, valued less for the esthetic experience it provides than for the prestige its ownership or even viewing confers. The works of the mind, if they are not laid to rest in a professional journal or a university press, must meet the exigencies of mass sales and the standards of book-club juries of selection. And nothing is more materialistic than the obscenities of the spirit with which in Southern California it is the custom to bury the dead.

Yet this core of truth in the falsehood of the caricature is not distinctively American. It is a by-product of civilizing agencies at work throughout the world. The deadening of the spirit and the corruption of the moral life with which America is charged is not an American invention; it is a concomitant, as Ortega y Gasset has persuasively argued, of mass man everywhere.[20] It is easy to present oneself as a member of the elite by sneering at mediocrity; none more loyal than those who denounce traitors! But the American middle class is no worse, though no better, than the middle class anywhere else. It is true that the push button and assembly line are destroying that sense of effort and sensitivity to materials essential to the creation and appreciation of works of art. But it is sheer prejudice that dismisses as untutored Yankee ingenuity the American contribution to the world's technology, while the contribution of other nations is supposed to attest to the high scientific level of their cultures.

But the defense that American "materialism" is largely a product of the conditions of life in the twentieth century is by no means an endorsement of the clichés which condemn twentieth-century civilization wholesale as a soulless technology. Without this technology, the soul might not have a body with which to live the life of the spirit. Lecky is a thousand times right when he declares that probably "the American inventor of the first anaesthetic has done more for the real happiness of mankind than all the moral philosophers from Socrates to Mill." [21] Care for the body, in America at any rate, has not been in the service of that hedonist sensuality which is so loathsome to the ministers of the spirit; the American ideal may be comfort, but it is certainly not pleasure—save perhaps in those backwashes of the South where the self-image of a decadent aristocracy is perpetuated. Technology has meant, for the most part, more food, clothing, and shelter—and must mean still more. European moralists must not be allowed to forget the wisdom of their own Aristotle: before a man can live well, he must be able to live.

Moreover, material achievement has made possible the widest access in history to the products of culture, and the widest sharing in its production and appreciation—in music, theater, letters, and the other arts. Behind the recurrent charge of Philistinism is perhaps no more than the fact, of which America can be proud, that we have no recognized leisure class of aesthetes and connoisseurs to serve as established arbiters of taste. And American standardization, after all, serves for society as a habit does for the individual: it may confine energies to a stifling routine, but it may also release them for creative effort.

America's material achievement needs no apology. What *is* indefensible is our failure to integrate the perspectives of this achievement with those in which our other values are defined and pursued. An age of material vigor is not necessarily backward in culture: it is usual to refer here to Pericles, Augustus, and the first Elizabeth. But what we have done is to dissociate values from their material embodiments, so that worth has become unreal, and much of our material reality worthless. This dissociation I call *cultural dualism*, and the value judgments it engenders the *dualistic code.*

Not every duality marks a dualism: there *is* after all a difference between an ideal end and the means realistically available for its attainment. But for the dualist this difference is thought to be absolute and irreconcilable, the distinction is drawn only to set the one against the other in far-reaching conflict, and the two are conceived as belonging to disparate metaphysical categories. The dualisms of spirit and matter, ideals and expediency, art and science, thought and action can be traced from Plato and Pauline Christianity through Descartes into modern times; in America today 'they are of enormous importance.

To the degree that ours is in very truth an acquisitive society, it is because of the separation we enforce between creation and ownership, between the instrumentality for the good life of what is acquired and the status mistaken for that life the mere acquisition confers. Work is unceasingly contrasted with leisure and few occupations pursued as a calling, so that occupational choices present the continuing dilemma—genuine only in the dualistic perspective—between prostituting a talent and burying it. One man is idealistic, another practical. Art is often treated, in Dewey's apt phrasing, as "the beauty parlor of civilization," moving out from the museums only to serve as irrelevant decoration. In short, beauty versus utility, thought versus action, theory versus practice—a Noah's ark of antediluvian pairings!

The situation with intellectual values is representative, and of particular importance in its own right for a political morality consisting in the best application of intelligence to the resources of political experience. The charge that America's worship of matter has cast mind into outer darkness is absurd. The United States today is undeniably a world center of scientific research and free scholarship. True, much of its creative effort is European in origin; but so is America itself. This great intellectual activity is now an integral part of the American scene. Our libraries, laboratories, and institutions of higher learning, taken all in all, rank with the best anywhere. European education is perhaps more intensive at an earlier age; but in my experience the difference disappears later on. And that so much education is here made available to so many is an intellectual as well as social gain which is not to be dismissed with cynical clichés about quantity and quality.

There is more basis to the criticism that intellectual effort in America is largely utilitarian in spirit, and that the mind is cultivated, not for its own sake, but in the service of government, industry, or individual ambition. The true and the beautiful are swallowed up in a utilitarian good. In many quarters philosophy and the humanities have taken up a defensive posture, seeking justification by claiming a contribution to science as "methodology" or to society as a way of filling the vacuum of increasing leisure. Yet the ideal of a "humanistic" education, when this is contrasted with a "technological" one, has been—as Dewey has tirelessly argued—not genuinely liberating, but a perpetuation of the standards of a leisure class, standards which are truly "materialistic" because they are derived from the status of those sufficiently wealthy to be spared the necessity of doing anything useful.

What remains true is that in America there is a continuing strain of anti-intellectualism, a persistent dislike and distrust of ideas and the men who live for them, possibly no stronger than in the past, but politically more influential. If any attitude be "un-American" *this* one is, for the Republic was founded by men of ideas who prized the works of the mind. Jefferson wished to be remembered as the founder of the University of Virginia; a college presidency today is a step to higher things, and too marked a literacy is a serious political handicap. It is not political partisanship to recognize that in America the capacities of the human mind often evoke fear rather than pride and hope—fear not just of the physical destructiveness they might engender, but also of the dissolution they may bring about of traditional patterns presumed to be too sickly to resist the germ of an idea.

For in this perspective, "ideas" are equated with "ideologies," ideas about "social" institutions identified with "socialism." Nor is this only a semantic blunder of illiteracy. The National Science Foundation encourages the study of "human resources" but not of "social science"—or it would encounter Congressional opposition. And a distinguished man of letters recently declared in a well-received book on American life that "our absence of ideas, the exclusion of ideas from American political life, gives us a superior kind of public morality," for ideas are the stuff of ideology, and ideology in turn makes for enforced and undemocratic unity.[22] I hope I have misunderstood him. But our hysterical fears of "subversive scientists" are expressed in actions that cannot be misunderstood. Perhaps these fears give ground, after all, for insisting that it is we who represent Athens and Europe, Sparta; for it is here that Socrates might have been put on trial for his security clearance.

The problems of military security are special, to be sure; but what is involved is the general question of the social and political role of ideas.

I am not arguing for the privileges of a caste of "intellectuals"; I am arguing against the emasculation of intellect which condemns it to social sterility. It is hard to believe today that so shrewd an observer as Bryce was at one time able to report that in America "intellectual eminence . . . is more admired and respected than in Europe." [23] In the last quarter-century, since the early days of the New Deal and its "brain trust," intellectual eminence, whatever admiration it has commanded, has occupied a steadily declining place in government. The makers of policy are increasingly recruited from business, finance, and industry, less and less from science, art, or education; the occasional exceptions are markedly more infrequent than their counterparts in Europe. There are in government, of course, considerable numbers of "symbol specialists" (as they are called by contemporary analysts of "elite structures")— which is to say: lawyers, publicists, and the like. The question, however, is not one of facility with words but with the ideas for which words are instruments. From this point of view, the philosopher Sri Radhakrishnan, the Vice President of India, provides almost a symbolic contrast with our own. We may not need to import the wisdom of the East; but we need desperately the domestic article.

I do not mean to say that contemporary anti-intellectualism is something new in American life. There has always been a civil war on this front, and the strategic position of the man of ideas is no worse today than it has been on several occasions in the past. Western agrarianism, with its hostility to intellection, has been as much a part of American politics as the high culture of New England. The fact is that the American attitude toward intellectuals has always been ambivalent. The problem becomes acute only when the chronic inner conflict is externalized; and what is then crucial is the character of the culturally acceptable ways of resolving the conflict. What I am protesting is the tendency to seek such resolutions by a partition of sovereignty between the thinkers and doers. This is why I speak of our code as dualistic: not that we reject the life of the mind but that we insulate it from the world of action. In Santayana's words, the dualism consists in "that separation which is so characteristic of America between things intellectual, which remain wrapped in a feminine veil and, as it were, under glass, and the rough business and passions of life." [24] Things intellectual we confine either to the selection of appropriate means—the myth of scientific neutralism—

or else to the purely verbal specification of abstract ends too remote to have any effect on policy. In our important choices, we largely disregard the intelligent habits, skills, and attitudes so effectively cultivated within the scientific enterprise. The dangers of such separatism are not just those of an amoral intellectuality, but even more those of an unintelligent, unrealistic morality. As it has been from the beginning, we might be able to deal with the scoundrels—if only we are not first destroyed by the fools.

What is foolish is the simple-minded morality which is indifferent to mere matters of fact, the thoughtlessness of Shaw's Sergius in *Arms and the Man* who with flashing saber leads a cavalry charge against a battery of machine guns. What sublime heroism! Yes, and what disastrous stupidity! There is no question that Americans are idealists: we have Wilson's word for it that "America is the only idealist nation in the world." [25] But it is idealism of a peculiarly adolescent kind—unyielding, unrealistic, otherworldly—in a word, romantic. It starts out, not from where we are, but from where we *would* be, if only we had the making of the world in our own hands; and it ends where it should begin. We undertake to bring to their senses whole nations, but not the necessary majority of the United States Senate. And what then! We may lose the good fight, but it will be well fought, and to the very end we will keep— our white plume. Alas for these childhood dreams of glory!

Such romantic idealism has played a considerable part in American reform movements and in American political life generally. "Sometimes people call me an idealist," Wilson says again. "Well, that is the way I know I am an American." [26] And he is right. Domestically, the idealist's image of himself has been that of a St. George attacking the dragons of Big Business, Crooked Politics, and Vested Interests. The familiar cycle of municipal reform in the United States documents in full both the ideal impulse and its realistic failure. In foreign affairs we picture ourselves as actuated only by moral considerations, while other nations go whoring after the false gods of their own self-interest. "In each of the two world wars," Laski comments, "American participation has seemed to some millions of its citizens not a necessary policy of self-defence, but a genuine act of charity, in which the president and Congress were deliberately casting their vote for right against wrong." [27] More recently, our policy in the Middle East has been presented to the world as the path of international righteousness from which our friends, alas, have strayed. But we will teach them self-denial for the sake of moral ideals.

This is as far as the idealist goes in his analysis of the moral problem: moral conflict is always between duty and desire, and morality stands unequivocally on the side of duty. For the adolescent, perhaps, this analysis may have elements of realism: his maturation rests on his coming to terms with powerful impulses. But in the world of men, such formulations are superficial and simplistic. There are conflicts among desires and among duties as well as between them. The problem is not how to carry out an easily recognizable idealistic policy, but how to reconcile conflicting ideals in a concrete context of their incompatibility, how to satisfy conflicting desires in circumstances that threaten to frustrate one or another of them. These are the conflicts which make a situation realistically problematic; and with regard to these, moralizing idealism is silent. It has recourse instead to a rhythm of sin and repentance, a sporadic self-righteousness which leaves us afterwards free to sin again. We alternate between a resolute response to the call of duty, until we win the war, and a return to the free indulgence of desire, until we lose the peace.

Here we come to the core of the dualistic code. It formulates conflicts as lying always between moral ends and immoral means. Success, it enjoins, must never be purchased at the expense of principles—which is to say that principles have nothing to do with realistic possibilities of attaining projected ends. In consequence, ethereal moral losses are counterposed to concrete though immoral gains; the resultant imbalance suprises no one but the dualistic idealist himself. When ideals are so conceived that in their very nature they stand opposed to expediency, it is foreordained which will give way. Necessity knows no law, and least of all a moral law. Dualism, in divorcing fact and value, seeks to place morality above necessity, and thereby puts it out of reach altogether of action enmeshed in causal necessitation.

The editors of an influential American magazine proclaim to other nations that we have learned how to have the best of both worlds: "Americans live on two planes at once—the practical and the ideal. The conflicts created by this ambivalent existence, which worry other people so much that they often feel constrained to reject one plane or the other, bother the American scarcely at all." [28] Might we not feel constrained instead to overcome the gulf between these two planes? No man, not even an American, can serve two masters. If we are not bothered it is because we have fragmented our lives, institutionally and individually, to accommodate both. We look to practicality in business and politics, and to the realm of the ideal in religion and morality. As businessman, scientist, politician, I have one responsibility; as father, husband, citizen, another. It is all a question of the role I am to play. And a play of shadows is what the pursuit of ideals then becomes, especially in the context of public policy. "Do-gooder," "world-improver," "reformer," Riesman perceptively observes, are "terms of contempt or friendly dismissal: to want to 'do good' in politics is obviously to be naive"[29] —as it must be, if we act naively. And so the final outcome is cynicism and disillusionment. But to be disillusioned there is one thing necessary—that we first be victims of illusion.

Vulgar Pragmatism

America has often been charged with being a nation of opportunists— a half-truth which ignores the important element of idealism in American life. But the dualistic code does give ground for the charge up to a point. When ideals are confined to the determination of ultimate ends, "practicality" remains the only standard for the choice of proximate means. But action is an unending sequence of such proximate choices; we touch the ultimate only in death. The core of truth in the charge that America worships success lies in this bent of the man of affairs: not for him only success counts, but that he looks to it for the opportunity afterwards to apply it to ideal ends. The revised American version is: Seek ye the kingdom of this earth; and all these godly things shall be added unto you.

It is useless to pretend that we do not largely accept success on its own terms: only the bankrupt has engaged in sharp practices, just as only the defeated candidate was guilty of dirty politics. Virtue always triumphs when triumph is the supreme virtue, and the triumphant the recognized arbiters of public morals. The history of the great American fortunes is ethically less interesting for the immoralities of their acquisition than for the moral force they were able to exert when acquired. Some recent distinguished political careers bring this documentation up to date. Yet what is often overlooked in this condemnation is that success is rarely in American life an end in itself. It is pursued, in a pathetic dependency on social acceptance, not for pleasure or power, but for admiration, love, and even self-respect.

In all this there is nothing of the philosophical pragmatism of Peirce, James, and Dewey, but only a vulgarized caricature. The emphasis on what works was meant by them as an insistence on the instrumentality of ideas for the enrichment of immediate experience. This is not the place to examine the persistent European misunderstandings of American pragmatism, but it is tiresome to have even Americans rationalize expediencies as a healthy "pragmatism," in the way in which a libertine might lean on Freud. Pragmatism is no more the working philosophy of America than the teachings of Jesus are its working religion. When Russell characterizes pragmatism as the philosophy of American business it is hard to say which of the two he has more seriously misunderstood. (Dewey was once moved to reply to this characterization with the remark that one might with equal justice attribute Cartesian dualism to the Gallic propensity for keeping a mistress as well as a wife—to which Russell rejoined, "Precisely!")

What cannot be denied is that there is something in pragmatism which lends itself to this vulgarization. An ethics which demands only the continuing application of intelligence to the problems of men without recourse to principles or powers outside experience does not invite spectacular acts of courage and devotion. It calls rather for that quiet heroism which so easily gives way, as was recognized long ago, to a quiet desperation. But there is nothing in pragmatism of the frame of mind for which the paradigm of the pragmatic lies in meeting a payroll or winning an election.

The issue here is not one of philosophical exegesis; what is at stake is not the correctness of a philosophical interpretation, but the morality of a pattern of action. In holding up the ideal of success, vulgar pragmatism does not ground values in existence, but takes as valuable whatever is existent. The test of success is essentially the same as the test of survival applied in "social Darwinism." What survives is the fittest—the fittest, of course, to survive; but competitive success is taken to be at once the sign and the substance of worth. This is the morality of the trial by combat, with the God who ensures that the right will prevail replaced by natural forces. When success is its own justification, the moral order is reduced to a purely historical one—retrospective, as in Hegel's "whatever is, is right," or prospective, as in the fascist or communist Wave of the Future. To be sure, a good which cannot be made to work is no good at all to us; but the Devil also has his triumphs, and when we have hit upon what works, the question still remains: whose work have we done?

To the ideal of success vulgar pragmatism also adds the ideal of efficiency, the most economic adaptation of available means to given ends. The vulgarization lies in the narrowness with which both means and ends are conceived. Economy implies the conservation of some values whose expenditure is required to achieve others. It becomes a false economy, a mere show of efficiency, when important values are left out of the accounting. This is the usual fate of the so-called human values which are the domain of morality. It characterizes the efficiency on which the fascist states prided themselves: the trains to the gas chambers ran on schedule.

In America efficiency is the fetish of the business world, and the operation of a business the model for politics and personal life. The promise of a business administration is almost irresistible to the American electorate, and a balanced budget is the Holy Grail of presidential Galahads. That the budgeting for a state rests on wholly different economic considerations than that for a private enterprise is a subtlety left to the long hairs of functional finance. The plain man will stand for no nonsense: he wants the most for his money. And the prudent politician will convince him that that is what he is getting.

In personal life this is the morality of double-entry bookkeeping. For such a morality, honesty is a matter of policy, generosity is good business, friendship pays off. We have risen above the nadir of a few decades ago when the Man of Sorrows was presented in a best seller as a cheerfully successful Rotarian. But efficiency remains a compelling ideal. I have forgotten which of the English utilitarians it was who chose his wife by listing in order of desirability all the eligible women of his acquaintance and proposing down the list until he was accepted. Such a man in America today could be a member of any Team in the country, and would even be admired for the sureness of his taste. Sense and sensibility are one. The same writer who found moral values in the exclusion of ideas from our political life finds aesthetic values in the standard of efficiency: "Americans' lust for possessions satisfies not a physical, but a metaphysical need. The pleasure is in having the instrument that works, in fitness. Efficiency is after all an artistic criterion—economy of matter and sufficiency of form." [30] No doubt it is this artistry which is responsible for the overpowering economy of matter and sufficiency of form in the American automobile.

There is no gainsaying the real efficiency achieved in American technology, and no intention here to derogate its value. The question is whether morality itself is a branch of technology. Vulgar pragmatism here unites with another important stream of contemporary American life: that misplaced and misconceived admiration of science aptly called *scientism*. Pragmatism yields to no philosophy in its emphasis on the significance of science for human affairs. But for it, science is a method— a temper of mind and a habit of action. Scientism identifies science with transitory results taken to be definitive and, even more, with special instruments and techniques taken to be the method itself.

Prominent among these are the procedures of quantification. The alleged American worship of bigness is itself a victim of European exaggeration; but Americans do attach excessive importance to exactitude. Nothing is so real as a measurable quantity. And if what is measured is good, the more the better. Under the impact of scientism, formation of policy is unduly influenced by considerations of dollars, votes, units of production; the data of a problem are those things that can be summarized in tables to appear in memoranda prepared by the experts. We can sympathize with that subject of Kinsey's who complained bitterly of the deflation of his masculine ego: "No matter what I told him, he just looked me straight in the eye and asked, 'How many times?' " Love is dealt with as sex and sex as ejaculation. Here at last we have something we can count. It would be well if we could measure the extent to which such reductionism affects our thinking on problems of health, education, housing, and employment—to say nothing of the mysteries in the trinity of peace, prosperity, and progress.

Applied social science can point to impressive success in such fields as marketing, personnel selection, and even labor relations. But there is often more impressiveness than success. If government suffers from the disease of bureaucracy, the bureaucrat himself is infected with scientism. Decisions are not the product of judgment and imagination, prudence and courage, but of surveys, questionnaires, graphs, and charts, of endless memoranda and reports, and, at last, of studies by special commissions just below the august policy-making level. One would almost suppose that to be scientific means not to think at all: the gadget, in the hands of the proper expert, will do it for us.

But this travesty of science is paralyzed in the face of imponderables, and for the morality of public policy the imponderables are everything. It is for just this reason that the brave new worlds of Huxley and Orwell are so morally repugnant. In them, not the scientific but the scientistic treatment of man has been carried to its conclusion: human engineering is at last totally and hideously efficient, without the saving absurdities of Chaplin's *Modern Times* or René Claire's *A nous la liberté*. The standard of efficiency leads inexorably to the treatment of man as a means, one among others. And because morality must take man as an end in himself, the moral impulse in American life is often expressed as a generalized hostility to science and all its works. Such admiration as the scientist receives is generously compounded with fear and distrust. In the end, scientism does not serve the cause of science, but enlists against science all the agencies of morality, within the self and in social institutions. And morality it condemns to be molded only by tradition, prejudice, and sentimentality.

What is called the "pragmatic" temper of the American mind is thus very far from pragmatic, however plausibly it is rationalized as the "scientific" treatment of our problems. It is efficient only if we do not count the cost, successful only in attaining the values we have fixed upon beforehand, not those in fact implicated in our actions. To simplify choices we isolate ends, confident in our innocence that what we have put asunder God will not join together. In any situation we suppose only one value to be at stake; what is essential in the light of the end we have in view becomes the essence of the matter in very truth, and the essence, in turn, not the heart but the whole. And on the unanticipated consequences of action morality goes aground. To the childish mind the adult is only more successful, more efficient, in the pursuit of childish things.

We are at war? Who does not know that the aim of war is victory! Its object, then, can be nothing less than unconditional surrender. To achieve that object all effort must be bent: total war for total victory. On the American banner is inscribed not "Exclesior!" but "Eccessivo!" More and still more—everything for victory, only the victory! This is the breathless virility Europeans mistake for mere braggadocio. But, for all that, it is a grievous fault, and grievously do we answer for it: in World War I, the hysterical renunciation of the German language, German poetry, German music; in World War II, the inhumanities of the up-rooting of the Japanese from the West Coast, to say nothing of the atom bomb; and in the Cold War, the immolation of friendship, faith, and even family—all in the name of loyalty. Loyalty to what? to values genuine in themselves, but pitiable things when torn loose from the body of living democracy.

Perhaps, after all, it is the American division of labor, and not American vigor, which must bear the blame. The expert on military strategy or foreign affairs, on the farm problem or labor relations, is just that and nothing more; in government an expert on morals would be an archaic absurdity. In arriving at policy, we calculate with precision half the distance, and content ourselves with a casual guess at the rest—and it is usually the second half which is exactly measured. The philosophy of American decision making is not pragmatism but utilitarianism, in the spirit of Dewey's characterization of the latter as "an intricate calculus of remote, inaccessible and indeterminate results." I propose to call this isolation of value the *utilitarian fallacy*: the appraisal of means by calculation of their effects on partial and perhaps secondary ends.

It is a cruel misunderstanding to charge Americans with immorality. Few peoples are more scrupulously righteous than we, when we recognize an issue as moral. But how seldom we recognize it! Our approach to the day-to-day decisions of government is largely utilitarian in the sense I have just given it. Ethics is thought to bear on policy, not from within, but only at the edges. Our conception of political morality is legalistic: we usually suppose morality to be threatened only when the law is violated. For the mass of the citizenry, policy raises moral issues only when its adoption or administration involves bribery, corruption, or venality. If from the wholly legal workings of policy patent injustices result, we suppose morality to be served by acts of philanthropy or executive clemency. Morality demands mitigation of effects; correction of causes is not the domain of morals, but of hardheaded practicality.

Alas, morality of this kind is a luxury product and will give way whenever we can no longer afford the philanthropies. It is easy for the rich to be generous and the powerful forgiving. "Does Job fear God for nought?

Have You not made a hedge about him, and about his house, and about all that he has, on every side? You have blessed the work of his hands, and his possessions are increased in the land." [31] What happens now that the hedge about us has given way? One recourse still remains. Morality is still important as the basis of morale: our own, our friends', and the morale of neutrals whose friendship is to be won by our show of morality. Today, desegregation is as often urged for its effect on neutralist Asiatics as on Americans themselves. Not our own ideals but someone else's idealizations become morally decisive.

This transformation of morality to morale accords well with the tough-mindedness on which American "pragmatism," so called, prides itself. For morality appears to many Americans as properly a feminine preoccupation, like elementary schoolteaching, social welfare work, or indeed any serious cultivation of intellectual and aesthetic values. De Tocqueville had already noted that morals are "the work of women"; [32] and various surveys, in this country and abroad, have shown that it is women who are especially concerned with morality in politics—at least in the sense in which this involves such matters as liquor, gambling, and political corruption.[33] Whether the greater interest of women in these questions relates, as has been suggested, to their greater participation in religious activities, or has some other basis—independent of the facts— the image of morality as feminine is well established in American life.

In these terms, the appeal to morality in politics faces the deep-rooted resistance of anxiety as to one's masculinity. To be a man is to be successful, efficient, even ruthless; sympathy, gentleness, and consideration are restraints imposed by the tender sensibilities of woman. A man, in short, is thought to prove his masculinity by his capacity of aggression, not for love; but it is love that morality calls for. Thus moral impulses find themselves blocked, as generosity, for instance, is inhibited by the fear of being shown up as a sucker. Americans are often more deeply motivated by moral considerations than they themselves pretend to be: we may rationalize our virtues even more than our vices. Our "pragmatism" may be a pretense to preserve the masculine ego.

Thus morality is first feminized, then rejected. In politics, to be conspicuously moral is to be not good but goody-goody: a boy scout, a Sunday school teacher—in a word, unmanly. The political leader must above all never be naive or a soft touch. A streak of femininity is toler-

ated and—by the female electorate—even welcomed: he may be gentle
with children, animals, and Mother. But he may not under any circumstances go soft on matters of policy. Here he must be unwaveringly hardheaded, hard-boiled, hard to get, and even harder to get around. I am
tempted to conclude that in the perspectives of vulgar pragmatism, the
affairs of the country would be in the best hands if we could turn them
over to a "private eye."

MORAL ABSOLUTISM

American morality is largely a morality of principle—so much so that
we may find it hard to imagine that a morality could be anything else.
We are self-consciously moral; to do what comes naturally is to be
wicked or, at best, irresponsible. Though our idealism is romantic, we
have rejected the romanticism of natural innocence, with its belief that
we can do right by instinct if this is uncorrupted by civilized sophistication. We are too divided within ourselves to be able to trust our native
impulses. We let conscience be our guide, but only because conscience
rests on moral principles. Our moral philosophy has a strongly Platonist
cast: generalized abstractions come first. The particularities of concrete
choices do not justify the principles but are justified by them. The logic
of morals is deductive; facts, not values, are arrived at inductively.

Such an appeal to principle has several important contributions to
make to morality. To start with, it precludes that unexamined life which
Socrates condemned as not worth living. If decisions are to be justified
by principles, they must be preceded by reflective appraisals of alternatives. Principled action, whatever its shortcomings, is not heedless,
makeshift, or arbitrary. As moralists, Americans are likely to feel that
life is real and earnest; and while this often imposes on our morality a
leaden solemnity and even grimness, it saves us from the emptiness of
pure caprice and the deadly necessities of meaningless routine.

What is more, principled action deepens the significance of personal
decisions by basing them on universalized standards. The principle will
not countenance the irrelevancy that my choice is, after all, mine. If an
act is not obligatory on all men in my position it is not an obligation on
me; and I have no moral right which would not belong equally to any
other man situated as I am. Kant, the superlative exponent of the ethics

of principle, counters the moral aloneness of the autonomous will by the shared rationality of the principles to which that will subjects itself.

To act on principle is to universalize action in another dimension: not only from person to person but also from case to case. It is to decide on the basis of what is usually involved, on the outcome in the long run, in general. To appeal to "the principle of the thing" is to take the special instance as representative of a class; whatever the outcome in *this* instance, what is decisive is the consequence that would follow if the whole class were to be treated on the basis of the principle in question. Principles thus provide an element of conservatism in action, binding each case as it arises to patterns already established as preserving the values sought for. Moral values disclosed by the Prophets are sustained by the Law; legal institutions perform this function of conservation for societal values. But, in both cases, the forces of conservatism may be so great as to stifle the creative morality, the transvaluation of values, continuously called for in a changing world. In science, too, the generalizations we designate "laws" do not legislate for nature, but set down conditions new truths must meet to conserve the facts accommodated by the old.

What principled action preserves in the individual we call character, the integrity that unifies the personality as it faces successive moral decisions. The betrayal of principle in any decision is morally subversive, for action leaves its residue in habit, and habit in character. The generality of the principle by which action is to be guided answers to this generalizing tendency in action itself. The moral collapse of character is not a single dramatic event, like the schoolboy's fall of Rome, but a gradual corrosion of the mainsprings of action. The barbarian is first a hired guardian of the frontier, then a general of the army; and at last the emperor himself is no longer a Roman.

Choices can thus find justification in principles. To act on principle is to act in moral self-defense. Or, rather, it is to act in defense of the wished-for self, the self in the making. American insistence on principle is a species of moral ambition, a determination to live up to our own ego ideal. Virtue, to be sure, cannot be forced; even its nurture is attended by the sin of spiritual pride. Yet the lure of the ideal, to be effective in action, must be joined by some drive within the personality. What begins as a role to be played may in the end define the character itself, as in Max Beerbohm's fable of the Happy Hypocrite. That the

American appeal to principle may be insincere signifies nothing; the moment of truth transpires in action. It is here that our morality of principle may be found wanting.

American principles are likely to concern themselves with ultimates, while action is a matter always of the next step. Principles define inherent values, but the assessment of instrumental values leads to concrete choices. A code of principles is not a map of action but a guide-book for ultimate destinations. Thereby it serves the armchair traveler and provides an escape from responsible commitment to the decisions actually before him. That American folk hero, the henpecked husband, boasts that in his household *he* makes the important decisions: his wife selects his job, his house, his children's schools; he has sole authority on questions of foreign policy, presidential candidates, and nuclear tests. The idlers of Pershing Square and Columbus Circle discuss only the largest issues: "Do you believe in God?—take either side!" The morality of principle, as Kant saw, turns on motives, not consequences; thus a debate on principles offers the incomparable advantage of irresponsibility. Weber points out: "There is an abysmal contrast between conduct that follows the maxim of an ethic of ultimate ends—that is, in religious terms, 'The Christian does rightly and leaves the results with the Lord'—and conduct that follows the maxim of an ethic of responsibility, in which case one has to give an account of the foreseeable results of one's action." [34] The man of principle is, to be sure, morally invulnerable; but for a reason that also makes him politically irresponsible.

The ultimates of principle ignore not only consequences but also conditions. Ideals are in the nature of things abstract; everything concrete is actual. Principles necessarily abstract, therefore, from the particular conditions in terms of which alone ideals can be actualized. Specifically, they are likely to localize moral problems in the character of the individual, without regard to societal pressures and possibilities. This error Laski has called "the fallacy of abstraction," and finds it "a central element in Americanism." "The individual is not seen in his context as a member of a particular society at a particular time; he is seen as an individual standing outside society who can by an act of will, sometimes called faith, assure his own regeneration." [35] Real problems are thus given unreal formulations which substitute artificial questions of principle for the genuine issues of the specific circumstances. Such questions resemble the sophomoric riddles of moral choice. I am in a boat with my wife and my mother; it capsizes; whom do I save? Alas, I cannot swim! How would I spend a million dollars? That depends on how I get it; perhaps the wisest course would be to set aside half for my legal defense. Such childishness is given a sophisticated cover in political debate; but at bottom—may I say, "in principle"?—the error is the same. What is relevant to moral choice is treated as settled beforehand, and so tacitly assumed; but just this is the real issue.

Too often the statement of the moral problem is mistaken for its solution. The underlying assumption is that we already know all the answers to our moral problems. Man, it is said over and over again, "knows thoroughly well what moral conduct is, has known for thousands of years." [36] The task, then, is thought to be only one of applying this knowledge— that is, of getting others to do so, for, of course, those who support my policies have already applied it. In this perspective, political morality is essentially a matter of police action; it calls for rigorous enforcement of the law, not wisdom in legislating it. Such wisdom has already been provided—by Moses and Solon, by the fathers of the church and of our country. And if enforcement itself raises problems, we do not ask whether something might be wrong with the law. It is taken for granted in America that morality is unpleasant and unpopular, in accord with the miscalled "Puritanism" of American ethics.

This fantastic belief in the sufficiency of our moral knowledge is sustained by the abstractness of our principles. Surely we have been shown what the Lord requires of us: that we seek justice, love mercy, and walk humbly with our God. How we are to do these things is no longer, we imagine, a moral question but a matter of expediencies. And thus in the name of justice and mercy we may in all humility make secure our supply of Middle Eastern oil. In our foreign policy we presuppose what it is the task of moral action to create: a real community of men and nations which can give content and direction to the moral obligations of the members of that community.

The abstractness of principles thus makes them as useful politically as they are useless morally. The image of morality can be preserved in the abstraction while expediencies govern concrete choices. In this way "natural rights" have been used to resist the real extension of rights in welfare legislation, just as today restrictive clauses and covenants take

refuge in the morality of "the principle of free choice of associations."
We can enjoy the satire in Orwell's "All men are equal, but some are
more equal than others"; but we fail to see through our own rationalizations. In a democracy these have a particularly important function: the
politician seeks the widest possible support and avoids positions so
definite as to alienate part of his constituency. Popularity requires that
he take his stand on the virtues of the American Home and the viciousness of Foreign Aggression. The most partisan critic of our policy makers
cannot accuse them of favoring Sin.

Policy itself becomes in a real sense unprincipled when it fails to recognize the contextualism of moral laws. For these, like scientific generalizations, have their conditions and limits, not exhaustively formulable in
additional generalizations, but requiring operational anchorage in the
particular case. No one has seen this more clearly than Aristotle in his
devastating attack on Plato's Idea of the Good. "I am at a loss to know
how the weaver or the carpenter would be furthered in his art by a
knowledge of this absolute good, or how a man would be rendered more
able to heal the sick or to command an army by contemplation of the
pure form or idea. For it seems to me that the physician does not even
seek for health in this abstract way, but seeks for the health of man, or
rather of some particular man, for it is individuals that he seeks to
heal." [37] With characteristic restraint Aristotle concludes, "In discussions
on subjects of moral action, universal statements are apt to be too
vague, but particular ones are more consistent with truth; for actions are
conversant with particulars; and it is necessary that the statements
should agree with these." [38]

Generalizations have their place in moral reflection, and we cannot
generalize without abstracting from the differences which individuate
particulars. But to the empirical temper, generalizations depend on the
individual case. A particular decision is not right because it accords with
principle; the principle is valid only as it is warranted by the rightness of
the particular decisions it encompasses. In scientific inquiry an established law may be used to discredit an alleged fact incompatible with it;
but in the end the law must be verified by such allegations or lose its
empirical standing altogether. In the same way, the principles which
Americans regard as the backbone of character are not wholly without
moral application. But character itself must be capable of growth. Ameri-

cans speak always of "building" character, as though once erected it need only be periodically strengthened but never be redesigned to meet the challenge of new situations. It is this point of view that I call our moral absolutism.

The rigidity of character is expressed politically in a fixation on policies successful in the past, without regard to present conditions, which are tacitly assumed to have remained as they always were. Every neurotic pattern is realistic in relation to some situation which once was actually experienced, in fact or symbol. The core of the pathology is a disturbance of memory—not that the past is forgotten, but that action is determined by a remembrance which is mistaken for a present perception. Moral rigidity is easily rationalized by an appeal to the permanence of fixed principles. Conversely, such changes as occur in the conceptions of good and evil are presented as nothing more than the application of the old principles to new situations. Americans are as reluctant to recognize that new principles might be called for as Communists are to admit the reality of a change in party line. Our periodic return in politics to the paths of righteousness is uncommonly like the Communist rescue of Marxist-Leninism from betrayal by crypto-fascist traitors.

The notorious American worship of novelty is thus at best a superficial truth. Just as every drunk argues his sobriety, every conservative prides himself on being forward looking, and in both cases the self-image betrays the reality. America is essentially a conservative nation, and nowhere more than in its morality. What the world knows as "modern" is French art, German science, Swedish design. Americans prize novelty of expression but not of substance—her dress must be in the mode, but the little woman would look good in anything! We are married to our morality, and stick to our principles until death do us part. "When [Americans] have accepted a principle," Bryce observes, "they do not shrink from applying it 'right through,' however disagreeable in particular cases some of the results may be. . . . They prefer certainty and uniformity to the advantages which might occasionally be gained by deviation." [39]

Moral absolutism also expresses itself in treating its values as unconditional. The morality of "my country right or wrong" is not altogether groundless. Loyalty knows no reasons, and love is not love which alters when it alteration finds. Yet some moral limits are surely presupposed by the morality of loyalty and love. Absolutism sweeps these limits aside or, rather, is blind to their existence. In defense of loyalty we have attacked public men for sticking by their friends, private citizens for insisting on their constitutional rights, and reformed sinners for exhibiting the virtues of forbearance and Christian charity. Even if a man be wrong in refusing to name his suspect associates, surely moral issues must be resolved before he can be flatly judged wrong. Absolutism does not disentangle these issues but cuts through them. It goes further and, like Heaven itself, rejoices more in the repentant sinner than in the righteous man whom it suspects of sins yet to come.

That no values are absolute means only that conditions and consequences are always relevant to our appraisals of them. Every end is also a means: it is the utilitarian fallacy all over again to suppose that a value can be isolated from the matrix of its causes and effects. Would we have a Russian act on the morality of "my country right or wrong"? Is my loyalty an unquestionable virtue and his a damnable fault, the patriotism of my party an absolute good and the patriotism of the opposition the refuge of scoundrels? If conditions must be met in the one case, why not in the other? God Himself looked upon His creation before He pronounced it good.

Absolute values are likely to be extremist as well as unconditional. Our morality is sharply etched in black and white. Its paradigm is the TV western where virtues are all on one side, vices all on the other, and the distinction between the two easily apparent even to a child. And the distinction is entirely a question of character, not of specific acts and their consequences. These signify only as expressions of character: the villain is immediately recognizable because he is not clean shaven and beats his horse. It is this childish morality which we often project onto the political scene, and especially in our foreign relations. Its outcome is a continuing sense of betrayal by our friends and bewilderment by our enemies, as the former reveal human failings and the latter some qualities of human decency. And as for ourselves, anything less than moral superlatives borders on subversion. Justice Holmes recognized this immaturity when he criticized the absolutism of the doctrine of natural law: "It is not enough for the knight of romance that you agree that his lady is a nice girl—if you do not admit that she is the best God ever made or will make you must fight." [40] In sum, the absolutist forgets too easily that even a saint falls short of the Godhead, and even Satan, though fallen, is a fallen angel.

Absolutistic—that is to say, unconditional, unqualified, unquestioned. American morality is likely to be presented as indubitably certain; it follows the Cartesian logic of the incorrigible premise. If our premises are unsure, how can we have confidence in our conclusions? We must begin with what we cannot doubt, or the cancer of skepticism will prove fatal at last. Thus moral principles are rarely thought of as hypotheses, for this would make them "merely" hypothetical. To say that they are warranted in the light of all the evidence we have is to admit that as experience grows, new evidence may call for their reappraisal and even—who can say?—their rejection. But then what would be left for our guidance? If the stars in the heavens are no longer fixed, by what shall we set our course?

In terms of this logic we are strongly motivated to treat our values as beyond question, lest we be left without an answer. "To the good American," Santayana says, "many subjects are sacred: sex is sacred, business is sacred, America is sacred, Masonic lodges and college clubs are sacred. This feeling grows out of the good opinion he wishes to have of these things, and serves to maintain it. If he did not regard all these things as sacred he might come to doubt sometimes if they were wholly good." [41] It is this which gives the dogmatic cast to American morality. Dogmatism does not consist just in the bareness of our affirmation: we cannot forever be giving grounds for all we assert. What is dogmatic is the refusal to countenance questions, the frame of mind which regards doubt as foolish and even wicked. In many quarters today our accepted values are beyond discussion—either because, like labor relations, they are too "controversial," or because, like the relations between the sexes, they are too sacred for controversy. An absolutistic morality is always accompanied by an absolute authority, a chaperone to preserve inviolate its fragile virtue. This accords well with the current distrust of the freely questioning intellect which we have already noted. Authority does not speak as frankly today as did the seventeenth-century governor of Virginia who declared, "Thank God, there are no free schools or printing; . . . for learning has brought disobedience and heresy . . . into the world, and printing has divulged them. . . . God keep us from both." [42] The words sound harsh to modern ears; but few in America today do not recognize the tune.

True, disrespect for authority is also an American tradition, stemming from our Revolution, our ideology of distrust of government, the spirit of the frontier, and the individualism expressed throughout our culture patterns. Yet freedom from authority is not easily come by, and what is won by one generation cannot easily be handed down to the next. American reliance on conscience and the personal moral sense provides an inviting domain for the sovereignty of an introjected authority, which may rule even more tyrannically than the despots alien to the self. Since Freud, the destructive potentialities of conscience—the despotisms of the ideal—have been widely recognized. Erich Fromm and others have directed attention to the powerful anonymous authority which finds expression in the mass media and elsewhere in our conformist culture. As a result of its working, the immature personality, escaping from a dreadful freedom, may insist on subservience to principle with the compulsiveness of a child's anxiety over bedtime rituals. There is even a danger that psychiatry in its turn will be elevated into a new moral authority; it is easier for the slave to change masters than to achieve emancipation.

An absolutistic morality cannot take hold on democratic politics, for politics in a democracy is essentially pluralistic, tolerant, compromising. In the absolutistic perspective moral intolerance is a virtue and even a duty. "Absolute principles are intolerant of dissent," Dewey has pointed out, "for dissent from 'The Truth' is more than an intellectual error. It is proof of an evil and dangerous will." [43] If one side represents the good—wholly, unquestionably, and unconditionally—the other side must serve the Devil; and compromise with Satan is a sin, particularly in America, where the Devil is doubly damned as a foreign power. In democratic politics, compromise must be seen as more than an avenue that leads to the good; politically speaking, it is the good itself. A scientific measurement of a magnitude, say a length, is spoken of as an approximation to the "true length," but this "true length" is an abstraction constructed from an unending sequence of such measurements, or it has no meaning at all in experience. The good in a democracy must be operationally defined by democratic procedures. Granted that the working of these procedures is unsure, conditional, and approximative, and that their results are almost surely wrong in some respects and perhaps even altogether. Nevertheless, a free man must be free to go where he wills, even to perdition, if it lie on a road of his own choosing.

Americans recognize the usefulness of compromise in matters of expediency, but cannot countenance it in matters of morality.[44] What is a prudent concession in the one case becomes a cowardly appeasement in the other. If moral compromise be given a place in politics, what becomes of the crusade? And every political movement must be moralized as a crusade to enlist the support of right-thinking people. The work of the politician, however, is nothing but compromise; this is what it means to say that politics is the art of the practical. Practicality without compromise defines dictatorship. What the absolute moralist calls "dirty politics" is its natural condition; the adjective is redundant. The contempt in which the American politician is so often held today is not a mark of the deterioration of American statesmanship. Politicians have always been held in contempt. This is their business, as it is one of the functions of the psychiatrist to serve as a target for displaced hostility. The politician is the scapegoat for what an absolute morality regards as the sin of compromise. But when a necessity of nature becomes sinful, it is the morality that is unnatural.

In the end, an absolutistic moral code lowers the level of political morality, just as scientism weakens the genuine scientific impulse. It is not just that the standards absolutism imposes are impossible ones. The point is rather that in focusing on these standards in opposition to "relativism," it deflects attention and energy from the approximate values which political action can and must secure. The best is the worst enemy of the better, as Dewey has it. In human affairs, and certainly in democratic politics, more or less is the most that can be asked for. "Never hope to realise Plato's Republic. Let it be sufficient that you have in some slight degree ameliorated mankind, and do not think that amelioration a matter of small importance." This is the sentiment of Marcus Aurelius, himself a philosopher-king. It is a moral sentiment. And for all its air of Stoic resignation, it is a sentiment on which courageous men can act with determination on behalf of their political ideals.

MORALIZATION

American morality has a strong legalistic cast. Public morals are thought to be satisfied by conformity to public law, though the grounding of this law in "nature" allows morality to transcend purely political arrangements. But such arrangements are widely regarded as the proper instrument to secure moral values. Confronted with injustice, indecency, or iniquity of any kind, the American reaction is likely to be: "There oughta be a law!" The mere existence of the law is thought to suffice: the commandment—prohibition or a peace pact—magically brings about its own fulfillment. More accurately, it is a moralistic aspiration which is fulfilled. The enactment of the law, like a New Year's resolution, puts us on record on the side of morality, and thereby allays anxiety and guilt concerning our immoral impulses. It has been estimated that some ninety per cent of the population would be in jails if all our statutes were enforced. It is difficult even to imagine the enforcement of some of them—for instance, those regulating details of conjugal intimacies. Such statutes are empty, legally and—what is more to the point— morally. This hollow shell of morality is *moralization*.

The shell is largely verbalistic in character. In these matters Americans put great emphasis on the word, especially the written word. American constitutionalism, for example, contrasts markedly with the British, possibly because the younger and more heterogeneous society cannot rely so well on long-established custom. Whatever the reasons, in America concrete practices turn to abstract symbolisms for their justification. Legal issues are argued and decided by "the law" and "the courts," not by lawyers and judges. Conformity, whether social or moral, is sustained by appeal to "public opinion," "good citizenship," "civic responsibility." And in politics, the label is crucial—from "the New Deal" to "Modern Republicanism." There is no question here of cynical propaganda, like the use of the term "socialism" by European fascist parties. Americans believe what they say: in its own perspectives the Liberty League of Roosevelt's day was defending liberties, not privileges. His "economic royalists" were convinced democrats, that is to say, republicans—I mean equalitarians. And on the other side, the real constraints imposed by the state to maximize the range of real choices were verbalized as involving no loss of liberty at all. "The thousand dollar fur coat," Blondie explains, "was on sale for five hundred; but I saved five hundred, so it really cost me nothing!"

Philosophy has endorsed and even participated in such logic. An important part in American life is played by the grand occasions on which philosophers are called upon to make cosmic pronouncements. Few Americans would venture to deny that their politics and ethics, their whole scheme of values, rest upon what is called a "metaphysical basis." And to be really profound, it seems that such a metaphysics must be largely unintelligible. When Martin Buber accepted an appointment to the Hebrew University, he faced the task of learning to lecture in Hebrew; to a friend who some time afterward inquired about his progress in the language he replied, "I know enough now to make myself understood, but alas, not enough not to be understood!" Party platforms, preambles to constitutions, charters and declarations, solemn editorials—all play roles akin to that of the invocations of the Congressional chaplain. They have no bearing on the decisions to be made; but Americans would be uneasy at their absence.

In a word, moralization is the ritualistic use of the symbols of morality. Verbalizations are abstracted from their contextual references and felt to have a life of their own. The words go their own way and, far from being instruments of moral effort, can themselves bend moral aspirations to their own ends. The basic values of our public policy are thought to be embodied in "the American dream," "the American way of life," or simply "Americanism." But to our ears "the French dream" sounds obscene, "the German way of life" rigidly inhuman, and "Britishism" connotes snobbery and priggishness. Yet the interpretation is as projective in the first case as in the others. In the concrete, "the American way" is the way of Americans and nothing else; what way we are to choose as we face particular decisions is in no way defined by appeal to the ritualistic symbol. Anthropologists have long been aware that rituals precede the dogmas which rationalize them and also survive changes in these dogmas. But the wisdom of moral choice is independent of ritual and dogma alike.

What is at work here is the belief in verbal magic, in the power of the word itself to bring about a desired result. The magic, of course, lies in the mechanism of efficacy; there is no magic in achieving an open door by asking someone to open it. The magic lies in the open sesame which suffices of itself. The word imprisons the essence of the thing, which is released to do its work when the word is uttered; we are masters of the demon if we can speak his secret name. These are the fairy tales that we act out in politics when we rely on "free information" and the power of "the truth" for world-wide accord with our policies. This is the magic of securing loyalty by oaths, good citizenship by singing the national anthem at ball games, and patriotism by repainting our mail boxes in the colors of Old Glory. It is the superstition of the gentleman's agreement to a conspiracy of silence, lest the mention of discrimination give it an actuality it otherwise would not have. Nothing is fully real, we suppose, until it is verbalized. The facts of life need not be faced if we can find euphemisms by which they can be magically transformed.

The danger of these fantasies lies not in ritualism itself but in our taking the word for the deed, in ascribing to ritual an effectiveness in action which it does not have. In America, Laski points out, "there is an excessive love of the rhetoric of rights and a too easy belief that their declaration is their fulfillment." [45] Ringing pronouncements are mistaken for moral courage, the verbalization of ideals for moral achievement. It is in this perspective that Americans put so much reliance on promises as political instruments. The campaign promise is recognized in our own country for the ritual that it is, but in foreign affairs we distress other nations by habitually promising more than we intend to deliver, more even than we could deliver if we wanted to. In our own childishness we treat other nations like unruly children to be quieted with assurances of future delights.

All this is by no means exclusively American. In no other age have language and symbolism been so central to important developments in science, art, philosophy, and politics. Austrian psychoanalysis, French poetry, British philosophy, and nationalist politics everywhere have in the present century all turned on the uses and misuses of words and symbols. Other nations have relied much more than we on the clichés and stereotypes, the equivocations and empty abstractions of totalitarian Newspeak. Nevertheless, in America the formation of public policy, not just its public presentation, has been deeply infected with the virus of verbalism. We are recurrently tempted to formulate the problem of "understanding" the Russians as a disturbance of "communication," just as we suppose our national security to be threatened by subversive writings and defended by scientific "secrets."

In part, this cast of mind may be traceable to the fantastic growth of our mass media, all out of proportion to the development of our critical skills and our education in habits of reflection; to the unceasing impact of advertising on our lives; to the need for symbols by which to unify our heterogeneous subcultures, with no time for the slow growth of an organic unity; and to the immensity of the challenge to our survival, which stimulates search for a sign in which we can conquer. But perhaps most of all, our verbalism is an expression of what we call our youthful vigor and what others identify as our emotional immaturity. It is the infant to whom language is a most magically wondrous thing; the infantile adult finds it hard to realize that what he reads into his morality is words, words, words.

My objection to moralization is not simply the disparity between words and deeds. The semanticist fad which attacks all abstractions as unreal and all ideals as fictions betrays a fundamental misunderstanding of both science and morals. The function of ideals depends on their divergence from fact, as that of abstractions depends on their transcending the irrelevancies of concreta. An ideal is a direction of action, an order along a dimension; it is a moral objective as guiding action, not as specifying a point to be reached. The unattainability of ideals is a tautology, not a tribulation of the human condition. What is objectionable in a verbalistic morality is that its symbols function not as ideals but as utopias. They are points at infinity, unspecified both as to distance and direction. They do not guide moral action, but substitute for it.

It is a blunder to take the symbol for the fact that it symbolizes. But it is equally a blunder to fail to recognize the factuality of the symbol itself. Meaning is not another dimension perpendicular to reality, but adds a degree of freedom to our movement on the plane of reality. The recognition of the symbol as a fact of political life is perhaps the major contribution of twentieth-century political science—from the work of such European sociologists as Pareto and Mannheim, through the Chicago school of Merriam and Lasswell, to the countless contemporary studies of propaganda, public opinion, and political behavior. The belief in the effectiveness of symbols is not magical when these effects are mediated by human responses to the symbols. The self-fulfilling prediction of the propagandist is beginning to be understood in terms of the mechanisms of social psychology; and Lasswell and others have illuminated many facets of political life by conceiving them as resulting from the displacement of private affects onto public objects—for instance, through the symbols of family life so common in politics.[46]

Ritual as a cultural fact is to be neither dismissed nor deprecated. It serves to intensify emotions and to make vivid meanings and values grounded in the life of the culture. It is objectionable only when its significance shrinks to its own performance, when it no longer draws nourishment from realities outside the symbols. Such realities are the sole source of the vitality of ritual; cut off from action it becomes a dry husk, the letter that killeth. What ritualism is to the religious spirit, moralization is to morality.

The words of the moralizer have no purchase on reality, and are not intended to. This makes them objectionable, not their vagueness and ambiguity, and certainly not their emotive force or appeal to the imagination. The moralist's conception of propaganda, within the framework of the dualistic code, is to drop on the satellite populations either the Sears catalog or the Bible, presumably according to the day of the week. The trouble with the Russian leaders, we say, is that they are godless men; if only they could be brought to read the Sermon on the Mount and share our conviction that the meek shall inherit the earth! But until then—what? Moralization, in cutting off morality from the springs of action, leaves action without moral guidance. It has often been argued against political verbalizations that historically they have been used in defense of reaction, while the semantic critique has been a weapon of reform. Maybe so. But the real danger here to morality is not that verbalizations will be invoked in support of the wrong policies. It is that verbalistic moralizing will interfere with deciding which policy *is* the wrong one.

In moralistic perspectives, not policy but people are judged. The moralist views politics as a drama of good and evil. His interest focuses on character. The moralistic analysis is directed to persons, not institutions, and to policies only as expressions of personality, not as the outcomes of institutional constraints. Whatever happens is ascribed to human agency, benevolent or malicious. The task of politics is only to throw the rascals out; with the right men in office there is nothing to worry about. People are good or bad and therefore policies are; the measure of the policy is the moral stature of the policy maker. Thus politics is personalized, personality moralized.[47] Governments are reacted to in terms of their representatives, and these, in turn, on the basis of the moral categories we project onto them. If our allies take important steps without consulting us, we respond with a sense of personal injury, not with a reappraisal of the policies that forfeited their trust and confidence. The moralizer, in short, formulates moral issues in terms of character and motive, not action and consequences. That is why verbalization is so congenial to him: it allows morality to be abstracted from action, internalized, and refined—until it becomes an altogether ghostly thing.

I do not mean to deny the importance of character in both politics and morals. On the contrary, I have already identified character as the element of unity in moral action, the integrity of political decision. But the moralizer misconceives character as an agglomeration of moralistic virtues, and he allows these to replace the wisdom of the moral agent and the judgment of the political leader. He looks for religiosity, patriotism, and simplicity; and if to these homey virtues there is added a driving sense of duty, the moralizer in politics asks for nothing more. His ideal among American statesmen is not Lincoln but William Jennings Bryan.

On the contemporary political scene, such stature as Bryan had has shrunk altogether to the level of boyish charm; moral indignation has given way to sentimentality, the old-time evangelist to the moral salesman for a mass market. The passion for ideals and principles which animates the moralizer is hard to distinguish, in its most distinguished representatives, from soap opera emotionalism. Moral sentiment, however, is not necessary to even the most elevated morality, as Buddha, Socrates and Spinoza attest, by what they were as well as by what they taught. And it is not sufficient either: the maudlin Christmas card and Christmas carol do not make a Christian life. But sentiment is easy to express, easy to recognize, easy to share; and, in a democracy, the pure of heart whom the moralizer calls for must wear his heart on his sleeve. The patriot must broadcast his patriotism on a national hookup. Liza

Doolittle might have become a congresswoman with her repeated declaration, "I'm a lady, I am!"

This is to say that moralization provides only a projected image of the moral life, as glamour objectifies only the fantasy of love. The bifurcation of appearance and reality thus reappears in the metaphysics of morals, as an expression of an ambivalence within the moral self, an inner conflict between private practice and public standards, between what we do and the shared pretense of what we are. The advertiser sexualizes every commodity (except breakfast cereals), but no one must notice it; just as the movie queen must look seductive while preserving the image of underlying chastity. We glorify the home whatever the rate of delinquency and divorce, and sentimentalize childhood while refusing to rent to couples with "children or pets." We condemn gambling and quote the odds, abjure state lotteries and take our cut at the track. As I have said elsewhere, conventional moralization is tyranny tempered by hypocrisy. And it is hard to say whether we are more hypocritical in our virtue or in our vice.

In the light of the great political problems of our time all this is trivial, but just this is the important point. Moralization trivializes morality, reducing virtue to a denial of the senses and moral principles to the prohibitions of a backwoods boardinghouse. Bryce reports that in America ". . . the average of temperance, chastity, truthfulness, and general probity is higher than in any of the great nations of Europe." This is probably still true; but a simple-minded eunuch with stomach ulcers would also be a paragon of these virtues. There is great moralizing zeal in America, Bryce continues, but it is directed to the same trivial ends: ". . . to suppress vice, to prevent intemperance, to purify popular literature." [48] Such morality, as I stated earlier, is felt to be feminine or childishly submissive. Its virtues are those of the "good little boy." The moralizer can neither wholly reject them, for they are virtues, nor wholly accept them, for he is a man. So he preserves self-respect by isolating virtue from effective action.

Where in this trivialized morality can we find the prophetic grandeur of social ethics? Moralism thinks to emulate Lincoln with passion toward none and philanthropy for all. Its code is essentially the control of libido, but not of aggression. Yet if we are to speak—as the moralist continually does—of the decay of morality in the present age, surely "free love" wears an incomparably less hideous aspect than "free hate." The American novelist and screenwriter may portray in detail a man killing a woman, but not one making love to her. To be sure, the pornography of violence is also condemned: the moralist has taken up arms against it, he will fight it to the death, he will destroy it utterly. And thus the hatred of evil can become an acceptable excuse—for hate. This is not to say flatly that aggression in all forms is wicked, as gentler versions of moralism have it. The moral problem is to externalize aggression and direct it against its proper objects. That is the moral problem with libido as well. The moralist feeds his prurience in his search for purity, and tries to master his own impulses by censoring the impulses of others. "Thou shalt not love, thou shalt not hate"—no wonder the moralist is felt to be lacking in simple humanity!

It is not Puritanism which is here in question. As a religious tradition, Puritanism is perhaps less influential in America than are the various evangelical, revivalist denominations. Just as Plato's Eros was scarcely platonic but in fact the creative principle, what is often called "puritanical" is not an austere self-denial but a single-minded devotion to self-advancement. In this ethic, sensory gratification is condemned, not because it is an indulgence, but because it interferes with work—its price is exorbitant, its pleasure is transient. But if it can refresh the tired businessman, it has its place. What is preached is Theodore Roosevelt's doctrine of "the strenuous life"; even William James defined moral action as "action in the line of greatest resistance." [49] These are the perspectives invited by an expanding frontier and an equalitarian society that provides an unlimited opportunity for advancement of the self through mastery of the environment. Such perspectives are much less important today, though something of Prometheus and Faust has been an enduring and admirable strain in the American character. But that strain, absolutized and moralized, degenerates to the fault Shaw (in Man and Superman) so incisively laid to the British—"Your pious English habit of regarding the world as a moral gymnasium built expressly to strengthen your character in, occasionally leads you to think about your own confounded principles when you should be thinking about other people's necessities." What the Devil later in the play remarks about the Englishman applies to the American moralist as well: he "thinks he is moral when he is only uncomfortable."

The political impact of these perspectives is considerable. American politics has often been characterized as combining both religion and sport. But in recent years much of the sportsmanship has disappeared; what remains is the ritual and a highly charged moralistic rhetoric. Self-righteousness has been carried to such a point that the opposition party is almost made to feel immoral for carrying on a campaign at all. Other countries are understandably dismayed by our offensive pose of unswerving rectitude. "A nation forgives if its interests have been damaged," Weber wrote some decades ago, "but no nation forgives if its honor has been offended, especially by a bigoted self-righteousness." [50]

Worst of all, this attitude leads to the preposterous analysis of political problems as turning solely on ethical considerations. How many times have we been told that "the crisis of the times is moral, and the only hope for democracy depends upon whether it can revitalize itself as a moral force"! [51] We have been using enough and more than enough of this "moral force" in Hungary and the Middle East; I am not aware that it was "moral force" that carried the day in Korea. Yet the cry endlessly goes up for "spiritual regeneration." When the diagnosis is unvarying—a moral failing—moralization becomes the irresistible prescription. [52]

Yet moralization is not without a genuine moral quality—far be it from me to deny that there is any good in men of virtue! Though the moralist does not recognize the Devil in his most effective guises, still he fights the powers of hell wherever he encounters them. He may be lacking in moral insight, but he does have a species of moral courage. There is no quietism in the moralistic outlook, no passive resignation to the evil that men do. Wherever something calls for betterment, the moralist stands ready to answer the call. His efforts may be misdirected to amelioration of immediate consequences rather than to removal of underlying causes—as in his vast philanthropies—but they are moral efforts nevertheless. The continuing myth that Americans worship the dollar is a European—and now also Asiatic—defense mechanism against the actualities of American generosity. The moralist may be right after all: it is more blessed to give than to receive.

Most truly moral is American sympathy for the underdog, the underprivileged, the man who has been left out. European observers have always been struck by our kindly good nature; what is really striking is that they find it so noteworthy. "Nowhere," Bryce says, "is cruelty more abhorred. Even a mob lynching a horse thief in the West has consideration for the criminal and will give him a good drink of whiskey before he is strung up." [53]

It is even possible that Bryce was in dead earnest. Americans, at any rate, are in earnest about their kindliness. Though our policy of being a "good neighbor" is a typically moralistic formulation, it verbalizes for politics a real constituent of our personal lives. "If it were given me to look into the depths of a man's heart, and I did not find goodwill at the bottom, I should say without any hesitation, You are not an American." [54] No American, I think, will quarrel with this opinion of Santayana's; no one who knows Americans will lightly dismiss it. But the question is still to be asked whether goodwill alone can bring peace on earth.

THE CODE OF CONFORMITY

For all the talk of modernism, scepticism, and the collapse of moral authority, the working morality of America is largely traditional. Of course, there have been changes in customs and manners, as well as persisting differences among our many subcultures. The importance of such changes and differences is often underestimated; some kinds of diversity continue to be welcomed. But by and large, the American moral code follows traditional lines.

To say that it is traditional is not to say that it is mistaken. I am bringing into question not the content of the morality, but its basis— its warrant, not its worth. Morals everywhere are the outgrowth of mores: the right way of doing things is the way they have "always" been done. But from its beginnings America has prided itself on a willingness to subject tradition to rational scrutiny. In one of the Federalist Papers Madison asks, "Is it not the glory of the people of America that, whilst they have paid a decent regard to the opinions of former times and other nations, they have not suffered a blind veneration for antiquity, for custom, or for names, to overrule the suggestions of their own good sense, the knowledge of their own situation, and the lessons of their own experience?" [55] It can scarcely be denied that something of this glory has faded. Veneration for antiquity, custom, and names makes up a considerable part of the impassioned and sometimes hysterical defense of "the American way of life."

Our adherence to the authority of tradition is not overt and self-conscious. On the contrary, in both religion and politics the tradition itself is explicitly anti-authoritarian. Individual conscience and personal experience are called upon for support of policy, moral intuition rather than received dogmas of Church and State. But moral intuition has a social history; when it becomes absolute and moralistic it provides an internalized channel by which the authority of tradition can take effect. The right way is what conscience proclaims to be right; but conscience proclaims it because it is the way followed in the culture by which conscience itself was shaped.

The morality of conscience is thus still, in terms of the classic contrast, a customary rather than a reflective morality. Virtue is taken to be a matter of heart and soul, not sense and intellect. The eighteenth-century program of summoning tradition before the bar of reason has been replaced in the twentieth by a pervasive fear for traditional values felt to be threatened by the critical intelligence. The successful candidate is the man who appears safe, the conservative with the forward look. Only when traditional patterns collapse in crisis is there a disposition to turn to the man of boldness and imagination. As for the critical and reflective temper, it has little place in politics at all.

What makes a morality a matter of custom is more than respect for tradition. Not only the past but also the present fixes its content. In both cases the content derives from a source external to the moral agent. His way of life is determined by submission to a standard set by others. What begins as "a decent respect for the opinions of mankind" ends in a thoroughgoing "other-directedness." Thereby morality is brought back to its starting point in the mores. It becomes a matter of good form, good taste, respect for the conventions—in a word, conformity. An immoral act is simply something which is "not done," righteousness reduces to propriety, and the good is nothing other than the established order of things. The sense of wrongdoing is marked by shame rather than by guilt. And there is no need for a man to decide whether he would rather be right than president; the majority that elects the president thereby determines what is right. If only you conform to the majority, he is right and you are right and all is right as right can be.

But is Emerson no longer to be counted an American? "Whoso would be a man must be a nonconformist!" Oh yes, Emerson is quoted often enough; quoting Emerson—and Jefferson and Lincoln—is itself a propriety, one to which I have already paid my respects and will again! But the slogans of nonconformism usually function in fact only to strengthen the patterns of conformity. We are all alike in priding ourselves on being different; we enforce uniformity in the pretense of inviting deviation. When Russell was jailed as a pacifist in the First World War he identified his religion as "Atheist," to which the bailiff replied, "Ah well, I suppose we all worship the same God whatever we call Him!" Conformism reaches its limit when noncomformist patterns are beyond understanding.

American love of diversity is a traditional verbalization (and perhaps the same is true of my own criticism of conformity!). Orators and editors speak at length about the harmonious orchestration of our many cultural themes, about the beauty of the American mosaic fashioned from bits and pieces of such divergent cultural origins. But our practice often accords with the more traditional metaphor of the melting pot, which is boiling more furiously today than during the years of heavy immigration. In recent polls, two-thirds of the population would not allow anyone to make a speech in the community against churches and religion; only one in eight would allow such a person to teach.[56] Russell was thought to be unfit to hold a position at the City College of New York; and when Laski was in this country a few years ago, a great university found reason to cancel his scheduled lecture.

These are isolated cases, to be sure, and of foreigners besides; but no purpose would be served here by statistical documentation. Regardless of ritualistic reassurances, we are not in competition for an Olympic award as the freest nation on earth. Will we never judge ourselves by standards of our own making? In willing unity as an end we have bound ourselves to conformist pressures as means, and these, in turn, can grow into the regimentation we detest as tyranny. The zone of privacy has been steadily shrinking before the inroads of the police, the press, the advertiser, the employer, and officious persons everywhere. Let us by all means congratulate ourselves that Big Brother is not yet watching; but we must also commiserate with each other for prying cousins.

In the name of "Americanism" the right to private opinion is most often sacrificed. What a man reads, with whom he associates, how he understands foreign affairs—these are not his own concern, in the perspective of the Americanists, but must be brought into public view and scrutinized for any possible threat to the security of our way of life. "To be an American is of itself almost a moral condition, an education, and a career." Santayana wrote these words over thirty years ago.[57] In the last decade several careers—of men without either morals or education— have consisted of little else. For a time the forum of public discussion was closed to any arguments but those leading to foregone conclusions. Everything else was proscribed as "controversial"—to defend a system of government by controversy, for democracy is just that. We remain free of the despotism of censorship; but pre-censorship—the fear of subsequent reaction—operates strongly still, especially in the mass media. Our laws guarantee freedoms which are weakened by informal pressures before ever the courts can be invoked in their defense. We are still to achieve a "moral emancipation" which as yet "is but nominal with us. The inquisition of public opinion overwhelms in practice the freedom asserted by the laws in theory." The American whose help I am calling on is—need I say it?—Thomas Jefferson. There are few who would claim that since his day the inquisition of public opinion has lessened in intensity.

The Americanist proceeds by personalizing the basis of political debate. What is brought into question is not only the opponent's program and policies, but also his motives and character. Issues come to be formulated solely in terms of the comparative loyalty of the conflicting parties. Political ideas are appraised only according to whether they are safe or dangerous. I do not mean to deny that loyalties have been betrayed in the Communist conspiracy, that security faces risks, or even that ideas can be dangerous. The danger of ideas, as of every other instrument, is inseparable from their efficacy. The same force that makes any instrumentality a power for good can also work corresponding evil. The Americanist's conclusion follows logically from his premise; if we are to be secure from this danger, we must either proscribe ideas altogether or remove them from the plane of action. Democracy, in my understanding, rejects the premise; it is committed to living dangerously, compelling assent only by the force of ideas. To achieve greatly we must dare greatly. Above all, we must dare to live with heresy and even, as our individual judgments dictate, to be occasional heretics ourselves.

If only God Himself identified the orthodox! But in a democracy there is no agency external to the democratic process to serve as absolute judge of right and wrong. Orthodoxy is simply the view supported at a given historical moment by the preponderant force of the community. To fix Americanism forever in that moment is to deny its past and destroy its future. Life is defined once for all only in death; a way of life is as variable and plastic as the people who live it. It may be frozen in ideology, but even that demands interpretation, an act *within* history, for each day as that day declares it. Orthodoxy and heresy may change places—and revert again—as values find actuality or lose it in the specific choices of concrete action. The Americanism of the Americanists is as bleak and immobile as the shadows etched in concrete at Hiroshima.

The code of conformity, in binding the future to the past, betrays its lack of a sense of history. In offering itself as the sole standard of right and wrong, it reveals its blindness to the present as well. Differences in American values can as easily be found by moving from one person to another as from one time to another. We each define the good in our own perspectives, as our own experience dictates. "Every man, for his own part, calls that which pleases and is delightful to himself, *good*; and that *evil* which displeases him; in so much that while every man differs from another in constitution, they differ also one from another concerning the common distinction of good and evil." This analysis of the moral judgment is in the words of Hobbes; it is fundamental in Spinoza's ethics, and has been reaffirmed by almost every naturalistic philosopher since. Shaw's Revolutionist drew from it the moral that we should *not* do unto others as we would have them do unto us: their tastes may differ. We must either respect these differences or else forgo democracy to impose a code from above. We will not protest if the imposed values be to *our* taste; but how if *their* tastes govern?

The code of conformity takes for granted the superiority of the orthodox values. The question is, however, not which is "really" better, but what meaning can attach to a comparison at all? To speak of "better" is to presuppose someone *for* whom it is better—not the person in whose judgment it is such, but the person whose experience of good is being judged. It is the relativity of value I am urging, not its subjectivity. Comparisons of value are odious when they overlook the essence of the values compared: the needs, interests, and tastes whose satisfaction is the very ground of value. Objective differences in these make for objective differences in value, however great the conformist pressures forcing valuations into a single mold. In our Father's house are many mansions; the plurality of values does not undermine the worth of any. The bogey of relativism is frightening only when we mistake it for subjectivism—as though the dependence of value on differing human desires makes the satisfaction of desire a matter of mere think-so. The varieties of human value are just beginning to be empirically explored; in the perspectives of conformism, such an exploration will produce only a catalog of human folly and perversity. Fortunately, only a minority of Americans have yielded this much to conformist pressures.

Critics of American culture have been given to loose talk about the evils of "standardization" and have made of difference itself an absolute good. There has been much foolish romanticism in connection with defiance of convention and self-conscious "originality." American technology, however, has demonstrated to all the world the human worth of standardized means, interchangeable parts, instrumentalities designed for application under the widest range of conditions. The resultant increase in the productivity of labor contributes significantly to the good life however that be conceived. The criticism has been superficial because it directed itself against standardization as such; and it has been futile because the value of standardization is now a commonplace of universal experience. What is objectionable is the unthinking extension of these technological perspectives to ends as well as means, to the values sought as well as to the ways pursued in the seeking. We have succeeded brilliantly in providing the one right tool for every job; but we have too often supposed that there is only one job for every right-thinking man, only one way of life, only one set of values.

Differences here are felt to be even more distressing than in the gauges of adjoining railroads. "We must . . . dissolve particularism," the conformist tells us, "vary the mixture indefinitely, disseminate all traits, enrich ourselves by permutation and combination. Anything else is the vicious circle of neurotic irritation and neurotic fear." [58] It is in this attitude itself that I find the irritation and fear. Differences in value engender conflict only in the perspectives of a conformism irritated by difference, not in the view of an accepting pluralism. We are impelled to destroy differences only when we are fearful of our capacities to live with them. In truth, the life of a democracy is a continuing conflict of values and its continuing resolution. The conformist is intolerant of difference because he has no tolerance within himself for the give and take of democratic decision making. If he can be sure of agreement beforehand, there will be no decisions to make. Failing this, he can at least look to a happy future when all differences will have disappeared in a realm of value rich and creamy with homogenized goodness.

It is always possible to make it appear that values are uniform, by concealing real differences behind a verbal sameness. Is not the emancipation of man from bondage to other men a communistic as well as a democratic ideal, social justice the aim of both patterns of social organization? In the abstract, yes; but the concrete meanings given to these ideals by specific practices and institutions are very different. If freedom of the press, for instance, is conceived as the right of the people to know the truth, and truth is held to be definable only by governmental authority, a state-controlled press will be thought to be free. We are ourselves the victims of this Soviet semantics if we identify values only because they bear the same names (or distinguish them only because they are differently labeled). Everyone, surely, seeks "justice," or at any rate recognizes that he ought to do so. But this is to say only that the desirability of the thing is part of the meaning of the word; what does not answer to our aspirations we do not recognize as being "really just." Similarly, we can produce a show of unity by focusing on "ultimate" ends, sufficiently remote for crucial differences in proximate policy to vanish in the distance. No doubt Israel and Egypt both want a resolution of the crisis in the Middle East. But it would be naive to suppose that this ultimate end of enduring peace represents the basis for agreement; on the contrary, the concrete meaning of "peace" for each of them is precisely what divides them. Two chess players both wanting a draw can quickly agree on the outcome of the game; but to say that they both want a checkmate is to point precisely to what makes them antagonists.

The logic of such situations is absurdly simple; alas, policy formation sometimes seems to follow a peculiar logic of its own, particularly when moral considerations come into play. I propose to call this blindness to real differences in value because of abstract and verbalistic sameness the *eudaemonian* fallacy, from Aristotle's term for happiness as the universally acknowledged good. Nietzsche's aphorism that man does not desire happiness, but only the Englishman does, is more than a jibe at bourgeois values. It directs attention to a narrower sense of the term in which it designates values that are far from universal. This duality of meaning is basic to the structure of the fallacy; in its broader sense the fallacious generalization is true but empty, and in its narrower sense significant but false. This equivocation has been pointed out many times with respect to the view that all men are fundamentally selfish. This confuses the truism that the satisfaction of each of my desires satisfies me, with the falsehood that what I desire is only my own satisfaction. The alleged universality of the profit motive is another case in point. In the broad sense of "profit" as any accession of good, it is tautologous that all action is undertaken for profit. In its specifically economic sense, this is patently false, even with regard to action in the economic sphere. Work is motivated also by what Veblen called "the instinct of workmanship," by ideals of service, by a desire for self-respect or the respect of others, by devotion to the good of the organization or even to the greater glory of God. In short, the *eudaemonian* fallacy finds a singleness of purpose behind the multiplicity of concrete values only by artificially abstracting values from the context of action which alone gives them meaning.

By such an abstraction the conformist can assure himself that American values are universal, that underneath it all other peoples prize just what we do. Such differences as he recognizes he ascribes to ignorance, to the lack of natural endowments—especially of character—and, most of all, to the pernicious influence of wicked leaders. Of course he can tolerate minor differences in political forms, as in the British monarchy or French parliamentarianism—though unquestionably the American political system is the best. But the basic values to which he demands domestic conformity he also expects to dominate the international scene. The American Way is intended for export, and for the best of reasons: America has, in Theodore Roosevelt's words, "a responsibility for the moral welfare of others which cannot be evaded." [59] Notice: not a moral responsibility for their welfare as *they* conceive it, but a responsibility for their *moral* welfare as *we* conceive it. America is the custodian of world morality, on behalf of history, posterity, or God. If we cannot see to the establishment of American values everywhere, we must at least secure their existence here. There is continuing pressure on our foreign policy—though it has progressively lessened in recent decades—to address itself only to this limited objective and let the rest of the world go hang. But if we are to concern ourselves with the welfare of others, there can be no real question what their welfare consists in: it is to be as much like Americans as they can possibly manage.

This is the posture in which for decades Europe and Asia have stereotyped the American: a moralistic imperialist imposing on others his puritanism and vulgarity to cover his sordid material interests. It is understandable that other nations should regard as insufferable conceit the presumption that only the American way of life embodies the true faith, while everything else is sin and superstition. The irony is that what the posture really expresses is a deep-seated insecurity. Our missionary zeal is rooted in a hope for our own conversion. When conformity serves as the standard of value, the mere existence of other values brings our own into question. *Therefore* there must be no others. The conformist wants nothing so much as to be accepted, to be liked. Popularity marks him as one of the Lord's anointed; it is at once the sign and the substance of his Election. This is what motivates the tendency to universalize American values; it is a wish-fulfilling fantasy to allay the anxieties of being left alone with values whose worth depends on others.

Accordingly, American foreign relations are conducted in the perspectives of salesmanship: we must "sell" our policies to other nations, and we can do so only by selling ourselves. The superiority of American values thus becomes a primary theme of American diplomacy as well as one of its working presuppositions. But we cannot quite believe in this superiority ourselves unless it is first acknowledged by others. The important thing, then, is to make ourselves liked, and it is to this end that we direct our efforts. It does not occur to us, however, to formulate policies that are also in the interest of those we want as allies. Instead we undertake to buy friendship, then rightly distrust the love that is for sale. We are forever looking for the prostitute with the heart of gold.

Conformism itself lays bare the dynamics of this insecurity. In the last century, the great mobility of American society made it hard for a man to know what his place was, what was rightfully his, and what was expected of him. In the present century, the narrowing of opportunity has made it doubly unsure where a man can get to, and whether he can remain at whatever height he reaches. Intensified competition engenders hostility, evokes fear both of failure and of reprisals for competitive success, and leads finally to the insecurities of emotional isolation. This line of analysis goes back at least to Spinoza: a man's security can rest only on what he is in his own nature. To measure ones' worth by a comparative standing, by conformity to norms externally imposed, is precisely what constitutes human bondage.

The final cost of the code of conformity is the sacrifice of leadership. The role of the leader it assigns to the most successful follower, the man whose features can best reflect at every moment the changing face of the crowd. Bryce was surely prescient when he wrote, "In America the practical statesman is apt to be timid in advocacy as well as infertile in suggestion. He seems to be always listening for the popular voice, always afraid to commit himself to a view which may turn out unpopular." [60] We have had some very "practical" statesmen, and television and the polls make them more "practical" every day. Leadership requires the maintenance of a certain distance from the followers, enough to give scope for independent judgment and decisive action. But this in turn calls for courage and self-confidence, not the sheepish virtues of conformity to a preformed opinion. Such a man may not always be liked; he may even expect to make some enemies. But to be able to lead others a man must be willing to go forward alone.

MORALITY AND POWER

In many ways the American moral code is absolutistic and conformist. Yet a great gulf divides it from the absolutism of the dictatorships, the regimented conformity of the totalitarian states. The key to this difference lies in the relationship of morality to power. In America the force of the state does not define morality but is itself continually subjected to the moral judgment of the citizen. Granted that in many areas of action American legalism tries to reduce morality to law; in business and politics whatever is within the law is conventionally acceptable. But this holds true largely for such peripheral matters as a corporation's payment of taxes or a legislator's acceptance of gifts. A critical business policy or political decision may at any time raise moral issues recognized as not settled—or, at any rate, as not yet settled—by the law. Our dualistic perspectives make for a tendency to polarize morality and power. In foreign affairs we are likely to rely on the affirmation of abstract moral principles together with the use of amoral economic pressures; a habit of thought which would concretize the principles and give moral significance to the pressures is foreign to us. Yet there remains a real sense of moral responsibility in political commitment. We may distrust as "propaganda" explicitly ideological formulations—even our own. But there is an unwavering insistence on the application of moral standards to political action. The will of the state is an expression of one kind of power; but morality lies in the power expressed as the will of the people.

Only the will of the people democratically justifies the action of the state. The power of the state rests on a moral basis; democracy agrees with Aristotle and Aquinas in viewing the state as an agency of moral order. This is the significance of the American tradition of natural rights; it is to secure these rights that governments are instituted among men. Once established, of course, governments define legal obligations to themselves. But these are morally binding only as the government, for its part, discharges *its* moral obligations. When government becomes destructive of moral ends, it is the right of the people to alter or abolish it. There is no autonomous political obligation distinct from moral obligation and its legal offspring. Democratic political theorists from Locke to Laski have insisted on this moralizing of power, in contrast to the totalitarian practice of politicizing even morality.

The historian of political ideas may rightly point out that Marx too had a moral objective. His materialism was metaphysical, not moral; there is no hedonism in it. It is a dangerous error to suppose that the appeal of communism—to the literate, at any rate—lies in its offer to fill the belly. The promise that Marx held out was rather to free the worker from wage slavery and to liberate the works of the human spirit from the status of mere commodities.[61] But there is also a danger here of succumbing to the *eudaemonian* fallacy. The question is not one of ultimate ends but of the proximate policies pursued in the name of these ends. Whatever its principles, in fact the communist elite treats the mass as something to be manipulated. The mass constitutes the means and the material by which the elite is to attain the ends of the state. Democratic ethics falls back on Kant rather than Hegel: in accord with Kant's categorical imperative, man is never to be treated as a means only, even if it be for the ends of history as Hegel conceived it. The concept of "exploitation" does not derive from the economics of surplus value; it is a moral category. Man is exploited when he is subjected to power without moral restraint.

The American moral code insists on limiting power by this restraint. Justice is not simply the interest of the stronger, the decision of the sovereign, or the policy of the ruling class. On this score American ethics has no use for Thrasymachus, Hobbes, or Lenin. The concept of "bourgeois morality" may make sense as designating the particular values of a particular social class, but not as identifying the ground of moral value with class interest, just as "class science" may point to what a class believes to be true without in the least undermining the objective basis of scientific truth. The reduction of morality to power pushes the basis of moral appraisal into a region wholly inaccessible to experience—the relation of the sovereign to God or of the proletarian dictator to history. Confronted with tyranny, Americans are not content with the assurance that history will provide its ultimate justification. Our attitude to the tyrant is not "Leave him to Heaven" but "Leave him to us!" The people must judge, and they must judge now.

It is not the political organization of the economic system that distinguishes the "People's Republics" from government of, by, and for the people. Democracy can accommodate whatever degree of economic planning or socialization emerges from the democratic process itself; some degree may even be necessary for the preservation of the process. The decisive question is whether the power applied in the economic sphere is subject to appraisal by the moral values underlying both politics and economics. What constitutes "statism" is not the range of welfare functions assumed by the state but the moral claim made by the state in performnig those functions. Similarly, a sense of history is as necessary to democratic statesmanship as it is to any other; but in a democracy, historical fact does not of itself define moral value. In these terms, the multiplicity of social philosophies can be brought into intelligible order without the crude simplifications of "freedom versus authority."

The theories of the organic state of English absolute idealism give primacy to the state as more metaphysically "real" than the empirical individuals that compose it. The locus of morality is thought to lie in this larger whole, the national community whose actions produce the movement of history. In fascism, the career of the state not only constitutes history but also defines the substance of morality, which is identified with the needs of the state at each historical juncture. Other social philosophies make history primary. For the social Darwinists, as for Nietzsche and Spengler, morality is defined by the historical process, the state being one expression among others of the spirit of the age. Hegel and Marx view history as working through the state; morality is meaningful only in relation to the dialectic of reason or the forces of production which provide the dynamics of history. Finally, morality may be put in first place. Judaeo-Christian thought conceives of history as embodying a universal moral order instituted by Divine Providence; the state is an instrumentality of this order. Democracy shares this insistence on the primacy of the moral. But it interprets the state directly in terms of moral ideals, and not through a chiliastic philosophy of history. For democracy, history is forever in the making. The Fall and the Redemption are enacted anew in each moment of moral choice.

Every state brings power into some relation with morality. Naked power must somehow be clothed in the robes of authority so that coercion can be internalized. The stability of the state depends on a widespread sense of the legality of its power, by which obedience to law is grounded in something more than fear. Unless a revolution is, in Lasswell's phrase, a rupture of conscience, any shift in the balance of power in the state can provide the basis for a new structure of authority. The state, in short, requires a principle of legitimacy by which it can command the continuing loyalty of its subjects and not just their passing obedience.

The possession of power, together with the capacity to exercise it, can itself be made to serve as such a principle. The sword belongs to him who has the strength to draw it and the courage to wield it. Might makes right when the maintenance of order is given primacy among political values and the evils of anarchy are thought to outweigh any others. Machiavelli is only superficially amoral: the unification of Italy was for him the political ideal by which the power of the prince was legitimized. Similarly, fascist political thought must obviously be understood in terms of the social disorganization of Europe in the decades following the First World War. In America order is not an absolute value, and scarcely even a major political concern. Yet our ideals of efficiency and success lend themselves to a similar political application. Between the wars our vulgar pragmatists have had a grudging—and sometimes even wholehearted—admiration for Hitler and Mussolini.

The identification of de facto with de jure power is not wholly absurd. American moralism has sometimes thrust out of consciousness the facts of political life, so that empirically recognizable power is denied formal recognition far beyond the point where the formality is serviceable as an instrument of diplomacy. Recognition may be withheld on moralistic grounds, rather than on the basis of a realistic appraisal of the moral values that are politically possible in the situation. The enduring contribution to political thought of the Machiavellians—Mosca, Michels, and Pareto, as well as their eponym—is their insistence on the facts of power as basic to any realistic morality of power. What is morally objectionable in Realpolitik is not that these facts are made central in politics but that they are identified, as is, with political values. Power politics is politics that takes power as an end in itself and as the sole and absolute end of political action. The refusal to countenance power as having any moral standing at all is not the antithesis to power politics but its moralistic counterpart. Political idealism which renounces power altogether achieves only the empty virtue of the impotent.

There is another principle of legitimacy: the conception of the state as fulfilling a mission accepted as moral—and even as defining morality—by the subjects of the state. Such a principle secularizes the divine right of kings, replacing God by history and the workings of Providence by historical forces. The Marxist dialectic is a political Manicheism: the class struggle re-enacts on earth the cosmic conflict between God and Satan. Politics in this perspective becomes a calling, and the vanguard of the proletariat serves as a priesthood—dedicated and self-denying. In the light of this personal asceticism, the moralistic concern with "corruption" sadly misconceives the moral issues raised by the exercise of power.

In the politics of Destiny it is still the Judaeo-Christian drama of man's fate that is being enacted, but in a secular production. Hitler's

Teutonic mythology and the New Order, Mussolini's Caesarism, primitive communism and world socialism—all these have the moral significance of paradise lost and paradise regained. The drama differs from the religious version chiefly in its holism: its protagonist is not the individual soul but the race, nation, or class. In American political life historicism reveals itself in the appeal of policy to historical patterns for meaning and justification: a linear pattern in the progressive's perspectives of continuous improvement in an unending future; cyclical in the reactionary's longing for a golden past to which we must return; or shrunken to a fixed point in the present, in the conservative's defense of a closed social order. For liberal democracy, past, present, and future are all three implicated in public policy. Paradoxically, historicism denies the reality of time, making of it, as Plato did, a moving image of an eternity where the solution to all human problems is already prefigured.

It is tempting to formulate policy by reference to a cause which must ultimately triumph, and Americans of many political persuasions have yielded to the temptation. We have usually rejected not the politics of destiny but only the mission claimed by other nations. It is the secularism that has offended our moral sense, not the historicism. We have not always seen clearly that a historic mission, whatever its content, divorces power from morality.[62] Policy that is realistically concerned with human values cannot be formulated in terms of Causes, but only in terms of the real possibilities for good in concrete political situations. We cannot discharge our moral obligations once and for all simply by pledging allegiance to America's mission of morality. We cannot realistically hope to succeed in our moral aspirations unless our fantasies of predestined success give way to sober appraisals of the risk of failure.

For most Americans what legitimizes power is the doctrine of representation. A man has the right to do as he chooses for himself; that right is transferred to the state insofar as the state represents him. What this presupposes, as Locke and Rousseau saw, is that there is no fixed social order into which the citizen is born, for otherwise his choice would be limited from the outset in ways which representation could not justify. It presupposes also a code of representation, a standard of performance by which the constituency can judge whether their representative is indeed representing them. It is in this responsibility to the people that the moral restraint on power is localized. Power is legitimate when it governs by consent of the governed. The doctrine of natural rights does not go deep enough in its attempt to provide a moral foundation for power. For what the rights come to in experience requires interpretation; if power is to be justified by its efforts to secure these rights, their interpretation must rest with the people. Morality is inseparable from freedom; the moral use of power is inseparable from a free consent to its exercise.

American moralism, however, sentimentalizes "the people." It imagines that popular sovereignty and civil liberties will inevitably result in the right decision. And so they will—provided that the "rightness" of the decision is recognized to be procedural and not substantive. A belief arrived at on the basis of the available evidence is necessarily a rational belief, but it is not necessarily a true one. The democratic process of decision making is justified by the moral aim of developing free and mature personalities. It does not and cannot find justification by a pretense of unerring wisdom in the people. Plato's arguments for a philosopher-king are logically sound—how could I deny it! But they are entirely beside the point. There is no doubt that an elite might make better decisions; but the question is whether it is better even so that they do the deciding. The voice of the people *is* the voice of God; only, what the people speaks in that voice is its own mind.

The American insistence that popular support for a policy is necessary to its morality seems to me unexceptionable. But we believe too easily that the consent of the people is sufficient for morality. We suppose that the force of public opinion itself provides the moral restraint on power, and particularly do we think so with respect to what we call "world opinion." What this belief overlooks is that consent can be cajoled as well as coerced; virtue is lost to seduction more often than to rape. Hitler was elected by a democratic majority under the Weimar Constitution; Communist candidates would win even free elections behind the Iron Curtain as long as the voters themselves are not free. Spinoza's rationalism is as important for democratic theory as Locke's empiricism.

The moralistic doctrine is that "the people" everywhere are good, kind, wise, and friendly. Only their leaders exhibit moral failings; quarrels between nations are really only between governments, not peoples; secret diplomacy is immoral, though of course security secrets must be kept. Direct access to the people of other nations would solve all our diplomatic problems. For the people of these nations have basically moral goals—that is to say, our own. Yet leaders are as good as their followers make them, and every people has the government it deserves. This tissue of contradictory sentiments has nothing to do with the political realities of terror and indoctrination; of the helplessness of goodwill before a monopoly of violence; of the manipulation for political ends of prejudice, insecurity, and fear. Moralistic democracy never misses an opportunity to pay homage to the people; it is less concerned about opportunities to make the people worthy of it. We worship an idol fashioned in our own image, and risk the punishment of being condemned to live in a social order not of our own choosing.

The American morality of power is under continuous tension between our moralization and our vulgar pragmatism. The uneasy equilibrium between what we think of as "idealism" and "realism" periodically gives way to the one tendency or the other. Like a character in Dostoevski, we hang suspended between bursts of religious ecstasy and drunken debauchery. Power is to be used by men of conscience and integrity for the common good, and its exercise guided always by the ideals of justice and humanitarianism, sympathy and fair play. At the same time, power is intrinsically immoral, corrupting those who have it, and in its very nature destroying the freedom of those subjected to it. Politics, in short, we regard as a succession of necessary evils; we play with words to make virtues of these necessities, rather than apply our energies to reconstituting either the facts that make them necessary or the valuations that make them evil.

For the moralizer, power of any sort is a trust, public office an opportunity for public service. Nothing must be allowed to override the restraints on power of legality and conscience. Yet, Americans pride themselves on their toughness, too. Mercy is subordinated to justice, and justice in turn to public safety, especially under the rubric of national security. We must not coddle wrongdoers or be soft on our enemies. Though the ideal of power is service, politics is felt to be unsavory. Politicians, by and large, are incompetent; they are office hungry, and once they secure office will do anything to keep it; what they look for are sinecures or opportunities to exploit power for their personal advantage. From its beginnings American political thought has distrusted government, and this distrust has undeniably served to strengthen our freedoms. But while emphasizing the dangers of governmental interference we have also pictured government as foolish and ineffective, riddled with inefficiency, and incapable of coping with problems solved daily by private enterprise.

When power takes the form of actual violence, the American moral code condemns it unhesitatingly: violence is inadmissible as an instrument of policy. What can be identified as overt aggression is monstrous and shocking, regardless of provocations. (On the other hand, the drive for individual competitive success is admirable.) Our own military must be carefully watched to ensure its subordination to civil government; the military does not represent the nation, especially in peace time. Even in war, an all-out effort must still be subjected to moral restraints; total war belongs to totalitarianism. For all that, violence is justified and is even a duty when it is inflicted on an immoral enemy. In that case the war becomes a crusade; the Church Militant has the blessings of the Prince of Peace. Peace, after all, is secondary to righteousness. What is more, the fight against evil purifies its participants. During the past twenty years the acceptable American attitude toward Soviet institutions and practices has been a matter of delicate timing, not of realistic social analysis. A just war aims at nothing else than victory over the forces of evil; morality condemns any negotiated peace with aggressors— they must surrender unconditionally. Our military men, viewed "realistically," exhibit the acme of loyalty, courage, efficiency, and leadership. In short, violence is damnable, but the instruments of violence guarantee peace and are the symbols of security.

Symbols themselves may serve the ends of power. As such, they are thought to constitute "propaganda," which is vicious in its very nature: it deals in falsehoods, inflames political passions, and interferes with the right of the citizen to think for himself. Propaganda makes for conflict and confusion when it is used by the enemy; when used by us, however, it is largely without effect. On the other hand, it is necessary to refute the enemy's lies about us, and to compete with him for the friendship of neutrals. Besides, our own citizens must be indoctrinated with democratic ideals and principles. This is a matter of "education," however, not "propaganda." It must be scrupulously factual, limiting itself to providing the information from which the citizen can draw his own conclusions. The best propaganda is the simple truth; the facts can speak eloquently for themselves. Yet, not all the facts should be disseminated. A free flow of information is necessary so that the people can participate intelligently in the making of decisions; but military security, efficient governmental operations, and delicate diplomatic maneuvers all necessitate justifiable measures against excessive or ill-timed disclosures. A free press, of course, is a bulwark of democracy, provided it recognizes its public responsibility—that is, provided it is not divisive or so self-critical as to injure our standing in the eyes of other nations. In sum, the American code for political symbols, as for political practices and for the use of violence, allows us to keep our shining ideals untarnished in the parlor while we live our lives being "practical" in the kitchen.

In the conventional sense, the level of political morality in America is high. True, even conviction of a crime does not altogether preclude the holding of political office, including membership in the United States Congress.[63] And there are recurrent incidents in both major parties of bribery and corruption. But public morality in this sense only reflects the general level of morality in the country. Regardless of the quality of men in public service, no public officer, as Harold Ickes once pointed out, has ever bribed himself.[64] The point I have been urging, however, is that conventional political morality relates only to the externals of public policy, not to its substance. Policy honestly administered after having been formulated without undue influence by special interests is thought to raise no other moral issues. But it is just here that the important values are at stake, in the decisions made by honest men on behalf of what they sincerely believe to be the interests of those they represent.

The success we have so far attained in securing human rights and promoting social welfare—and it is considerable!—has too much inclined us to view our political and economic system as automatically guaranteeing moral achievement. Moral responsibility has too often been thought to be limited to keeping the mechanism in good working order; when it is running smoothly, moral values will take care of themselves. In the last few decades Americans have become widely aware of the moral bankruptcy in the totalitarian escape from freedom by submission to the will of the leader, the state, or the party. We are not yet equally conscious of our own moral escapism by submission to the will of the people as embodied in our political and economic institutions. We cannot restrain power by moral standards except as we free those standards themselves from amoral political restraints.

POLITICAL IDEALS

The substance of political morality relates to the content of public policy rather than to the honesty of its formation and administration. This substance is crystallized in political ideals—for America, as for the rest of the democratic world, in the classic ideals of liberty, equality, and fraternity. Whatever the failings in our conception of political morality, our practice with regard to these ideals justifies much of the praise we commonly bestow on it. I have little patience with the moralism that has eyes only for our shortcomings, never our achievements. Such moralism, especially in European appraisals, often invokes ideals only to rationalize a hostility to America whose motivation is far from ideal. Yet the misuse of criticism by others need not keep us from being critical ourselves. The point to which criticism must be directed is not, of course, the empty tautology that our actuality falls short of our ideals. It is, rather, that our moralistic misconception of these ideals continuously interferes with realistic moral achievement.

The most basic of the ideals is liberty, since it is not only an inherent value but is also instrumental to securing the others. To the Communists it is of no consequence, because in the perspectives of their historical determinism liberty is an illusion: individual choice is bound by historical necessity. To be sure, history does impose constraints on the individual; but it does not bind him altogether. Choice remains free within a range of possibilities that history provides. The past exerts a force that cannot be ignored, but it is not wholly irrestistible. On the other hand, the metaphysical free will with which this determinism is frequently countered in America is equally irrelevant to action. Free choice is as subject to causality as is any other event. What makes it free is that among its causal agencies is included a symbolic indication of the future consequences of present alternatives. We are free when our choice is the product of full awareness of the needs to be met and of the resources and constraints of the situation in which we find ourselves.

Such psychological freedom is a necessary condition of political liberty. American dualism tends to view liberty as a matter either of political mechanisms or of "character" conceived in isolation from its formative elements in society. The emphasis we put on our tradition of freedom helps to overcome this dualism: tradition is constituted by both personality and institutions. It becomes a political force only as it constitutes in turn the basis of widespread participation in the political process. The importance of such participation for the maintenance of liberty has been recognized by political theorists since antiquity—most eloquently in Pericles' funeral oration. That the proportion of voters is lower in America than in most other countries does not necessarily signify a dangerous political apathy; it may also mark our contentment with the workings of our political system. Yet some measure of irresponsibility cannot be denied, or at least a sense of helplessness in the face of what is felt to be a vast and unmanageable political mechanism. "Go fight City Hall!" is as American as "You can't do this to me!"

In the last half century the development of depth psychology as well as the rise of authoritarian regimes has made Americans increasingly aware of the importance of personality in politics. The fact that thousands of ex-Nazis became Communists, as many ex-Communists turned to the authority of religion, we begin to find intelligible in terms of personality dynamics. The many studies of "the authoritarian personality" trace in character the roots of authoritarian institutions. Political liberty demands psychological independence, as against both conformism and rebelliousness; an integrated self, as against the internal conflicts of a dualistic code; and inner security, as against the neurotic quest for certainty that ends in absolutism. It is this dependence of political institutions on personality traits that justifies Dewey's insistence that democracy must be achieved anew by each generation.[65]

But freedom is a consequence as well as a condition of liberty. A purely psychological analysis is as inadequate as a purely institutional one. Independence is difficult to achieve in a society where the real dependencies of a complex division of labor are extended to the absurdities of reliance on "the expert" in every phase of life, and where "expertness" itself is only socially defined. Integration is not easy in a culture which unremittingly stimulates desire while withholding and even moralistically condemning what is necesary to its satisfaction. The insecurities that make this an age of anxiety owe as much to continuing economic and political uncertainty as to the traumas of personal history. This interdependence of free personality and libertarian institutions need not be seen as the working of a vicious circle of futility. It can equally be made the basis for a perspective of successive approximation.

The right of free speech may be viewed as uniting freedom and liberty in a single ideal. It is a right that is rooted in the core of personality by way of the beliefs and values for which it allows expression; and it reaches out to society in the act of expressing them through social channels. America still adheres, by and large, to the classic defense of this right, as formulated by Milton, Jefferson, Mill, and Holmes. The value of free speech is inherent as constitutive of the free personality, which cannot grow without expression. And it is of instrumental value in two ways, both as defending other liberties by allowing grievances to be heard and as necessary to the discovery of truth. Whatever truth authority may lay hold on is beyond correction if inquiry itself is subject to authoritarian control. And its truth cannot even be recognized outside of free inquiry, for there is nothing outside experience with which we can test its correspondence. The control of opinion, if it is not monstrously thorough, only dramatizes the forbidden belief. Like loyalty oaths, which are most oppressive on the most loyal, the denial of free speech, in creating a suffocating fear of heresy, robs even orthodoxy of its vitality. At this writing the public schools of our country's third largest city cannot freely discuss, for fear of undermining patriotism, an international organization which enjoys the active support of the Republic to which the patriot daily pledges allegiance.

Americans have been aware from the beginning of the dangers of political interference with their liberties, but we tend to overlook or underestimate the dangers outside the political mechanism. We recognize at once the viciousness in a pronouncement by the Communist Party on the correctness of a theory of genetics. We are not so quick in recognizing and resisting economic and social pressures on free opinion, whether from the monopolistic control of the mass media, the influence of advertisers, or the power of pressure groups. Not only the totalitarian governments have their captive audiences.

Yet it is, after all, the political factors that are basic to liberty, for the others are themselves subject to control by political power. Liberty in America derives from our constitutionalism. The legitimizing of power by the principle of representation leads to majority rule; it is the constitutional limits on power that guarantee minority rights. In detail, these limits constitute a system of juridical defense: innocence until guilt is proved; guilt for actions only, not for thoughts or intentions, and actions counter to predictable law, not to personal caprice; and the whole apparatus of due process of law. What this system comes to is the possibility of effective challenge to decisions. What makes challenge effective is our political pluralism—the existence of more than one party; the focusing of power in other institutions than the state, the press, the church, the unions, and organizations of every description; and the separation of powers within the state, for power can be limited only by power. In this respect the investigating committees of the past decade threatened our liberties in the act of trying to preserve them. They exercised all three powers of government at once: legislating by defining the offense of subversion, judging whether the offense had been committed, and punishing what they judged offensive by public defamation.[66]

The preservation of liberty thus requires the sharing of power by the citizenry. Conventionally, this is distinguished as the "positive" liberty which must supplement the "negative"; more accurately, it is a matter of a causal analysis supplementing a description of effects. The political mechanisms of universal suffrage, proportional representation, the initiative, referendum, and recall, and all the rest are only external marks of liberty. Its substance lies in access to the bases of control and the channels of influence in society: wealth, education, public office, media of communication, and the association of like-minded citizens into groups organized for common ends.

It is here that the fundamental problems of liberty in America must be localized. The individual alone cannot effectively counter the power to which he is subjected; he must organize with others. But the paradox of organization is that every organization acquires its own instinct of self-preservation, which drives it to sacrifice the principles for which it was established to the expediencies of its own survival. And the power within the organization, by what Michels called "the iron law of oligarchy," tends to become so concentrated as to threaten liberty anew. There is an even more pressing paradox within which democracy is caught up, the paradox of liberty: liberty itself must pay the price of more liberty. We must somewhere yield the right to choose in order to create a world in which elsewhere there is more right to choose. The continuing problem of democracy, for which no formula or mechanism can provide a permanent solution, is to find liberty *within* the system of power. Liberty must turn to power for resources as well as restraints. It is not enough to love liberty or any other political ideal; one must love with a maturity which is capable of living with the ideal as well as worshipping it.

The ideal of equality impressed de Tocqueville and countless other observers as most characteristically American. As a political ideal, equality of course is not a matter of personal attributes or possessions but of rights and opportunities. To be born equal is to be limited in opportunity only by native endowments and by restrictions universal in the society. The basic right of equality is to be taken into the community without conditions. The conception of separate but equal facilities is self-contradictory; the separatedness is itself an inequality. It is an exclusion from the community with an implied inferiority, a guilt by dissociation. Similarly, immigration quotas are defensible only when based on factors, like labor skills, relevant to a place in the community; formulated in terms of ethnic origins they betray the equalitarian ideal. There seems to be some confusion as to what is truly alien to the American spirit.

Equality of opportunity cannot be guaranteed once for all by any arrangement of the social mechanism. The stereotype of America as the land of unlimited opportunity did not derive from a literal absence of any limits; there have always been limits, and in the present, century-old opportunities have vanished while new ones have come into being. What was felt to be important, what *is* important, is the equalization of whatever opportunities are available at any moment. This is not an automatic consequence of a pre-established harmony, as was postulated in classical economics; it calls for policy wisely directed to just that end. To be born equal is to be born with a right to contract freely for privileges by the free acceptance of duties, rather than into a determinate status of a fixed social order. But freedom of contract may become only a name if the pressure of economic necessity denies genuine choice. This is the significance of minimum-wage legislation and the apparatus of collective bargaining. As new pressures develop, new policies will be called for to maintain equality.

Equality is thus fundamentally an economic ideal as liberty is a political one and freedom a spiritual one. Of all the forms of discrimination, the economic has been judged to be the most serious, the most bitterly resented, and the one most markedly at variance with democratic ideals. Satisfaction of the primary economic needs is basic to an equalitarian society, for otherwise there is no genuine freedom to contract for further opportunities. These primary needs include more than food, clothing, and shelter; what the American economy can take pride in is its increasing recognition of the rights to educational betterment, productive work, and creative leisure.

Traditionally, the idea of equality has been conjoined with that of social justice, and they are still associated in the American moral code. We abhor the idea of "classes," so much so that it is difficult for us to consider it even as a category of purely descriptive social analysis; almost all Americans think of themselves as belonging to the middle class. To have no desire for getting ahead in the world, and especially for our children to be even better off than we are, is almost un-American. Social mobility in America is probably less than it was a century ago; but whatever the actuality, the aspiration remains. We are distrustful of the concentration of economic resources; moralistic support is always forthcoming for "the small businessman" and "the family farm." More effective is our determination to preserve equality with regard to values too important to be left to the inequities of economics—health, education, and the exercise of talent. Most Americans are prepared to meet the Communists on their own terms with the equalitarian ideal of a classless society.

An important component of this ideal is what Aristotle called "distributive justice," the distribution of goods on the basis of merit. To the American mind the bestowal of a privilege always evokes the question, "What has he done to deserve it?" Behind this colloquialism is Locke's justification of property by reference to the labor that was "mixed" with it in its production. Ownership is defensible only as it meets a moral obligation in terms of which it is judged to be deserved. The ideal of equality cannot countenance privilege which seeks justification only by allowing its benefits to trickle down to the less privileged. In a complex economy there is a correspondingly complex mixture of labor in all property. The continued attack by the extreme right on the income tax is met in the American moral consciousness with the insistence that the ability to pay is itself an index of benefits received: we pay the tax as the last obligation discharged in order to deserve the income.

What is at issue is the moral commitment of economic practice. But this commitment is only obscured in the moralistic dualism of "property rights" and "human rights." Property in the abstract is itself a human right; ownership is increasingly coming to be seen as a relationship among men, not between men and things. The entity that owns property is socially defined, even when we think it to be a concrete individual rather than an abstract corporation; and the fact of ownership consists of the enforcement by society of certain privileges of use. I say *certain* privileges, for the rights in property are in fact always far from absolute, however we verbalize them. The system of restrictions in force at any moment are taken to define the abstract and "natural" rights of property. When concrete values require changes in this system, such changes are either attacked as denying "property rights" or else defended in the name of contrasting "human rights." Morality does not call for a compromise between these spuriously contrasted claims, but for their integration in a humanized economy. Whether, how far, and in what respects our present economy should be subjected to planning, governmental controls, or even socialization, is a moral question, as are all questions of public policy. But it is not a moralistic one, which is to say, it is not a question of abstract principles. It is a question of concrete fact: how American values can best be achieved, in each situation as it arises, in accord with our own professed ideals.

The ideal of fraternity completes the classic trinity. "Democracy," Bryce wrote, "has not only taught the Americans . . . how to secure equality, it has also taught them fraternity. That word has gone out of fashion in the Old World. . . . Nevertheless there is in the United States a sort of kindness, a sense of human fellowship, a recognition of the duty of mutual help owed by man to man, stronger than anywhere in the Old World." [67] This is perhaps less true today than it was a century ago. A sense of human fellowship is a virtue of the frontier, and has almost vanished with the frontier. The conditions of urban life, even if they preserve the sense, provide few channels for its expression.

There is also a darker side to American history which must be faced. The history of bigotry in the United States is perhaps less shameful than in Europe, but not because it was any nobler in intent, rather, because it lacked the power to achieve its intent. Yet this in itself is a significant fact about American values. Bigotry today usually takes the form of prejudice by projection: "I myself am without prejudice, but unfortunately, my clients, employees, administrative superiors, . . . leave me no choice." A rationalization, to be sure; but by that very token a mark of acceptance of the ideal, even though it be an ambivalent acceptance.

There is no need to rehearse here once more the now familiar—alas, too familiar—explanation of prejudice in terms of scapegoating, insecurity, ego-enhancement, and the rest. More to the point is a recognition of the futility of the attempt to reinstate the ideal of fraternity on purely moralistic grounds. Too often the moralist bases his appeal for brotherhood on a reference either to a shared divinity or to the commonality of human nature: "After all, they're really just like us!" Such an appeal confuses community with identity, and reinforces prejudice by conceding the logic which derives a prejudicial conclusion from the premise of difference. To love another only because he is like me is to love not him but myself reflected in him; and to preserve my appearance I must at last destroy his reality.

Nor can fraternity be grounded in an appeal for "tolerance." This, too, concedes the implied objectionableness of difference and, what is worse, calls only for a passive permissiveness, not an active absorption of difference into the sense of community. There is an experiment in animal learning in which a hungry pike is put into a tank with minnows but separated from them by a sheet of glass. Again and again the pike dashes himself against the invisible glass, until he is conditioned to passivity. When at last the barrier is removed, the minnows can swim unmolested all around him. This is the state pictured by the philosophy of tolerance—live and let live. It cannot serve as an ideal for human society. In the relations of man to man, alienation and indifference may be even more disruptive of community than is hatred.

Perhaps the basic problem posed by the ideal of fraternity derives from the dehumanization of interpersonal relations in modern culture.

What is said in one of Silone's novels about fascist Italy comes uncomfortably near the mark with reference to the American business world: people do not have friends any more, only contacts and connections. Aristotle's *Ethics* devotes two long chapters to the goods of friendship; a comparably realistic treatise today would scarcely mention the subject. There may be widespread endorsement of Aristotle's dictum that "without friends no one would choose to live, even if he had all other goods." But its meaning is betrayed by our linking the goal of making friends to the goal of influencing people.

The depersonalization of politics is of particular relevance here. The bosses and ward heelers of the old-time machines related on a personal plane to the voters, and performed a variety of personal services for the large immigrant populations of the Eastern seaboard; the country candidate made himself personally known to his constituents. Today the mass media provide the channels for political appeal, and mere symbols of human relatedness replace the real thing—the nickname, the family pet, the image of the devoted wife. Such folksiness is of a piece with the moralistic verbalizations about brotherhood. In Plato's ideal *Republic* family life was to be replaced by a community structure in which every contemporary is a brother, every elder a father. Aristotle's criticism is refreshingly down-to-earth: "How much better is it to be the real cousin of somebody, than to be a son after Plato's fashion!" [68]

What part the state can play in sustaining the ideals of fraternity and equality is limited by its commitment to the ideal of liberty. But while prejudice may be politically inviolable, discrimination is not; at the very least, the state cannot be a party to discrimination by legally institutionalizing it. What more can be done America is now in the course of learning. The experimental temper of the American mind evokes both moralistic impatience and traditionalist denunciation. But in the long run nothing else than this temper can be relied on to ground our ideals in the realities of our daily life.

In American thought the ideals of liberty, equality, and fraternity are summed up in a single comprehensive ideal: individualism or, perhaps better, "individuality." Respect for the rights of the individual and recognition of his inherent worth imply all the rest. Democracy in America has conceived the values to be achieved by social action in terms of goods to be enjoyed in individual experience. Historically, this conception must be understood in connection with the perspectives of classical economics: the right of the individual entrepreneur and laborer to join in the economic process, and of the individual consumer to enter the market, when and how each of them sees fit—which is to say, on the basis of the individual satisfactions afforded each of them by the economy. Whatever the shortcomings of this economics, the theory of social value to which it led is basic to democracy. The aims of a democratic state must be specified in terms of distributive values—that is, values that can be referred to the individual members of the state. Collective values are significant only as instrumental to the distributive ones; the only justification for action directed to the wealth and power of the state is the well-being and security of its individual citizens.

But democratic individualism is misconceived when it is dualistically counterposed to "collectivism." That the basic democratic values are distributive does not imply that collective action is ruled out as a means of attaining them. An economy whose workings are appraised on the basis of the individual satisfactions it provides is not thereby predetermined to be an individualistic economy. American individualism has a marked element of romanticism in it—not a mature declaration of independence in our ends, but an adolescent determination to refuse any help from others in the means for their attainment. We condemn totalitarian hero worship, yet conceive of democracy as aiming at a nation of "heroes," each a law unto himself, and scorning cooperative effort as a reflection on the adequacy of his own manliness. What such a miscalled "individualism" expresses is not self-confidence but insecurity. Socialized action is not at issue between democracy and communism; what is at issue is the conception of the values at which such action aims, and, thereby, the proximate policies to be followed in securing them.

The danger of this anxious individualism is that its actions serve only to counter the anxiety, not to promote the individualism. We are so fearful of collective measures to secure a distributive good—for instance, adequate housing—that we forgo the good, then rationalize our fears with moralistic claptrap about self-reliance or absolutistic verbalizations about regimentation. What is worse, our anxieties have even brought about some degree of reversion to tribalism. To preserve individualism citizens have sometimes been dealt with not on their individual merits but only as members of dubious organizations, and condemned not for their individual actions but for those of their guilty associates. We have undermined individualism in our anxious efforts to stamp out collectivist heresies, evoked insecurities in the name of security.

The paradox is that we have not taken individualism seriously enough. We are so preoccupied with preserving a way of life that we sometimes lose sight of the individuals living it. The words of de Tocqueville have a prophetic ring:

It would seem as if the rulers of our time sought only to use men in order to make things great; I wish that they would try a little more to make great men; that they would set less value on the work, and more upon the workman; that they would never forget that a nation cannot long remain strong when every man belonging to it is individually weak, and that no form or combination of social policy has yet been devised to make an energetic people out of a community of pusillanimous and enfeebled citizens.[69]

America's ideals of liberty, equality, and fraternity will yet make us strong—as individuals, not just as a nation, only if we have courage as individuals to face the realities of their pursuit.

METHODOLOGY OF MORALS

The formation of policy without regard to moral considerations is sometimes defended on the ground that the ethical principles on which public morality rests are a private matter and differ from person to person. There is no official ethics in America any more than there is an official religion. But agreement on ethics is not necessary for a moral consensus, just as differences in epistemology do not prevent acceptance of the same body of scientific truths. The same public morality can be grounded in a belief in God, man, or nature— at least sufficiently to make possible agreement on policy. Social philosophies are not expendable, but philosophers have each exaggerated the indispensability of their own social doctrine. Since Kant we have talked presumptuously of saving science or morality when it was our own philosophies that needed to be saved. Scientific and moral judgments are among the data of the philosophical problem; knowledge and valuation are the stuff of daily experience. A philosophy that ends by denying the existence of what it set out to explain reduces itself to absurdity. To be sure, the claim to knowledge and virtue in each particular case requires justification; and to formulate with philosophical adequacy what such justification consists in calls for the utmost care and subtlety. But we may know many things without knowing how we know them, and certainly without knowing much about the process of cognition itself. In America policy makers worry too much about philosophy, while philosophers do not worry enough about policy.

It is certainly true that not only its basis in ethical theory but also our moral knowledge itself is vague and unsure. But it is the part of an educated man, Aristotle says somewhere, to require exactness in each class of subjects only so far as the nature of the subject admits. If our requirements are realistic, we may even find that the situation is not so bad as in self-justification we are inclined to paint it. That the principles of public morality are far from definite and certain has not kept America, in a time of greatness, from applying them in public policy. The diagnosis in the *Federalist Papers* is still to the point:

> Though it cannot be pretended that the principles of moral and political knowledge have, in general, the same degree of certainty with those of the mathematics, yet they have much better claims in this respect than, to judge from the conduct of men in particular situations, we should be disposed to allow them. The obscurity is much oftener in the passions and prejudices of the reasoner than in the subject. Men, upon too many occasions, do not give their own understandings fair play; but, yielding to some untoward bias, entangle themselves in words and confound themselves in subtleties.[70]

Morality is rarely a matter simply of applying an unquestioned principle to a case that indubitably falls under its scope. The moral problem is to weigh conflicting principles and to act on a balance of probabilities on behalf of the preponderant values. Totalitarian contempt for the democratic way of muddling through attacks precisely what is most defensible in our practice. Statesmanship is nothing other than muddling through; in politics the straight line is the shortest distance to perdition. To move unswervingly toward predetermined objectives is inevitably to bypass morality. Circumstances alter cases, and whatever be true of abstract principles, concrete moral values are nothing if not circumstantial. God Himself repented His creation when confronted by the generation of Noah. In a democracy, at any rate, policy must reconcile conflicting values, especially conflicting judgments of value, among the makers of policy. We talk too loosely of "government" and "the people" as though each were unitary and of a single mind. For government, the locus of moral issues is in such encounters as that of a secretary of state facing a senatorial hearing. For the people, it is in the encounters, not only among a multiplicity of overlapping groups but also within the individual, among the fragmentary selves whose integration is the achievement of moral maturity.

The desire for absolutes and the pretense of certitude are not a personal failing of American leaders. They are a constitutional weakness of democracy where everything turns on popular support. We do not often hear a politician admit that he has made a mistake. The politician, unlike the scientist, cannot rejoice in a disproved hypothesis, or he will do so in retirement from public life. But our predisposition to this weakness must put us all the more on our guard against it. To raise the level of public morality we must learn to tolerate a wider margin for error in public policy. If the spirit were not quite so willing the flesh might be not quite so weak.

I am not defending a particular political program that might be attacked as lacking in "idealism." I have no program to offer at all, and that is just my point: there is no such thing as a programmatic morality. When policy is wholly predetermined, moral values inevitably become absolute and abstract, and action is bifurcated into the amoralities of a vulgar pragmatism conjoined with an ineffectual moralism. In a democracy there are no recipes for the moral life. Democratic values can be defined procedurally, not by a content fixed beforehand. In terms of this procedure morality can be assimilated to science, in spite of the dualistic ethics which polarizes value and fact. Policy must be scientific to be effective; if morality is ineffective, it has no place in policy. But to say scientific is not to speak of the paraphernalia and techniques of the laboratory; it is to say realistic and rational—empirically grounded and self-corrective in application. Policy is scientific when it is formed by the free use of intelligence on the materials of experience.

American moralism has been so fearful of *realpolitik* that it has sometimes forgone being realistic altogether, especially in the field of foreign relations. Over and over again we have watched dictatorships rise, and even given them support, formulating our policies toward them by wishful thinking rather than by assessing consequences in the light of our past experience. We are realistic with respect to such limited and isolated objectives as obtaining military bases; but the larger values of peace and freedom we are inclined to pursue only by verbalizations. "If people loved humanity as genuinely as they loved their children," Bertrand Russell has recently said, "they would be as unwilling in politics as in the home to let themselves be deceived by comfortable fairy tales." [71] To be realistic does not mean resigning ourselves to the facts; it is not necessarily a matter of lowering our aspirations. The facts may also point to unrealized potentialities of value, to opportunities and resources as well as to limitations and constraints. The confusion of realism with resignation is a product of the childishness which complains that there is nothing to eat but food. When facts are prejudged as inimical to value, values are predestined to remain in the world of fantasy.

On a more fundamental level, moralists have argued that to ground values in the facts of experienced goodness is to reduce them to the crudities of desires as they are, not as they ought to be. It is to destroy morality by identifying it, at bottom, with nothing other than the satisfaction of animal instinct. In a democracy especially, realism, so the argument runs, subjects values to the vulgarization of the mass. This is the fallacious logic, however, which mistakes empirical science for a brute empiricism, as though respect for the facts precludes interpreting them, appraising their significance. A scientific hypothesis must stick to the facts, but it does so precisely by distinguishing them from superficial appearances. The realist bases judgments of value on what experience discloses to be good. But the disclosure requires assessment in the light of ideals that point beyond any given experience, though not beyond experience as a whole. The norms of the dictionary follow the facts of usage, but they are norms because there is such a thing as misusing words. Moral norms, if realistic, conform to the facts of experienced goodness; but there is such a thing as insensibility in the experience and irrationality in its assessment. When Aristotle says that political science does not make men but takes them from nature and uses them, he is a realist in what he affirms but not in what he denies.[72] Realistic politics must take men as they are at any given moment, but it must also create conditions in which men can grow to their full moral stature. In short, realism is not limited to the conservation of values already achieved; it can also

aspire to the good which is not yet achieved. The realist will not leap
into the void, but he is not for that reason earthbound.

Realism is above all contextualist. The distinctive quality of parlor
politics, apart from its irresponsibility, is just this failure to refer issues
to specific contexts. "Do you support a tough policy toward Russia?"
is a meaningless question until both the toughness and the form of support are made concrete and specific. The lessons of operationism are as
important for policy as for science: to be able to guide practice, theory
must be formulated in terms that connect it with determinate behavior.
The totalitarian criticism of the democratic state as a debating society is
not altogether without substance. The floor of Congress has increasingly
become a platform for empty verbalization; as the work of congressional
committees becomes more responsive to its coverage by the mass media
the same tendency appears. We face the serious problem of creating and
maintaining conditions under which the issues of public policy can be
realistically debated in public.

Contextualism implies not only that values can be appraised only in a
concrete setting, but also that *there is always an appraisal to be made*.
The moralist supposes that once the side of the right has been identified
no further moral problems remain; there is left only the practical matter
of ensuring that the right will prevail. What is good he supposes to be
wholly good; there is no red ink in his ledger. If his dualism did not
stand in the way, his moral judgment might benefit from a consideration
of the practicalities of business enterprise. The operation of a business
inevitably involves risks, and losses, too. Sound policy minimizes them
but cannot eliminate them; simple prudence demands that they be carefully taken into account beforehand. This means a contextual appraisal,
not a reliance on general and abstract principles. Weber's warning seems
to me unanswerable:

No ethics in the world can dodge the fact that in numerous instances the
attainment of "good" ends is bound to the fact that one must be willing to
pay the price of using morally dubious means or at least dangerous ones—
and facing the possibility or even the probability of evil ramifications. From
no ethics in the world can it be concluded when and to what extent the
ethically good purpose "justifies" the ethically dangerous means and ramifications.[73]

Morality desperately needs intelligence as well as virtue, good judgment as much as good intentions. It has seemed at times that our State Department was more concerned with sterling qualities of character than with ability. At the height of the Americanist purge an applicant for private employment was said to have admitted that he had been fired from the State Department, but he assured his prospective employer that it was only for incompetence! The Victorian advice, "Be good, sweet maid, and let who can be clever," is scarcely a foundation for twentieth-century morality. The sweet maids of today have found that they must be clever to remain good. In politics, at any rate, America cannot preserve its virtue unless it abandons its innocence. I am not making the Socratic identification of virtue with knowledge; but I do not see how we can hope to arrive at morally defensible policy unless we know what we are about. Our difficulties in foreign affairs surely stem in part from the fact that other nations are so often politically more knowledgeable than we are.

Granted that sometimes the morality of an action seems clear even when its consequences are not clear. This does not justify, however, the claim of moral intuition to be independent of such knowledge. What seems right may afterward turn out not to be so. Moreover, if our intuition is not mistaken, it is either our good fortune or else we are indebted to the cultivation of our intuition by what was already known to be right in the relevant circumstances. A scientific hypothesis may be assigned an antecedent probability prior to the outcome of the experiments by which it is tested. This is not an a priori probability, however, but one derived from the experience sustaining what has already been verified. What remains true is that often we know enough to recognize what is bad but, alas, not enough to recognize what is good. Here is where courage is called for—to be able to take thought without undermining the resolution to act. We need not choose between the yogi and the commissar or, in American terms, between the pedant and the goon. That an enterprise of great moment has been intelligently based on the best knowledge availible to us need not lose it the name of action.

When virtue is detached from knowledge it becomes easy for everyone to suppose that he already knows enough for the purposes of moral choice. It is in the American tradition for each man to be convinced that he has nothing to learn about politics, sex, or religion. But the conviction rings hollow, and in fact we are as a people unusually receptive to authoritative pronouncements on these matters by the experts. All three areas have their pundits, held in a popular esteem which can be given a rational justification only in very exceptional cases. Democracy does not presuppose that every citizen is an expert on morals nor does it necessarily succeed in making him one. But it does put the responsibility for moral choice on the individual citizen. The expert in a democracy must be only a consultant, not the decision maker. It is the citizen— directly and through his representatives—who must decide among con- flicting expert opinions and how much weight to put on even a con- sensus of experts. Plato assigned this responsibility to a philosophical elite because only they, in his philosophical judgment, decided on the basis of thought, while the mass was swayed only by feeling. But the one duality is a reflected image of the other. The problem is as much to put feeling—responsible commitment to values—into the thought of the intellectual as it is to put thought—intelligent consideration of real conditions and consequences—into the feelings of the mass of the citi- zenry.[74]

It has become fashionable for the intellectuals to join with the less re- flective members of the community in submitting to a religious or political absolute which can lighten the responsibility for individual moral choice. The position is still essentially Plato's: in his epistemology a proposition which is not universally and necessarily true is not knowl- edge at all but mere opinion. For Kant, universality and necessity are the criteria by which we can identify a priori principles, on which morality as well as science must rest. But the only such principles that have withstood the growth of knowledge and the changes in social pat- terns are those of pure mathematics. Logical analysis has shown, how- ever, that pure mathematics pays for its absolute truth by sacrificing all its empirical reference. Judgments bearing on matters of fact can achieve no more than some degree of probability. What is hard to accept is that this probability suffices as a guide to life. Will men fight for a mere probability? They have and they will. A mature man does not demand ironclad guarantees from God or nature, and seldom even from other men; and surely he does not deceive himself with illusions of certitude to make bearable a life of uncertainty. Platitudinous though it be, there is profound wisdom in the Americanism that in this world nothing is certain but death and taxes. We do not always remember that Franklin wrote these words in a passage appraising the prospects of survival of the newly adopted Constitution. The courage of the men who established our republic was no whit lessened by their realistic perspectives on politics as a succession of calculated risks.

We often hear today the argument that "confused liberals" condemn absolute values as authoritarian and fascistic, while on the contrary the belief in such absolutes is necessary to the survival of democracy. The moralist urges again and again that our vulnerability to communism is basically "the collapse of our moral values," "the loss of faith in our principles," "the weakening of moral authority by the corrosion of scepticism." Heterodoxy in religious belief or in ethical theory is in some quarters condemned as downright subversive or dangerously near it. The ideals of democracy, it is insisted, are themselves absolute, distinguished from the absolutes of the authoritarian regimes in having been freely chosen rather than imposed by the state. According to this argument,

The crucial point is whether the absolutes are imposed from without or are voluntarily observed. Personal absolutes personally maintained are the essence of democracy and the antithesis of dictatorship. Freedom is itself one of the absolutes, a standard by which men can measure their lives, and only men who can maintain firm values can maintain freedom.[75]

Firmness in the maintenance of our values is one thing; the supposition that the values themselves must be unconditional and beyond question is quite another. The argument confounds the function of an absolute with its substance, its role in action with its status in nature. This confusion transformed Kant's empirical liberalism into Hegel's metaphysical authoritarianism. Ideas which Kant analyzed as regulative in experience the idealists treated as constitutive of a transcendent reality beyond experience. To say "standard" or "norm" is to say "functioning as an absolute"—used as a measure while not itself measured. But it functions as such only in that use, not intrinsically. As a result of its use, in other contexts it may itself be subjected to appraisal and modified or replaced. A standard is only a *relative absolute*, relative, that is, to the contexts of its normative function. Even the most basic principles of science are not eternal and unqualified truths, but instead the most powerful heuristic instruments so far known. A principle like that of the conservation of matter was for a long time presupposed in the design and interpretation of chemical experiments; but it itself rested on an experimental foundation, and indeed has been falsified in Einstein's identification of matter and energy. Cannot the "absoluteness" of the moral law be construed in the same way? I do not see how the values basic to a democratic social order are undermined when they are conceived as resting on an empirical basis. What is undermined is only the value *theory* which insists on construing these values as a priori, intuitive, and transcendental. It is not democratic morality that benefits from the absolutist's defense but only the absolutist's own ethics. To ground the value of freedom on all that experience has taught us of what is good for man in society is surely not to weaken its claims. And such a grounding points at once to the mode of connection of moral values with concrete political policy.

The absence of such a determinate connection is the most pressing objection to moral absolutism from the standpoint of its bearings on policy formation. I am directing attention to the futility of the belief that all moral problems have been essentially solved, and that the task for policy is only to translate these solutions into action. Where is the dictionary for such a translation? Just this is the problem; it is precisely in this task that statesmanship is called for. But here the moralist can make no contribution other than an exhortation to virtue. The American reputation for hardheadedness is well deserved by our rejection of panaceas for the social and economic core of public policy. But with regard to its moral penumbra, as we conceive it, we are, by contrast, extraordinarily simple-minded and naive. We tend to rely too much on the magic formulas of democratic theory. The maxim of the greatest good for the greatest number, for instance, is useless as a basis of choice when, as is almost always the case, one alternative provides a greater good for some while the other benefits more people though to a lesser extent; what, on this basis, is an equitable distribution of the tax burden? To take another example, reliance on the rule of the majority is not always even logically consistent, as has recently been demonstrated in a penetrating mathematical analysis of the theoretical relation between social choice and individual values.[76] And as a matter of practice the rule of the majority is certainly not always consistent with other democratic values. A few years ago an oriental under pressure to give up his home in a "restricted" residential area in a California city agreed to submit the question to a vote of the community; a majority voted against him. It is well said that there is no safety in numbers, or in anything else. In short, the moralist who can do no more than reaffirm his faith in the ideals of liberty, equality, and fraternity ignores the real problems occasioned by the use of one of these ideals to undermine the others.

Problems are also set by the necessity to compromise some of our values for the sake of the others, as in the paradox of liberty already mentioned. There is a comparable paradox of equality. The administrator of a public housing project may be concerned to break down a pattern of segregated housing in the community. But unless he himself imposes quotas on the occupancy of the public housing, the minority group which has been discriminated against, being under greater pressure, will fill the project completely, and instead of destroying segregation he will have contributed to it. But the quota is itself a discriminatory practice. Such dilemmas have no simple resolution, and certainly none in terms of abstract and absolute moral principles. In dilemmas of this kind, however, the moral problems of public policy largely consist.

There is no escaping the dependence of moral values on realistic contextual analyses of the situations in which they are to be secured or achieved. When Stephen Undershaft in Shaw's *Major Barbara* is interviewed by his father with regard to his career, he reveals neither aptitudes nor interests; but he does claim to know the difference between right and wrong. To which his father replies: "You don't say so! What! no capacity for business, no knowledge of law, no sympathy with art, no pretension to philosophy; only a simple knowledge of the secret that has puzzled all the philosophers, baffled all the lawyers, muddled all the men of business, and ruined most of the artists: the secret of right and wrong. Why, man, you're a genius, a master of masters, a god!" And when later in the scene Stephen identifies the power that governs England as "the best elements in the English national character," it is decided that he is a born journalist. In America he might have been recognized as destined to become a secretary of state.

American philosophy today must certainly share the blame for the sorry condition of contemporary thought about the relations of morals and policy. In the last few decades marked advances have been made in the empirical study and theoretical analysis of values, by such disciplines as anthropology, psychiatry, economics, and even mathematics. The contribution of philosophy to the understanding of social values has been slight. We have been preoccupied with the moral problems of the individual rather than with the problems of social ethics. Fifty years ago there was widespread agreement with Aristotle's dictum that "to discover the good of an individual is satisfactory, but to discover that of a state or nation is more noble and divine." [77] Today, except for occasional textbooks on "the conflict of ideologies," ethical treatises focus entirely on the analysis of a single paradigmatic moral judgment. Just as a political theory, however, cannot be appraised without regard to its moral consequences, so an ethical theory cannot be appraised without regard to its political implications. For the working morality which the ethical theory is intended to explain and justify is, under the conditions of modern life at least, inescapably political. As Croce has said, "Moral man does not put into practice his morality except by acting in a political manner and by accepting the logic of politics." [78] To have bearings on action ethics must take into account the social determinants of both the ends and the means of action. The fact that ours is preeminently the age of politics has not yet been sufficiently reflected in contemporary American philosophy.

What is worse, the philosophical theory of value seems to be completely caught up in the problem of subjectivism. There is a virtually exclusive preoccupation with the analysis of the justification for judgments of value. For two decades our philosophical journals have been filled with interminable discussions of whether value judgments are factual or only express the attitudes of the judger. The semantics and epistemology of ethics have been explored in detail, but not its specifically ethical content, and especially not the political bearings of such content. I do not mean that philosophers should abandon philosophy for politics; but I am pleading for a restoration of the social relevance of philosophy. We have focused so closely on the logical foundations that we are in danger of losing sight of the cultural superstructure which makes the foundations important.

It is true that philosophy has no special competence to deal with the problems of the superstructure. But it does have a special responsibility, surely as great as that of the journalist, priest, and psychiatrist to whom we have abandoned these problems. The philosophical task here, as I see it, is not to provide a "democratic ideology" or the "philosophical foundations" for such an ideology. It is to provide conceptual instruments which can be applied by the citizen himself to the materials of his own experience and the products of the human sciences so as to arrive at more realistic and intelligent perspectives on values in society.

Conclusion

The "moralist" whom I have been attacking is, of course, a fiction, as is every consistent representative of a philosophical position in all its purity. No life is limited to the concrete embodiment of a philosophical abstraction; the political behavior of living men and women is inevitably more subtle and complex than any political theory can pretend to picture. But the fiction is useful, nevertheless, as an "ideal type" in Max Weber's sense—a point of reference for the analysis of cases which all depart more or less widely from the type. If moralism has played too small a part in American policy for this reference point to be useful, so much the better! It is more useful than the usual fiction of the "materialist" who disregards moral values or pays them only lip service and who must therefore be enjoined to elevate his morality. That American policy leaves *something* to be desired from a moral point of view we can surely admit without compromising our loyalty. Democracy needs its critics today as much as its apologists. And for my part, what I find to criticize here is neither insensibility nor insincerity but rather their opposites. We have been so sincere in our devotion to the good that we have confronted the world in a posture of self-righteousness which we cannot maintain indefinitely without discomfort. There is no doubt, at any rate, that it makes other nations uncomfortable in their dealings with us.

As good a case can be made out for the charge against America of moralism as for the familiar charge of materialism. It is not that one myth will cancel out the other; both tendencies are at work and intensify rather than cancel one another. Walter Lippmann has recently held that

. . . the radical error of the modern democratic gospel is that it promises, not the good life of this world, but the perfect life of heaven. The root of the error is the confusion of the two realms—that of this world where the human condition is to be born, to live, to work, to struggle and to die, and that of the transcendent world in which men's souls can be regenerate and at peace. The confusion of these two realms is an ultimate disorder. It inhibits the good life in this world. It falsifies the life of the spirit.[79]

In essence, he is quite right. But perhaps the more radical error still is not in confusing the two realms but in conceiving them as two, in separating them at all. So long as they are distinguished, the good life on earth will inevitably be thought to derive from the perfect life of heaven, and the earthly city will either be abandoned to wickedness or else forced into the pattern of what is presumed to be the city of God.

It is in these dualistic perspectives that we supplement our moralism with a vulgar pragmatism. We promise earthly goods as well as heavenly ones, and often even deliver them. But having separated "practical" interests from "moral" ones, we find that even the fulfillment of the earthly promises fails to win us friends. Our philanthropies are suspected to conceal our self-interest, while the frank defense of our interests is condemned as immoral. In the minds of many people around the world, whatever the action, we are damned if we do and damned if we do not. In part, of course, it is Soviet diplomacy and propaganda that have maneuvered us into this position. But in part also, the extent to which they have succeeded points to the vulnerability of our own dualistic dilemma: what is moral is unreal, what is "realistic" is immoral. We may succeed, nevertheless, in establishing alliances, but we will not have friends among other nations. The transformation of an uneasy balance of power into a genuine international community must of course be a matter of slow growth, and our statesmen deserve the world's gratitude for every extension of time they can provide for this growth. But to make good use of our time we must extend and deepen our sympathetic understanding of other values, other ways of life.

What is genuinely pragmatic in America is our willingness to apply science to the problems of technology. Americans are widely stereotyped as having an intense and ever-present desire to improve ways of doing things, provided we see the improvement as only a change in means for established ends. But it is true that with regard to ends we are remarkably conservative. The scientific outlook of our technology continues to undermine traditional conceptions of value, but that outlook is usually regarded as incapable of replacing those conceptions by more adequate ones. The achievement of nuclear fission has not suddenly made science a threat to civilization. It has only stepped up the magnitude and urgency of a problem faced by civilization since science first became a significant force in society. Some years before the atom bomb Dewey wrote: "A culture which permits science to destroy traditional values but which distrusts its power to create new ones is a culture which is destroying itself." [80] Not science itself but the leaden shield that insulates it from ethics and politics is deadly. We must either leave science alone altogether and forgo its transformation of means, or else integrate it with our moral aspirations and forgo the fixity of traditional ends. This is the spirit in which I have been urging a realistic political morality, which is to say, a continued reassessment of traditional moral values in the light of contemporary political actualities. A belief is not scientific because it has been "proved" but because it is continuously tested, and tested by conformity to experience rather than to axiomatic truths. It is in this spirit, too, that I have pressed the claims of an empirical, naturalistic theory of value. An ethics which provides a religious or metaphysical foundation for political morality has still to solve the problem of bringing that morality into connection with the world of political action revealed in experience.

I have viewed political morality, therefore, as a matter of proximate choices, not of ultimate goals. It is customary to criticize politicians for lacking statesmanlike vision; statesmanship, however, consists in seeing clearly what here and now bears on long-run values. Communism has plenty of vision—focused on a utopian future, but not on the miseries and brutalities of the present. American moralists may be equally vision- ary when they prefer the ultimate virtue of uncompromising principle to the day-to-day gains of a compromised good. "The path of duty lies in what is near, and men seek for it in what is remote." What a political realist Confucius was! Political morality lies in the everyday shaping of policy, not merely in the heroic stand at a time of crisis. The association of morality with heroism and martyrdom is not intrinsic to morals, but is a part of the contemporary crisis mentality. We talk so much of "the crisis of our time" that we come to think that some single stroke of statesmanship will put an end to our problems—one way or the other— once for all. I do not believe that the atom will destroy all life on earth, nor do I believe that the latest Peace Plan will forever remove its de- structive potentialities. I do not believe in the Apocalyptic Moment in

politics: every day is the Day of Judgment. In the politics of crisis law
and morality are both endangered.

I have attacked conformism, not because I reject the values pressed
upon us but because the pressures interfere with the realistic appraisal
of values. Even when the conformist judgments of value are sound, they
can scarcely lay claim to rationality; for rationality cannot be defined by
the content of belief but only by the procedure for arriving at the content. What is worse, conformism has an appetite for power that grows
by what it feeds on; orthodoxy has devoted itself more and more only
to the stamping out of heresy. Political morality depends on voices of
protest. To silence them is not only an immorality in itself but also
makes for other immoralities as policy becomes exempt from critical
appraisal. We rightly condemn Communist "elections" in which there
is only one set of candidates; but many Americans take for granted that
only one set of values suffices for democratic choice.

Quite apart from the possibility of public protest, we must surely allow
for private reservations. The individual must be able to find a refuge
from the conformist pressures of society. "The right to be let alone,"
Brandeis has said, "is the most comprehensive of rights and the right
most valued by civilized men." In American life this right is continuously threatened, not so much by political instrumentalities as by the
more subtle invasions of privacy in a variety of social patterns and practices. The teacher, the business executive, the government employee,
and even the research scientist are all subjected to a code of conformity
whose requirements increasingly extend beyond the range of their professional activities. Competitive advertising has been attacked many times
for its wastefulness and its degradation of public taste. More fundamental is its weakening of our sense of the right to be let alone, to live our
lives as we choose. It is not what the advertiser says, but the frequency
and intensity with which he says it, the inescapability of his urging,
which is truly degrading.

When the conformist directs himself to the preservation of "Americanism" his efforts are self-defeating. More and more his "American"
comes to be defined only negatively, as a noncommunist. Our prestige
abroad may suffer more from this negativism than from the stupidities
and injustices with which the negative definition is applied. It offers
nothing to the neutrals save the assurance that if they join us they will

be on our side. But what side is it? It is not surprising that other nations think of us as materialists: it is our materials that we most freely export. As for our values, when we have descended from the clouds of moralistic generalities, they are not clear in our own minds; in that condition, we can hardly expect to be able to state them clearly to others. And, above all, our values are not clearly embodied in our actions. De Maupassant tells a story of a young man challenged for the first time to a duel, who is thrown into such an agony of fear of the outcome that on the morning of the duel he takes his own life. Negative "Americanism," by a kind of defensive subversion, destroys what it is most fearful of losing. I do not mean to say that if we conquer our fears our problems will vanish. The problems of democracy are rooted in more than our own anxieties; we now have more to fear than fear itself.

The preservation of liberty calls for leadership, as important in democracy as in the totalitarian states. Edmund Burke long ago called attention to the paradox of representation: the representative owes his constituency his own judgment as well as a representation of their will. The demands of democratic leadership cannot be side-stepped by policies aimed at giving the people "what the people want." America has had world leadership thrust upon it, it is often said, and the next century may look to the Pax Americana as the last one looked to the Pax Britannica. The problem is to outgrow our political adolescence in time to discharge this mature responsibility.

The ideal of equality confronts us with the continuing task of operating our economy in the general welfare, which means recognizing all the special interests that make up the generality, without identifying the general welfare with any one of them—even the special interest of General Motors. We cannot side-step this problem by a verbalistic appeal to an abstract "national interest" unrelated to the needs of concrete individuals. "The art which discovers the public interest by eliminating the interests of successive sections of the public," Tawney once pointed out, "smacks of the rhetorician rather than of the statesman." [81]

The problems of fraternity, finally, are not solved by desegregation alone; it is integration that is called for, the creation of genuine community, both nationally and internationally.

What gives all these problems a peculiarly moral cast is that they are constituted by man's relations to man. We need not share Schopenhauer's pessimism to recognize that "the chief source of the evils which affect men is man himself." The real world, he continues, "surpasses Dante's hell in this respect, that one man must be the devil of another." [82] Moral revivalism will not suddenly transport us from hell to heaven. When we have solved one moral problem, another will arise to take its place; the Divine Comedy plays forever in the second act.

All this will probably be regarded by many as nothing but old-fashioned liberalism which has long ago been exploded. But the the old-fashioned liberalism was victimized by the dualism of ideal aspirations and material interests, it was given to moralization, and it tended to absolutism with regard to its own values. Laski's characterization seems to me a fair one:

Liberals viewed Americanism less as a concept of power than as a concept of ethics. They still thought . . . that there was a natural law, expressive of a natural order, which man breaks at his peril. . . . They still laid . . . far more emphasis on the free individual than upon the free society. They retained the illusion of a security for the American which could be enjoyed by all other peoples if they would only exercise the virtues of reason and goodwill. And there was an inner conviction, inevitably strengthened by their sense of overwhelming power, that it was their mission to lead the world to righteousness. They still had, despite the experience of two world wars, what Emerson called "the disposition to trust a principle more than a material force." [83]

But I have been as critical of *this* liberalism as of the political philosophies it set itself against. My aim has been to reinstate the connection between morality and power, to give political force to moral principle.

If, nevertheless, it is felt that the position of this essay is old-fashioned liberalism still, I will not protest too much. If it is a matter of labels, I do not mind being politically identified as a pre-Raphaelite. We are all of us living on the moral capital of the liberalism of a generation or two ago, whether or not we find it politically expedient to acknowledge the source of our riches. Whatever its shortcomings, it is the old-fashioned American dream that brought America moral greatness. There was a time when we said to the nations of the world, "Give me your tired, your poor, your huddled masses yearning to breathe free." Today this is embarrassing sentimentality. And it is even more embarrassing politically, for it is written on the Statue of Liberty but nowhere to be found in our immigration code. Simple decency—to say nothing of the friendship of other peoples—demands that we remove it from the one or restore it to the other.

I am myself an immigrant, from a family of immigrants, and I see America still as those huddled masses saw it—so various, so beautiful, so new. When my father visited Washington for the first time, I stood with him under the dome of the Capitol and watched what he saw of America struggling with what he remembered of tsarist Russia. Then he asked, "Does it really belong to us?" It does indeed—it belongs to the people, to all the people—if we but choose to make it our own.

NOTES

[1] Cotton Mather, Diary, 1716; quoted by Harold J. Laski, The American Democracy (New York: Viking, 1948), p. 432.

[2] Max Weber, The Protestant Ethic and the Spirit of Capitalism (Chicago, Ill.: University of Chicago Press, 1930), p. 87.

[3] George Santayana, Character and Opinion in the United States (New York: Doubleday, 1956), p. 103.

[4] This appears to be belied by R. W. Davenport and the editors of Fortune: "The American character and tradition will never be satisfied with a merely defensive or even preventive foreign policy. We seek ways to be creative and constructive. . . ." U.S.A.: The Permanent Revolution (New York: Prentice-Hall, 1951), pp. 249–250. But the passage continues: ". . . ways in which we can feel we are extending the American Proposition [sic!] to other peoples." It is not this extension that I had in mind by an "ideological offensive"; see pp. 00–00 below.

[5] Walter Lippmann, The Public Philosophy (New York: Mentor, 1956), pp. 80, 123, and throughout; Benedetto Croce, Politics and Morals (New York: Philosophical Library, 1945), p. 145; John Dewey, German Philosophy and Politics (New York: Holt, 1915), p. 44; Jacques Maritain, Man and the State (Chicago, Ill.: University of Chicago Press, 1951); Zevedi Barbu, Democracy and Dictatorship (New York: Grove, 1956), p. 58.

[6] Charles Stevenson, Ethics and Language (New Haven: Yale University Press, 1947).

[7] UNESCO, Human Rights: Comments and Interpretations (London: Allan Wingate, 1949), p. 11.

[8] Charles E. Merriam, Political Power (New York: McGraw-Hill, 1934), p. 113.

[9] James Bryce, The American Commonwealth (New York: Macmillan), vol. 2, p. 278; Gunnar Myrdal, An American Dilemma (New York: Harper, 1944).

[10] See George R. Stewart, American Ways of Life (New York: Doubleday, 1953), pp. 69–70.

[11] Bryce, op. cit., p. 632.

[12] Job, XXXI, 13–15.

[13] "The number of human beings sacrificed in late prehistoric and historic times must be reckoned in thousands of millions, all of them immolated to the gods in behalf of the welfare of the community." Homer W. Smith, Man and His Gods (New York: Grosset and Dunlap, 1956), p. 134.

[14] See, for instance, M. J. Hillenbrand, Power and Morals (New York: Columbia University Press), 1949, p. 69: "No system of political ethics which demands the obedience of men on the basis of moral obligation can have validity unless it involves

certain concepts which, taken together, equal the natural law, no matter how reluctant men are to use that designation."

15 Jeremy Bentham, Introduction to the Principles of Morals and Legislation (New York: Oxford, 1923), p. 18 n.

16 John Dewey, Freedom and Culture (New York: Putnam, 1939), p. 29.

17 John Dewey, "Theory of Valuation," International Encyclopedia of Unified Science, vol. 2, no. 4 (Chicago, Ill.: University of Chicago Press, 1939).

18 C. I. Lewis, An Analysis of Knowledge and Valuation (La Salle, Ill.: Open Court), 1946.

19 Dewey, Freedom and Culture, op. cit., p. 104.

20 J. Ortega y Gasset, The Revolt of the Masses (New York: Mentor, 1950).

21 W. E. Lecky, History of European Morals (New York: Appleton, 1929), vol. 1, p. 88.

22 Jacques Barzun, God's Country and Mine (Boston: Little Brown, 1954), p. 90.

23 Bryce, op. cit., vol. 2, p. 458.

24 Santayana, op. cit., p. 27.

25 Quoted by David Riesman et al., The Lonely Crowd (New York: Doubleday, 1953), p. 200.

26 Quoted by D. W. Brogan, The American Character (New York: Vintage, 1956), pp. 75–76.

27 Laski, op. cit., p. 738.

28 Davenport, op. cit., p. 19.

29 Riesman, op. cit., pp. 207–208.

30 Barzun, op. cit., p. 81.

31 Job, I, 9–10.

32 Alexis de Tocqueville, Democracy in America (New York: Longmans, 1889), vol. 2, p. 179; see also Brogan, op. cit., p. 16.

33 Martin Lipset, "The Sources of the 'Radical Right,'" in Daniel Bell (ed.), The New American Right (New York: Criterion, 1955), p. 224 n.

34 Max Weber, "Politics as a Vocation," in H. H. Gerth and C. Wright Mills (eds.), From Max Weber (New York: Oxford, 1946), p. 120.

35 Laski, op. cit., p. 737.

36 Barzun, op. cit., p. 113.

37 Aristotle, Nicomachaean Ethics, I, 1097 a.

38 Compare also Aristotle's dictum: "The time when, and the cases in which, and the persons towards whom, and the motive for which, and the manner in which, constitute the mean and the excellence."

39 Bryce, op. cit., vol. 2, p. 477.

40 Oliver Wendell Holmes, "Natural Law," in his Collected Legal Papers (New York: Harcourt Brace, 1921). The passage continues: "It seems to me that this demand is at the bottom of the philosopher's effort to prove that truth is absolute and of the jurist's search for criteria of universal validity which he collects under the head of natural law. . . ."

41 Santayana, op. cit., p. 106.

42 Quoted by Carl L. Becker, Freedom and Responsibility in the American Way of Life (New York: Vintage, 1955), p. 51.

43 Dewey, Freedom and Culture, op. cit., pp. 90–91. He continues: "Arbitrary irresponsibility varies in direct ratio to the claim for absoluteness on the part of the principle in behalf of which power is exercised."

44 Compare Daniel Bell, op. cit., p. 17: "Throughout our history, Americans have had an extraordinary talent for compromise in politics and extremism in morality. The most shameless political deals (and 'steals') have been rationalized as expedient and realistically necessary; yet in no other country were there such spectacular at-

tempts to curb human appetites and brand them as illicit—and nowhere else such glaring failures."

45 Laski, op. cit., pp. 719–720.
46 H. D. Lasswell, *Psychopathology and Politics* (Chicago, Ill.: University of Chicago Press, 1930); *World Politics and Personal Insecurity* (New York: McGraw-Hill, 1935).
47 See James Burnham (ed.), *What Europe Thinks of America* (New York: John Day, 1953), p. 43.
48 Bryce, op. cit., vol. 2, p. 278.
49 William James, *The Principles of Psychology* (New York: Holt, 1927), vol. 2, p. 549.
50 Weber, "Politics as a Vocation," op. cit., p. 118.
51 A. Valentine, *The Age of Conformity* (Chicago, Ill.: Regnery, 1954), p. 177.
52 Compare Daniel Bell, op. cit., p. 20: "The singular fact about the Communist problem is that an ideological issue was raised in American political life, with a compulsive moral fervor only possible because of the equation of Communism with sin. A peculiar change, in fact, seems to be coming over American life. While we are becoming more relaxed in the area of traditional morals . . . we are becoming moralistic and extreme in politics."
53 Bryce, op. cit., vol. 2, p. 273.
54 Santayana, op. cit., p. 106.
55 James Madison, *Federalist Papers*, No. XIV.
56 Nathan Glazer and Martin Lipset, "The Polls on Communism and Conformity," in Bell, op. cit., p. 145.
57 Santayana, op. cit., p. 104.
58 Barzun, op. cit., p. 99.
59 Quoted by Laski, op. cit., p. 747.
60 Bryce, op. cit., vol. 2, p. 352.
61 See, for instance, Sidney Hook, *Toward the Understanding of Karl Marx* (New York: John Day, 1933).
62 Compare Croce, op. cit., p. 188: "Whenever we hear someone refer to 'historical necessity' rather than to his conscience to justify an impending decision about some line of action, we can be sure that we are faced with a case of lack of moral sensibility, or with an attempt to defraud the uncheatable law of duty."
63 See George A. Graham, *Morality in American Politics* (New York: Random House, 1952), p. 89 and throughout.
64 Quoted by Graham, ibid., p. 49.
65 John Dewey, *Problems of Men* (New York: Philosophical Library, 1946), p. 39.
66 See Alan Barth, *The Loyalty of Free Men* (New York: Pocket Books, 1952).
67 Bryce, op. cit.
68 Aristotle, *Politics*, II, 3.
69 De Tocqueville, op. cit., vol. 2, p. 301.
70 Alexander Hamilton, *Federalist Papers*, No. XXXI.
71 Bertrand Russell, *The Impact of Science on Society* (New York: Simon and Schuster, 1953), p. 87.
72 Aristotle, *Politics*, I, 10.
73 Weber, "Politics as a Vocation," op. cit., p. 121.
74 Compare Dewey: "The conclusion is not that the emotional, passionate phase of action can be or should be eliminated in behalf of a bloodless reason. More 'passions,' not fewer, is the answer. To check the influence of hate there must be sympathy, while to rationalize sympathy there are needed emotions of curiosity, caution, respect for the freedom of others."
75 Valentine, op. cit., p. 174.

[76] Kenneth Arrow, *Social Choice and Individual Values* (New York: Wiley, 1951).

[77] Aristotle, *Nicomachaean Ethics*, I, 2.

[78] Croce, *op. cit.*, p. 24.

[79] Lippmann, *op. cit.*, pp. 109–110.

[80] Dewey, *Freedom and Culture*, *op. cit.*, p. 154.

[81] R. H. Tawney, *The Acquisitive Society* (New York: Harcourt Brace, 1920), p. 135.

[82] Schopenhauer, *The World as Will and Idea* (London: K. Paul, 1896), vol. 3, p. 388.

[83] Laski, *op. cit.*, pp. 736–737.

THEORY VERSUS PRACTICE IN AMERICAN VALUES AND PERFORMANCE

by J. Robert Oppenheimer

THE conflict with Communist power from time to time throws a harsh light on our own society. As this conflict continues, and its obduracy, scope, and deadliness become increasingly manifest, we begin to see traits in American society of which we were barely aware, and which in this context appear as grievous disabilities. Perhaps the first thus to come to attention is our inability to give an account of our national purposes, intentions, and hopes that is at once honest and inspiring. It has been a long time since anyone has spoken on behalf of this country of our future or the world's future in a way that suggested complete integrity, some freshness of spirit, and a touch of the plausible.

More recently two other national traits have attracted attention. The conflict with Communist power is taking place concurrently with an extreme acceleration of a technological revolution. In particular, these last few years have marked the maturing of the military phases of the atomic age. Public attention has inevitably been drawn to a comparison of the relative effectiveness of the Soviet system and ours in the training and recruiting of scientists and technical people. This comparison has shown that in a field where once we were better than the Russians, we may soon be less good. The Soviet system, by combining formidable and rare incentives for success in science and technology with a massive search for talent and rigorous and high standards in early education, appears about to attract to scientific work a larger fraction of its population than we shall be doing. When we learned this, it was natural to turn our attention to its causes. Some of the causes lie in the relatively low esteem in which learning is held in this country and, above all, in our indifference to the profession of teaching, especially teaching in the schools. This low esteem is both manifested and caused by the fact that

111

we pay our teachers poorly and our scientists not too well. The grimness
of life in Soviet countries makes it easy to translate prestige into luxury
and privilege. We do not want it so here. Yet on closer examination we
have seen that educational standards in our own schools for languages,
mathematics, and the sciences are far lower than in their Soviet counterparts. We have learned that many of our teachers are not really versed
in the subjects which it is their duty to teach. In many cases, their lack
of knowledge is matched by their lack of affection or interest. In brief,
by matching ourselves against a remote and unloved antagonist, we have
come upon a problem of the greatest gravity for the life of our people.

Something of the same kind appears to be happening in a quite different area. This has to do with the ability of our government, and, through
our government, the ability of our institutions and our people, to determine national policy in those areas that have to do with foreign affairs
and strategy, military and political. To quote Mr. Rostow's address to
the Naval War College in 1956:

I do not believe we as a nation have yet created a military policy and a civil
foreign policy designed to fulfill [our purposes] and to exploit the potentials
for social and political change favorable to our interest within the Communist Bloc.

Historically, the United States has thrown its energies into the solution of
military and foreign policy problems only when it faced concrete, self-evident
dangers.

Or again, as Mr. Kissinger wrote in the April 1957 issue of *Foreign
Affairs*:

By establishing a pattern of response in advance of crisis situations, strategic
doctrine permits a Power to act purposefully in the face of challenges. In its
absence a Power will constantly be surprised by events. An adequate strategic
doctrine is therefore the basic requirement of American security.

It is now a widely held view that, despite the organization of the
executive branch of the government to cope precisely with long-range
problems, foreign policy, and military strategy; despite the role assigned
to the Joint Chiefs of Staff, the National Security Council, and the
Policy Planning Staff of the Department of State; despite the availability
to these organizations of the technical and intellectual talent of the
whole of this country and, to a more limited extent, of the whole free
world, the United States has not developed an understanding of its pur-

poses, its interests, its alternatives and plans for the future in any way adequate to the gravity of the problems that the country faces. There is a widespread impression that we live from astonishment to surprise, and from surprise to astonishment, never adequately forewarned or forearmed, more often than not choosing between evils, when forethought and foreaction might have provided happier alternatives. Why should this state of affairs exist in a country rich with wealth and leisure, dedicated to education, with a larger part of its citizenry involved in education than in any other land at any other time, with more colleges, universities, institutes, and centers than anyone cares to count, and at a time when unparalleled powers in the hands of a dedicated and hostile state threaten us more grievously than ever since the early days of the Republic?

There are, of course, other national traits of which we can scarcely be proud, on which neither the atomic age nor the conflict with Communism has put much emphasis. We may think, for instance, of our great wantonness with our country's resources; we may think of the scarcity of instances in which a concern for public beauty and harmony has made of the physical environment in which we live the comfort to the spirit which the loveliness of our land and our great wealth could well make possible.

All of the traits in which we judge ourselves harshly could have been drawn by historians comparing us with past cultures or by observers of the current scene comparing us with those contemporary to us. We should perhaps note that no people has ever solved the educational problem which we have put to ourselves, and that no government, in a world in which few governments succeed for long, has ever succeeded in meeting a problem of the scope and toughness of the one facing ours. Indeed, we could recognize the traits of weakness in our society in terms of a norm or an ideal and hear of them from the philosopher or prophet. I believe that these ways are the more constructive because the traits that bother us are signs of a rather deep, refractory, and quite unprecedented cultural crisis. In the end they will yield not to symptomatic therapy but to changes in our life, changes in what we believe, in what we do, and in what we value.

In historical times the problems of our country and our age could hardly have arisen in anything like their present form; certainly they were never resolved. Although our adversary may appear to have solved them better than we, it would hardly be healthy for us to adopt his means. He knows what he wants, because he has a simple theory of the meaning of human life and of his place in it. With the strength of that confidence, he has a government prepared to take, at vast human cost, the steps to his ends. That there is only a small, fragmentary, largely obsolete taint of truth to his theory, that it excludes the greater part of truth and the deeper, should give us some confidence that he will not succeed. That his failure may be marked by a vast, if not universal, human involvement and an unparalleled devastation and horror should temper our pleasure in this prospect and return us to the solution of our problems on our own terms, in our own way, in our own good time.

For the traits of weakness in our society we can see grounds that are at once multiple, intelligible, and ironic. I think that the three weaknesses—in our education, in our faltering view of the future, and in our difficulties in the formulation of policy—have some common grounds. But they are not the same, and to follow them all is not the purpose of this paper. Certainly egalitarianism and our traditionally cherished tolerance of diversity—diversity on the fundamental issues of man's nature and destiny, of his salvation and faith—long held as virtues, have much to do with our troubles. In education egalitarianism and diversity define, as it were, the insoluble problem. They have much to do with the difficulties of prophecy and policy, which traditionally rest on consensus in those matters where we are dedicated to difference. The good fortune of the country, speaking in large terms and over the centuries, and its consequent optimism and confidence, have something to do with our troubles. Perhaps we would not change these things, but we must give weight to them, when we compare ourselves with Athens, or Elizabethan or Victorian England, or seventeenth century France.

Our weaknesses, of course, have a touch of irony. It is our very confidence in education, our determination that it should be available to all, our belief that through it man will find dignity and freedom that have played so large a part in reducing our educational system to the half-empty mockery that it now is. When, for the first time in years of formal peace, we have devoted effort, study, thought, and treasure to the quest for military security, we have brought about the most fearful insecurity that has been known to man in what we know of his history.

After this preamble, we turn to the terms of reference of the present paper. The words evoke a certain diffidence: they are Mr. Millikan's:

Theory versus practice in American values and performance. The origins of the acutely pragmatic national style; its consequences for American military and diplomatic performance, and the pattern of domestic life. The relation of pragmatism to the American difficulty in dealing with foreign policy problems until they become full-blown crises might be examined, and, more generally, the costs and advantages of the traditional national premium on operations rather than staff functions, on engineering rather than basic science. The extent to which there has been a significant change in the classical American pragmatic bias in the past twenty years might be considered, including changes in education.

Perhaps a few comments are needed on the word pragmatic. It can refer, of course, to Peirce's doctrine, according to which the meaning of a more general statement lies in the relatively more concrete and particular statements which follow from it, and in which the truth of the general statement is to be determined by testing the truth or falsity of the particulars. This is a view which well describes the cognitive activities of all the sciences, taking the word science in its oldest and broadest sense. It was proposed by an American, and that is probably no accident. It has found favor not only with scientists but also with the logical empiricists among the philosophers. It is a view of the nature of knowledge and of truth which clearly could not be harmful to the conduct of foreign affairs; indeed, when we are met with uncomfortable general statements of intent and policy, we should be grateful if the American habit were in this sense pragmatic.

I do not believe that this is what Mr. Millikan had in mind; nor do I believe that he was referring to James, although here I am not so sure. James had moments, at least, when he argued that a statement was true if belief in it led to good results—good in this case, however, not being confined to verification, good in this case having the full generality of ethical judgment. There are merits to this doctrine, but there are dangers too; and its application to the formulation of policy or the conduct of international affairs is full of such dangers.

A government may, for more or less valid reasons, reach a conclusion as to what its action should be, as ours does when we declare war, or when we adopt such relatively well-defined policies as the Truman Doctrine. Such decisions, reflecting the best estimate of the evidence available when they are made, are acts of will; clearly, further evidence which supports the decisions reinforces the will, makes the prosecution of the war or the execution of the doctrine more likely to be effective. Evidence that the decisions may have been in error or may no longer be timely has a contrary effect. The human commitment to its own decisions, the human reluctance to learn and to change should not be reinforced by any doctrine which deprecates the truth, and therefore the value, of what is inconsistent with past evidence and past judgment. The danger lies not so much in that the new and conflicting evidence may be weighed and given too little weight; it is that it will not even be seen, that our organs of intelligence and perception will be coded, much as our sense organs are, by our commitment, so that we will not even be aware of inconsistency and novelty.

My impression, however, is that in using the word pragmatic, Mr. Millikan meant something less formal and more colloquial: a favoring of practice versus theory, of action versus thought, of invention versus contemplation. There is some truth to the thesis that this is a national trait. It should not be exaggerated. For one thing, the balance between operation and reflection must always, everywhere, numerically favor the doers as compared to the reflectors. Even in Athens there were quite a few Sophists for one Socrates; and I find it hard to imagine any society in which the world's work does not occupy more people more of the time than does an understanding of the world. For another, the balance between these aspects of life has been accented by circumstance, in that the doers in our country have had great good fortune to mark and celebrate their deeds: the country's wealth, its spaciousness, its wide measure of freedom, and, on the whole, its prevailing optimism. It would take considerable accomplishments of theory and understanding to match the brilliance, often the near impudence, of our material creations.

Yet it is true that our past has been marked by a few original and deeply reflective minds. Though part of the intellectual tradition of Europe and the world, their work nevertheless has a peculiarly national stamp, as in the names of Peirce, Gibbs, James, and Veblen.

Today, in almost all fields of natural science, and in some others as well, our country is as pre-eminent in theory as it is in experiment, invention, and practice. This has meant a great change in the educational scene, so far as higher education is concerned, in the graduate schools, in post-doctoral work, in the institutes and universities. Part of this, it is true, has come about because of misfortunes abroad: the two wars in Europe, the advent of the Nazis, and the initial effects of Communist power in Russia, which for a time at least made conditions of serious study very difficult. It has been brought about in part by the coming to this country of scholars in refuge from tyranny and trouble abroad. Nevertheless, it is true that while three decades ago a young man wishing the best training in theoretical physics or mathematics, theoretical chemistry or biology, would have gone to the schools of Europe, today he would be likely to come to this country.

After the Second World War, there was much public interest in the successes in applied science which the war years had brought about in this country. It was important to combat any exaggerated sense of American superiority by pointing to the great contributions for which we were in debt to individuals from Europe and other lands. But to repeat today what was only partially true, namely, that Americans excel in practical undertakings but are weak in theory, is to distort the truth. It should, of course, be added that the number of men engaged in theoretical science has always been small, even today. Their work and their existence can have little direct bearing on the temper and style of the country.

Having said all this, it does seem to me that, in comparison with other civilizations, that of the classical days in India surely, that on the continent of Europe, and probably even that of England, where theory is brilliantly made but largely ignored in practice, ours is a land in which practice is emphasized far more than theory, and action far more than contemplation. In the difficult balance of teaching, we tend to teach too much in terms of utility and too little in terms of beauty. And if and when we "do it ourselves," it is unlikely to be learning and thought.

To see the bearing of this trait, we should recognize another feature of the American landscape: in important, deep, and complex ways, this is a land of diversity. It tolerates, respects, and fosters diversity in the form of a true pluralism. There is much theory made in the United States—cosmological theory, theory of genetic processes, theory about the nature of immunity, theory about the nature of matter, theory about learning, about prices, about communication. But there is no unifying theory of what human life is about. There is no consensus as to the nature of reality or the part we are to play in it, no theory of the good life, and not much theory of the role of government in promoting it. The diverse talents, skills, beliefs, and experiences of our people contribute effectively to the solution of a concrete problem, to answering the well-defined question, to the building of a machine, a structure, or a weapons system. In such concrete and limited exercises, the diversity and strangeness of the participants is harmonized by the community of the concrete undertaking. The team of experts, sometimes including experts from social science, was an immensely successful invention for wartime research, and continues to be in many forms of technical enterprise. It continues to be inappropriate, and tends to languish, in the general undertakings of academic life.

American pluralism can no doubt in part be understood in terms of our history and of those features in which we differ from most of the communities of Europe and of much of Asia. We may think of the relatively primitive communities in the Indian villages of the Southwest, which some of us still remember from the earlier years of this century. Life there was relatively static and highly patterned; all of its elements were coherent and were rendered unified and meaningful by religious rites and religious doctrine. Change was slow and their communication was adequate to the limited experience of the villagers. Such communities represent almost an ideal of unity, of common understanding, and of a monistic view of the world.

There has been little of the village in American life. The frontier, the openness of the country, and, later, the immense rapidity of change and the tumult of motion and traffic have given us a very different national experience. Probably for two centuries, New England had the stability of village life; and I believe that we see today, in the coherence, firmness, and mutual understanding of its survivors, one of the most stable and unified elements in our country. Probably, although I know less of this, one could find a similar story in the South, though the fortunes of the last hundred years have dealt harshly with it.

Even if we turn our thoughts to Europe, the site of so much of the commotion, disillusion, and variety which characterizes our own land, we see important differences. There is a long past of limited mobility, culminating in the thirteenth century in the unified view of all matters important to man, with a universe determined by God, an omnipresent

God, the unvarying nature of all finite things, and the ever-present end and purpose of man's life. When this world began to break, it broke slowly, and first of all in the minds of the philosophers and scientists. It was not until the seventeenth century that the turn from contemplation to action can be seen with any completeness; its consequences were still troubling to John Donne, who said long after it occurred, "'Tis all in peeces, all cohaerence gone, All just supply, and all Relation." Man's awareness of his power came slowly to Europe; it came to people bound by a common tongue, a common habit, and common traditions in taste, manners, arts, and ways.

Compared to all this, Americans are nomads. There is, of course, much in common in what brought people to this country. In overwhelming measure, what was common was either negative or personal and practical—the desire to escape repression, or the hope of making a new fortune. In the formative years of our history, emptiness, the need and reward for improvisation, variety, and the open frontier endowed the differences between men with weight and sanction. Our political philosophy undertook to reconcile the practical benefits of union with the maximum tolerance of diversity. Complementing the closing of the physical frontier, there has come within the last century a new source of change, more radical and in the end more universal than those before. This lies, on the one hand, in the unprecedented growth of knowledge, whose time scale, estimated apprehensively as a half century two hundred years ago, could better now be put at a decade; and with this, based partly upon it, partly upon accumulated wealth, and partly on the tradition of freedom and mobility itself, a technological explosion and an economy unlike any the world has seen.

Early in this century, William James wrote: [1]

The point I now urge you to observe particularly is the part played by the older truths. . . . Their influence is absolutely controlling. Loyalty to them is the first principle—in most cases it is the only principle; for by far the most usual way of handling phenomena so novel that they would make for a serious rearrangement of our preconception is to ignore them altogether, or to abuse those who bear witness for them.

In our time the balance between the old truths and the new has been unhinged, and it is not unnatural that most men limit, in the severest possible way, the number and the kind of new truths with which they will have to deal. This is what makes the intellectual scene a scene of specialists, and this is what makes our people, for all the superficial evidences of similarity, more varied in their experience, more foreign to each other in the tongues which they use to talk of what is close to them than in any time or place which comes to mind. This is what limits consensus to statements so vague that they may mean almost anything, or to situations so stark and threatening and immediate that no theoretical structure, no world view, need intervene.

Perhaps the most nearly coherent of all our large theoretical structures is that of natural science. It is hardly relevant to many of the questions of policy and strategy with which our government must be confronted; to some it is. This coherence is, however, of a very special sort. It consists by and large in an absence of contradiction between any part and any other, and in a pervasive, often only potential mutual relevance. It does not consist in a structural coherence by which the whole can be derived from some simple summary, some key, some happy mnemonic device. It is not known, and probably cannot be known, by anyone. Small parts of it are; and in the world of learning there is mediation in the great dark of ignorance between the areas of light. But when our government calls on the community of scientists to advise it, even for instance in so relatively limited a field as the peacetime hazards of atomic radiation, it cannot turn to an expert for the answer. It turns to the National Academy of Sciences, which assembles a series of committees, both numerous and populous, whose collective knowledge and collective recognition of ignorance is, for the time being, our best answer.

In other aspects of intellectual life, more relevant to policy and to strategy, we find a situation not wholly dissimilar, though less formalized and less clearly recognized. In our own internal affairs, the government's knowledge of the situations in fact with which it must deal is complemented by a traditional safeguard in our political institutions. If, in fact, the executive and legislative branches of the government have erred in their assessment of the problems of Northwestern lumbermen, or of maritime labor, or of Marine recruits, there is opportunity for those who are specialists in these problems, because they live with them, to be heard. And there is an underlying tolerance, sometimes violated, sometimes ignored, which yet gives to the voice of those most deeply concerned and most intimately and immediately knowledgeable the grave weight of the doctrine of the concurrent majority. In foreign affairs, in matters affecting other lands and people, no such protection and no such redress exist. Here the government must rely most heavily on what is essentially scholarship—what the historian, the linguist, the artist, and all others who, with the slowly learned historian's art of judging, evaluating, and understanding, can give as an intimate glimpse of what goes on in foreign and often very strange lands. It would not be easy to assemble committees, comparable to those created by the National Academy for its radiation studies, to give to the government an intimate professional insight into the state of affairs, the aspirations and divergences, hopes and probable behavior of contemporary South Africa, or Egypt, or Indonesia.

Faced with all this, faced with the complexity, the variety, and the rapid change which characterize both the intellectual scene and the world itself, there is a terrible temptation for us to seek the key that is not there, the simple summary from which all else might follow. We have tended to do that in the wars of this century, with, it would seem most probable, consequences of great trouble when we have come to the end of the war. It was probably bad even in the First World War, when our government had a relatively elaborate and learned theory which was widely accepted by our people, but which was not quite true. It was probably bad in the Second World War, when the theory seemed to be very primitive and to consist of the view that evil, however widely spread in the world, was so uniquely concentrated in the governments of the hostile powers that we could forget it elsewhere. I believe that we are now deeply injured by the simplifications of this time. The cold war is real, it is bitter, and it is deadly; it is not the only issue in the world, and for countless other peoples and their governments, it is not the issue they see in the brightest, harshest light. The greatest danger of such global views lies in the fact that they inhibit the reception of information which cannot be categorized in accordance with them; that they lose for us essential knowledge because in the light of our dominant doctrine this knowledge appears irrelevant or somehow does not fit. That we are indeed in this danger seems to me clear from the extent to which the unfolding of history finds us always surprised.

It seems to me that certain features of the situation I have attempted to sketch need special comment. Both the variety and the rate of change in our lives are likely to increase. Our knowledge will keep on growing, perhaps at a faster and faster rate, and change itself will tend to be accelerated. In describing this world, there will probably be no synopses to spare us the effort of detailed learning. I do not think it likely that we are in a brief interval of change and apparent disorder which will soon be ended. The cognitive problem seems to me unprecedented in scope, one not put in this vast form to any earlier society, and one for which only the most general rules of behavior can be found in the past.

It also seems to me that we must look forward to a world in which this American problem is more nearly everyone's problem. The beginnings of this are perhaps as important in the present moods of Europe as are the history of the two World Wars, Communism, National Socialism, and Europe's loss of political, military, and economic power. The problems seem clearly implied in the determination of peoples in Africa and Asia, and in Central and South America, by means not yet devised and not at all understood, to achieve education, learning, technology, and a new wealth. They form a part of the unrest, which is newly apparent in the intellectuals of the Soviet world and perhaps especially among their scientists, and increase the somberness of any prospect of change from tyranny to freedom.

Thus there are the most compelling external reasons why we in this country should be better able to take thought and to make available in the pressing problems of policy and strategy the intellectual resources now so sorely lacking. They are needed in the struggle with Communism; they are needed if we are to have some understanding and some slight influence on all the rest of the world in the great changes that lie ahead for it. Awareness of this need will do us good; and I do not underestimate the value of its general recognition by the people of the country or of official recognition by their government. It can only help to make money available to education and to teaching; it can only help to make the learned as well as the facile welcome in the proceedings of government policy making. But though these measures are bitterly necessary, and though they are long overdue, the real thing will not, I fear, come from them alone.

There may be valid grounds for a difference of opinion as to whether an official recognition of a need, or even a generally understood recognition of a need among our people, will evoke the response to that need.

What we here need is a vastly greater intellectual vigor and discipline, a more habitual and widespread openmindedness, and a kind of indefatigability not inconsistent with fatigue but inconsistent with surrender. It is not that our land is poor in curiosity, in true learning, in the habit of smelling out one's own self-delusion, in the dedication and search for order and law among novelty, variety, and contingency. There is respect for learning and for expertness. There is a proper recognition of the role of ignorance, and of our limits, both as men and as man. But of none of these is there enough, either among us, or in the value with which they are held by us, if indeed government by the people is not to perish.

NOTE

1 William James, Pragmatism (New York: Longmans, 1948), pp. 61–62.

AMERICA'S ADMINISTRATIVE RESPONSE
TO ITS WORLD PROBLEMS

by George F. Kennan

THE manner in which, in a complex modern society, the efforts of great numbers of people are harnessed to the performance of a single function is obviously something that reflects in the most intimate way the basic cultural and spiritual tenets of the people in question. Concepts of the proper mutual approach as between subordinate and superior and among colleagues, methods of selection and promotion, modalities of decision taking and command, the manner in which the dignity and enthusiasm and initiative of the individual are to be treated within a complex disciplinary framework—all these flow, inevitably, from philosophic concepts, assumptions, habits, and traditions that strike to the heart of the entire personality of a people and run through every phase of its life where large-scale organization is practiced: governmental and nongovernmental alike.

To attempt to make an assessment of a nation's concepts and habits of administration generally would be to undertake a sociological study of vast dimensions, and would far surpass the possibilities of this paper. What can be done within this framework can be only suggestive and illustrative. It must be confined to limited examples; and it can serve, at best, to indicate on the basis of these examples the nature of a problem that assumes a host of other forms throughout the entire panorama of American life.

Confronted with this necessity, I have chosen to address this paper simply to problems of administration within government, rather than in our society at large; and only to that part of government which deals with the external relations of the country. The discussion relates, therefore, primarily to the Department of State and to the other civilian agencies that perform work generally concerned with external relations, as well as to those branches of the executive offices and of the Pentagon that deal primarily with problems of foreign affairs.

The Problem

In the course of the past half century the portion of the United States government in question has grown to fifty to sixty times its original size. In the last twenty years alone, the growth has been somewhere upwards of 1000 per cent. This expansion has occurred, for the most part, in a few great spurts, the two World Wars and the period of Cold War in the late forties being the principal occasions.

With this stormy growth, spelling as it did the transition from the small, intimate organization to the vast, impersonal one, there came all the normal concomitants of bigness and complexity: a greatly increased coefficient of internal friction within the governmental machinery; an elaborate cumbersomeness of the decision-taking process; a sacrifice of timeliness and incisiveness in the decisions taken; a ponderous inertia in the apparatus as a whole; a loss of flexibility; mechanical, impersonal personnel procedures, with attendant loss of efficiency in utilization of personnel.

It is not surprising that today, when a state of relative, if precarious, stabilization has been reached in the development of this particular segment of the governmental machinery, there should be questions in many minds about the reasons for and implications of this rapid growth. Does this enormity signify health or disease? Is it really all necessary, or could it have been avoided without damage to the national interest? Are its drawbacks trivial or are they seriously harmful?

In the entire realm of public affairs there are few other questions of such importance which have been subjected to so little systematic study, about which so little is scientifically known, and for which the statistical background is at once so vast, so unordered, and so inadequate. Judgments about it can be, in the face of this situation, only subjective and intuitive, based on personal experience rather than on scientific analysis.

Reactions to the questions just mentioned tend to polarize into two opposing views, the reassuring one and the anxious one. Let us glance at them in that order.

THE REASSURING VIEW

The great majority of senior officials and administrators in government probably would take substantially the following position: bigness is unavoidable and is here to stay. It is a normal expression of the new role and the new responsibilities the United States has assumed in world affairs. It flows from the demands of the Cold War; from the increased number of clients of American policy; from the introduction of new devices of American diplomacy—alliances, propaganda, foreign aid. Neither size nor complexity of the present governmental apparatus could be appreciably reduced without real damage to the national interest. Those who yearn for the days of small staffs and intimate circles of participants in the policy-making process are indulging a sentimental nostalgia for the horse-and-buggy days of American diplomacy. The only practical course open to us today is not to attempt to abolish bigness but to find ways of living successfully with it and of making it work.

In support of this view, the following points would be made:

1. The growth in governmental machinery merely corresponds to the growth in function.

2. There has been comparable growth in other branches of government, in private activities affecting foreign affairs, and in the corresponding machinery of other governments. Not only does this prove that there is some overriding necessity involved in the phenomenon of rapid growth but also it creates a liaison and communication requirement which would compel the United States government to resort to something resembling the present large staffs, even though it were otherwise disinclined to do so.

3. Even with governmental employment at its present levels, almost all responsible officials in executive position complain of overwork; the answer to present problems may thus turn out to be not less personnel but even more.

4. The problems with which American statesmanship has to deal in the foreign field have achieved a degree of complexity which renders them no longer fit subjects for individual judgment and insight, no matter how perceptive or otherwise qualified; these problems must, to be correctly solved, be subjected to highly organized collective study in which a variety of technical skills, funds of specialized knowledge, and

governmental interests can be brought to bear on their solution. This necessitates large staffs and intricate organization. Concentration of authority in the hands of a single individual, to be exercised without full use of the established machinery for collective study and decision taking is, in fact, positively dangerous. Authority thus concentrated is apt to be exercised on inadequate information, to lack roundedness of judgment, and to ignore the interests of departments and agencies of the government other than just the one taking the action.

5. The yearning for the small organization, in the field of foreign relations, is usually connected with a nostalgia for the compact elite career group, self-perpetuating and self-administered, removed from the management of governmental personnel in general, and operating largely on its own standards and traditions. But this is undemocratic. It means the cultivation of a governmental entity alien to the spirit and background of the American people. It would be separated administratively from the remainder of the American governmental services, where popular tastes and interests find their normal expression. It tends toward snobbishness, arrogance, and a conspiratorial method of operation. It forfeits the resources of specialized knowledge and skill now essential to the formulation of an adequate judgment on policy matters, as also to the proper execution of programs and decisions.

6. The need for uniformity of administration and personnel management throughout the entire government leaves no room for the quaint, parochial administrative devices of the old State Department and Foreign Service. The administrative and managerial function must be laid out on a large scale; and the various departments and agencies operating in the foreign field must be required to adjust to the general governmental standards, instead of developing methods of administration and personnel management geared merely to their own particular functions.

7. Such deficiencies as do exist in the large governmental entity can be ironed out by improvement of the machinery itself. What is needed is further study by experts professionally trained in problems of personnel management and administration and the devising of better systems of coordination, control, and utilization of human resources through the entire field of activity.

8. To the extent large-scale organization might have drawbacks that would not yield entirely to the correct human engineering approach,

these are ones of secondary importance. Having a few people too many could not be a serious burden to an economy of the dimensions of that of the United States today; having many too few could easily cripple the programs to which the government is committed and on which the security of the nation depends.

THE ANXIOUS VIEW

Opposed to this school of thought is another which sees bigness as a dangerous evil in itself, is suspicious of the soundness of the causes that have produced it, and does not believe that adequate remedial measures could be found short of a basic change in the spirit of administration and a drastic reduction in the scale of the operation.

Addressing themselves to the first point cited above as substantiation for the reassuring view, namely, that growth in personnel has merely kept up with the growth of function, the adherents of this second school would deny that there is adequate proof of this assertion. They would cite numerous examples of instances in which the opposite would appear to be the case. The London *Economist*, in its witty and only semi-facetious article (November 19, 1955) on "Parkinson's Law," drew attention to the fact that whereas the Royal Navy had 67 per cent less ships in commission in 1928 than in 1914, and 31.5 per cent less officers and men on its lists, the shore establishment used to support this was greater in all categories—78 per cent greater, in fact, when it came to Admiralty officials. American critics would find similar illustrations. They might question—to take a random example—whether the functions of the American Foreign Service in Germany are really five to ten times greater today, as the personnel complement would seem to imply, than they were in the first years of the recent war, before Pearl Harbor, when the American official staff there handled not only American interests but also those of a number of belligerent countries, not just for the present reduced territory of Germany but for the entire united country, and not even for this alone, but for a number of German-occupied territories as well. They might question why the Mosow Embassy, having substantially the same functions now as it had twenty years ago in a country where there are no American investments and no appreciable colony of American residents, should have in the bosom of its official family today more children alone than it had official staff and dependents together in 1937. Any number of other examples can be found.

The adherents of this second school would not deny that both America and its world environment have become bigger and more complex in these twenty years, or that America's role in the world has grown. They would be prepared to admit that the Department of State has a great deal more to do than it had in those earlier years. But that the growth in the Department's functions has been upwards of 600 per cent they would greatly doubt. They would cite a number of indices—population, number of foreign governments, extent of commercial and financial exchanges, foreign investment, travel by Americans, rate of immigration—to show that in no instance does the rate of growth approach anything like this figure. They would argue that this means one of two things: either a great deal of machinery has been created needlessly or there is a law of diminishing returns in the efficiency of governmental organization as size increases. One would eventually reach a point (and some would say it had already been reached) where masses of new personnel could be added without any appreciable increase in the genuine work output of the organization. In either case, these people would point out, bigness is an evil.

As to the second point—that the growth in this sector of government only parallels similar growth elsewhere—the adherents of this second school would not deny this for a moment. Nor would they deny that this circumstance constitutes one of the few valid and unanswerable reasons for bigness, in that it raises liaison and communication requirements far greater than anything that would otherwise exist. That the administration of foreign affairs proceeds today in a general climate of bigness, they would not dispute; and they would recognize that for this reason the chances of combating it successfully are poor unless the effort is made on a very wide scale indeed. They would point to the armed services as probably the main source of contagion. They would cheerfully concede the difficulty involved for other departments and agencies in attempting to exist even in *proximity* to the Pentagon without resorting to bigness in self-defense.

But all this, they would argue, only proves what everyone knows: that bigness is contagious and that the bad organization tends to drive out the good. And they would question whether the over-expansion in other places is not the product of precisely the same dangerous and unhealthy tendencies that have produced over-expansion in the State Department itself.

To the argument that people are overworked, the adherents of the second school would reply that this proves nothing: that it is precisely the inordinate internal friction of the great organization—its muscle-bound quality—which consumes the energies of its people in so appalling a proportion. If the organization is large enough it can be given only the most rudimentary function to perform and it will still keep masses of people overworked in the performance of it.

As to the alleged superiority of the collective method of decision taking: representatives of the anxious school would—again—not deny that decision must be refined by expert advice or that the interests to be kept in mind today in most decisions of foreign affairs are complex in the extreme and not readily familiar to any single person. But they would argue that thought is, by its very nature, an individual process, not a collective one; that to be useful thought must be communicated; that to be communicated it must be filtered through the single mind that puts it into words; that it cannot, therefore, be greater than what a single mind can comprehend and state. There is thus no such thing as collective judgment; there is only individual judgment, enriched and refined by the advice of others and commanding, in certain cases, the approval of a wider body. This being the case, the pretense of a collective wisdom, underlying so much of the governmental committee system today, is simply a form of play-acting and self-deception—an elaborate exercise which fragmentizes responsibility without broadening thought. It leads—these people would argue—to a complete sacrifice of incisiveness and style. And this applies not only literally, in actual effectiveness of communication, but also in the broader sense of the style of statesman-ship itself, which can never be expressive and convincing unless it is the product of a single human personality.

As for the criticism that the small, compact organization is snobbish and undemocratic: the adherents of this second school would maintain that this criticism was merely the reflection of a prevailing jealousy on the part of Congress, the press, and other branches of the government of any genuinely select service which insists on putting quality before quantity, which has its own administrative integrity, which is impervious to domestic political influence, which defies the leveling hand of the professional administrator, and which cannot be entered laterally at higher levels by people who would not be able to meet the normal requirements for entrance at the bottom. It would be denied that there is anything undemocratic about the cultivation of a tightly organized professional corps which could stand at the center of the government's foreign affairs work and which would be based on superiority of background, intelligence, education, and performance. They would not claim that the old Foreign Service had adequately met this requirement; but they would consider that it would be wholly possible, given observance of the correct principles, to create a service that did. They would hold that such a unit would—for reasons of discipline, personal excellence, and ease of internal communication—be a more effective aid to the President than what we have today; that the President has a right to the best he can get in the way of assistance; that the Executive Branch of the government is supposed to be a disciplined institution, not a debating society or a forum for the manifestations of the virtues of the average citizen; and that to fear excellence and exclusiveness in this form of work is to confuse democracy with doctrinaire social egalitarianism aimed at the suppression of talent and individuality rather than the achievement of maximum efficiency. They would claim that the tendency today is to achieve administrative arrangements geared completely to the workings of mediocrity—arrangements which, as the saying goes, "the least talented can operate, and the most intelligent cannot disturb."

Leaving the field of rebuttal, and turning to the attack, the members of the anxious school would point to the obviously unsound and, in some instances, disreputable causes that enter into the creation of the elephantiasis which now marks governmental machinery. They would call attention to the way in which government is geared to favor expansion rather than contraction, to the psychological and sometimes legal or procedural factors that make it so much easier to hire than to fire. They would point to the rampant empire building—to that inconquerable human tendency to feed the ego by cultivating the trappings of bureaucratic power even where the substance is lacking. They would point to the excessive paternalism—borrowed from the army, initially justified by wartime conditions, but preserved almost undiminished today. They would point to the insistence of the government on providing its charges with housing, transportation, education, medical service, parking places, stores, shopping discounts, recreational facilities, literature—practically everything but romantic love. All of this, again, is at the cost of more personnel, more machinery. In all such things, the skeptics would find justification for the suspicion that a great deal of governmental growth is the product of certain unhealthy immanent processes—involuntary and subconscious—that take hold of organizations once a certain border of intimacy and compactness has been left behind.

BASIC FAULTS IN PRESENT ADMINISTRATIVE METHODS

The author of this paper is, in general, himself a proponent of this second school of thought. This being so, he would like to state in his own words where he believes the greatest dangers of the present administrative principles to lie.

The present system is based, throughout, on what appears to be a conscious striving for maximum fragmentation and diffusion of power. This operates on each of the two major planes by which all governmental work is ordered—administrative and substantive.

On the administrative plane it takes the form of the divorce of administrative functions from the substantive chain of command and their subordination to special independent hierarchies of administrators, managers, and security officials. With respect to inanimate things—supplies, premises, communication channels—this practice is unexceptionable. With respect to persons, it is wholly misconceived. It deprives the superior officer in the substantive chain of command of one of the most vital tools for the proper accomplishment of his own work: the right to select and control the personnel who are to assist him. By divorcing personnel control from the substantive aspects of a man's performance, it assures that personnel decisions are made on the basis of every sort of judgment other than the one most qualified, most informed, and most intimately associated with the man's usefulness to the government, namely, that of his immediate superior in his regular work. The individual officer or employee is left with the impression that strive as he may to please those who are his visible superiors during the hours he spends at the office, his fate will nevertheless be determined by members of an invisible fraternity of administrators and security agents whose identity he does not know, who do not know him, and for whom he is only a card from the business machine, bearing certain perforations intelligible only to another business machine. With the achievement of this state of affairs, the sense of pride in work suffers, along with the hope of any genuine and reliable relationship between effort and reward. In their place there is left only an uncomfortable sense of being at the mercy of forces unknown and unseen—a condition that grips subordinate and superior together in a Kafka-esque nightmare to which there is no end and from which there is no escape. If, in these circumstances, enthusiasm and devotion survive—as fortunately they often do—this is usually the result of a mutual respect and sympathy among associates and a common devotion to the government's interests. Both must be strong enough to override the sense of insecurity and the dimness of the connection between effort and recognition.

I am aware that the opinions of the immediate superior are consulted and do enter theoretically into personnel decisions, if not into security control. But the decision lies, after all, with a third party; the opinions of the immediate superior are utilized only at second hand; and the devices for the communication of those opinions (forms, questionnaires, multiple-choice questions) are in many instances so miserably inadequate and misconceived that they would stand as barriers, rather than conveyers, to the transmission of any apt and subtly informed judgment.

This impersonal system of personnel control rests on the desire to find ways of judging people that get away from personal opinion and personal responsibility. This tendency is almost inevitable whenever numbers get so large that the persons doing the judging cannot have any personal knowledge of the subjects. But it rests, unavoidably, on the assumption that there exist such things as adequate and fully comparable objective criteria, divorced from personal opinion, for judging a man's worth as an employee of the government. This could not be more mistaken. There is no such thing as an abstract, objective evaluation of a human being, independent of the personality of the one who judges. The only definition of a man's worth that has reality is the image as seen by another man; and that image is a reflection of—and a reflection on—both of them. The judgment, in other words, is valueless without a knowledge of the judger as well as of the judged. This is why one cannot realistically depart from the human personality in its most intimate sense as the basis of selection and promotion and handling, generally, of personnel. To attempt to make this departure is to operate in a world of unrealities. It would deal not with men themselves but with distorted shadows of them, at the price of inefficient, wasteful use of their talents, and at the sacrifice of the enthusiasm and devotion that come from the assurance that one's official fate is likely to be a reasonably faithful reflection of the quality of one's effort.

The cultivation of an impersonal system of personnel control rests, of course, on the understandable desire to achieve maximum fairness and uniformity in the terms of competition. No personnel system can be properly operated, even in a moderately large organization, without some centralized system of record keeping and without the invocation of some general criteria designed to guard against the aberrations of the biased, unjust, or erratic superior. One cannot leave men exclusively to the mercy of the man they happen to work for at any given moment.

But what is involved here is the question of the weight to be given to the various components of a personnel decision. The preponderant voice should always lie with a superior who knows the man personally, who has firsthand knowledge of his work performance, and who is interested in him as a human being—not with remote, unseen individuals, devoid of experience in the substantive aspects of the work of the man they are judging, and protected by their anonymity from the real responsibility that resides in the shaping of the fate of individual employees of the government. So long as the latter system prevails, the premium, for the individual employee, will continue to lie not in boldness, not in individuality, not in imagination, but in the cultivation of that nice mixture of noncontroversialness and colorless semi-competence that corresponds most aptly to the various banal distinctions of which, alone, the business machine is capable.

As for the fragmentation and diffusion of power on the substantive plane? This begins, of course, at the very top, with the fragmentation of the responsibility for conducting—under the President's direction—the foreign affairs of the nation. The very fact that there are several departments and agencies involved in this work, and none with real authority over the others, sets the tone for the distribution of responsibility all the way down the line. There is, of course, the National Security Council; but this is a body capable only of sporadic, solemn decisions, laboriously prepared and negotiated among the various government offices prior to their submission to the President. It does not yet have, to my knowledge, the independent professional staff it would require for the kind of decision which is needed; and the very nature of its composition (the executive heads of various government departments) militates against detached judgment. What the foreign affairs segment of the government needs is not primarily an occasional NSC paper but intimate day-by-day, hour-by-hour direction, sensitive to the smallest significant change in the world situation. It needs, in the language of the day, to be ridden herd on; and this is precisely what the National Security Council cannot do for it.

From this center, the system of diffused authority spreads downwards into a thousand branches and twigs of the governmental tree. At every level, decision taking proceeds by the cultivation of consensus among various units in committees which operate on the veto principle, each unit represented being effectively in a position to bar or at least to delay action not acceptable to it. Whether it was the original intent that committees should operate in this manner I do not know. A Department of State handbook on committees, from about the year 1949, affords no evidence that committees were conceived to operate in any other way than this; and this is certainly the way most of them functioned in Washington at that time. This is, of course, only an extrapolation of the internal initialing system of the Department of State, where outgoing communications usually require the initials of a number of offices, each one of which can hold up the communication if it withholds approval. The fact that a single office may be designated as the one with primary responsibility does not give that office the power to act independently. The system thus operates on the principle embodied in the words so frequently heard from senior officials of the Department: "Anything you fellows can agree on is all right with me."

Now if what were at stake were only action, this might, in some instances, have its virtue in assuring that action was sound and that all the aspects of the government's interests had been taken into account. But when it is a question of thought and analysis and political philosophy, this method has grievous handicaps. The result, as everyone in government knows, is usually a least common denominator of opinion: compromised language, platitude, obscurity, a hodgepodge inferior to any of the individual views out of which it is brewed. A great portion of the lack of authority and incisiveness in the positions taken by the government can surely be laid to this method of decision taking.

Opinions on the origin of this curious committee system vary. It has flourished particularly on the military side of the river, and particularly in the relations between the three services. There is a plausible theory that it was in large measure a somewhat misconceived importation of the British committee system with which our armed services came into extensive contact during World War II. There are other analogies drawn from the separation of powers in our government as a whole, and from the unbelievable obscuration of responsibility achieved by the legislative committee system.

The basic assumption underlying this fear of a rigid, clear allotment of responsibility is surely the belief that it lends itself to dictatorship and to curtailment of the liberties and rights of others. There is a feeling that concentration of authority is in some way undemocratic—that the allotment to a single individual of the power to decide something is in some way incompatible with the spirit of the American political system. What is ignored is the fact that authority is required to protect freedom just as it is required to assail it. Beyond this there is the failure to realize that what is involved in the conduct of external relations is merely the exercise of a personal authority which already constitutionally exists and which is absolutely essential to the transaction of the country's international business. The inter-divisional and inter-agency squabbles in Washington represent a form of insistence on fragmenting at lower levels a power which the fathers of the Constitution meant to unify when they invested it in the President of the United States.

The amount of time and manpower consumed in the effort to arrive at consensus in this manner among numbers of governmental entities in an endless series of questions has to be seen to be believed. The portion of each day spent by higher officials in committee meetings while papers, telephone calls, and messages accumulate at their desks is a part of the price paid for this method of decision taking, as is the great volume of internal written correspondence about such matters: the chits, the opinions, the position papers.

The aggregate result of these deficiencies—the flight from the individual, the striving for the creation of machinery to replace individual insight and judgment, the labored diffusion of power—is to give to the governmental apparatus an inflexibility, an inertia, a sluggishness, and an incoherence in communication that render it an inferior instrument in the hands of the senior officials of government.

No one who has worked in the immediate vicinity of the Secretary of State or the President can fail to have been impressed with the difficulty involved for either of these officials in making use of so vast and complex a machinery. They cannot apprehend it. They cannot memorize or picture its table of organization.

The regular governmental machinery was designed to serve the President and the Secretary of State in two ways: first, as a source of information, stimulus, and recommendation with relation to the exercise of their responsibility; and, second, as a channel for the implementation of their decisions.

So far as the first is concerned, it is plain that the contribution the regular apparatus is capable of making bears no proper relation to its size and to the enormity of its effort. This is partly the result of the very limited time that the senior officials have in which to absorb information and impulses of all sorts brought to them through the regular channels;[1] but it is also partly a consequence of the inferior form in which this information is produced—inferior, that is, from the standpoint of its effectiveness in engaging and impressing the mind of anyone so busy, so overwhelmed with ulterior preoccupations, and so constituted by education and intellect as most presidents and most secretaries of state are apt to be. On countless occasions subordinates have been surprised and disappointed—sometimes even personally hurt—to find that the Secretary or the President has been more decisively influenced by some chance outside contact or experience than by the information and advice offered through the regular channels. Either he has talked with someone from outside whose statements seemed somehow simpler and more striking and appealing than anything he had heard from his own subordinates, or the same effect has been produced upon him by some newspaper or magazine article he has read, by something he has heard on the radio, or something he has seen in the newsreels or on television.

There is, admittedly, a real injustice here, in most instances. The statements of the fascinating outsider often prove in retrospect to have been less sound and balanced than the final product of official judgment; and the items purveyed by the mass media are found to be dangerously over-simplified and inadequate as a basis for official action.

But the regular subordinates are inclined to forget or to ignore the deadening effect of the bureaucracy on all forms of communication, oral and written. Whereas the products of the mass media are designed to strike and to hold briefly the attention of busy people, and whereas the statements of the outside visitor are apt to have at least the charm of the expression of a single human mind, with all its directness and fresh-ness, the products of the official machinery are almost invariably dull and pedestrian, drafted or spoken in the usual abominable governmentese, and even—in many instances—intellectually inferior by virtue of the extensive compromising of language which has preceded their final for-mulation. In short, the busy senior executive frequently finds more use-ful and meaningful to him the product of the individual mind than the product of a tortured collective effort; and it is only the latter that he gets from his assistants.

In the execution of policy, we see the same phenomenon. Anyone who has ever had anything to do with the conduct of foreign relations knows that policies can be correctly and effectively implemented only by people who understand the entire philosophy and world of thought of the per-son or persons who took the original decision. But senior officials are constantly forced to realize that in a governmental apparatus so vast, so impersonal, and so lacking in any sort of ideological indoctrination and discipline they cannot count on any great portion of the apparatus to understand entirely what they mean. The people in question here are in large part ones they do not know personally and cannot hope to know in this way. Considerations of security alone would make it difficult, in many instances, to attempt to initiate into the reasons of action all those who might be involved if one were to attempt to use the regular chan-nels. The expansion of the governmental apparatus has led to a steady inflation of titles, roughly matching that of the growth of the apparatus itself. The result is that the stature of many titles and offices has been reduced in everyone's eyes; and dozens of officials who ought, by virtue of the titles they hold, to be able to serve as vehicles for the execution of policy, are prevented from doing so in consequence of the fact that they would now be considered too low level to be acceptable to other governments, or even other departments of our own government, as interlocutors and negotiators. Try as one will, one simply cannot make the vast organization absorb or replace the small circle of responsible officials as the center for the formulation and execution of policy.

For all these reasons, there is a growing tendency to have policy executed personally at the top. There was once a day when matters of world-shaking importance were carried forward, discussed, and negotiated by counselors of embassy and chargés d'affaires. Today the Secretary of State or the President feels obliged to jump into a plane and do the job himself. The governmental machinery is simply too unwieldy, too cumbersome, too unknown, and too deflated of meaning by its own vastness to be useful as an instrument of policy. The facelessness inflicted on a horde of officials by the vastness and complexity of the organizational framework in which they are buried has deprived them of personal status in the eyes of foreign governments, or even of other American agencies, and has thus reduced their usefulness to those they are supposed to serve.

These realities raise the question as to the value of the great organization, per se, as an aid to the President in the execution of his most solemn responsibilities with respect to the conduct of foreign relations. The damage is not only that the President tends to bypass it: the damage is that he does not have at his side what he needs to do his work and this is most serious of all in the conceptual field.

It need hardly be pointed out that the position of the United States in the world today is of such a nature that its diplomacy, to be successful, must be based on the most subtle and literate comprehension of world realities. Furthermore, it must be animated by a single rounded and consistent political philosophy, must be refined at its inception by the processes of private and intimate discussion, and must be executed in such a way as to permit maximum flexibility, instantaneous adaptation to changing world realities, and delicate shifts of emphasis in response to new situations. It must even operate with contradictory policies, deliberately and simultaneously, in order to permit the rapid exploitation of the shifting external scene.

Such a diplomacy cannot and will not emanate from the workings of a great bureaucratic apparatus. It requires, necessarily and properly, too much of the personal, too much of the private, too much—if you will—

of the conspiratorial, to be conceived and implemented in this way. The chief executive is faced today with the choice of bypassing the regular apparatus, both as a source of information and inspiration and as a channel of execution, or of forgoing effective diplomacy altogether and contenting himself with the monumental inflexibility, the philosophical shallowness, the ideological obscurity, and the unimaginative execution which the great organization assures.

Up to this time, the tendency has been to compromise, giving the edge to the latter alternative. The result has been the situation we have today: a diplomacy that comes alive as and when the President can give it personal expression. Otherwise it is a diplomacy insensitive to external developments and stimuli—a diplomacy which speaks but scarcely hears —a diplomacy which, as a consequence of its own inertia and inflexibility, represents for other governments more of a topographical feature on the horizon of world affairs than a sensitive, reacting, and feeling partner in the great process of action and discussion that constitutes international life. Such a diplomacy is something other nations have to take into account as an important reality; it is not something they can hope to influence extensively by words and ideas.

And this is a shame; for words and ideas work both ways. America's self-centeredness and hardness of hearing hamper her effectiveness as a speaker in the councils of the world.

CONCLUSIONS

There can be no question but that the present size and complexity of the governmental apparatus are in part a response to real requirements, and thus in part unavoidable. There has been a considerable real increase in function. There can, of course, be no total return to the past. What has been written above should not be taken as in any way a denial of this fact.

A distinction must be drawn, furthermore, between essentially me-chanical processes, such as the issuance of passports, where staffs can be and must be expanded to meet whatever the requirements may be, and purely intellectual processes, where bigness runs into the law of dimin-ishing returns. Even here, there is an important distinction to be ob-served between the process of intelligence gathering and initial analysis, on the one hand, and the synthesis and final utilization of intelligence, on the other. For the first, large-scale organization is unquestionably essential; and it must admittedly draw on a large variety of technical skills and specialties. For the second, compactness and intimacy of association are necessary.

The problem narrows down, therefore, to the essentially intellectual processes of synthesis and evaluation of information available to the government and of the formulation and execution of high policy. And the question which it is intended to raise in this paper is whether, for these processes, the massive organization can be useful at all—whether, in fact, the attempt to solve problems in this field by large-scale organization does not rest on certain basic misunderstandings as to what can and cannot be accomplished by the working together of many people.

One would not have to go far to seek the origins of these misunderstandings. The past quarter of a century has seen the gradual and eventually overwhelming rejection by official Washington of the very concept of the diplomatic professional as a source of guidance for the organization of this work. The present pattern of organization is largely the work of wartime administrators, using ideas borrowed from the armed forces or from business—in both of which fields the processes involved are largely mechanical rather than intellectual, and ones in which there is room, or appears to be room, for utilization of great numbers of people, selected solely on the basis of technical qualification, without much relation to their general qualities as human beings. I say "appears to be room," because I do not know whether here, too, this principle is not actually subject to limitations not readily visible to the outsider.

The evils of our present system for conducting external relations could be mitigated, if not entirely eliminated, by remedial measures taken just within the foreign affairs sector of government. A beginning could be made by the concentration in the hands of the Secretary of State of the authority (under the President's direction) for the entire foreign affairs field, subordinating to him all civilian activity relating primarily to external affairs. There could then be a much clearer and firmer allotment of responsibility and power right down the line, involving abandonment of the present negative-veto committee system, and a systematic assignment of individual operational authority, if necessary on an arbitrary basis, where specific questions bridge existing competencies. Personnel and security control could be restored to the normal chain of command—which would not mean that specialists would not be needed or that there would not be centralized, functional record keeping procedures, but would mean that these services would be used as adjuncts to the normal discipline of the work, not as competing empires. The foreign affairs work could be removed from the general civil service administration and organized, once more, in accordance with its own specific requirements. An end could be put to the effort to base a professional foreign affairs service—in the name of democracy—on educational and personal mediocrity; and a beginning could be made once more at the creation (it would take at least two decades to complete) of a professional service commensurate in quality with the tasks to be performed. All these things would help—though none would fully overcome the effect of contagion from the official environment in which this branch of the government has to exist.

Actually, it would be the height of irrealism to suppose that any of these measures will be—or could be—taken in the intellectual and official climate of the present epoch. For this, the misunderstandings are too deep, too ubiquitous, and too dearly held; in many instances the formal commitment to contrary courses has already been made; the vested interest in what now exists is far too great to permit of serious preoccupation with what ought to be. In the governmental machinery of the present day the American people have a commitment of relentless finality. No deliberate human hand will now dismantle it or reduce it to healthier dimensions. Only some form of catastrophe—natural disaster, financial collapse, or the atomic bomb—could have this effect.

The foreign affairs sector of government will remain, then, for the foreseeable future, substantially what it is today. Of itself, it will tend to continue even to grow; for there will be continued growth in the functions to which it must address itself, and beyond this it will continue to breed activity internally, according to its own peculiar laws. This growth will find its limits, at any given time, in the readiness of Congress to provide funds. But regardless of what motions of investigation the Congress may go through, its final decisions will not be based on any real effort at exact measurement of what is required to meet the demands in question. For this, the organization is already too vast, too impenetrable, too inscrutable; it is no less baffling to Congress than to anyone else. What is appropriated will represent, in the last analysis, a combination of what the Congressmen have become accustomed to and what they feel they can provide in the face of competing demands. And the final product will continue, if past experience is any criterion, to grow greatly in times of crisis and to hold on to the bulk of its gains in the periods between.

This being the case, we must expect that the regular apparatus of the government will become, with time, of less and less value to the President and the Secretary of State as a source of intimate guidance and as a vehicle for the promulgation of policy in really delicate, important, and urgent situations. Increasingly, in situations of this sort, American statesmen will have to take refuge in a bypassing of the regular machinery and in the creation of ad hoc devices—kitchen cabinets, personal envoys, foreign offices within foreign offices, and personal diplomacy—to assure the intimacy of association, the speed, the privacy, and the expression of personal style essential to any effective diplomacy. This will always be in some degree demoralizing to the regular echelons of government, but not too much so. Many of the values of the regular apparatus are self-engendered in any case, and are already separated from the reality of real decision taking by distances so great that a bit more or less makes little difference.

Both government and high policy will go on, then, much as they have in the past, but with a tendency toward increasing separation. Presidents, for want of suitable institutionalized assistance, will continue to improvise—some well, some less so. The muscle-bound bureaucracy will do its chores, some of which are important. It will continue to wage the endless exhausting encounter with itself which is implicit in its over-intricate structure. Beyond this, it will continue to be what it has been in these past years: a unique educational institution, second to none in its pedagogical effect—a place where, through the course of many frustrations and bewilderments, just close enough to responsibility to feel its bite and just far enough from it to be safe from real harm, many men may learn many things. They learn about world affairs, about how people are governed, about how people's interests can be represented, and about how the human animal behaves in the political context. A few of them also learn something of the evils of large institutions as instruments of analysis, judgment, and discriminating execution in the field of foreign policy. Perhaps some day the number of those who learn this last lesson will grow to a point where they will rebel successfully against the jungle of superfluous relationships in which they are now confined.

NOTE

[1] Who has not seen, for example, at international conferences, the huge black briefing books remain idle and unused because the chiefs have no time to look at them? Who has not seen experts, by the dozen, cool their heels through such conferences, unconsulted and unused because the chiefs have no time to talk to them?

HAVE THERE BEEN DISCERNIBLE SHIFTS IN AMERICAN VALUES DURING THE PAST GENERATION?

by Clyde Kluckhohn

> We float on mystery
> And the wise man knows it better than the fool.
> But having said as much, most men forget
> What they have just said, forget that mystery
> Is just what they have called it. They go on
> When they have granted the unfathomable,
> To pitch their petty plumblines overboard
> and fathom it.
> THEODORE MORRISON, "The Dream of Alcestis"

> Es ist schwer, die Wahrheit zu sagen, denn des gibt zwar
> nur eine; aber sie ist lebendig und hat daher ein lebendig
> wechselndes Gesicht.
> FRANZ KAFKA

I. INTRODUCTION

ELSEWHERE I have attempted (nor very successfully) a somewhat rigorous definition of "value" for social science purposes (Kluckhohn, 1951).* Here I shall deliberately use the term loosely, ranging from those culturally defined and affectively toned conceptions of the right and the good which the philosophers have generally considered "social values" to widely shared "goals" and "aspirations" that have a more psychological tinge. Since I agree with Northrop (1947) that normative and existential propositions are almost always intimately linked and their separation is, at best, a convenience of abstraction, it is necessary to deal with conditions and the cognitive maps of Americans as well as with their orienta-

---

* Note: Throughout this essay, source materials are indicated merely by author and year of publication. See pp. 208–214 for a more complete reference to the sources cited.

tions, "moral" and "emotional," toward standards of what is deemed desirable. While "values" are always manifested in the behavior (including the verbal behavior) of individuals, the interest in this paper is in those values that are in some sense attributable to the group and in those isolable similarities characteristic of a large segment of the society. I am quite aware that no single value is held in literally identical form by even two different persons; indeed it may be presumed that "the same" value undergoes changes in a single individual as he matures and as his environing situations alter. Such variations, such developments and innovations (for, after all, "new" values take their origin, concretely, in particular individuals) are extremely significant processes, but they are not our concern here. It may also be well to state explicitly at the outset another assumption that I make (contrary to most Communist theorists): values are something more than "epiphenomena," verbal rationalizations of existing conditions. Values influence and, on occasion, determine action.

As I shall neglect purely private variations in values, so also I shall discuss regional, ethnic, and class variations only insofar as they illuminate by contrastive perspective the "dominant" values of American society. One gets variant values in some segments of the South, New England, Texas, California; in ethnic and religious minorities; between various social classes. In certain particulars the values of these groups are unique; in more cases they represent a shading, a heightening or lowering of a value emphasis distinctive of the dominant American culture. For example, Japanese-Americans ordinarily exhibit an allegiance to middle-class conformity, hard work, striving for "success" that is exaggerated to the point of caricature; certain American values put upon pleasure and special forms of recreation reach their present climax in identifiable portions of the population of California. My eye will be primarily upon the Middle Atlantic states, the Middle West, the Far West (excluding Texas and California), Protestant "Old Americans" whose ancestors came predominantly from Western Europe, and upon the middle class. Substantially all students, American and foreign, agree that American culture in its distinctiveness is overwhelmingly a middle-class culture. In a recent *Fortune* poll, three-fourths of those interviewed identified themselves with the middle class,[1] although in the community studies where the whole population has been class typed, the proportion assigned to the middle class runs to about forty per cent.[2]

While variations in values along regional,[3] ethnic-religious,[4] and class [5] lines (these categories interlock at more than one point) are important for some kinds of analysis, I am convinced that without going to an empty level of abstraction one can talk about American values. National advertising, national communication media, national political life can be effectively operative only on the premise that some values (and the related motivations) tend to prevail in a manner that cuts across—to a considerable extent—the varying lines of differentiation. An impressive validation of this assumption rests in an examination of the consistently contrasting ways in which the same products were advertised by the same companies in the same year in British, Canadian, and American periodicals directed at audiences of roughly equivalent economic, educational, and social position. The dominant American values are recognized, however implicitly so far as verbalization is concerned, by virtually all adult Americans. They affect political and every other type of behavior even where one or more of these values is consciously or unconsciously rejected or regarded ambivalently by an individual as an idiosyncratic organization of experience or by individuals who are mainly reflecting the values of a particular group. All of my study confirms Myrdal (1944, vol. 1, p. xliv) as being fundamentally correct when he says ". . . most Americans have most valuations in common though they are arranged differently in the sphere of valuations of different individuals and groups and bear different intensity coefficients." We shall keep these "valuations in common" to the forefront while never forgetting completely that what Murray (1940, pp. 160–161) says of personality is equally true of society:

A personality is a full Congress of orators and pressure groups, of children, demagogues, communists, isolationists, warmongers, mugwumps, grafters, logrollers, lobbyists, Caesars and Christs, Machiavellis and Judases, Tories and Promethean revolutionists.

Just as I shall center on broadly American values with little attention to their personal and group variations, so I shall concentrate upon those changes that I deem secular rather than ephemeral or cyclical. This means, for example, that the hysterical phenomena attendant upon Mc-Carthyism will be considered only insofar as they appear to reflect longer ground swells, that the reactive swings back and forth between "isolationism" and "internationalism" will be discussed only from the viewpoint of a smoothed curve.

II. BACKGROUND

It may be useful to give a candid picture of the work upon which my documentation and interpretation rest. I have had occasion from time to time since 1940 to attempt, for purposes of both teaching and writing (Kluckhohn, 1941, 1949, 1950, 1951; Kluckhohn and Kluckhohn, 1947), critical analysis and synthesis of empirical and impressionistic writings on American culture and especially American values by social scientists and others. Building upon this previous experience, I have, specifically for this paper, done a great deal of additional reading and rereading and have also put to work on this subject three Harvard tutorial groups, two able Harvard seniors writing distinction theses, and a research assistant. While our combined coverage of pertinent sources is far from complete —this would be a lifetime task for a research team—it is much more massive than anything my wife and I had previously accomplished. In addition, I have since 1948 been continuously working upon value theory in general.[6]

My own reading for the present task was systematic in the following respects:

(1) Review of previous work upon American values (at many different time periods) by social scientists, historians, philosophers, and literary figures.

(2) Saturation in writings upon American history, going back into the eighteenth and nineteenth centuries but focusing upon twentieth century history and especially the period since 1918.

(3) Reading widely in the literature on changes in American values during the past generation, produced by writers of various (or no) disciplinary affiliation who based their reflections on their own experience rather than upon specifically pointed and systematic research.

(4) Intensive study of the empirical investigations, however miniscule the topic and range of the research, which have dealt with value changes involving at least a portion of the 1935–1955 epoch.

The economic and political sources I have not covered systematically, but many of them have been summarized and interpreted in general works (e.g., Allen, 1952; Valentine, 1954; Goldman, 1956). All in all, I have used as basic sources upwards of fifty books and monographs and two hundred articles. In addition, I have sampled roughly another hundred books and at least several hundred articles. Before going into detailed discussion, let me state my general reactions to the sources (grouped by the four categories above) and anticipate some over-all findings.

1. The available materials which explicitly and implicitly state, analyze or interpret, or provide empirical data upon American values are overwhelming in their magnitude. Most, however, are "impressionistic" or "literary," written from the angles of the writer's personality or peculiar experiences. The "solid" materials have been provided primarily by historians and social scientists, with a few exceptions. Morris (1956), a philosopher, has supplied highly empirical data on the preferred "paths of life" of American college students and the corresponding choices of a number of foreign college populations. Unfortunately, for our purposes, we have no strictly comparable American data for the period of a generation ago.

In broad outline there is remarkable agreement as to what American values are or have been and agreement upon their stability through more than a hundred and fifty years. The words vary somewhat with the fashions of the time of writing and with the language associated with the writer's field. One analyst will include one or more central values that another omits or expressly rejects. The shadings, the historical derivations, the linkages vary appreciably in some instances. But the agreements and overlappings on central points are vastly more striking than the disagreements, stated or possibly inferable on ground of omission. W. W. Rostow called my attention to an extensive survey by Coleman (1941) of traits and values held to be "characteristic of the country as a whole" by authors writing in four periods (Pre-Civil War, Civil War to World War I, World War I to Depression, Depression to 1940). Coleman found almost complete agreement on 27 characteristics and more support than dissent for an additional 13. Of these about one quarter were mentioned in all four periods, and almost all of the rest were asserted in three out of the four periods.

The convergences between authors may be spurious for one or both of two reasons. All observers may have been too much influenced by a

prevalent *Zeitgeist*. This seems unlikely in view of the congruence between statements written during Victorian optimism, the pessimism of
the depression period, and the confusion after 1939; between assertions
of English, French, American, and Asiatic writers. The second objection,
that of intercontamination between sources, is more serious. It would
be an exaggeration to speak of all subsequent discussions of American
values as a series of commentaries upon de Tocqueville because some
American social scientists have never heard of de Tocqueville and there
is no evidence that certain foreign observers have read him. Nevertheless,
there are many indications that some of the characterizations which crop
up again and again derive directly or indirectly from de Tocqueville,
Bryce, and a small number of other acute and fundamental works. On
the other hand, one can point to a number of cases where at least the
direct derivations came out of quite distinct sources and intellectual
backgrounds and where there is no question but that the authors wrote
in complete ignorance of the work of the others. As an instance, let me
give the findings of a United States senator, an historian, a philosopher,
and two social scientists.

Clifford Case (1957) lists individualism, pragmatism, work, optimism,
change-as-desirable, generosity (compassion) as "principles in which most
Americans believe deeply." Arthur Schlesinger, Sr. (1949) likewise includes individualism, pragmatism (especially "mechanical ingenuity"),
"worship of work," optimism, high valuation of change, generosity
("idealism") but adds a few others such as emphasis on deference to
women, "wasteful living," pursuit of pleasure, geographic and social
mobility (which can perhaps be considered part of the "change-as-desirable" syndrome), "the acquisitive spirit," overstatement (especially in
humor). Ralph Barton Perry (1949) considers as "characteristically American" a "physiognomy" based upon the interrelations of the following
elements: individualism, achievement (work), "hope of perpetual and
limitless improvement" (optimism), change, generosity. He has passages
that are roughly parallel to those of Schlesinger on the special place of
women in American society, "materialism" ("wasteful living"), recreation ("pleasure"), wealth ("the acquisitive spirit"). He introduces the
high values upon education and "moralism" which are not so explicit
in Schlesinger and comments upon the unusual mixture of lawlessness
and respect for law which Schlesinger touches upon in a different con-

text. Kluckhohn and Kluckhohn (1947) list the following orientations
and sub-orientations:

1. "Effort and optimism"
   a. "Moral purpose"
   b. "Rationalism"
2. "Romantic individualism"
   a. Cult of the average man
   b. Tendency to personalize
3. Change a value in itself
4. "Pleasure principle"
5. "Externalism"
6. "Simple answers"
7. Humor
8. Generosity

The four publications summarized above vary greatly in length, in
the audiences to which they were addressed, and in degree of systematization. Reduction to catchwords does not do justice to the qualifications
which are presented (e.g., both Perry and Kluckhohn and Kluckhohn
make it clear that American "individualism" is of a very special type)
or to the linkages which are postulated. But the lack of overt contradiction and the congruence of what is explicitly said is striking. Making
all necessary bows to *Wissensoziologie* and some reservations as to the
possibility that many restatements and refinements derive ultimately
from a few original interpretations, we must conclude that, in the main,
the agreements of these authors and of many others are based upon
stubborn and irreducible facts of repeated observations that have amazing continuity through time.

The attention, both of scholars and of the general public, has been
preponderantly focused upon the diversities in the American scene.
Schlesinger (1949, pp. 2–3) notes that "the detached observer from
Europe has always been less impressed by these regional deviations than
by the evidences of fundamental kinship" and that "the preoccupation
of American historians with local and sectional diversities has tended to
obscure this underlying reality." He quotes Bryce:

Scotchmen and Irishmen are more unlike Englishmen, the native of Nor-
mandy more unlike the native of Provence, the Pomeranian more unlike
the Wurtemberger, the Piedmonteses more unlike the Neapolitan, the Basque
more unlike the Andalusian, than the American from any part of the country
is to the American from any other part. . . . It is rather more difficult to

take an assemblage of attributes in any of these European countries and call
it the national type than it is to do the like in the United States.

Perry (1949, pp. 4–5) very properly says:

It might be supposed that the continental vastness of America, and its unparalleled variety of climate, natural resources, race and creed, would make
such an enquiry both impossible and unprofitable. But the fact is that identity is more easily traced when it dwells amidst variety. It is because there is
something common to life in New England and California, Montana and
Florida, in the arid deserts of Arizona and the lush Mississippi and Ohio
lowlands, in great cities and small towns, that it is possible to find a meaning for Americanism. It is because this thing which is common within our
boundaries stops so abruptly at the Mexican border, and so unmistakably
though less abruptly at the Canadian border, and begins when one disem-
barks either at New York or at San Francisco, that it can be detected and
set apart from the rest of human life, however similar this life outside may
be. . . . The melting pot has not merely melted; it has cooked a broth with
an unmistakable flavor of its own.

Of course it remains true that it is very easy to be wrong about America. As Perry says, there is a "paradoxical balance of opposites" and "it
is impossible to make any statement to which exception may not be
taken." Yet I finished my study of what others have written upon American values surer than ever that ". . . America has not hidden its face;
its character is not mysterious, but palpable—there are those who would
say, flagrant." (Perry) This "character" may legitimately be attributed
to the whole of the United States, remembering always that there are
group and individual variations in intensity of acceptance or rejection.
Though there were shadings through time, the central and distinctive
aspects of the American value system were remarkably stable from the
eighteenth century until the thirties [7] and, in spite of some changes that
have occurred and are in process, the characteristic American values remain highly influential in the life of the United States.

Some of the vast literature (e.g., Lynd, 1946; Sirjamaki, 1947) deals
extensively with the "contradictions" in the American value system.
Since it is unpublished but based upon considerable research, I shall
quote Naegele (1949) at length:

Values, as constituent elements of a system, are related in several ways: they
may enforce one another, limit each other, be segregated from one another,
contrast with one another, contradict each other. In general these various
relations have not been elaborated for America's system of values, yet there
has been a marked tendency to "discover" in America a series of paradoxes

and conflicts . . . descriptions of a value system of as complex a society as that of the United States are bound to be rich in paradoxes since the general propositions in terms of which such descriptions must be made always have a logical extension that exceeds the facts. One must, in other words, proceed by way of assertion and qualification. This process of apparent "undoing," or better of continuous assertion of opposites is useful and legitimate only as long as one specifies clearly the locus, level of abstraction and temporal extension of one's analysis. Otherwise paradox breeds confusion. Paradox, however, can yield profundity. It can also substitute for clear thinking and merely flirt with profundity. There is therefore always a danger that paradoxical statements about America are merely clever and not really valid.

The following represent the range of paradoxical characterisations relative to American values as found in the literature examined for this report:

1) *Achievement vs. passivity.* Bryce, Myrdal and others have commented how Americans combine a belief in individual achievement with a general mass passivity, a certain fatalism and a belief in luck. In actual fact these characterisations do not conflict, since they are exhibited in segregated areas of conduct (business vs. politics). One is probably dealing here with contrasting manifestations of America's individualism.

2) *Liberty vs. conformity.* The publicly acknowledged ideal of freedom is silently and effectively limited by the anonymous and ubiquitous public pressures for conformity to present standards. One's own liberty, by having to be made consonant with the liberty of another, is frequently limited to the absence of ties. From the point of view of the observer there is indeed a conflict here which Americans, paradoxically enough, may not define as such.

3) *Equality of opportunity vs. "uneven breaks" and "pull."* The ideal of equality of opportunity is never sufficiently spelled out to show what precisely this would mean for two different people at the same time. Daily details, however, document again and again the reality of "pull" and the reality of unequal handicaps and the advantages which are created by man and not by the nature of things.

4) *Equality of status vs. caste and class.* There is disagreement over the meaning of the term "equality." Does it refer to opportunity only or to all rights and social conditions? For many observers the belief in "equality" and the existence of social distinctions contradict one another on the level of value and on the level of behavioural pattern. It is worthwhile to add that one observer interpreted the meaning of "equality" to imply a condemnation of "tipping" (and called it an aristocratic hangover) and yet found that in "the minds of American city dwellers . . . tipping is *not* generally looked upon as an undemocratic practice." Myrdal sees America in a dilemma valuing both equality and the advantages of specific inequalities, yet judging its conduct and producing its rationalizations in accordance with the American Creed. Hollingshead sees the paradox weighted in favour of the conflict of class and inequality.

5) *Competitive success vs. brotherly love.* Conflicting standards of means have been reconciled and segregated in many ways. The other contrast, between America's dislike to be the aggressor and the sanction of individ-

ual aggressive initiative, also raises the general problem of the structuring of legitimate and illegitimate patterns of aggression in American society.

6) *Spending vs. saving.* It remains to be shown for whom this is a conflict and whether we are dealing here with values designed for different occasions or with values encouraged as general goals.

7) *Love and fear of bigness vs. the emphasis on the Little Man.* This seems a matter of psychological ambivalence rather than of valuational conflict. High goals in accomplishment are in America combined with a demand for a human comparability dissociated from the extreme differences of wealth.

8) *Simplicity and sincerity vs. extravagance and "show."* "Plain living" as well as superlative experience of all kinds are valued in America. One wants to reach the top and is praised for not leaving the ground of virtue and common sense. Truth is a value and honesty the best policy, but to "use a bit of psychology" (and double-talk) is a sign of (coveted) "maturity."

9) *Determinism vs. responsibility.* It is right to distribute blame and to judge events or people as "good" or "bad." It is right, too, to look for the cause of things and to go beyond will or choice as an explanation for conduct.

10) *Incompatible demands.* Hughes has shown the dilemmas of a lady engineer and of a negro doctor where "biological" limitations militate against professional requirements. Komarovsky has documented the conflict between the patterns of being glamorous, a good companion, mother and housewife. Whyte has described the delicate balance of the values of law and illegality which policemen must often maintain.

11) *Inappropriate opinions.* For some observers it is incongruous that the poor of America are often conservative and share their outlook with the rich. The perception of such incongruities derives from the concept of "objective interest" and often assumes that the observer, not the actor, possesses the "true" definition of the situation.

12) *The stimulation of needs vs. the possibility of satisfaction.* This paradox raises the problem: where does such a contrast lead? To resentment? To displaced envy? To in-turned feelings of inferiority?

13) *Novelty vs. constancy.* It is right to value the new things and to value constancy rather than unreliable moodiness in people. "To be always the same" (and to be "the same to everybody") is a value. Yet novelty, too, is a value. Novelty can, however, proceed in a very narrow range of style and represent yet another constricting norm rather than some unique emancipation in thought or style of life.

14) *Concern for others vs. looking out for oneself.* There is a certain ambivalence in America which challenges one to "play the game for all it is worth and get as much out of it as possible" and to play according to rules of honesty and fairness. Both approaches call for some justification in America where moral purpose is a general need.

15) *Efficiency vs. "the human factor."* The realization that "it is actually more efficient to make allowances for the human factor, for then people

seem to work much better" has helped to produce the instrumental part
of America's interest in "psychology."
16) *Playing safe vs. taking risks.* The values of responsibility and adventure are both emphasized and can on occasion conflict.
One might add to these the more general contrasts between: "theory and
practice," universal vs. particularistic standards, the ethic of responsibility
(where consequences matter) vs. the ethic of intention (where motives
alone matter) and the contrast between Americans' gift at organization and
hatred of bureaucracy.
Clearly such a list contains contrasts and contradictions on several levels. Not
all of them produce incongruous meanings or structural strains. Yet here
probably lie some sources of change in the American system of values.

2. My readings in American history did not except for Potter (1954)
much enlarge my conceptions as to the principal situational conditions
that presumably defined the environmental press of the last generation.
Potter's historical treatment of the influence of economic abundance
upon the shaping of the American character is very penetrating indeed
and demands more systematic attention from behavioral scientists than
it has thus far received. One hardly needs to be reminded of the consequences for Americans of this country's involvement in two world wars,
of the Great Depression, of the emergence of nuclear and thermonuclear
weapons. Nor can I say anything upon the significance of these factors
that has not already been said better.

There is, however, one point upon which a mythological view still prevails in well-informed circles and which is a situational circumstance
directly relevant to changing values. This is the widely held belief that
occupational mobility in the United States has sharply decreased.

In the first place, it was never as high even in the last century as the
myth alleges. In the 1870s among 303 top executives in the largest textile, steel, and railroad companies only 25 per cent were the sons of
farmers and only 8 per cent the sons of workers (Miller, 1952). In the
Warner-Abegglen (1955) study of 8300 executives in the largest firms in
the United States in 1952, 15 per cent turned out to be sons of laborers.
Comparing these figures with those of Taussig and Joslyn for American
executives in 1928 and those of Newcomer (1955) for company presidents and board chairmen in 1925 and 1953, it is evident that the percentage of workers' sons who become executives has actually increased
during the past generation, though the proportion attaining the very
top may have decreased slightly in recent years. Newcomer, however,

notes that while the percentage of presidents and board chairmen coming from poor families has declined, the decline in wealthy origin is even more marked. Direct inheritance and nepotism have likewise fallen off sharply. Since it is relevant to a postulated value change which will be discussed later, I shall mention here another fact which emerges from these studies: the decline of entrepreneurship from roughly 44 per cent in 1900 to 15 per cent in the early 1950s. Newcomer shows that two-fifths of today's executives began as salaried bureaucrats—a doubling since 1900. Only 5 per cent of the Warner-Abegglen group were self-employed owners of their firms.

3. In general, there is also considerable agreement in the interpretative literature as to the directions in which American values have changed or are changing. Many authors (laying varying stress upon economic opportunity, ability to count upon the future in any respect, and conceptions of the "evil-good" balance in human nature) have commented upon the "devaluation of the future" or "increasing pessimism" or "weakening of the value of optimism" (e.g., Mead, 1942; Morris, 1947; Allen, 1952; Sutton et al., 1956). Parrington (1927) suggested thirty years ago that American values had passed from Puritan pessimism through romantic optimism into mechanical scepticism.

Taking not a single value orientation but the whole constellation, when Brogan's (1957) article appeared I immediately compared it with a tentative list I had drawn up only a week earlier on completing the intensive reading I had mapped out for myself. While, once again, there were variations in emphases and in phrasings and each of us had included one or two items not discussed by the other, the goodness of fit was so nearly perfect that my initial impulse was to stop work on this paper at that point. For the most part there is rough consensus as to what is going on, but much less so as to whether the changes are temporary, cyclical, or secular. Still more, those who see approximately the same things interpret them differently in accord with their own personal values. A book like Allen's (1952) and an article like Galantiere's (1950) are cheerful in tone, whereas Morris (1947) is nostalgic and pessimistic and Valentine (1954) is angry and pessimistic. Such works reach broad conclusions on bases that in the nature of the case involve "intangible" factors of the author's appraisal and judgment. These factors also influence certain more technical—but still not systematically empirical—publications which inform us, for instance, about shifts in values relating to sex (Kardiner, 1954; Himmelhoch and Fava, 1955[8]) and women (Mead, 1949; F. Kluckhohn, 1952). All of these writings are useful and exceedingly stimulating. None of them, however, fully lend themselves to testing in terms of standard operations for assessing the evidence and the procedures by which one moves from evidence that is agreed upon as to its validity and pertinence to unarguable conclusions.

4. Here, where I searched for big trees, I found underbrush. Some of it indicates where stalwart trees will eventually be discovered. But present data are very limited in scope. Allport (1950) provides useful information on alterations over a generation but only with respect to the religious values of college students, and his populations are not strictly comparable. When one moves to severely technical research where the evidential procedures are subject to scrutiny in accord with rather generally accepted canons, one sacrifices breadth and generality in favor of some rigor. One goes from the realm of the "wise man" to that of the technician. In the behavioral sciences at present the technician can deal reasonably adequately with only a restricted area and a very limited number of variables. Thus we have, for example, Lee's (1954) intriguing little study on a few small points of changing linguistic usage, Scodel (1957) comparing the emotional themes in the lyrics of popular songs of the twenties and the fifties, Hopson (1952) and Collins (1957) systematically analyzing the values accented in best sellers at pertinent time periods, Schneider and Dornbusch (1957) on changes in "inspirational religious literature," Dornbusch's unpublished results of an attempt to test empirically certain aspects of the Riesman "inner-directed" versus "other-directed" hypothesis. There are also some impressive investigations of other questions (e.g., Stouffer, 1955) which make partial but highly significant contributions to our problem.

Summary on Materials. A vast amount has been published on American values and upon topics immediately relevant to the study of values. A large amount is well-documented history; a large amount consists in interpretations and generalizations which often appear enlightened but which are loose so far as operational analysis and demonstrable factual background are concerned; an amount which is relatively small but absolutely fairly large is based upon somewhat rigorous empirical studies. In general, there is quite satisfying consonance as to what American values

are or have been at given epochs. There is likewise rough congruence
as to the directions in which values have shifted or are shifting. But the
few studies systematically designed to test changes in values over the
past generation give us only tiny and restricted baselines for inference.
We shall have to rely largely on a critical sifting of opinion and of im-
pressionistic observation.

III. SOME RESULTS OF RESEARCH

In this section I want to bring the reader a little closer to representative examples of actual investigation of contemporary American values
and value changes over the past generation and differences between
living generations. By quotations and paraphrase-digests I hope to give
the reader an idea of the range and variety of these studies and also of
their limitations for our purposes. I shall be selective, not including
everything drawn upon or mentioned in Parts II and IV.

Contemporary Values. There are a number of excellent reports from
values in single American communities (e.g., Vogt, 1955), but the task
of analyzing and correlating all of these proved too formidable. I have
likewise not had time to work out adequately the value implications in
Mills' studies of the labor (1948), "white collar" (1951), and "power
elite" (1956) segments of our population, for Mills has organized his
materials primarily in terms of economic, political, and organizational
factors.

I shall draw from selected empirical studies which I consider "firm"
within the limits of their conceptual schemes and the particular populations examined. These studies fall into two categories: "miscellaneous"
and those directly pertinent to our interests. In the latter category there
are two bodies of data of considerable substance on the ideology of
American business and on the values of college students. Actually, we
could be much worse off. For, as has often been said, this is "a business
man's civilization." The college group has the advantage of being a
sample from a population that will presumably give this country a large
share of its future leaders. We may even hope to gain some hints as to
value drifts because of the age difference between business leaders and
students, though allowance must always be made for the alterations that
occur with aging—quite apart from secular variations in values.

First, however, to give perspective, I want to present a deliberately miscellaneous selection from materials that are not easy to relate with confidence to our central questions.

Miscellaneous. This first statement (primarily in psychological terms) is based on a small (69) but very carefully selected sample of adult American men from the Boston area and comes from a report (Roseborough and Phillips, 1953) on but a single instrument used in the Russian Research Center study of Americans. These findings fit beautifully with the results of other instruments administered to the same group and with the conclusions of other investigators working at about the same period in other parts of the country and using different methods:

In viewing others the Americans place emphasis upon the relationship they have with others. They perceive others either in terms of themselves or in terms of the other's performance. They want others to think well of them; they want the affection of others; they want others to be easy to get along with. They admire others who perform well and successfully, or for that matter, who just perform. They admire people who are sociable, sensible, strong and sincere. They are critical of inadequate or no performance by others, of unsociable people, of irresponsibility, of indecision. They are critical of overbearing people and of people with unusual or defective physical appearance. They are critical of themselves, of their own inadequate performance and physical appearance and of their failure to live up to the expectations of others.

This emphasis on social relationships and on performance coincides with the action choices the Americans make in strain situations in which other people are involved. The two major responses are to perform more adequately or to become upset . . . both imply the concentration of attention on the job and on the relationship of the actor to the people involved in it. These are precisely the foci for their judgment of other people. The Americans tend to view the qualities of positions rather than the qualities of the people filling those positions. Other people are therefore conceived representatively rather than uniquely. Yet the self is conceived uniquely. With these two points of view, one can be very hurt if one discovers one is not thought well of; one can be very angry if the duties of a position are not fulfilled and one is let down. But the importance of performing well and the lack of importance of the unique qualities of other people prevent, on the one hand, letting one's "hurt" affect one to the point where all is lost and withdrawal into a suffering aloneness the only solution, and on the other, directing one's anger against the culprit and causing him to suffer for his "personal" sins. Hurt is a possible response but if the Americans want people to think well of them they cannot remain hurt: they must perform better. Anger is also possible but they cannot remain angry for to do so anger must have a particularistic focus. Irresponsibility, indecision, poor performance are qualities of others about which something can be done; they are not qualities which must leave the actor in a helpless state of rage which nothing but punishment can assuage.

Second, let us turn—even though it may be questioned how applicable this is to the college-educated, middle-class group I have taken as my central point of reference—to the Wolfenstein and Leites (1950) content analysis of the plots of all American A films with a contemporary setting released in New York City for the year following September 1, 1945 and all American A melodramas released in New York City from September 1, 1946 to January 1, 1948:

The major plot configuration in American films contrasts with both the British and the French. Winning is terrifically important and always possible though it may be a tough fight. The conflict is not an internal one; it is not our own impulses which endanger us nor our own scruples that stand in our way. The hazards are all external, but they are not rooted in the nature of life itself. They are the hazards of a particular situation with which we find ourselves confronted. The hero is typically in a strange town where there are apt to be dangerous men and women of ambiguous character and where the forces of law and order are not to be relied on. If he sizes up the situation correctly, if he does not go off halfcocked but is still able to beat the other fellow to the punch once he is sure who the enemy is, if he relies on no one but himself, if he demands sufficient evidence of virtue from the girl, he will emerge triumphant. He will defeat the dangerous men, get the right girl, and show the authorities what's what.

When he is a child, he is the comic hero, showing off, blundering, cocky, scared, called on to perform beyond his capacities, and pulling through by surprising spurts of activity and with the help of favorable circumstances. He is completely harmless, free from sexual or aggressive impulses, and the world around him reflects his own innocuous character. Its threats are playful and its reproaches ridiculous. When he is a man he is the melodrama hero and the world changes to reflect his changed potentialities; it becomes dangerous and seriously accusing, and launches him on his fighting career. The majority of the melodramas show him coming through successfully. A minority reveal various perils which lie off the main track; they are cautionary tales. The hero may succumb to his attacker; this is his bad dream. The men around him may be less dangerous than he suspects. Under the delusion that he attacks in self-defense, he may initiate hostilities; then he will lose. In this case he is crazy. Without being deluded to this extent, out of greed and overconfidence, he may try to get away with murder; he commits the crime of which he is usually only suspected and he has to pay for it. The girl may turn out to be worse than he believed. He will have to go off without her; then he is lonely. He may not be able to produce anyone on whom to pin the blame for the crimes of which he is falsely accused; then he is a victim of circumstances. If circumstances fail to collaborate with his need to blame someone else, he may even end by blaming himself. These are the various hazards which the usual melodrama hero safely passes on the way.

The fantasy which provides for defeating dangerous men, winning the right girl, and coming out in the clear, is produced under the auspices of two major mechanisms: projection and denial. Self-accusations are embodied in the blundering police and destructive impulses in the unprovoked attacker. The beloved woman seems to be involved with another man but investigation ends in the gratifying demonstration that she never loved anyone but the hero. The love disappointment to which the French movie hero is repeatedly exposed is here denied.

The external world may be dangerous but manageable, or, at other times, uncontrollable but gratifying. Where things seems to get out of control the results turn out to be wish-fulfilling. The overturning automobile throws the girl into the hero's arms, the rocking boat tosses the heroine's rival into the waves. The world that is uncontrollable but gratifying expresses an omnipotence fantasy while at the same time eliminating guilt. As soon as the internal problem is replaced by an external one, we can see the promise of success. The hero suffering from kleptomania becomes involved in investigating the activities of a gang of thieves; the amnesiac hero pursues his memories only long enough to unearth clues of someone else's crime before he rises impatiently from the psychiatrist's couch to embark on a successful detective job.

The world, which is not effectively policed, does not need to be policed at all. The hero, the self-appointed investigator and agent of justice, is able to set things right independently. The world thus appears as a kind of workable anarchic arrangement where, although hostilities are far from eliminated, life need not be nasty, brutish, and short, at any rate not for anyone we care about. The unofficial supervisors of private morals, the comic onlookers, are just as superfluous as the police. No one has any intention of doing anything naughty; only the mistakenly suspicious onlooker fails to recognize the natural goodness of the clean-cut young people.

American film plots are pervaded by false appearances. In this shadowy but temporarily vivid guise, the content of what is projected and denied tends to reappear. It is in false appearances that the forbidden wishes are realized which the hero and heroine so rarely carry into action. In a false appearance the heroine is promiscuous, the hero is a murderer, the young couple carry on an illicit affair, two men friends share the favors of a woman. This device makes it possible for us to eat our cake and have it, since we can enjoy the suggested wish-fulfillments without empathic guilt; we know that the characters with whom we identify have not done anything. The contention of American films is that we should not feel guilty for mere wishes. The hero and heroine are threatened with penalties for the incriminating appearance but in the end are absolved. The misguided police or the foolish onlooker in comedies conveys a self-accusation from which the hero and heroine struggle to dissociate themselves, a vestige of archaic conscience which is to be dispensed with.

What the plot unfolds is a process of proof. Something is undone rather than done: the false appearance is negated. The hero and heroine do not become committed to any irretrievable act whose consequences they must bear. Nor do they usually undergo any character transformation, ennoblement or degradation, gain or loss of hope, acceptance of a new role or the diminution and regrets of age. They succeed in proving what they were all along. They emerge from the shadow of the false appearance. What has changed is other people's impressions of them. In so far as the hero and heroine may be unsure of who or what they are except as they see themselves mirrored in the eyes of others, they have succeeded in establishing for themselves a desirable identity. In so far as they struggle against a projected archaic conscience that persecutes the wish as if it were the act, they win a victory for a more tolerant and discriminating morality.

From Stouffer's impressive book (1955) a few major points seem most pertinent:

Without exception, each of the 14 types of community leaders tends to be more willing to respect . . . civil rights. . . . Women tend, with small but consistent difference, to be less tolerant than men with respect to nonconformists . . . the West seems to have the largest proportion of relatively tolerant people on the scale of willingness to tolerate nonconformists, and the South the smallest proportion. The East and Middle West are in-between . . . metropolitan areas and other cities tend to have a larger proportion of relativly tolerant people than rural areas. . . . The less educated were less tolerant than the better educated. . . . Very few Americans are worried or even deeply concerned about either issue [the internal Communist threat and loss of civil liberties]. These issues do not even compare with issues like personal or family economic problems, personal or family health, or other family crises. . . . If very few are deeply worried about Communism or civil liberties, there are, nevertheless, many who are interested in the news about such matters.

Business Ideology. Sutton et al. (1956) base their "Values of a Good Society" (chapter 12) upon a scrupulous examination of "public statements of business leaders, the institutional advertisements of large corporations, the literature of such business associations as the United States Chamber of Commerce, the Committee for Economic Development, and the National Association of Manufacturers." The following quotations cover the principal points:

A note of individualism sounds through the business creed like the pitch in a Byzantine choir. . . . Individualism has two main aspects, an injunction of responsibility and an affirmation of freedom. First, it involves individual moral responsibility in the sense that each individual must direct his actions according to moral norms and be prepared to accept the consequences of his actions. . . . Second, it asserts the desirability of autonomous choices by individuals in their own interest.
Materialism complements individualism. As consumption goods, material

riches gratify individual needs. More important, the material emphases on thrift, saving, and capital accumulation are a necessary condition of personal autonomy. Both material advantages and productivity are based on moral qualities. . . . The business creed becomes ambiguous over the ultimate significance it assigns to material abundance; it certainly does not advocate a sybaritic enjoyment of wealth.

Practical realism complements individualism. It stresses the importance of those problems which no adult can avoid, and it demands that each individual meet them with competence. . . . Close attention to the practical side of life demands a kind of relentless activity. . . . The emphasis on sheer activity and effort in the creed has its natural complements in high valuations of rationality, adventure, and progress.

It is because of its stress on fair competition and equal opportunity that the business creed may be called egalitarian or democratic.

The achievements of American capitalism vaunted in the creed are nearly all concerned with the common welfare; they imply an ideal of a democratic distribution of rewards and opportunities.

A favored means of justifying values and working out their relative priority in our society is that of linking them to our religious heritage . . . the place of religion in the business creed is an honored, but ill-defined one. The creed bows to the importance of religion, admits seeking religious guidance, but continues to be a predominantly secular ideology.

This picture is quite close to many statements of American values from the early nineteenth century onward that have been mentioned in Part II. Though there are some obvious continuities, the contrasts with the values of post-World War II college students may be significant *if* one assumes tentatively that the variations are not entirely due to temporary attitudes of youth.

Contemporary college students. Jacob (1957) states that:

The values of American college students are remarkably homogeneous, considering the variety of their social, economic, racial, and religious backgrounds, and the relatively unrestricted opportunities they have had for freedom of thought and personal development.

Jacob holds that the following profile applies to 75 or 80 per cent: [9]

A dominant characteristic of students in the current generation is that they are *gloriously contented* both in regard to their present day-to-day activity and their outlook for the future. Few of them are worried—about their health, their prospective careers, their family relations, the state of national or international society or the likelihood of their enjoying secure and happy lives. They are supremely confident that their destinies lie within their own control rather than in the grip of external circumstances.

The great majority of students appear unabashedly *self-centered*. They aspire for material gratifications for themselves and their families. They intend to look out for themselves first and expect others to do likewise. But this is not the individualistic self-centeredness of the pioneer. American students fully accept the convention of the contemporary business society as the context within which they will realize their personal desires. They cheerfully expect to conform to the economic status quo and to receive ample rewards for dutiful and productive effort. They anticipate no die-hard struggle for survival of the fittest as each seeks to gratify his own desires, but rather an abundance for all as each one teams up with his fellow self-seekers in appointed places on the American assembly-line.

Social harmony with an *easy tolerance of diversity* pervades the student environment. Conformists themselves, the American students see little need to insist that each and every person be and behave just like themselves. They are for the most part (with some allowance for sectional difference) ready to live in a mobile society, without racial, ethnic or income barriers. But they do not intend to crusade for non-discrimination, merely to accept it as it comes, a necessary convention in a homogenized culture.

The traditional *moral virtues are valued* by almost all students. They respect sincerity, honesty, loyalty, as proper standards of conduct for decent people. But they are not inclined to censor those who choose to depart from these canons. Indeed they consider laxity a prevalent phenomenon, even more prevalent than the facts seem to warrant. Nor do they feel personally bound to unbending consistency in observing the code, especially when a lapse is socially sanctioned. For instance, standards are generally low in regard to academic honesty, systematic cheating being a common practice rather than the exception at many major institutions.

Students normally express a *need for religion* as a part of their lives and make time on most weekends for an hour in church. But there is a "ghostly quality" about the beliefs and practices of many of them, to quote a sensitive observer. Their religion does not carry over to guide and govern important decisions in the secular world. Students expect these to be socially determined. God has little to do with the behavior of men in society, if widespread student judgment be accepted. His place is in church and perhaps in the home, not in business or club or community. He is worshipped, dutifully and with propriety, but the campus is not permeated by a live sense of His presence.

American students are likewise *dutifully responsive towards government.* They expect to obey its laws, pay its taxes, serve in its armed forces—without complaint but without enthusiasm. They will discharge the obligations demanded of them though they will not voluntarily contribute to the public welfare. Nor do they particularly desire an influential voice in public policy. Except for the ritual of voting, they are content to abdicate the citizen's role in the political process and to leave to others the effective power of governmental decision. They are politically irresponsible, and often politically illiterate as well.

This disposition is reflected in *strangely contradictory attitudes towards international affairs.* Students predict another major war within a dozen years yet international problems are the least of the concerns to which they expect to give much personal attention during their immediate future. The optimism with which they view their prospects for a good long life belies the seriousness of their gloomy prophecy. They readily propose some form of supranational government as a means of preventing war, but a very large number display only a limited knowledge of and confidence in the United Nations as an instrument of cooperative international action.

Turning to their immediate preoccupation, the pursuit of an education, students by and large *set great stock by college* in general and their own college in particular. The intensity of their devotion varies quite a bit with the institution and sometimes with the nature of the students' educational goals. And the real point of the devotion is not the same for all. Only a minority seem to value their college education primarily in terms of its intellectual contribution, or its nurturing of personal character and the capacity for responsible human relationships. Vocational preparation, and skill and experience in social "adjustment" head the rewards which students crave from their higher education.

Against the background of earlier generations, these values of today's students look different. The undergirding of the Puritan heritage on which the major value assumptions of American society have rested is inconspicuous, if it is present at all. Perhaps these students are the forerunners of a major cultural and ethical revolution, the unconscious ushers of an essentially secular (though nominally religious), self-oriented (though group-conforming) society.

The values of the college graduate do differ in some respects from the rest of the society. He is more concerned with status, achievement and prestige. Proportionately more college graduates distrust "welfare economics" and "strong" government than in the country at large. Paradoxically they tend to be somewhat more tolerant and less repressive of "radical" ideas and unconventional people, also less prejudiced towards minority groups and alien cultures. They share few of the cold-war suspicions of the subversiveness of college faculties, nor do they support the popular stereotype of the colleges' godlessness. Religiously, they may be less superstitious or other-worldly than their fellow countrymen. The college man or woman thus tends to be more self-important—more conservative—more tolerant—and less fearful of evil forces in this world and outside than those who have not been "higher-educated."

Morris (1956), comparing American students with samples from Canada, India, China, Japan, and Norway, finds "orientation to self" is somewhat stronger than in any other national group and "orientation to society" somewhat weaker. Americans stand out for their emphasis upon personal possessions. The factor analysis scores give the impression that the American students are activistic and self-indulgent, less subject to social restraint and less open to receptivity than students from the other nations. On the other hand, the Americans in their choices of "paths of life" emphasized flexibility and many-sidedness (with an explicit place for contemplation and enjoyment as well as for action) far more than any other group.

Gillespie and Allport (1955) say:

The American pattern, in spite of a prevailing individuality among documents, includes a predominant value which we may call "search for the right, full life." It reflects, however, relatively little interest in the life of the group or nation, and little awareness of the political and social context of the American student's existence. A strong flavor of privatism marks the sample.

In studying "paths of life" Charles Morris discovered that Americans, more frequently than Indians, Chinese, and Japanese, subscribed to a way of life that he calls "dynamic integration of diversity," a finding strongly supported by our study. David Riesman offers a similar picture. His "outer-directed" modern American is a person who seeks adjustment to his peers, security, the pleasant variety of suburban living with family and business interests, hobbies, travel, and sociability. The "inner-directed" American is, he holds, outmoded. Such "gyroscope" attributes as risk-taking and ambition are less prominent than formerly. While we have no evidence on earlier American character, our picture of present value-orientations is not inconsistent with Riesman's description.

By contrast, the qualities often ascribed to Americans—competitiveness, desire for success, and personal ambition—are mentioned rather more often in autobiographies by students in countries of newer nationalism, where aspirations for achievement are high, viz., Mexico, Egypt, and among the Bantu. We are faced here with the question whether the American character, as represented in youth born during the Great Depression, grown up during a world war, and living since the war in a nation where prosperity and fear are both widespread, is not in fact markedly altered from what it was in earlier times.

The American pattern of values seems to contrast also with the European pattern represented by students in France, Italy, and Germany who more often mention their desire to "form a character" (former, formare, Bildung), to "become a distinctive personality." . . . Americans, by contrast, seem less concerned about self-consistency and more disposed to welcome diversity even at the expense of firmness and integration.

Another prominent American characteristic is the relatively low interest in social problems. Poverty, delinquency, politics, and race relations are less frequently mentioned in American documents than in those of most other lands.

In keeping with his search for a rich, full life, and with his unconcern for social problems, we find other evidence that the American student, by and large, manages to separate himself from the political and social context of his existence. The term privatism has been used to label this particular state of mind. G. A. Almond describes the trait this way:

The American is primarily concerned with "private" values, as distinguished from social-group, political or religious-moral values. His concern with private, worldly success is his most absorbing aim. In this regard it may be suggested by way of hypothesis that in other cultures there is a greater stress on corporate loyalties and values and a greater personal involvement with political issues or with other-worldly religious values.

Our data tend to prove Almond right in his hypothesis, except that our American students are not conspicuously low in religious interests.

Spindler (1955), working with several hundred Stanford students, finds that the following complex of values characterizes the personality type regarded as most desirable: balance, outward-orientedness, sociability, and conformity for the sake of harmony.

Allport (1950) reports upon the religious values of Harvard, Radcliffe, and Miami University students in 1946–1947:

1) most students feel the need of including a religious sentiment somewhere within their maturing personalities;
2) for the most part they believe in a God, though their view is not usually that of the traditional theistic variety;
3) a bare quarter are in essential matters orthodox and historically faithful to theological dogma;
4) the majority maintain some of the forms of traditional religious practices including prayer;
5) but the majority are clearly dissatisfied with institutional religion as it exists, so much so that 40 per cent of those who feel a religious need yet repudiate the church in which they were reared. If we take the entire student population who have had a religious upbringing, including those who feel no religious need and those who do, we find that 56 per cent reject the church in which they were trained.

Changing values and generational differences. Stouffer's (1955) data showed that "the older generation was less tolerant of non-conformists than the younger generation." He also notes that within each group the less educated were less tolerant than the better educated and remarks that, "Not only are more of the people who are moving from youth to middle age better educated than their elders, but also they are products both of child-rearing practices and of a school system which is more apt to foster tolerance." Stouffer's tentative inference that values are in the direction of tolerance of diversity squares with the evidence presented by Morris (1956) and Jacob (1957).

Allport (1950) compares some of his findings made in 1946–1947 with Syracuse students in 1926 and University of Wisconsin students in 1930. Attitudes of the Syracuse group on the need for religion and on the current state of institutional religion were not very different from those of Allport's samples, though the Wisconsin students exhibited more unfavorable responses to the church. Only 10 per cent of the Syracuse students abstained altogether from church attendance and devotional practices as against nearly a third in 1946–1947. Not more than ten or fifteen per cent of a group of Colorado students expressed the opinion that man has a spiritual as well as a biological and psychological nature (Chambers, 1956).

Hopson (1952), comparing best sellers in the 1907–1916 and 1940–1949 periods on the basis of a content analysis of "leading characters" and their kinship and courtship roles and relationships, discovered two dimensions in which there were no statistically significant differences between the two periods. In both, male leading characters outnumber female leading characters by a ratio of two to one. Female leading characters are more involved in kinship and courtship relationships than are male leading characters. Six shifts were discovered in the second period:

(1) Interest in kinship and extra-marital relationships rises;
(2) Sex is discussed more frequently and openly;
(3) "The world" often takes precedence over romantic love;
(4) Relatives rise in importance versus objects of romantic love;
(5) Many leading characters are old or middle-aged, whereas in the earlier period they were almost entirely young;
(6) Hostility is common between Group B leading characters and their numerous close kin.

Dr. Dornbusch has provided the following summary of the Schneider and Dornbusch (1957) content analysis of inspirational religious literature, 1880–1955:

1) The view of religion as promoting a better world hits its stride about 1940. Correlative findings which reinforce the pattern are recent emphases on religion providing a moral base for action and linkage to fellow man.
2) About 1940 there is a very sharp decline in the number of statements that one of religion's functions is the promotion of optimism. The books do not endorse a pessimistic view of the world, but they stop being as optimistic.
3) There is some tendency for reconciliation to the inevitable to become more important in recent years, again beginning about 1940.
4) Up to 1910 there is no concern with the meaning of existence. The existential problem gets some attention after that date.
5) Before 1940 only a single paragraph related religion to national leadership and victory over our enemies. World War II and the post-war Communist crusade often found religion linked to national aspirations.

6) The pragmatic test for the existence of God is most emphasized during the depression. God is known to exist because belief in him produces positive results. Before and after this period non-humanist conceptions are most prevalent.

7) The evidence is slight, but the theme of thought conquering or influencing matter is found most often during the depression. The Christian Science view hits a peak then.

8) The use of testimonials from scientists for the worth of religion does not begin until the end of the 1920s. The identification of religion and science, religion being science applied to a specific sphere, begins at the same time. A further corollary is the view of religion and science as neutral, dealing with different fields, which appears during the same period.

9) With a couple of exceptions, psychological and psychiatric orientations enter the literature in the 1930s and remain important.

10) Beginning about 1930 there is a sharp increase in religion's role in changing the world, in contrast with the emphasis on only the individual's salvation in the earlier period.

11) The early period finds more emphasis on faith, and faith as more important than reason. The later period has a greater weight on the interdependence of faith and reason, with faith no longer viewed as standing on its own feet and requiring no support from reason.

12) Although subjective religious experience is more important in this literature than either dogma or ritual, there is a clear trend in recent years toward a more favorable evaluation of the latter two elements of religion. The shift seems to have taken place toward the end of the 1930s, and is probably not unrelated to the so-called "religious revival."

13) The view of religion as alleviating suffering and promoting health is more pronounced in more recent years with a shift occurring at about the year 1932. The shift is more pronounced for mental ills than physical ones, but the change is present for both.

14) The view that religion brings wealth was present in the early period and comes to a peak in the depression. Since then it is ignored, with the exception of Peale and Fox. The Calvinist link between riches and moral excellence follows exactly the same pattern, even to the point where Peale and Fox are the lone exceptions.

15) Endorsements of attending church, reading the scriptures, and consulting a spiritual counsellor all increase in recent years, in accordance with finding Number 12. The greatest increase has come in the post-war period.

Collins (1957),[10] comparing the five best sellers of the 1930–1935 period with those of the 1950–1955 period, notes these shifts in the latter period:

1) more present-oriented; a trend from dominantly future-oriented to a more even emphasis on present and future;
2) more "outward conformity but inward seething";
3) romantic love themes replaced by interest in "sex, loneliness, rebellion";

4) more preoccupation with "the individual within the organization" or "the individual as a member of the group"; more stress upon conflict of autonomy versus group benefits;

5) while more of these novels deal explicitly with the subject of religion, attention is given more to "the organizational dilemma" than to religion as an intimate personal experience; stress upon religion as "good" for the individual in that it provides emotional security;

6) value placed upon "being" rises with a concomitant lowering of the value placed upon "doing";

7) more explicit concern with problems of the changing role of women; an "almost universal condemnation" of the present role of women as competitors against men;

8) the values present in novels of the thirties show considerably more variation; in those of the fifties, American values appear to have "jelled" appreciably.

9) a decrease in the importance of the conflict between generations which become mere "family squabbles";

10) a lowering of economic success goals to an upper middle class minimum standard;

11) a continuation of the "man-over-nature" theme as primary, with a shift in the secondary "nature-over-man" theme to group dominance over the individual;

12) essentially unchanged "mixed" concept of human nature as neither completely bad or good, with a tendency toward environmentalist excuse for "bad" behavior.

Kangieser (1957) summarizes her exploratory study:

In their social implications and the treatment of their themes the best sellers of the postwar decade suggest that the ethical problems inherent in the social power derived from the possession of wealth—problems arising from the fact that the value system which is expressed as Money as Power is less acceptable to the modern American than it was in the society of his father's day—are of widespread current concern. One finds an ambiguity in the presentation of the Money as Power value: it constitutes a fictive reality for the characters in these novels, but they deny or reject it.

Their denial or rejection sometimes implies another value: the greater importance of man as a group animal than as an individual. One aspect of the acceptance of this other value is the fear of isolation. A concomitant of this fear is the need to be part of the group—from which is drawn the almost inescapable inference that man alone is powerless, that as an individual he cannot act upon his environment. Moreover, aware of the structure of his society, and feeling powerless to act as an individual, he attaches guilt to his state of separateness. Even the Titan of business, who symbolizes the Money as Power ideal, experiences withdrawals from or rejections of the role of individualism and dedication to the power structure.

Current popular literature appears, then, to emphasize a choice of two courses of action open to the individual. Feeling powerless to act alone, he may delegate his power to one to whom he feels psychologically close; or he may withdraw from the older power structure (as embodied in the figure of the Titan) in favor of the more personal, more specific value system of the group man. The exegesis of these choices in current literature may indicate the emergence of an altered form of the democratic ethic.

Dornbusch and Hickman (1957) have tested Riesman's hypothesis using a periodical (*Ladies Home Journal*) that had a stable (class and otherwise) audience of women from 1889 to 1955. Random samples (examined in random order to avoid the possibility that the criteria of the investigators would change in a manner loaded to favor negative or positive results) of advertisements were studied to determine the extent of use of "other-directed" themes to pressure the readers. I am indebted to Dr. Dornbusch for communicating these tentative [11] results in advance of completion of the study:

1) "Other-directed" advertisements are much more frequent in the second half of the period. The order of magnitude is 2 to 1.
2) The peak of "other-directedness" is reached in the 1920s and 1930s.
3) The difference is not a function of different types of advertisements. Testimonials, quantitative, and "people will like you if . . ." etc. approaches *all* reached their apex in the twenties and thirties.
4) Very recent materials are approximately half-way between those of the nineties and those of the thirties.
5) Variations within periods is slight: nine to eleven per cent in the early period; 23 to 24 per cent at the peak; 14 to 15 per cent in recent years.

The following findings [12] of Foster's (1956) quantitative study of the content of third-grade readers, 1900–1953, are of especial interest:

1) Beginning about 1930, "non-fiction" materials started on a downward trend, until at the present time, in fact since 1948, there has been practically none. Just the reverse was found in regard to "realistic fiction" which made a rise from 23 per cent in 1930 to 62 per cent in 1948.
2) The subject of "how others live" was used very little from 1900 to 1920, but by 1953 occupied 30 per cent of the subjects used.
3) "Social activities" has made a very noticeable increase. The graph shows practically no use of this topic during the first period considered, but by the final period it made up 32 per cent of the reader content.
4) From 1900–1920, the theme of "winning friends" occupied only four per cent of the content of the readers. However, by 1953, 35 per cent of the content was taken up by this theme.
5) Graph III shows that since 1930 "obedience and thoughtfulness," as well as "honesty" have declined as themes.
6) "Learning and cleverness" reached a low point in 1930, while the high point marks the close of the period, 1953.

7) The theme of self-control appeared in from zero to six per cent of the material scored. The highest per cent occurred in the 1930 period.

8) Success now depends upon approval by the group and adjusting to the group standards; thereby winning friends becomes important if one is going to fit into his selected group. This theme comprises a good percentage of the content of present-day readers. . . . Doing as one's group does is usually a sign that one is adapting successfully.

Lee (1955) studied the frequency and context of usage of certain words that seemed to her important (free, freedom, must, have to, got to, have got to, up, out) in ten American plays from the eighteenth and nineteenth centuries and in a great variety of sources in the twentieth century (especially 1942–1952). She began with the conviction that "freedom and spontaneity were decreasing, at any rate as values, in American society, and that the desire for limit was increasing." Her data, however, forced her to more complex conclusions:

I found corroboration for the assumption of this growing spirit of personal inquiry in another linguistic usage. The use of [the] must in recent years has been mainly limited to a reference to logical necessity; that is the speaker uses the must as a way of figuring out the given. In Macbeth, out of thirty occurrences of must, I find no occurrence of the must of logical necessity. Throughout the nineteenth century, I find it both in English and American literature; but in this country, the occurrences of the must of logical necessity increase and soon outnumber the use of the other must; whereas, in my little reading of English literature through the nineteenth century, I find the opposite to be true for England. This development, then, is recent, and mainly American; and it is, I should say, another indication that the American individual does not merely accept the given, but applies himself personally to it; that he tries to figure it out.

I concluded from all this that the up does not refer merely to limit, as I thought at the start of my inquiry. It refers to a personally chosen end, an end to which the individual applies himself with decisiveness and vigour. Speed is a part of its meaning; but as part of it, it is not merely a temporal quality. It is now a quality of the person, of upsurging strength. Perhaps it contains something of the meaning of quickening, which identifies speed and life. Freedom, on the other hand, is not in the picture; it is the limit which provides backbone which evokes the personal involvement of the individual, in terms of motivation and spontaneity. In fact, when this limit is absent the response of quickening does not seem to occur.

I had begun my inquiry into the up with a feeling that I would not like what it led me to. I had considered the limit contained in the meaning of the up as restricting and depriving. I found it, instead, challenging and motivating toward temporary enhancement of the self, calling out an answering upsurge of the self. I found it the expression of the peculiarly American version of spontaneity and vigour.

An exploratory study was next attempted to find out what are the factors underlying the use of the up by a specific individual, or in a specific situation; or, to phrase it according to my conclusions, what situations challenge an individual to a responding mobilization of the self and what kind of person does an individual have to be to recognize and rise to the challenge.

This exploratory study has only suggested lines of investigation so far. For example, analysis of non-directive counseling material indicates a less frequent use of the up in proportion to the use of the verbal out, than is common elsewhere (37 up to 32 out in one series of interviews; 58 up to 20 out in another series; whereas in two plays from 1950, I find 36 up to 8 out and 22 up to 1 out). Does this mean that a permissive situation does not evoke in the individual a response of vigour? A parallel investigation of compositions of children in a progressive school in comparison with those of children in a conservative public junior high school was attempted as a possible control; and here the up was found to be more frequent in the former group of compositions. The progressive school, however, was not non-directive in its approach. It was permissive in the sense that it allowed children to use language as they knew it; whereas the conservative school was opposed to the use of up as not good English, that is, it provided restriction, not challenge. So that I found that when children in a structured situation were allowed to use the verbal up, they did use it. On the other hand, the counseling situation, like the progressive school, also afforded the freedom to use speech according to the speaker's wish; yet the speaker did not choose to use the up frequently. I remained with the question: was it the situation that did not evoke the response of up? or was it the individual who, in self-doubt and conflict, could not respond in terms of up? That it may be the individual is suggested by the following: twice when one of the speakers used the up of spontaneity or creativity, she qualified it with an apologetic or belittling "just something I just built up myself." In opposing the individual to the situation here, I merely want to emphasize shift of focus; I do not mean to separate the one from the other.

In children's books the verbal up is curiously rare or absent, though the language used is a simple vernacular and other post-positions such as the verbal over or through are present. This is the case also with the writing in popular magazines, pulps, popular Sunday supplements. Even the whipped up vernacular of the sports pages which I investigated, rarely, if ever, makes use of the verbal up. Does this mean that the self is not fully mobilized when we address ourselves to children and to those whom we consider our inferiors in education? Is this equivalent to the way we mute ourselves when talking to those who are lesser than ourselves, speaking in modulated and sweetened tones to children, slowly and with less vigour to the old, the lost, the needy? It is not simplicity of speech which calls forth the use of the verbal up, I think. English writers of children's books use it more frequently than American writers—at least among those whose books I analysed.

The conclusions I reached on the basis of my inquiry into the use of the verbal up are supported through my parallel inquiry into the have to. Briefly, the use of the have to also has been increasing, in fact more rapidly than that of the up. In Jonathan Postfree, an American play from 1807, it occurs once; in *Come Back Little Sheba*, 1949, it occurs over sixty times. A detailed study of its use as compared with the use of equivalent ways of relating the individual to his situation, indicates to me that this, like the *up*, is self-oriented, and is, to use an apparent paradox, to some extent spontaneous. The meaning of the *have to* ranges from the voluntary personal assumption of responsibility (I've got to do it, as equivalent to: it's up to me to do it) to the recognition of the personal application of a generic necessity; that is, of the translation of the *must* of environmental necessity, or the *ought to* of moral necessity to the *have to* of the personally chosen necessity, or personally assumed responsibility. The *have to* carries force. I have recorded the expressions: "I *must* . . . but I am not going to"; "I know I *should*, but I won't"; "I *ought* to do my chemistry, but I *don't have to*." The *have to* is the only "compulsive" that leads surely to the act. When the Vassar students, whose after-dinner conversations were recorded over a period of two weeks, said "I've got to" all but once before they left the group, they used the only phrasing of their situation which could express a force strong enough to move them to the sequel: "and I'm going to."

On the basis of the conclusion to which I was led through my study of the verbal *up* reinforced by the study of the *have to*, I would suggest that the question of the freedom of the self is of little or no concern here. If the rare occurrence of the terms *free* and *freedom* indicates small preoccupation with inner freedom, it may mean that freedom is irrelevant, or perhaps assumed and therefore out of mind. Or it may mean both of these. This conclusion would suggest that what is of concern, what is sought and prized is that which moves to the vigorous, the strong act. The participant in American culture then finds this motivation in the defining and stiffening limit. Free time does not motivate him to strong action, neither does the mere freedom to act. The schedule to which he has committed himself, the deadline he has assumed, the appointment he has made, these are the things which move him to act. Having taken the *must* as personal obligation or responsibility, it is up to him to carry it through.

In recent years, we have been impressed by the need for limits, because we believe that unlimited freedom is frightening. But to the American self, I do not know that the reaction to the unlimited "I can" is necessarily one of fright. Rather, the unlimited freedom to may mean a condition of inertia, and, I think, one lacking in value. The linguistic clues discussed here, suggest the meaningful situation is the precise, delimited, defined situation; and it is this which calls forth the upsurge of spontaneity and strength. (Pages 12 to 14.)

Scodel (1957) examines one hundred popular songs of 1925–1931 and contrasts them with the same number for 1949–1955. The differences are significant at (and beyond) the .001 criterion:

1) Contemporary songs are almost completely devoid of the themes of "domesticated sexuality" and "Latin and Oriental temptresses";
2) Marriage, if mentioned at all in the later period, is "deglamorized" by being made folksy;

3) Contemporary songs are much less likely to romanticize the love object, and there is much more preoccupation with the themes of loneliness, unanswered appeals, and psychological trauma should a partner be found.

Scodel connects this "more realistic, less repressed perspective," the demand that "love be viewed with more hesitancy and fearfulness since the possibility of frustration is perceived more clearly" with "the recent ascendancy of Neo-Freudian psychology." He also points out that the central themes discovered by Wolfenstein and Leites (1950) in 1945 Class A movies closely resemble those of the 1925–1931 songs and suggests that "movies may evidence a much longer cultural lag" or that "consumers of 1945 movies might well represent consumers of 1925–1931 songs."

Riesman (1956), on the basis of examination of 25-year reports from classes of Ivy League colleges and study of 183 *Time*-commissioned interviews from 1955 graduating seniors from nine colleges and universities, reached the following views on trends:

1) Hardly any of the class of 1955 would ever want to live in New York in order to make a million, or in any other big city. "No life in the ulcer belt for me," as one of them says, explaining why.
2) Going over our class reports, . . . I have detected a tendency to emphasize increasingly the non-vocation aspects . . . the family and hobbies and, markedly . . . the fabulous array of philanthropic and civic activities. . . . Many . . . have . . . moved to the suburbs for the benefit of the children, or even become exurbanites for the sake of a better family life.
3) Although they [the 1955 group] enter a far more prosperous and secure world in economic terms, they appear in more of a hurry—not from a driving ambition which, as we shall see, not many have, but because they have already made up their minds as to exactly who they are and exactly where they want to go on the superhighway of their chosen corporation or profession.
4) And he [a Princeton senior] points out that he doesn't have the brass his father had to be a lone wolf—a comparison a number of them make, in almost every case with detached admiration for the old man's toughness, but with hardly any despondency for not living up to him as a model.
5) These are the exceptions, however, the immoderates who want neither the fringe benefit nor the fringe suburb. Their idiosyncrasy is evident in the fact that they say more about their careers and less about their prospective wives and families than most. Rather than looking to a large corporation to advance them if they deserve it, they want to find a situation to which they make a difference—a situation small enough for them to make an impact on it. They want a ladder, not an escalator.
Most of them, however, as I've indicated, think of themselves as too mature —and perhaps of the economy as too mature as well—to be that interested

in self-advancement. The career they want is to find the good life, for which their corporation or profession serves as the good provider. These men already know they won't be president—they wouldn't want the job with its unpredictable demands, its presumptive big city locale, its disruption of family and recreational life. This is all the more striking since it is my impression that the interviewers tried to get "representative men," who were often big men on campus (a strategy which seems to have totally failed at Harvard, where the respondents—some of them prospective doctors—include neither the intellectual nor the social elite who would, I suspect, have avoided or kidded the whole "deal").

This relative subordination of career ambition goes together with the fact that for most of the respondents the girl they are to marry is already picked out in fact or fancy, and the style of life the family will lead is foreshadowed with equal clarity. Some sound rather psychological about it (like a Harvard man, already engaged, who declares: "Well, it's supposed to be psychologically bad for the middle child if you have three, so I suppose we'll have four"). Others are as uncomplex as the Michigan engineering student who says that he and his girl have "talked some about a family, and we're agreed that we'd like a pretty fair-sized one—maybe four or five kids. We're both fairly easygoing and a lot of noise wouldn't bother us."

6) To members of an older generation, this may sound like a young man on the make who wants contacts. But that is only a small part of it: the civic-minded life, the gregarious life, is at once felt as an obligation, seen as professionally useful, and anticipated as a pleasure and an end in itself. The wife is an indispensable auxiliary to this life which, even if it is a very outgoing, two-car life, is still centered in the backyard bosom of the family. This is an element in the resentment which appears again and again in the interviews toward the (almost purely hypothetical) career girl. One Harvard man says about the sort of girl he wants to marry:

She shouldn't be submissive, she can be independent on little things, but the big decisions will have to go my way . . . the marriage must be the most important thing that ever happened to her.

Another says what many feel:

My wife can work if she wants when we are first married, but she shouldn't work when we have children.

At the same time, they don't want a stay-at-home wife; they want a presentable date who, as we have seen, will be active in community affairs; she must be college-bred, she must understand her husband and know how to bring up children. There are contradictions lurking here; as one Harvard man says:

I want someone who would stay home and take care of the children, but on the other hand I want someone who can stimulate me intellectually, and I don't know if those things are compatible . . . if a woman goes to Radcliffe and takes up economics, she isn't learning how to bring up children.

In order to see what kind of mother their girl will make, a number of men say they will take a hard look at the girl's mother, to see what kind of a model mother she is—a rather awesome theme for those of us in the Class of 1931 who have eligible daughters and hopelessly impractical wives.

7) It is this vision of life on a plateau that perhaps most distinguishes the Class of 1955 from that of 1931. We who were graduated twenty-five years ago found our way by trial and error—and I emphasize the error as well as the trial—to many of the values and styles of life the Class of 1955 already begins with. We were, as I've suggested, more immature in many ways, and by the same token we expected to change and to be changed by our work and our experiences. The Class of 1955, judging by these interviews and for-getting their unreliability, would appear to expect to go on successfully adapting as they've already done, but not to change in any fundamental way, save that the family will take the place of the fraternity.

8) The girls in question, however, may find it harder to stay on the plateau —or if they're *that* good, they may not want these boys; after all, Grace Kelly has had a career and has married a prince. . . . In 1954, *Mademoiselle* magazine sent out questionnaires to women undergraduates at a number of colleges, and also to a few graduates. I had an opportunity to examine these, and the picture they present is not different from that presented by the men: they, too, want the well-rounded life, suburban and family-centered (but, like the men in the *Time* interviews, near enough to a big city for cultural advantages—it isn't clear who will populate the city), and fear ambition in themselves and their prospective spouses. Russell Lynes, in "What Has Suc-ceeded Success?" (*Mademoiselle*, September 1954), discusses these inter-views perceptively, pointing out how demanding and strenuous the goals of well-roundedness and contentment can become, and what effort it takes to be "cool."

9) I have the impression that hardly anybody seeks swank or social distinc-tion, and this seems not merely an artifact of the interview but an expression of the prevailing democratic ethos. A number who themselves went to prep school say they will send their children to public school. The suburb they aim for is regarded as the scenic backdrop for the happy family, not the locale of mobility as in *Point of No Return*. As I have implied, they have very few dreams, these young men; they dream of neither conventional prestige and social éclat nor, in general, of unconventional accomplishments. A fortune which can be passed on to children would be one sort of accomplishment, but very few of these seniors look for even modest capital accumulation; the capital is, as it were, society's, built into the schools and suburban develop-ments and Blue Cross plans and corporate reserves. A floor is under these men, a low ceiling over them (analogous to the ranch-type houses in which they will live, in contrast to the high-ceilinged Victorian home), and these provide a narrow and "constant level of happiness."

Dr. Dornbusch has also provided the following summary of his current researches upon changing values with respect to the position of women in American society (Dornbusch and Roberts, 1957):

As in my previous report on the inspirational religious literature, I will note only those phenomena which exhibit clear evidence of change. For the study of the role of women, we tested the significance of differences between the period 1890–1919 and the period 1920–1955. Using this split in time, all

differences reported here are significant beyond the .05 level when the chi
square test and the Fisher exact probability test are applied to the data.
1. In their relations with men, women during the early period are enjoined
to be feminine, while the later issues stress companionship. There is no
attempt to deny the differences between the sexes, but the later material is
not disposed to emphasize the delicacy of women.
2. Before 1920 women are viewed as morally superior to men. This theme
completely disappears.
3. Although love is emphasized throughout the period under analysis, the
early issues state that love is the only prerequisite for marriage. The more
recent issues note that love alone is not enough, bringing in more practical
considerations.
4. Working outside the home becomes somewhat more acceptable for
women without children. This middle-class journal does not exhibit a shift
toward more acceptance of working mothers.
5. There is a sharp decline in mention of charitable and religious activities
outside the home, with a corresponding increase of interest in political and
community affairs.
6. Housework is no longer viewed as an endless task, with the later issues
discussing saving time on housework in order to engage in other activities.
"A woman's work is never done" is not found in later issues.
7. There is a sharp increase in mention of father's supplementary role in
aiding the wife to raise the children.
8. Physical attractiveness is more stressed in the later period. A new sentiment is that "Wives must remain attractive in order to keep their husbands."
9. Divorce, although discouraged, is in recent years countenanced when unavoidable.
10. In the later period the view of women as subordinate to men disappears.

IV. RECONSTRUCTION

Let me start somewhat negatively by trying to expose some of the
fallacies or misunderstandings inherent in the three conclusions about
value shifts which, I suspect, appear most frequently in popular writings
and in private conversations. These we can label: the lawlessness of the
young, conformity, and return to religion.

There is always some conflict between generations, and this conflict
is exacerbated in rapidly changing societies of which the United States
has always been an extreme example. Each elder generation is disturbed
because the younger violates law and custom. One has only to dip into
a source like Calhoun (1945) to realize that outraged laments upon juvenile delinquency and the disintegration of the family have a very long
and repetitive history upon this continent. Moreover, there has always

been a distinctively "lawless" strain in American culture. A characteristically American rationale is found in *Huckleberry Finn:*

Well, then, says I, what's the use you learning to do right when it's troublesome to do right and ain't no trouble to do wrong, and the wages is just the same? I was stuck. I couldn't answer that. So I reckoned I wouldn't bother no more about it, but after this always do whichever come handiest at the time.

But I have encountered no hard evidence that this strain is on the increase in very recent times. If anything, one wonders if it is not less manifest than one might anticipate in this country in a postwar period of confusion and uncertainty.

Conformity must not be allowed to mask too many questions. Is it really, as alleged, a conformity of anxiety or of automatism? Or is it a fairly deliberate conformity of choice which follows upon the weakening of the Puritan ethic with its demands for exhibitionistic achievement, unbridled "individualism," and competition? An outward conformity of behavior or an inward conformity of thought and feeling? We must remember, as Mead (1956) points out, that much of the indignation over the conformity of the young comes from the intellectuals who in the twenties and thirties made nonconformity a rampant virtue and whose ego stature is thus diminished if their children reject this value.

Bird (1957) says:

Americans expect the young to overthrow—in the name of progress—at least part of the values of their parents. But those born in 1930 have found their parents largely without oppressive values. How are you going to rebel against a generation which made a cult of rebellion; which, in the confession of its spokesman Malcolm Cowley, felt that "our lives were directed by Puritan standards that were not our own, that society in general was terribly secure, unexciting, middle-class"?

Also, while conformity is probably a heightened value for the younger generation, the data indicate that this goes along with greater tolerance for diversity in others (Stouffer, 1955) and indeed a prizing of diversity as a value in itself (Gillespie and Allport, 1955; Morris, 1956).

Finally, we must avoid putting too much weight, consciously or unconsciously, upon a single distressing phenomenon (McCarthyism) which had complex and highly specific historical causes. Parsons (1955) remarks:

The strains of the international situation have impinged on a society undergoing important internal changes which have themselves been sources of strain, with the effect of superimposing one kind of strain on another. . . . It is a generalization well established in social science that neither individuals nor societies can undergo major structural changes without the likelihood of producing a considerable amount of "irrational" behavior. There will tend to be conspicuous distortions of the patterns of value and of the normal beliefs about the facts of situations.

The religious best sellers and the figures on church membership [13] and attendance do indicate some shift in the values placed upon religion. This trend [14] seems to be usual after a major war. However, there is more than this to the phenomenon. I doubt—except for the fundamentalist and emotional sects—that it means a return to religion in the meaning of daily search for divine guidance in one's daily life or of taking the pleasing of a personal God as one's primary goal. Rather, I think the return to religion a manifestation of two more fundamental value shifts: increasing stress upon affiliation with stable groups, and increasing recognition of the need for explicit and shared values.

The changes in American values during the past generation are in part a consequence of processes steadily affecting all "advanced" industrial societies (cf. Inkeles and Rossi, 1956), in part the result of more temporary political and economic currents playing upon the whole world in the mid-twentieth century. But in both cases the specific forms are recognizably American, and it is these that I shall treat rather than attempting to relate them to the world-wide context.

Let us summarize first three recent and independent overviews of value changes in the United States by an anthropologist, an historian, and a writer. Spindler (1955) is convinced that a radical shift in values has begun. He charts the contrasts:

TRADITIONAL VALUES	EMERGENT VALUES
Puritan morality (Respectability, thrift, self-denial, sexual constraint; a puritan is someone who can have anything he wants, as long as he doesn't enjoy it!)	*Sociability* (As described above. One should like people and get along well with them. Suspicion of solitary activities is characteristic.)
Work-Success ethic (Successful people worked hard to become so. Anyone can get to the top if he tries hard enough. So people who are not successful are lazy, or stupid, or both. People must work desperately	*Relativistic moral attitude* (Absolutes in right and wrong are questionable. Morality is what the group thinks is right. Shame rather than guilt-oriented personality is appropriate.)

and continuously to convince themselves of their worth.)

Individualism (The individual is
sacred, and always more important
than the group. In one extreme
form, the value sanctions egocentric-
ity, expediency, and disregard for
other people's rights. In its healthier
form the value sanctions independence and originality.)

Consideration for others (Everything one does should be done with
regard for others and their feelings.
The individual has a built-in radar
that alerts him to others' feelings.
Tolerance for the other person's
point of view and behaviors is regarded as desirable, so long as the
harmony of the group is not dis-
rupted.)

Achievement orientation (Success is
a constant goal. There is no resting
on past glories. If one makes $9,000
this year he must make $10,000
next year. Coupled with the work-
success ethic, this value keeps people moving, and tense.)

Future-time orientation (The future,
not the past, or even the present, is
most important. There is a "pot of
gold at the end of the rainbow."
Time is valuable, and cannot be
wasted. Present needs must be denied for satisfactions to be gained in
the future.)

Hedonistic, present-time orientation
(No one can tell what the future
will hold, therefore one should enjoy
the present—but within the limits
of the well-rounded, balanced personality and group.)

Conformity to the group (Implied
in the other emergent values. Everything is relative to the group. Group
harmony is the ultimate goal. Leadership consists of group-machinery
lubrication.)

Brogan (1957) deals largely with situational changes but concludes
that there has been a "reassessment of values," though he feels that the
alterations are mainly extensions of trends visible in 1925. Brogan's essay
is less systematic than Spindler's article, but the following will give an
idea of his most pertinent views:

There has been a revival of religion, but that ambiguous term does not imply
a revival of the sense of sin.
The American woman may not be as powerful as the advertisers tell her she is,
but she is out on the world.
To decide that a couple need children more than a new car, that a child needs

brothers and sisters more than an expensive camp or a "good" school, is a novelty. You can find in people of my generation either wonder and pleasure at the acceptance of the four-child family by their only child, or an irritated bewilderment at such indecently large families. A big family in modern society is seldom a good material investment. Is it not then important that so many young Americans are making this materially unwise decision?

It is linked with other decisions. One is the decision for leisure rather than for ever-expanding income . . . there can be no doubt that the American concept of "success" has widened . . . to climb too hard and too obviously, is not the best way to get on in the gray flannel world.

In a society in which the old unquestioning acceptance of the business "life of action" is no longer prevalent—in which a great many young men turn away from business not as something disgraceful, but as something dull without being adequately rewarding—will American business "tick" just the same?

Compare these excerpts from Bird (1957):

Religion? They go to the Presbyterian Church because they like the minister and the Sunday school is the most popular, even though he himself was born a Unitarian. . . . It seems likely that the generation born 1930 tends to view church-going, like psychiatry, as a means to general "adjustment" rather than as a spiritual end. . . . Religion, in short, now provides still another pattern for conformity.[15] Whether it does more than that remains to be seen.

It would seem significant of the new attitude to money that the once-sacred male prerogative of managing it has now fallen almost exclusively into female hands.

They are less interested in experiment than in building lasting marriages, and they fervently believe that the proper end of love is a child. . . . More young women are marrying. . . . Both men and women are marrying earlier. . . . They are also having babies sooner.

Money, in a capitalistic ethic, must have intrinsic glamour, or it cannot spur effort as it is supposed to do. But to the young it seems to have no symbolic value whatever. It has become merely a bookkeeping device.

Where are these silent, smooth young people going? To their elders, they seem to be building a somewhat savorless society, lacking in individual idiosyncrasy, intellectual vitality, or even political responsibility. . . . How . . . can our capitalist economy sustain its dynamism if so few are willing to take risks? What will happen to our culture if there is a continued decline in the American tradition of protest?

There is a chance that while the young seem tame, uncommitted, they may be invisibly moving in a direction so radical that we cannot as yet conceive it.

Many of the signposts detected by different observers point in the same direction. We have again, to be sure, the possibility that the consonance derives from Zeitgeist or from parrotings—with variations—of a few popular formulations. It is certain that Riesman's writings have been influential. On the other hand, some work (e.g., Morris, 1956) was done (though not published) prior to *The Lonely Crowd*, and it may be questioned whether Riesman's ideas (as opposed to his catchy phrases) were profoundly original: it seems more likely that he brought together and dramatized much that many others had already said in part on the basis of their researches or their more diffuse observations. The one small empirical test of Riesman to date (Dornbusch, 1957) confirms his hypothesis, but suggests that "other-directedness" actually had more salience in the thirties than at present.

This raises two broad questions:

1. The general question of time lag. For example, are the changes in value emphases manifested by the generation born in the late twenties and early thirties really currents pouring over a watershed from that period? Did the younger parents of that epoch—their own explicitly stated values to the contrary notwithstanding—communicate to their children (in the home, in the schools to which they sent them) a series of sets which made them less rampant individualists, less committed to hard work in a single direction and to success and the like?

2. The specific question of time lag between class and mass groups. Hopson (1952) showed that mass media of the 1940–1949 period reflected about the same value shifts which were perceptible in best sellers read by the college-educated classes in the 1907–1946 period. Differentials of this sort may well be the rule.

I can't answer these questions. But a few remarks may clarify what is to follow. First, when I speak of such matters as the decline of the Protestant Ethic I am merely calling attention to certain phenomena without making any dogmatic assumptions as to when and how this trend emerged or even—necessarily—any assumption that, if we knew enough, we could not discern the beginnings of a counter-trend among the young children of the "found" (Riesman, 1956) or "unlost" (Bird, 1957) generation. Second, as stated in the introduction, my eye is upon the middle-class (roughly equivalent to "college-educated") younger generation. There are highly vocal protests (e.g., Lindner, 1953, 1956; Fromm, 1955) against the gospel of adjustment, but those with which I am familiar come almost [16] exclusively from representatives of the older generation, those of European background, and/or from members of radical political groups.[17] I neither assert nor deny that my postulated value shifts apply to the lower classes and the lower middle class, though some studies (e.g., Friedmann, 1956) claim that the picture is quite different among those who have not been so richly rewarded by our society and, among these, especially within the subgroups adhering to fundamentalist or emotionalist religious sects. Yet the Schneider-Dornbusch book (1957) indicates that among those who read inspirational religious literature the weakening of the Puritan Ethic has already occurred.

The most generally agreed upon, the best documented, and the most pervasive value shift is what Whyte (1956) has called "the decline of the Protestant Ethic." This is a central theme in Whyte's book. It is a clear-cut finding of the Schneider-Dornbusch (1957) study of inspirational religious literature. It is noted by essentially all the serious [18] publications on recent value changes and on the values of the younger generation. No one questions that the sexual mores—especially those of women— have altered as have the attitudes toward deviations from the traditional mores. Stouffer (1949) has demonstrated the undercutting of moral values in certain areas. Wolfenstein (1951) brings out another dimension of the change. Comparing the Infant Care Bulletin of the United States government for 1914 and for 1942–1945, she points out the change from an earlier dread of strong and dangerous impulses in the child to a current view of infant impulses as harmless, needing no suppression but only to be safely channeled into a variety of activities. It was an essential premise of the Puritan Ethic that innate human impulses were largely evil and required harsh regulation.[19] Sutton et al. (1956) found the Puritan Ethic central to the business creed. "At the core of the Calvinistic, Puritan tradition as it worked itself out in social life were the linked values of *austerity, individualism,* and devotion to *occupations as callings.*" But in discussing "Changing Values and the Acceptability of the Business Creed" they observe that the values of industriousness, personal integrity, thrift, and self-reliance "have declined in relative importance."

Riesman and Glazer (1948) say:

We suggest the thesis that since the latter part of the 19th century there has been under way a fundamental shift, from the control of America by Protestants to the control of America by Marketers. This shift occurred in connection with well-known economic and social developments. First there is the decline in the relative numbers of people engaged in production and extraction—agriculture, heavy industry, heavy transport—and the increase in the numbers engaged in white-collar work and the service trades: the shift from working with things to working with people, and the growth of the "new middle class." Second, there is the concurrent relative decline of small communities, and the growth of metropolitan centers and their cultural dominance. Third, there is the change . . . in paths to success, and the requirement of more "socialized" behavior both for success and for marital and personal adaptation. Fourth, there is the secular change in family patterns and child-rearing practices which results partly from the foregoing changes and partly follows its own logic, for instance in making use of modern scientific teachings about permissive child-care; these tend to send the child out early into the personality-market of the peer-group culture, while the parents make him feel guilty, not about violation of Protestant standards but about failure to become adequately "socialized." . . . Fifth, the role of the school and the peer-group is assisted and continued by mass media, also following in part their own dynamic of development in serving as tutors in marketing techniques. . . .

Connected with and influenced by this fundamental shift are a number of others. The degree to which these shifts may plausibly be traced to a weakening of the Puritan Ethic varies considerably among them. Perhaps a more logical interpretation would be that all changes, including that in the basic ethical conception, are the products of still deeper processes not yet satisfactorily analyzed or named. At any rate, all of the shifts are interconnected and mutually reinforcing. The decline of the Protestant Ethic is peculiarly palpable and—at very least—a convenient point of central reference.

External (social) versus internal standards. This does not mean greater concern with social welfare, national and international politics, and the like. Brogan (1957) finds Americans more politically conscious in 1956 than he did in 1929, but Stouffer (1955) discovered apathy on civil liberties and the internal threat of communism; Jacob (1957): "Most American students desire to separate themselves from their political and social context. They shun civic responsibility and have little interest in public affairs"; Morris (1956) showed that American students exhibited considerably less commitment to social causes than Indian, Chinese, and other students abroad; Gillespie and Allport (1955) comment on the "privatism" of American students.

Nevertheless, there is a stronger drift toward what some (e.g., Perry, 1949) have called "collective individualism." This *does* mean a sensitivity to the approval of others, a strong need to be liked, a respect for the standards of the group with which one has one's primary identification rather than for the demands of one's own private "conscience." This is Riesman's "other-directed," [20] "radar-oriented" type of character. Riesman's "other-directed" is very similar to Fromm's "personality of the market place," just as his "autonomous" equates to Fromm's "productive" personality. It represents nothing new among American values but rather a heightening and an appreciably different form. De Tocqueville wrote:

I know of no country in which there is so little independence of mind and real freedom of discussion as in America. The will of man is not shattered, but softened, bent, and guided; men are seldom forced by it to act, but they are constantly restrained from acting. Such a power does not destroy, but it prevents existence; it does not tyrannize, but it compresses, enervates, extinguishes, and stupefies a people. . . . The majority no longer says: "You shall think as I do or you shall die"; but it says: "You are free to think differently from me and to retain your life, your property, and all that you possess; but you are henceforth a stranger among your people. You may retain your civil rights, but they will be useless to you, for you will never be chosen by your fellow citizens if you solicit their votes; and they will affect to scorn you if you ask for their esteem.
"You will remain among men, but you will be deprived of the rights of mankind. Your fellow creatures will shun you like an impure being; and even those who believe in your innocence will abandon you, lest they should be shunned in their turn. Go in peace! I have given you your life, but it is an existence worse than death."

It is true that American official standards have always been better described in terms of "public approval" than as either "materialistic" or "idealistic." There is also considerable truth in the saying that "standardization is the primal crime of democracy." Yet it is ridiculous to accept literally the statements of some superficial European observers about "the dreary uniformity of American life" [21] (cf., Drucker, 1952). We must only grant with Perry (1949) that while Americans do not easily accept authority from above, they have ever been "highly vulnerable to the impersonal and unorganized authority of their social environment."

This longstanding disposition has without doubt been enhanced in some respects both by irrational methods of persuasion (advertising— see McLuhan, 1949, for a devastating indictment of advertising and other mass media) and by the very economic and technological rationality of the last decade. The amount of external compulsion has been trifling, the mechanics of conformity have moved from the great corporations into other areas of society: schools, entertainment, politics. Not that the "blame" should in any simple sense be put upon "business." Greenwalt (1957) is at least partly right:

I realize that it is popular to regard the large business unit as a machine in which human tolerances are held within precise limits and some All-Seeing Eye charts the manners, dress, and political view of each candidate for advancement. . . . Conformity is not a special characteristic of business; it is a characteristic of all organizations of whatever nature. I am inclined to think that, man for man, the large business unit provides greater opportunities for individuality and requires less in the way of conformity than other institutions of comparable size—the government service, say, or the academic world, or certainly the military.

Greenwalt uses the word "individuality" rather than "individualism." Whyte and others who are protesting the most loudly are not clear as to the distinction between those two words. "Individuality" may entail —as in the French case—a very great deal of outward conformity, but this is a conscious protective device to guard the areas of life deemed really important—one's leisure, cultivating one's private garden. "Individualism," on the other hand, in its distinctively American form involved public and often aggressive assertion of the qualities the person wanted to exhibit—often at great loss to individuality in the French sense.

Today's kind of "conformity" may actually be a step toward more genuine individuality in the United States. "Conformity" is less of a personal and psychological problem—less tinged with anxiety and guilt. I have a hunch—from reading some of the literature on Puritanism in both its New England and frontier forms—that the only way the American Puritan could lower his guilt level was by participating in a group— especially (but not exclusively) a religious group. To the extent that the Puritan Ethic has declined one would therefore expect that the whole problem of conformity was less compulsive and emotional in both its affirmative and negative directions. If one accepts outwardly the conventions of one's group, one may have greater psychic energy to develop and fulfill one's private potentialities as a unique person. I have encountered no substantial evidence that this "conformity" is thoroughgoingly "inward." Nor am I convinced that even in the "McCarthy period" more than a tiny minority of Americans spelled loyalty: c-o-n-f-o-r-m-i-t-y.

There is some visible oiliness and slickness on the surface of American life as notably represented by Hollywood and the Luce publications.

McLuhan (1954) has a point when he suggests that the machine motif is a dominant one for the Luce publications, which bury the identity of the writers in anonymity. And we do have the largely anonymous creatures of "the gimmick society" (Fiddle, 1952):

. . . a disproportionate number of specialists who exploit peripheral devices for solving problems: huckstering, chicanery, and misdirection of inventions. Each is a device which elaborates a peripheral structural element at the expense of some other shared central element in the interest of a special occasion or special group. The gimmick specialist gets a dilemma and solves it by unsuspected indirection. Such a division of labor encourages some citizens to thrive by forcing open or widening the holes in the social and cultural fabric. Gimmick specialists prosper when the flaws in the social structure expand in number and size, and as the possibilities for spontaneous consensus on critical issues diminish. Indeed, even concealing the absence of shared values becomes the function of a gimmick: elections are run along sidetracked issues. Instead of party contests on broad issues, the citizen is bemused by the gulleys and sidings of political problems. Semantic confusions and cunning ambiguities—these are some of the familiar devices contrived to flour his vision. What is distinctively American is the stress, pervasiveness, and profitability of the gimmick pattern and its congeniality with other cultural patterns such as the emphasis on technological development. Tugging the rules of the game at their edges or pushing in the fabric's flaws characterize both the gimmick man and the demagogue.

But are these the main currents? I think not. Surely the last two presidential elections with their split votes indicate that Americans are not altogether at the mercy of either "gimmick specialists" or of a single-minded conformity. And on the contemporary American scene "conformity" itself takes two forms which—in their prevalence—are somewhat new. The second of these I shall comment upon under the rubric of "Value Placed upon Heterogeneity." The first is that "conformity" arises more from active choice that departs from a strengthened value put upon harmony within primary social groups, less from fear of social ostracism. This "social-harmony" value is in part a response to the much talked of "alienation" of contemporary men,[22] in part a response to chaos, confusion, and dispute in the world in general and to the abyss threatened by a potentially immediate future. They learn from the writings of many intellectuals that the best service that historical perspective can provide is that of preparing us for the worst (Muller, 1954, p. 362). If disorder is visible all about and impends still more, order in those circumscribed areas becomes immensely precious. Tillich (1953) says:

"There are periods in history in which the element of freedom predominates, and there are periods in which fate and necessity prevail. The latter is true of our day." The opening paragraph in *The Power Elite* (Mills, 1956) states: "Great changes . . . from every side . . . now press upon men and women of the mass society, who . . . feel they are without purpose in an epoch in which they are without power." Whether these generalizations be factually correct or not, they are prevalent and influential upon thought and behavior. What use to strive endlessly for achievement, to compete blatantly with one's neighbors and with one's rivals in the occupational sphere? Is it not, rather, more sensible to keep the surface of things harmonious, to enjoy what one can while one can? As Whyte (1956) says, "inconspicuous consumption" is now a higher value than "conspicuous consumption." ". . . the old urge to keep up with the Joneses has been replaced by the need to keep *down* with the Joneses." (Bird, 1957.) At any rate, I am convinced that much of the contemporary "conformity" springs from deliberate and somewhat reflective choice based both upon realization of the uncertainty of things and upon recognition of the implacable necessities of gigantic organizations. Possibly "conformity" may also be a reaction to exhaustion brought about by the speed and number of changes.[23]

Excursus on "machines." I have hinted earlier that I was dubious of the "automaton" or "robot-like" motives often imputed to the "conformity" of contemporary Americans. I remain skeptical of some of the too facile analogies that have been drawn. Yet there is something to Horkheimer's remarks:

The more intense an individual's concern with power over things, the more will things dominate him, the more will he lack any genuine individual traits, and the more will his mind be transformed into an automaton of formalized reason.

The allegations that Americans have unconsciously taken machines as their models have some resonance in facts. Constant metaphors reflect something of the underlying, the formative images of a culture. We are all familiar with slogans of the form, "You push the button; we do the rest." McLuhan (1949) has savagely documented the range and extent of these, and Kangieser (1957) calls attention to the same finding in a recent investigation by Whatmough. Sutton *et al.* (1956) give numerous and vivid examples of machines as models for the social organization of

American business. Even Frederick Lewis Allen uses the machine as a simile for American society: a machine that must be made to run while it is being patched and tinkered with. Looking to the future, this passage in Erikson (1950, pp. 253–254) has always troubled me:

This idea of a self-made ego was in turn reinforced and yet modified by industrialization and by class stratification. Industrialization, for example, brought with it mechanical child training. It was as if this new man-made world of machines, which was to replace the "segments of nature" and the "beasts of prey," offered its mastery only to those who would become like it, as the Sioux "became" buffalo, the Yurok salmon. Thus, a movement in child training began which tended to adjust the human organism from the very start to clock-like punctuality in order to make it a standardized appendix of the industrial world. This movement is by no means at an end in this country or in countries which for the sake of industrial production want to become like us. In the pursuit of the adjustment to and mastery over the machine, American mothers (especially of the middle class) found themselves standardizing and overadjusting children who later were expected to personify that very virile individuality which in the past had been one of the outstanding characteristics of the American. The resulting danger was that of creating, instead of individualism, a mass-produced mask of individuality.

Kouwenhoven (1956) sounds a more hopeful note:

We hear a lot . . . of the notion that our system "dehumanizes" the worker, turning him into a machine and depriving him of the satisfactions of finishing anything, since he performs only some repetitive operation. It is true that the unit of work in mass production is not a product but an operation. But the development of the system, in contrast with Charlie Chaplin's wonderful but wild fantasy of the assembly line, has shown the intermediacy of the stage in which the worker is doomed to frustrating boredom. Merely repetitive work, in the logic of mass production, can and must be done by machine. It is unskilled work which is doomed by it, not the worker. More and more skilled workers are needed to design products, analyze jobs, cut patterns, attend complicated machines, and co-ordinate the processes which comprise the productive system.
The skills required for these jobs are different, of course, from those required to make hand-made boots or to carve stone ornaments but they are not in themselves less interesting or human. Operating a crane in a steel mill, or a turret lathe, is an infinitely more varied and stimulating job than shaping boots day after day by hand. . . .
The apprehensions which many people feel about a civilization absorbed with process—about its mobility and wastefulness as well as about the "dehumanizing" effects of its jobs—derive, I suppose, from old habit and the persistence of values and tastes which were indigenous to a very different social and economic system. . . . To say this is not to deny the past. It is simply to recognize that for a variety of reasons people living in America

have, on the whole, been better able to relish process than those who have lived under the imposing shadow of the arts and institutions which Western man created in his tragic search for permanence and perfection—for a "closed system" . . . the past of those who live in the United States, like their future, is open-ended. It does not, like the past of most other people, extend downward into the soil out of which their immediate community or neighborhood has grown. . . . "America" . . . is not a fixed and immutable ideal toward which citizens of this nation strive. It has not order or proportion, but neither is it chaos except as that is chaotic which no single mind can comprehend or control. And in so far as people have been "American"— as distinguished from being (as most of us, in at least some of our activities, have been) mere carriers of transplanted cultural traditions—the concern with process has been reflected in the work of their heads and hearts and hands.

It is not that the traditional value placed upon "individualism" has completely disappeared. There is talk about it, even among the young adults. American parents continue to worry (among other things) about the possibility that "socialization will go too far and destroy individual impulses" (Farber, 1953, p. 247). But to the question as to why this parental generation has "submitted so tamely to this loss of individuality and independence," Bird (1957) not unreasonably replies:

. . . it has not seemed unnatural to them that their lives should be so regulated. From nursery school to executive training squad to housing project, they have been trained to conformity.

Howe (1954) says:

To what does one conform? To institutions, obviously. To the dead images that rot in one's mind, unavoidably. And almost always, to the small grating necessities of day-to-day survival. In these senses it may be said that we are all conformists to one or another degree. When Sidney Hook writes, "I see no specific virtue in the attitude of conformity or non-conformity," he is right if he means that no human being can, or should, entirely accept or reject the moral and social modes of his time.

But Howe—and most other critics—fail to see the potential dynamisms pointed out by Riesman (1952b):

I am sorry that many have read The Lonely Crowd too unambiguously, as simply another indictment of American conformity; . . . I do not regard other-direction simply as a malign growth of nouveaux types, but as an open type, to which in the course of historical development much may happen; that what is possible depends in part on who the others are who are taken for models; and that the growth of leisure gives Americans the opportunity greatly to develop the interpersonal competence by which they can, throughout the course of a long life, learn from others and emulate them. To be sure, I have posited a diffuse anxiety as characteristic of other-direction, that the radar-scanning sometimes becomes frantic, but I also try to indicate that to have anxiety may not be the worst offense unless one is to surrender to a Durkheimian decalogue for ranking our modern American sins.

If contemporary Americans are, as Whyte (1956) alleges, "imprisoned in brotherhood" and if America threatens to lose its characteristic genius by still more emphasis upon the long too accentuated social virtues, this trend is also not static. Friedmann (1956, p. 10) correctly observed that "the search for new forms of concreteness, for a revival of individuality, is symptomatically present in many forms."

Hedonistic, present-time orientation. Looking forward optimistically, planning and working toward the future—this hallmark of the Puritan Ethic has surely waned. At least the distant future has been drawn into the very near future. One [24] has children, several of them,[25] now while one can because who knows where the husband will be after the savings have been accumulated that will "provide properly" for them? A little later one uses one's meagre accumulations as a down payment on a comfortable house rather than putting them into annuities or other provision for the college education of the children, for "the house will mean a great deal to us and the children now, and you can't tell if inflation would wipe out our savings anyway or if all college education will be provided by the government when they are ready for it." [26]

I do not employ hedonism in the pejorative sense since it strikes me that there is considerably less hedonism of this sort than there was in the decade after World War I. I mean, rather, the values which the Puritan Ethic never placed upon recreation (except as a means to the end of more effective work), pleasure, leisure, and aesthetic and expressive activities. Americans enjoy themselves more and with less guilt than ever before. Moreover, there has been a remarkable diversification and broadening of the base of leisure-time activities within the population. Between 1940 and 1950 ticket sales for the legitimate theatre and the opera went up 85 per cent as against only 42 per cent for motion pictures. Attendance at concerts of serious music jumped 88 per cent; more dollars were spent for them in 1951 than for baseball. By 1951 there were 659 symphonic groups in the United States, and the number of towns and cities having regular concert series had doubled since 1940. Sales of paintings, attendance at art museums, the number of art museums had increased at an almost fantastic rate. The sales of art supplies were ten times as great in 1949 as in 1939. Gardening, photography, *participation* in sports, foreign travel—all gained fabulously.[27] In part—but only in part —these changes are a reflection of economic prosperity. Americans have long been comfort loving, and they continue to be, but their activities, aesthetic and expressive, have expanded greatly beyond mere comfort. There is "the boom in American history" (Hale, 1955), to mention only one further example.

As far as "taste" is concerned, I know, of course, that there is another aspect to the story. But Brogan (1953) is right when he says:

There are . . . no fundamental differences in the problem of popular taste in Europe and in America. . . . We are all in the same boat together or in the same kind of boats, for the American boat is bigger and better. But it is not fundamentally different. . . . We are the first civilization in which the canons of taste are laid down by the majority of the inhabitants of a civilization that has largely had its roots with its traditional culture cut and is busy manufacturing a new culture, with a speed and universality that modern technology alone makes possible.

And I would say that there is abundant evidence that popular taste in the United States is improving.

Barzun (1956) links the spread of aesthetic interests to the new value emphasis upon the immediate social group:

The new amateur, then, is very much a product of industry and social equality. But he is also moved by more obscure forces. Why, with the world's great artists mechanically at his beck and call, does he want to paint and play, as we say, personally? Why do communities increasingly prefer to be entertained by unprofessional talent nearby and even entrust their bare walls, private or public, to the perilous brush of the modern primitive in their midst? . . . one feels on all sides a growing community spirit which relishes what is local and of the group. Further causes are speculative: the family unit has perhaps been replaced by this larger aggregate. Again, the greater leisure and the desire to supplement the life of livelihood with the life of self-cultivation impel people into community enterprises. And what once might have been a religious endeavor is now secularized, taking the form of art, which for a century and a half has been the religion of the intellectual.

In spite of the admiration—sometimes extravagant—which cultivated Europeans have evinced for certain of the American arts, there remains a disposition on the part of both Europeans and Americans to judge the arts in this country on the basis of canons which may be inappropriate.

Kouwenhoven (1948, pp. 266, 268) talks interestingly of a distinctively American style (the "vernacular") which runs through various media:

. . . both [skyscrapers and jazz] are climactic achievements of the vernacular tradition in America. Neither implies anything resembling the cultivated tradition's negation of or contempt for the actualities of a civilization founded upon technology and shaped by democratic political and social institutions. . . . The important thing about the vernacular is that it possesses inherent qualities of vitality and adaptability, of organic as opposed to static form, of energy rather than repose, that are particularly appropriate to the civilization which, during the brief life span of the United States, has transformed the world.

Greater acceptance of governmental and other organizational control. This requires only brief comment, for it is both instigator and reflection of the value shift just discussed. Valentine (1954) sees the drift toward conformity flowing out of three trends affecting mass society all over the world: the economic trend toward highly industrialized and urbanized society; the political trend toward direct and centralized government; and the social trend toward the acceptance only of popular standards of culture. Protests continue to be made in the United States, even among the young. Harris (1949), reporting on the impressions of a group of Oxford students who visited many American educational institutions, says:

During many a debate one felt that if America went to war, it would be for Private Enterprise against Collectivism rather than for Western civilization against Eastern tyranny.

It remains probably true (Galantiere, 1950) that Europeans still ask what man ought to be, Americans what man ought to do (with a notion of individual independence and responsibility). But in 1957 Senator Case, a Republican, could write:

But since we believe in these institutions [private property and capitalism] pragmatically, not dogmatically, we have never permitted them to be ends in themselves. We do not shrink from governmental intervention to insure that our economy produce a constantly improved standard of living shared as widely as possible. And we insist that the Government intervene to protect the individual against hardships he cannot master through his own efforts. (Cf. Allen, 1952, p. 291.)

Value upon "psychological health." However much "conformity" may have increased, no one can argue that attention to the psyche of the individual has dropped out of the picture. On the contrary, concern with "mental health," with the proper psychological atmosphere at home and in the school, with psychotherapy, has risen to proportions that some have, understandably, regarded as obsessive. This has been associated with the domestication of psychoanalysis on the American scene and the immense increase in psychological self-consciousness in mass dimensions.

Little review is required, for the phenomena face us daily in conversation, in the movies, in almost every book or periodical we read. I shall only run through a few illustrations by way of reminder. Aldridge (1955) speaks of the "preoccupation with . . . psychological *problems*" in the novels of the forties and in the novels of the fifties of "signs of concentration upon rather thin childhood and domestic situations in which the drama tends to center in a subtle psychic conflict between characters. . . ." Sutton *et al.* (1956, p. 399) comment that:

To a remarkable degree, children are now raised according to what are currently conceived to be sound psychological principles rather than according to traditional moral norms.

Strunsky (1956) writes of "the cult of personality" in political life. Inkeles (1957) shows that Americans (both those with a college education and those with only a secondary education) attribute national characteristics to child-rearing and psychological factors more (by a considerable margin) than do samples from eight European countries and from Mexico.

Mead (1956) makes some perceptive observations:

. . . what increase in self-consciousness can be invoked to explain the present trend which so revolts our systematically and recurrently revolted critics of the American scene? . . . This increase in self-conscious reflexive response to partly accurate, partly contrived pictures of what young executives, career girls, Americans overseas or exurbanites do, think, say, feel, what they read, eat, wear and believe, may indeed have lamentable consequences, although they are not the consequences that are immediately prophesied by the critics.
It may also be suggested that this reflexive state in which we live is a kind of stepchild of some of the most important developments of the last quarter-century—of increased awareness of ourselves as individuals with a partly forgotten past, as members of a culture many of whose values are unformulated but nonetheless real. It would be easy to blame our present state on an exaggerated self-consciousness which has destroyed both innocence and spontaneity. But it may also be blamed upon those who have used the tools which have been developed by the therapist, the teacher and the research scholar

as implements of manipulation within a system which they despised and hated, often quite unfairly, but from which they continued to draw a livelihood. The frustrated novelist who sells his soul to an advertising agency or a public relations firm, the frustrated liberal who condones the use of sensational sex stories to sell a politically liberal newspaper, the cynical reformer who thinks the only way to get members of Congress to do a good deed is to offer them bad rationalizations—these are among the people who, out of disillusion, self-contempt, and contempt for their employers and their audiences, have helped to construct this world of semi-truths and manipulated backgrounds and faked shadows within which young people find the images on which to model their lives—and so seem to their elders to be "conforming."

Trilling (1955) sees psychoanalysis as a healthy counteraction to conformity, for Freud:

. . . conceived of the self as being not wholly continuous with culture, as being not wholly created by culture, as maintaining a standing quarrel with its greatest benefactor.
Freud is quite at one with literature. In its essence literature is concerned with the self; and that particular concern of the literature of the past two centuries has been with the self in its standing quarrel with culture. We cannot mention the name of any great writer of the modern period whose work has not been in some way, and usually in a passionate and explicit way, insistent on this quarrel, who has not expressed the bitterness of his discontent with civilization, who has not said that the self made greater legitimate demands than any culture could hope to satisfy. This intense conviction of the existence of the self apart from culture is, as culture well knows, its noblest and most generous achievement. At the present moment it must be thought of as a liberating idea without which our developing ideal of community is bound to defeat itself. We can speak no greater praise of Freud than to say that he placed this idea at the very center of his thought.

However, Trilling sees as "the crisis in our culture," the "progressive deterioration of accurate knowledge of the self and of the right relation between the culture and the self. . . ."

Heterogeneity as a value. Heterogeneity is itself becoming one of the organizing principles of American culture.[28] This tendency has two origins. One goes back to the realization of the bewildering rapidity of change and is reflected in an implicit premise of much American life and especially American education: you never can tell what strange oddment of information will be interesting or indeed useful in an unforeseen context. Americans are devoted to newspaper columns and drawings of the "Believe It Or Not" type and to TV programs of the "$64,000 Question" variety. Americans, perhaps, are following a way of thinking suited to a world in which generalizations are hard to apply.

The other origin lies in increased experience with cultural diversity and a diminished certainty about the infallible superiority of "the American way of life" in every last idea and detail. One of the massive facts of the last twenty years is the vast jump in the number of Americans who have actually seen other cultures. Twenty million have served in the armed forces, and a high proportion of these have been abroad. It would be naive to assume that a majority of these have been much affected one way or the other (one small study—Smith, 1945—indicates the effects are not great), and we all know from personal observation that sometimes the effects are negative.[29] Nevertheless, some are enlightened and the consequences of this in the body politic gradually become cumulative. It is difficult in the military setting to have other than somewhat artificial and superficial experiences though a surprising number of individuals manage to do so. Americans traveling in foreign countries since 1945 for pleasure and as civilian representatives of government or business have better opportunities, and the American masses are far less hermetically isolated from first-hand or one-remove contact with "foreign ways"—other than those of immigrants who were traditionally looked down upon and were, for the most part, not representative of the "higher" levels of their cultures. Finally, there is the circumstance that all fairly well-informed Americans, even if themselves untraveled, are aware—however grudgingly—that the realities of international politics will not permit the writing off of other values and customs as simply "ignorant" or "stupid."

These influences—and others of a more personal and psychological nature—have brought about, even in those who choose themselves to conform to the patterns of their American peer group, a diminution of the single-mindedness of devotion to "the American way" and that positive attachment to diversity as a value which the investigations of Morris and others have revealed. It may be symptomatic that an Easterner (Hughes, 1956) finds "tolerance of differences" a distinctive feature of California, that Stouffer reports the Far West "more tolerant" than the other three regions, that Morris discovered more "innovation" in the Far West than in his other five regions. Whether one happens to like California and the rest of the Far West, almost all students would agree that—for better or for worse—this is "the America of the future," the "climax" (in the technical anthropological sense) of American culture.

One must not, of course, be too cheerful. Erikson (1950, p. 374) warns that the tolerant appraisal of other identities endangers one's own. And not all soberly factual opinion agrees to the increase in acceptance of diversity. One of the investigations in greatest depth (Adorno et al., 1950) finds little spontaneity but much compulsiveness, whether this shows itself in apathy, surface piety, or active racism. They conclude that those Americans who are relatively free of ethnocentrism tend to be neurotic and indecisive. These authors believe the sado-masochistic type is growing in numbers because of a steady increase in monopolistic domination of American life. Likewise, they see the mass media as leading to increased confusion, cynicism, and conformity on the parts of Americans.

Having reviewed the evidence, however, I would put my money on Stouffer's appraisal:

Great social, economic, and technological forces are operating slowly and imperceptibly on the side of spreading tolerance. The rising level of education and the accompanying decline in authoritarian child-rearing practices increase independence of thought and respect for others whose ideas are different. The increasing geographical movement of people has a similar consequence, as well as the vicarious experiences supplied by the magic of our ever more powerful media of communications.

Even an article on "The New America" (Braverman, 1956) in *The American Socialist* comments that there is in this country generally "a considerable and growing body of humanism, toleration, sophistication, cosmopolitanism, and a general spread of a more mature mood and approach." Granted that it is not always easy to distinguish "tolerance" from "indifference."

The search for values. Among those who have rejected the Puritan Ethic or who are, at most, apathetic toward its tenets, there is often an extremely active search for explicit values that educated men who accept mass organizations as the normal centers of their lives can believe in and live by.[30] This is evidenced by the "return to religion," by the staggering number of articles on ethics and values in literary and middle-brow journals, by the fact that business groups (e.g., the Advertising Council and the Corning Glass Works) have staged expensive round tables on this subject. This trend is intensified by the concern of thoughtful citizens with the growing reaction abroad that American values are either negative or *status quo* ones (preservation of the eighteenth century values of the Founding Fathers—cf. Robinson, 1949). Indeed, I would say flatly that one of the outstanding differences between the climate today and that of a generation ago is the recognition of the need for positive and explicit values. Howard (1954) has remarked:

The prevailing characteristic of American literature 1919–1929 was its antagonism toward conventions and toward social conformity, glorification of individual independence. But the aggressive individualism of the period was an individualism without values: mere self-assertiveness, rebellion without faith.

Trend toward equalization of roles of men and women. Another aspect of the withering of the Puritan Ethic is that American fathers are seldom "patriarchs" any longer. There is rough agreement as to some of the main facts. Women are competing successfully in the occupational system (the percentage of women in the labor force has doubled in 65 years [31]); in all of the principal categories some women occupy leading positions. Women are more than ever "the social cynosure" (La Barre, 1946). Thurber (1954) after an analysis of plays of the last generation sees a "feminization" of the legitimate theatre in the United States: decreasing attention to actors, more to actresses, decrease in the number of plays centering on men. Men (or at any rate middle-class men) undertake domestic duties (cooking, changing diapers and other care of children, chores around the home) much more frequently than a generation ago. Some of this latter must be attributed to situational factors: shortage and expensiveness of domestic help, increased significance of wives' contribution to the family income. But value change is likewise involved.

Analysis by my tutees of the same comic strips in 1956 and in 1929 indicates that men are portrayed more frequently in 1956 as dominated by their wives, henpecked, less mature, and less practically intelligent than women. A U.P. dispatch of March 1957 reports that:

The farmer and his wife have combined jobs. . . . Once the farmer was king of his acreage, and his wife was queen of the farm home. But now the farmer and his wife plan and work together on long-range family goals.

Only on details have I detected any doubts as to the trend. On its significance, however, on what it means as regards marriage, the family, the present satisfactions and dissatisfactions of women and men, there is great argument. A special issue of *Life* (December 24, 1956) quotes representative women (and some men). A man says: "My wife works, and I like it." A woman gave up a good job "because something more important was always left undone." Let us look at some of the summary statements of the "experts":

Mary Ellen Chase (quoting an English friend): "Whatever is the matter with your American women? Everywhere I went I got the distinct impression that far too many of them are discontented, restive, and even complaining. They seem to me to have everything that every woman wants. They have beauty and brains, husbands who evidently adore them and are proud of them, more freedom of every sort than any other women in the world. They have opportunities for creative and constructive work which no other women in any other country could possibly have and yet they don't seem to be making use of them. In comparison, our British women are surely dowdy and maybe dull, but I honestly believe they've got more staying power than yours have, and even more resources within themselves. I can't help thinking that, as a whole, American women are just not doing their part in keeping your country where it has to be for the sake of the world. Am I right or wrong?"
I am afraid she is right. But I say this with definite reservations, for . . . I have known and still know thousands of American women who are clearly happy and contented, whether married or unmarried.
Thousands of us American women, young, middle-aged, and even elderly, are not merely wasting our time and disregarding our opportunities, which would actually be bad enough in all conscience. We are actually strewing destruction in our wake. Unless we shortly take strict account of our mental, moral and spiritual stock by examining ourselves with that common sense, integrity and wholesome fear of failure which apparently our mothers and grandmothers employed without the help of a psychiatrist, we are surely headed for far worse troubles than those which so many of us are unprofitably imagining. Our powers of warning will be directed largely against ourselves: we shall comfort no one; and instead of that respect and admiration which we must still want and ought to deserve, we shall command only disparagement and censure.
Margaret Mead: American women have come a long way on the road toward a role for women which is as dignified and responsible as the one assigned to men. Although she has made the home and marriage even more important than they should be, to the exclusion of other values and other roles, she has also given American life a special, unrivaled flavor. All over the world, in the harem, in the hut, in the peasant cottage, other women, who have never envied their husbands' positions, now envy and desire to emulate the American woman.
Emily Kimbrough: Since the rise and fall of Eve, women have not "had it so good" as American women are having it today. And since the wrath of God fell upon Eve, women have not been so excoriated as the American woman is today. She is an easy mark for the slings and arrows of her critics

simply because she is so conspicuous. She has asked for what she gets. She has pushed, shoved, shrilled her way into the open, demanding recognition. . . .
This trail-blazing has undoubtedly unsettled a great many people, including the American woman herself, but it has also accomplished something. . . .
Phyllis McGinley: On the other hand, though, I like our status too much to make the suggestion seriously. For everybody knows it's a man's world and they have not managed it very well, but at least it's their baby. If women took over, we might find ourselves threshing around in the very masculine morasses we have so far managed to avoid.
Cornelia Otis Skinner: Ladies, we have won our case, but for heaven's sake let's stop trying to prove it over and over again. By setting ourselves up as a race apart and special we lose many of the delights and fulfillments of being women. In the long run, we cannot do without men and men cannot do without us—not unless we drive them to it with our shrill cheering for our own accomplishments.

In the same issue there is a report from a panel of psychiatrists:

Spottily and sporadically, but increasingly, the sexes in this country are losing their identities. The emerging American woman tends to be assertive and exploitive. The emerging American man tends to be passive and irresponsible. As a result neither sex can give to or demand from marriage the satisfactions peculiarly necessary to each. They are suffering from what the psychiatrists call sexual ambiguity. This is not a peculiarly American disease but it is more prevalent here than any place else in the world.
Then, one day, the wife (it is almost always the wife) arrives at the psychiatrist's office for advice about her marriage. Her husband is drinking too much, she says. He doesn't take on his share of the responsibilities, whether it be writing the checks for the monthly bills or seeing about vacation reservations. He is not aggressive sexually; in fact he often seems indifferent to her. When they do have relations, she finds it difficult to get satisfaction. They quarrel a good deal, and one or two times, when he has been drinking, he actually hit her. She has lost a lot of her respect for him. She doesn't want to be a clinging vine, goodness knows, but at least she wants a man she can depend upon. Someone who does the things a man is supposed to do. A man.
Enter now the husband. He drinks a good deal more than is good for him, he agrees, and does things he is sorry for later. The marriage is not in good shape. But the trouble with his wife is that she tries to run everything. She has strong ideas and he . . . well, rather than get into a wrangle he had tried to see things from her point of view, and finally began letting her make most of the decisions. He was sexually attracted to his wife and still thinks she is a good-looking woman. But she expects him to respond to her mood. She is independent and assertive in all their other relationships, and then suddenly she switches to the role of yielding seductress; he cannot make the transition. He admires her as a person but does not think she is much of a wife. . . . She never gives much of herself to *him*. He wishes she would

do more of the things women are supposed to do. He wishes she were more of a woman.

Another psychiatrist (Kardiner, 1954) writes a chapter on "The Flight from Masculinity." Many interviews with soldiers who have married Japanese or German wives in preference to American have quoted them to the effect that "American women aren't really women" or "American women want to have it both ways."

Fromm (1956) takes a dim view of both sexes:

Automatons do not love; alienated men do not care. What is praised by marriage counselors is a team relation between two people who manipulate each other with the right techniques, and whose love is essentially a haven from an otherwise intolerable loneliness, an egotism à deux.

Bryson (1953) summarizes a chapter written by my wife as follows:

Florence R. Kluckhohn lays bare the general discontent of modern American woman, who is not generally pleased by the changes that have taken place in her status in the past two centuries. She may have lived a hard life, as a colonial wife and mother, but she had a place of practical and spiritual importance in her civilization and had her full share of honor. Now she has, with a measure of success, entered the competition for other values, hitherto reserved for masculine competitors, but she is still also housewife and not much admired for efficiency in either role.

About all we can conclude is that there is considerable tension over this change in value (and situation). As for family and kin, Schneider and Homans (1955) say:

Far from being "pushed to the wall" and "distorted by values from outside kinship," the American kinship system embodies in clear and communicable form the essence of the dominant values of the whole culture even while it manages to discharge those functions universal to kinship systems, those social functions which are prerequisite to the maintenance of any social and cultural system.

V. Discussion

What one makes of all the views that have been reported and of such research findings as there are depends a good deal upon one's own value system and personality perspective. The most controversial issue is: how much and what kind of conformity is there at present? I think I have marshaled some evidence to the effect that however much compliance there may be there is no complete "internal" acceptance of any one conventional point of view on everything or any general notion that the deviation of others from that viewpoint is "wrong" or "bad." Indeed I would argue that the evidence is to the effect that Americans have matured somewhat since de Tocqueville (vol. 2, pp. 275–276) wrote:

Not only does he mistrust his strength, but he even doubts of his right; and he is very near acknowledging that he is in the wrong, when the greater number of his countrymen assert that he is so. The majority do not need to force him; they convince him.

And I believe that Fromm (1950, p. 83) exhibits a European bias and a lack of comprehension of the American matrix of values when he says:

. . . the vast majority of people in our culture are well adjusted because they have given up the battle for independence sooner and more radically than the neurotic person. They have accepted the judgment of the majority so completely that they have been spared the sharp pain of conflict which the neurotic person goes through. While they are healthy from the standpoint of "adjustment," they are more sick than the neurotic person from the standpoint of the realization of their aims as human beings.

We can, of course, agree with Meyer (1955) that there exists a "lag":

The moral degeneration insofar as it exists today as well as our neurotic fears and desire for conformity are due to the fact that our social cohesion and mutual sympathies . . . have been shattered by a scientific and technological revolution without parallel in history for its rapid tempo and for the radical transformations it has brought about in our social structure. Man has been permanently and finally exiled from his comfortable anthropocentric, geocentric universe . . . the conditions of our lives have been basically more altered in the last fifty years than they were in the previous two or even three thousand years. But in our thoughts and feelings we are still living in a bygone era, anywhere from the thirteenth to the nineteenth century.

But perhaps there is equally a "lag" in our interpretations. Good observers such as Granville Hicks (1956) make observations of the following order: "When I look about at my neighbors, I see no evidence that they are leading standardized lives." Individuality is hard to extinguish. As Strunsky (1956) remarks:

Man does not easily surrender his autonomous nature or concede his irrelevance. When denied by circumstance, he creates his own occasions of individuality, contriving them out of the very forms which conspire to repress them.

Arthur Schlesinger, Jr. (1952) is right in saying: "The only answer to mass culture, of course, lies in the affirmation of America, not as a uniform society, but as a various and pluralistic society made up of many groups with diverse interests." The predilection for diversity appears to be developing, and changes in social structure seem to be moving in the right direction. Lynes (1953) says: "Society which once divided into something like a gigantic three-layer cake, now is broken up into a series of independent pyramids, each with its own interests, hierarchies, and rewards." [32]

A "new" set of values may be visibly emerging. In this freehand sketch I have made no pretense of discerning a final common path, but I shall recapitulate in slightly different language the trends I think to have detected over the past generation:

1. Strictly personal values have receded in importance at the expense of more publicly standardized "group values" whether those of an organization, a community, a social class, a profession, a minority, or an interest group. "Conservatism" has increased. It is possible that the machine is coming to be taken as the implicit model for human behavior.

2. But there has been a concomitant rise in the "psychological values" related to mental health, the education and training of children, and the like. However, as DuBois (1955) puts it, "Self-cultivation in America has as its goal less the achievement of uniqueness and more the achievement of similarity."

3. The value placed upon "future success" [33] has receded in favor of "respectable and stable security" seen in shorter time range.[34]

4. Aesthetic values have notably risen in the hierarchy.

5. The value of institutionalized religion is greater but primarily in terms of changes No. 1 and No. 3 above (need for group affiliation and stability) rather than in terms of intensified personal religious life.

6. "Heterogeneity" is becoming one of the organizing principles of the dominant American value system.

7. The ideal for American woman and her place in the society has altered as have our sexual codes.

8. There is an increased overt concern for abstract standards; greater value is placed upon explicit values.

VI. APPLICATIONS TO POLITICS AND INTERNATIONAL AFFAIRS

I am going to say very little about "applications," for there are those who are far better equipped in experience and wisdom than I to draw the moral—if any. The first memorandum from the Center for International Studies on the subject of this conference stated that the objective was "more to know ourselves than to change ourselves." I shall, however, permit myself a few "pessimistic" and "optimistic" remarks.

On the former side one must surely range the political apathy demonstrated by Stouffer, Jacob, and others for the vast majority, an unhappy conclusion not seriously challenged by any data—or even views—with which I am familiar. We must also put the devaluation of the future and preoccupation with the present on this side. Those who are mainly concerned with enjoying the here and now while they can, are not likely to expend the long-range effort or make the sacrifices necessary to build a strong United Nations or otherwise provide for stable world order.

On the positive side I would, on the whole, put the diminishing of tense and highly competitive striving in "the American character." If this continues into older age grades, some of the irritations Americans present to friends, neutrals, and enemies abroad should lessen. We may become more patient, less determined to transform much of the world into a replica of ourselves,[35] less intrigued by the image of "The American Century."

This grades into something which I am certain is positive: a greater tolerance of and even appreciation for diversity—manners and morals other than our own. Perhaps the view of a Catholic (Santayana) and a Protestant (Niebuhr) that the American people are not sufficiently mature to assume world leadership is based upon a value pattern that still dominates our elder leaders but may not dominate our future leaders. Possibly the eighteenth century quality of optimism and defect of naïveté and the nineteenth, early twentieth doctrines of "America First" and "the melting pot" will no longer prevail.

I am cheered by the fact that men who are better informed and who see more clearly than I (e.g., Bryson, 1952) have taken a long, close, and unflinching look at "the next America" and are undismayed—indeed, on balance, "optimistic." Though I dislike the tones of internal and external propaganda varyingly manifested, I do think there is something to the "Fortune line" of "the Permanent Revolution." [36] Galantiere (1950) is right in insisting that the critical views of our foreign friends are skewed in important respects. Perhaps because, like most Americans of my generation, optimism was ingrained in me as a basic value, I think Allen (1952) is far more right than wrong when he concludes:

The story of the changes in the contours of American life that we have hammered out in the first half of this twentieth century, is a triumphant story, however harsh may have been some of our experiences in the interim and however obscure may be the shape of the future. We would do well to think of our accomplishment thus far as but the preface to what we may accomplish in the second half of the century if we can continue to invent, improve, and change—and can keep a good heart. The courageous nation, like the courageous man, is not unhappy at the thought of dangers beside the road ahead, but welcomes them as challenges to be faced and overwhelmed along an adventurous course.

But these are "the old values" speaking! Let me conclude with a young American's reactions to England (Burdick, 1949):

In England there is none of the rise and fall, the massive brooding anxiety, the creative stabbing of self-doubt, the tortures of ethnic inadequacy that one finds to a marked degree in America and Asia and to some degree in France and Italy. It is impossible that England could today produce a Shakespeare while the United States or Asia might. In this man-eating neurotic America there are enormous creative currents. Those English who see only our chrome plating and assembly lines and love of big automobiles and our roaring vulgarity are, understandably, not attuned to something vaster that turns and weaves just below the surface of American life like some raging, caged and almost invisible beast. This beast may destroy us while England is still competent and serene.

To the Reader

By now you will have found notes toward a paper rather than a decently written document in which well-digested materials have been properly organized and economically presented. I spread my net too widely. I looked up too much and read too much. If any virtue can arise from my deficiency, it is this: perhaps from the long quotations, readers will get some direct feel for my sources both in their richness and suggestiveness and in their limitations, vagueness, and other inadequacies.

I present immediately a brief sketch of what I think I have learned. Those who want some idea of the tortuous paths by which I got there will have to wade through my longer notes and, much better, go to my original sources.

FINDINGS

Documented by some empirical data: *

1. Decline of the Puritan Ethic as the core of the dominant middle-class value system (Stouffer, 1949; Jacob, 1957; Sutton et al., 1956; Whyte, 1956; Kardiner, 1954; Himmelhoch and Fava, 1955; Kangieser, 1957; Foster, 1956; Lee, 1952; Riesman, 1956; Wolfenstein, 1951; Riesman and Glazer, 1948; Schneider and Dornbusch, 1957).

   a. Rise in value upon "being" or "being and becoming" as opposed to "doing" (Collins, 1957; Riesman, 1956; Spindler, 1955; Allen, 1952).

   b. Trend toward "present time" in contrast to "future time" † value-orientation (Collins, 1957; Spindler, 1955).

   c. Increase of aesthetic and recreational values (Riesman, 1956; Hale, 1955; Allen, 1952; Turck, 1952).

2. Increase in "other-directedness" (Dornbusch and Hickman, 1957; Schneider and Dornbusch, 1957; Foster, 1956; Whyte, 1956; Riesman, 1956), though the peak of this trend may be behind us (Dornbusch and Hickman, 1957). I see the "return to religion" as an aspect of this shift and of the following one.

3. Emergence of explicit value placed upon "psychological health" (Schneider and Dornbusch, 1957; Scodel, 1957; Sutton et al., 1956; Strunsky, 1956; Inkeles, 1957).

4. More prizing of some kinds of tolerance and of some kinds of diversity (Morris, 1956; Jacob, 1957; Gillespie and Allport, 1955; Stouffer, 1955; Foster, 1956; Spindler, 1955).

5. Drift toward equalization of the roles of the sexes (Collins, 1957; Scodel, 1957; Dornbusch and Roberts, 1957).

Possible interpretations **

1. The active search for explicit values.
2. "Individuality" versus "rugged individualism."
3. Increased ambivalence toward "science." ‡

---

* These findings are also in general accord with the more interpretative and im-pressionistic literature, but it seemed useful to segregate those points on which there is support from good—or fairly good—research designed to test these or closely re-lated hypotheses.

† My over-all impression is that this is accompanied by a decline in the American value placed upon "optimism." Some sources, however, (e.g., Jacob, 1957) submit data to the contrary.

** This category does *not* mean that my assessment is "no evidence" beyond im-pression for these propositions. On the contrary, I think there is substantial evidence for the first two and some for the third, but this "evidence" does not emerge from systematically designed research. Some of it is, however, empirical; the rest con-sists in the agreement of many (though not all) observers and interpreters of various kinds.

‡ The evidence I have here is not put together in an orderly fashion and is some-what conflicting. Advertising, numbers of young people attracted to science, etc. would suggest increased prestige. On the other hand, there are the currents to the

Some Queries and Skepticisms ***

From my readings and attempted analysis of the literature I have gained a strong conviction that there are some warnings to be kept constantly in mind:

1. Most of the comment on American values is by a special and highly articulate group that has its own biases of particular kinds.
2. In all "modern" societies, the intellectuals are assigned a role as social critics.
3. In the United States "literary" people strongly tend to be super-critical of academic people (are they motivated by resentment at being apart from their natural home, the universities?) and most especially of those trespassers on the traditional territory of poets and novelists, the social scientists.
4. There is a troublesome "time lag" problem, for example:
   a. Are older, vocal critics projecting their values upon a generation that is not yet so articulate?
   b. Are some of the canons (especially the implicit ones) of evaluation inappropriate to altered context, both of situation and of value matrix?
   c. Is the United States, as has been said, "the one culture in which silence gives dissent" or does the fact that the visible arguments about some problems (e.g., "feminism" and religion) are appreciably less heated mean that some "battles have been won" and some value changes have indeed occurred?
5. I believe there is a tremendous amount of "semantic confusion" on the matter of "conformity." In part, I would trace this to the circumstance that American intellectuals (at any rate, the older ones) feel compelled to talk as "non-conformists."

References Cited

Adorno, T. W., Else-Frenkel-Brunswik, Daniel J. Levinson, and R. Nevitt Sanford
    1950 *The Authoritarian Personality.*

Albrecht, Milton C.
    1956 Does Literature Reflect Common Values? *American Sociological Review,* December.

Aldridge, John W.
    1955 Gray New World. *The Nation,* June 25.

Allen, Frederick Lewis
    1952 *The Big Change.*

Allport, Gordon W.
    1950 *The Individual and His Religion.*

Andrews, Wayne
    1955 *Architecture, Ambition and Americans.*

---

effect that "science is leading to destruction," etc. Hence I have not treated this matter at all in the body of the text.

   *** John Gardner in a conversation in March helped me formulate some of these points, but he must not be blamed for the way I have expressed them here.

Arensberg, Conrad M.
  1955 American Communities. *American Anthropologist,* December.
Barzun, Jacques
  1956 The New Man in the Arts. *The American Scholar,* Autumn.
Berger, Morroe
  1957 What Do We Know About the Businessman? *Princeton Alumni
      Weekly,* February 1.
Bird, Caroline
  1957 The Unlost Generation. *Harper's Bazaar,* February.
Braverman, Harry
  1956 The New America. *American Socialist,* July.
Brogan, Dennis W.
  1953 The Taste of the Common Man. *Saturday Review,* February 28.
  1957 Unnoticed Changes in America. *Harpers,* February.
Bryson, Lyman
  1952 *The Next America.*
  1953 Introduction to *Facing the Future's Risks.*
Burdick, Eugene
  1949 An American in England. *Oxford Magazine.*
Calhoun, Arthur W.
  1945 *A Social History of the American Family.*
Case, Clifford
  1957 *New York Sunday Times,* Magazine Section, February.
Chambers, Clark A.
  1956 College Students and the Nature of Man. *Colorado Quarterly,*
      Winter.
Coleman, Lee
  1941 What is American? A Study of Alleged American Traits. *Social
      Forces,* May.
Collins, Jerome
  1957 Changing Values in the Best Sellers of the 1930–1935 and 1950–
      1955 Periods. Unpublished Distinction Thesis, Harvard Univer-
      sity.
De Tocqueville, Alexis
  1954 *Democracy in America.* (Edited by Phillips Bradley)
Dornbusch, Sanford M. and Lauren Hickman
  1957 A Test of Riesman's Hypothesis 1890–1955. Unpublished paper.
Dornbusch, Sanford M. and Caroline Roberts
  1957 Perception of Women in the "Ladies Home Journal," 1890–
      1955. Unpublished paper.
Drucker, Peter F.
  1952 The Myth of American Uniformity. *Harpers,* May.
Du Bois, Cora
  1955 The Dominant Value Profile of American Culture. *American
      Anthropologist,* December.
Erikson, Erik H.
  1950 *Childhood and Society.*

Farber, Maurice L.
    1953 English and Americans: Values in the Socialization Process. *Journal of Psychology*, volume 36.
Fiddle, Seymour
    1952 Our Gimmick Society. *The Nation*, July 26.
Foster, Margaret P.
    1956 A Study of the Content of Selected Third Grade Basic Readers Used in the United States from 1900 to 1953. Unpublished M. A. thesis, Wesleyan University.
Friedmann, F. G.
    1956 America: A Study in Contingency. Mimeographed paper.
Fromm, Erich
    1950 *Psychoanalysis and Religion*.
    1955 *The Sane Society*.
    1956 The Present Human Condition. *American Scholar*, Winter.
Galantiere, Lewis
    1950 America Today. *Foreign Affairs*, July.
Gillespie, James and Gordon W. Allport
    1955 *Youth's Outlook on the Future*.
Gillin, John
    1955 National and Regional Cultural Values in the United States. *Social Forces*, December.
Goldman, Eric
    1956 *The Crucial Decade*.
Goldschmidt, Walter
    1951 Notes. *American Quarterly*.
Greenwalt, C. H.
    1957 The Culture of the Businessman. *Saturday Review*, January 19.
Hale, William H.
    1955 The Boom in American History. *The Reporter*, pp. 42–45.
Harris, Kenneth
    1949 Visit of Oxford Debaters. *American Oxonian*, January-March.
Hicks, Granville
    1956 Liberalism in the Fifties. *American Scholar*, Summer.
Himmelhoch, J. and F. F. Fava (Editors)
    1955 *Sexual Behavior in American Society*.
Hopson, A. L. B.
    1952 Best Sellers: Media of Mass Expression. Unpublished Ph. D. thesis, Harvard University.
Howard, Leon
    1954 Society and the Individual in Twentieth Century American Literature. Lecture delivered at Tokyo University, Fifth American Studies Seminar.
Howe, Irving
    1954 This Age of Conformity. *Partisan Review*, January.
Hughes, H. Stuart
    1956 California—The America to Come. *Commentary*, May.

Hyman, H.
  1956 The value system of different classes: a social psychological con-
      tribution to the analysis of stratification. In: *Class Status and
      Power*, R. Bendix and S. Lipset, editors.
Inkeles, Alex
  1957 Unpublished research.
Inkeles, Alex and Peter Rossi
  1956 National Comparisons of Occupational Prestige. *American Jour-
      nal of Sociology*, January.
Jacob, Philip E.
  1957 *Changing Values in College.*
Kangieser, Helen G.
  1957 A Note on Changing American Values as Seen in Contemporary
      Popular Literature. Duplicated: Center for International Studies,
      M. I. T.
Kardiner, Abram
  1954 *Sex and Morality.*
Kluckhohn, Clyde
  1941 The Way of Life. *The Kenyon Review*, volume 3.
  1949 *Mirror for Man* (chapter 9).
  1950 Midcentury Manners and Morals. In: *Twentieth Century Unlim-
      ited*, Bruce Bliven, editor.
  1951 Values and Value-Orientations in the Theory of Action. In:
      Toward a General Theory of Action, Talcott Parsons and Edward
      Shils, editors.
Kluckhohn, Clyde and Florence Kluckhohn
  1947 Generalized Orientation and Class Patterns. In: *Conflicts of
      Power in Modern Culture*, Lyman Bryson, editor.
Kluckhohn, Florence
  1952 American Women and American Values. In: *Facing the Future's
      Risks*, Lyman Bryson, editor.
Kouwenhoven, John A.
  1948 *Made in America.*
  1956 What's American About America? *Harpers*, July.
La Barre, Weston
  1946 Social Cynosure and Social Structure. *Journal of Personality*,
      March.
Lantis, M. (Editor)
  1955 The U.S.A. as Anthropologists See It. *American Anthropologist*,
      vol. 57, no. 6.
Lee, Dorothy
  1955 Freedom, Spontaneity, and Limit in American Linguistic Usage.
      Explorations, no. 4:6–14.
Leites, Nathan
  1948 Trends in Moral Temper. *The American Imago*, April.
Lindner, Robert
  1953 *Prescription for Rebellion.*
  1956 *Must You Conform?*

Lundberg, George A.
    1955 Occupations and "Class" Alignments in the United States, 1870–
        1950. *Social Forces*, December.
Lynd, Robert
    1946 *Knowledge for What?*
Lynes, Russell
    1957 *A Surfeit of Honey.*
Manfredi, J. F.
    1950 The Relationship of Class-structured Pathologies to the Contents
        of Popular Periodical Fiction: 1936–1940. Unpublished Ph. D.
        thesis, Harvard University.
McArthur, Charles
    1955 Personality Differences Between Middle and Upper Classes. *The
        Journal of Abnormal and Social Psychology*, March.
McGranahan, Donald V. and Ivor Wayne
    1948 German and American Traits Reflected in Popular Drama. *Hu-
        man Relations*, vol. 1, no. 4.
McLuhan, H. M.
    1949 *The Mechanical Bride: Folklore of Industrial Man.*
    1954 The Psychopathology of Time and Life. *Explorations*, vol. 1,
        no. 1.
Mead, Margaret
    1942 Customs and Mores. *The American Journal of Sociology*, vol. 47.
    1949 *Male and Female.*
    1956 Our Documentary Culture. *The American Scholar*, Autumn.
Meyer, Agnes E.
    1955 Democracy and Clericalism. *The Christian Register.*
Miller, William (Editor)
    1952 *Men in Business.*
Mills, C. Wright
    1948 *The New Men of Power.*
    1951 *White Collar.*
    1956 *The Power Elite.*
Morris, Charles
    1947 *The Open Self.*
    1956 *Varieties of Human Value.*
Muller, H. J.
    1954 *The Uses of History.*
Murray, H. A.
    1940 What Should Psychologists Do About Psychoanalysis? *Journal of
        Abnormal and Social Psychology*, April.
Myrdal, Gunnar
    1944 *An American Dilemma.*
Naegele, Kaspar
    1949 From de Tocqueville to Myrdal: A Research Memorandum on
        Selected Studies of American Values. Unpublished; Values Study
        Project, Harvard University.

Newcomer, Mabel
 1955 *The Big Business Executive.*
Northrop, F. S. C.
 1947 *The Logic of the Sciences and the Humanities.*
Parrington, V. L.
 1927–1930 Main Currents in American Thought.
Parsons, Talcott
 1955 "McCarthyism" and American Social Tension. *Yale Review,* Winter.
Perry, Ralph Barton
 1949 *Characteristically American.*
Potter, David M.
 1954 *People of Plenty.*
Riesman, David and Nathan Glazer
 1948 Polls, Political Apathy, and Character Structure: Problems of Measurement and Analysis. Duplicated.
Riesman, David
 1952 Our Country and Our Culture. *Partisan Review,* May.
 1952b Some Observations on the Study of American Character. *Psychiatry,* August.
 1954 *Individualism Reconsidered.*
 1956 The Found Generation. *American Scholar,* Autumn.
Robinson, G. T.
 1949 The Ideological Combat. *Foreign Affairs,* July.
Roseborough, H. E. and H. P. Phillips
 1953 A Comparative Analysis of the Responses to a Sentence Completion Test of a Matched Sample of Americans and Former Russian Subjects. Unpublished: Russian Research Center, Harvard University.
Rosen, Bernard S.
 1946 The Achievement Syndrome: A Psychocultural Dimension of Social Stratification. *American Sociological Review,* 21:203–211.
Schlesinger, Arthur, Sr.
 1949 *Paths to the Present.*
Schlesinger, Arthur, Jr.
 1952 Our Country and Our Culture. *Partisan Review,* September.
Schneider, David M. and George C. Homans
 1955 Kinship Terminology and the American Kinship System. *American Anthropologist,* December.
Schneider, Louis and Sanford M. Dornbusch
 1957 Inspirational Religious Literature: from Latent to Manifest Functions of Religion. *American Journal of Sociology,* March.
 1958 Inspirational Religious Literature in the United States 1880–1955. In Press.
Scodel, Alvin
 1957 Changes in Song Lyrics and Some Speculations on National Character. To appear in *Psychiatry.*

Sirjamaki, John
    1947 A Footnote to the Anthropological Approach to the Study of
         American Culture. *Social Forces,* volume 25.
Smith, M. B.
    1945 Did War Service Produce International-mindedness? *Harvard Ed-
         ucational Review,* October.
Spindler, George D.
    1955 Education in a Transforming American Culture. *Harvard Educa-
         tional Review,* Summer.
Stouffer, S. A.
    1949 Analysis of Conflicting Social Norms. *American Sociological Re-
         view,* December.
    1955 *Communism, Conformity and Civil Liberties.*
Streik, G. F.
    1948 Idealism and War Bonds: A Comparative Study of the Two
         World Wars. *Public Opinion Quarterly,* Summer.
Strunsky, Robert
    1956 The Cult of Personality. *American Scholar,* Summer.
Sutton, Francis X., Seymour E. Harris, Carl Kaysen, and James Tobin
    1956 *The American Business Creed.*
Thurber, James
    1954 Get Thee to a Monastery. *The New Yorker,* August 21.
Tillich, P. J.
    1953 *The Protestant Era.*
Trilling, Lionel
    1955 *Freud and the Crisis of Our Culture.*
Turck, F. B.
    1952 The Great American Explosion. *Scientific Monthly,* September.
Valentine, Alan
    1954 *The Age of Conformity.*
Vogt, E. Z.
    1955 *The Homesteaders.*
Warner, W. Lloyd
    1953 *American Life: Dream and Reality.*
    1957 Symbol Systems of Yankee City. Manuscript.
Warner, W. Lloyd and James C. Abegglen
    1955 *Occupational Mobility in American Business and Industry 1928–
         1952.*
Whyte, William H., Jr.
    1956 *The Organization Man.*
Wolfenstein, Martha
    1951 The Emergence of Fun Morality. *Journal of Social Issues,* vol-
         ume 7.
Wolfenstein, Martha and Nathan Leites
    1950 *Movies—A Psychological Study.*
Woods, Sister Frances Jerome
    1956 *Cultural Values in American Ethnic Groups.*

NOTES

¹ The interpretation of these results is equivocal because the respondents were offered only three alternatives as opposed to the six-class system used by Warner and his associates. Nevertheless, it is an induction from my experience that Americans who would be typed by Warner as "upper" tend to place themselves as "middle" or "upper middle" class, while those from Warner's "upper lower" group often assign themselves middle-class position.

² In "Yankee City," Warner (1953) puts only 10 per cent in the upper middle class and 28 per cent in the lower middle; in "Jonesville" (Illinois), 11 per cent upper middle and 31 per cent lower middle. One study in Georgia does give 22 per cent in upper middle and 35 per cent in lower middle.

³ Arensberg (1955), Gillin (1955), and Riesman (1956) all provide useful materials on various aspects of regional differentiation with respect to values.

⁴ Sister Frances Jerome Woods (1956) has provided a good survey of the cultural values of American ethnic groups.

⁵ Recent investigations have shown that, contrary to our official ideology, the lines of social class are significant in the United States. From the social science viewpoint, the most interesting single finding of Kinsey and his group is the extent to which sexual behavior is class typed. Apart from McArthur (1955) I have found no published work that deals systematically with variations in values by classes. There are two interesting Harvard senior theses on the subject, and Donald Michael carried out in 1946 a study which clearly indicated that reactions to the atom bomb varied consistently with the values attributable to the distinct social classes. See also Hyman, 1953; Rosen, 1956.

⁶ Since my participation in the Comparative Study of Values in Five Cultures project (supported by the Rockefeller Foundation through its Division of Social Sciences) permitted me to do this background preparation in the literature on values generally, the present paper must be considered a contribution from that project as well as from the M.I.T. study.

⁷ A comparative study of 45 popular plays in the United States and Germany in 1927 (McGranahan and Wayne, 1948) shows the persistent values as still central. The only contrasts with a sample of American plays produced in 1909–1910 were: "the conflict between youthful lovers and parents is less pronounced, and there is a greater tendency for the parents to be morally right" (p. 449) in the earlier period.

⁸ See especially Chapters 28 and 29.

⁹ Jacob's data are drawn from five major (and independent) pieces of research embracing many thousands of students from many different institutions.

¹⁰ On the use of literature for values analysis, cf. Albrecht, 1956.

¹¹ Certain statistical problems remain to be ironed out; also the influence of the Depression. After this draft had been typed and the manuscript was due at M.I.T. for duplicating, Dr. Dornbusch communicated the following additional information:
1. The quantity of materials on the depression years was not sufficiently great to be confident as to the influence of the Depression.
2. The peak in "other-directedness" was in 1920–1940 with some decline after 1940.
3. If we compare the period up to 1920 and the post-1920 years, the early period has only two years out of twenty above the median in other-directedness. On the other hand, the more recent period has 19 out of 21 years above the median in other-directedness. The difference between the level of other-directedness up to 1920 and after 1920 is statistically significant at the .001 level. These figures are based on the use of testimonial, collective endorsements ("society women like"), and quantitative endorsements ("twenty million women like"). If one uses as data advertisements

which claim the use or non-use of a product will affect inter-personal relations, exactly the same figures appear in the cells of the resulting table.

[12] Foster's findings are similar to those of J. A. Hockett (*Encyclopaedia of Educational Research*, revised edition, 1950). This source was not examined by me.

[13] One source says 16 per cent of the adult population were church members in 1850, but 59 per cent were members in 1950. Standards for church membership had, of course, altered markedly. A Roper poll in 1954 found that nine out of ten Americans believe in the existence of some supreme being; that where in 1942 only two out of ten persons named religious leaders as doing the most good for the country, this percentage had doubled by 1954. A Gallup poll in 1954 "discovered" that 87 per cent of the adult population were church members. We must take such figures seriously but not *too* seriously.

[14] Evidence that this trend is not uniform has already been presented. Berger (1957) adds that 59 per cent of American business executives in 1950 indicated *no* religious preference, whereas the corresponding figure for 1925 was only 37 per cent.

[15] Cf. Fromm (1956): "religion becomes a self-help device for increasing one's own powers for success."

[16] For example, the *New York Times* for March 3, 1957 reports that students were asking themselves "whether they were giving sufficient thought on how to meet the pressures against individualism." But note: a) the college in question was Sarah Lawrence, and b) at this conference they were harangued by leading older men who are well-known for carrying this particular torch.

[17] I am not certain whether the little magazine *Dissent* comes from this category but it would appear so.

[18] Streik (1948) finds that whereas World War I propaganda stressed "conscience" and "duty," that of World War II emphasized "security and affection."

[19] The mother of John Wesley wrote: "In order to form the minds of children, the first thing to be done is to conquer their wills and bring them to obedient temper." Jonathan Edwards regarded children as "young vipers in God's sight and infinitely more hateful than vipers." Even the behaviorist psychologist, John B. Watson, said: "Learn not to talk to children in endearing terms lest dreadful neurotic conditions be initiated."

[20] Aldridge (1955) says that the last fifty years of the American novel show a gradual movement away from "inner-directed . . . toward the phase of at least incipient 'other-direction.' "

[21] Actually, as Riesman (1956, p. 50) says: "Two processes appear to be going on simultaneously in this country: homogenization and differentiation. Equalization is proceeding between city and country, between the social and occupational strata and between the sexes . . . by the same token, differentiation proceeds among the age-grades, and remains large . . . between North and South and between the college educated and those of lesser academic exposure."

[22] Goldschmidt (1951) reports "loneliness" a dominant theme in the romantic short stories of 1950 he studied.

[23] Cf. Goldman (1956, p. 259): "In the winter of 1953–1954, for the first time in twenty years, the term 'conservative' was being used in the United States widely and without embarrassment."

[24] Especially "the literate and hopeful."

[25] The number of women with three or more children has doubled in twenty years. The increase is particularly marked among college-educated women.

[26] Whether this be cause or effect or both, the tax law which encourages *using* earnings is significant.

[27] The figures in this paragraph are from Turck (1952) and Allen (1952). For other information and interpretation see the essays on leisure, aesthetics, and mass media in Riesman (1954).

[28] Schneider and Homans (1956) say: "Perhaps the fundamental characteristic of the American kinship system is the presence of a wide variety of alternate terms."

[29] Nevertheless, on the whole, contact does make a difference in the favorable direction. Stouffer attributes the fact that women are less tolerant of nonconformity than men to the circumstance that their social environments are more limited. Adorno et al. (1950) also found American women more ethnocentric than American men.

[30] There has been, as Leites says (1948, p. 4), a marked decline in "the degree of felt certainty in moral reactions."

[31] A Woman's Home Companion survey in 1950 showed that 52 per cent of American women asserted a preference to remain exclusively housewives. (Goldschmidt, 1951.)

[32] Cf. also Lundberg (1955). Riesman (1952, pp. 310–311) says: "Even the term 'mas culture' may beg the question; it is better to speak of 'class-mass culture,' because what I think we have is a series of audiences, stratified by mass and class, each (even that of PR devotees) large enough to constitute in psychological terms, a 'mass.' Moreover, I believe there is more critical judgment, at more of these levels, than is generally realized. And on one level there is perhaps too much. Our intellectuals do not, for instance, allow themselves to praise Hollywood movies as much as, in my opinion, they deserve; they are like psychiatrists who do not dare give a patient a clean bill of health lest some other doctor find a hidden flaw."

[33] Cf. Friedmann (1956, p. 6): " 'Success,' rather than being achieved by unique actions in the presence of unique situations, has to be sought now by more clever and more pleasing performance of what is socially or institutionally expected. This emphasis on a generally accepted or acceptable form of behavior (and the corresponding de-emphasis on the substance of an action), the obedience to an almost Kantian imperative of universal pleasantness, is rewarded today by 'position' (historically corresponding to 'rank') in the scheme of institutions which have risen in connection with the growth of efficiency and social engineering and the proliferation of administrative and managerial tasks."

[34] As Berger (1957) points out: "For some years the Luce publications, choniclers of business activity and guardians of business values, have been disturbed by the tendency of college seniors to prefer employment to enterprise."

[35] Riesman, however, suggests that we are increasingly stressing "mood engineering" —i.e., trying to persuade other nations to "like" us.

[36] Apart from the somewhat defensive and propagandistic tones, perhaps the most basic question is: are we (and the English) simply tinkering with and remodeling a structure that no longer is appropriate to contemporary conditions instead of examining fearlessly the most basic premises, explicit and implicit? Simone de Beauvoir in The Mandarins eloquently contends that this is the real difference between American and French intellectuals of the contemporary and recent period.

INDIVIDUALITY

by Henry A. Murray

A YEAR ago, in line with an ancient tactic, I planted "individuality" in the soil of the subconscious, trustful that after several months of incubation Nature would supply me with abundant produce. But, on finally returning to this plot of earth, I found, to my dismay, no vegetation that would bring a penny in the public market. Strange, because individuality—the myth, the concept, and the word itself—has been, for many cycles of thought and talk, a generating symbol compact with drawing power.

The prospect of arriving at the date line empty-handed gave rise to a discomfort bordering on panic, and instead of persisting in my faith that the ground would render up the wanted stuff, I turned to friends. In doing so I demonstrated—as I see now—that in a crisis other-directedness can prevail even against a veteran resistance. At the moment of decision I was reminded that nowadays—if not always—everybody repeats with bantering minor variations what everybody repeats with bantering minor variations. Why be so proud as to refuse to join? Why not partake of this communion?

What I did was to transcribe and edit an evening's conversation among three old friends of mine, Curt, Marc, and Dy, which I instigated and unintrusively attended.

CURT: Hasn't David Riesman already said everything that is worth saying about individuality? Can we bring this drowned value back to life with a pulmotor of vocal air no matter how inspired? The day of individuality is done. I was a pallbearer at the funeral.

DY: It isn't like you—protagonist of the unyielding will of man—to admit defeat. According to my core of values, it is ill-bred to stop fighting when you see that your cause is going under.

CURT: You can't strike your axe against the roots of a whole people.

Accepting the obligatory is prophylaxis against the inroads of misanthrope.

MARC: Are you two assuming that you know a *real* individual when you see one and would agree in all of your pickings? Highly improbable. I have studied personalities for years in great detail and in each case found uniqueness; but I have never had occasion to cry "Eureka! *Here* is individuality." It is all a matter of degree and emphasis. As Kluckhohn put it: "Every man is in certain respects like all other men, in certain respects like some other men, and in certain respects like no other man." Since the truth of this statement is self-evident, we must agree that everybody has some measure of uniqueness, distinctiveness, individuality. The question is, how common in our country today, compared to yesterday, are those who are unique to a significant degree in several significant respects? But the rub is that the respects which are significant to Curt may not be significant to Dy. There are so many ways in which a man may differ from the general run! He may be queerly featured, wear queer clothes, or have a queer speech or accent—be born with a harelip and a cleft palate. Or, he may be out of the ordinary in his tastes and hobbies—smoke nothing but Mexican cheroots and collect only pewter soup tureens. He may be a specialist in heraldry, Elizabethan ballads, Portuguese fados, or azaleas. Or, he may cleave to very odd convictions—affirm that the world can be improved only by S-R conditionings of young children—having them taught to be nice with electric shocks in place of Hell, and cheese in place of the milk and honeydew of Paradise. Or, a man might be unique in supporting a peculiar cluster of philosophic values or in feeling differently than others do when facing up to the totality of things, the personified impersonal. I could go on and on in this vein, but you already see my point. The issue is, what are the most relevant criteria and standards of individuality?

CURT: We can't waste time appraising surfaces and shows of individuality. There is only too much of that around. We must look for something substantial and unobtrusive—the real McCoy? And that, I claim, is out of fashion, dead.

MARC: So you say. But first tell me whether you insist that individuality be taken as a good thing and that we must therefore disregard uniqueness among criminals, delinquents, neurotics, and psychotics? I have a cabinet full of case histories of unusual deviants and abnormals.

The topic of the coming seminar, however, suggests that individuality is an acknowledged value, a value we are losing or in danger of losing. As you know, according to evolutionary theorists, numberless variations —perhaps the majority of variations—are deleterious to the organism, the society, or the species in which they first appear. In some cases it is impossible to tell whether an emergent variation will be harmful or beneficial to society; but in others it is less difficult. We could hardly disagree, for example, about the harmful effects of addiction to marijuana among children. Or, take an average community of honest, intelligent, and friendly citizens. Here it will be the most dishonest, stupid, and unfriendly person who will best exhibit individuality if degree of variation is your yardstick. The other day when I asked a superbly conventional old friend of mine to name twelve persons with decided individuality, everyone he mentioned was characterized by defects rather than by virtues. It seems that individuality, in the opinion of a representative member of our culture, consists of such traits as egotism, selfishness, wilfulness, defiance, arrogance, eccentricity, exhibitionism, irrationality, irresponsibility, and downright cussedness—all adding up to a high nuisance quotient. What do you two mean by individuality?

Dy: I suggest that we exclude lower-order variations from our definition of individuality. These appear to be increasing in frequency and in degree. We might distinguish post-socialized individuality from pre-socialized individuality and focus on the former—those who have internalized the values of their society and then transcended them.

Curt: That helps. But, in addition, I would suggest that we suspend the rule that discussants should define their terms. It is not possible to catch the crux of individuality in a net of words to which all of us would subscribe. Everybody has his own preferred type of extraordinary character which depends upon his standards of human worth more than it does upon the recognition of a public fact. Consequently, there will be no consensus in respect to individuality. But since we have, nonetheless, been urged to talk about it and since it is pleasanter to talk than to remain mute, we might as well come out with what comes up. As a starter, here is what comes up in me. A real individual is self-substantial, a man who builds on his own genes for better or for worse, a man who would hate to be anybody but himself, a man who likes the flesh that sticks to his own ribs, a man who shows his natural face and does not care too much how others like it. A real individual consults himself, waits for the inner lift or fall of feeling, the dependable intimation, the touch of ages, the daemon's voice, the vital omen—and consults others only at the end of his own wits. He is apt to find that an idea ceases to concern him as soon as it is generally accepted. He is a man who, like the Abbé Coignard, expands with joy in the heart of an enchanted solitude. He is a hive of surprising thoughts and judgments. It is not easy to predict what he will say. He cuts through a lot of chatter and gets down to fundamentals quickly. And when it comes to the last ditch, he may—thinking of William Lloyd Garrison—proclaim, "I will be heard," or cry out "No in thunder" as Herman Melville put it. By the way, have you got the works of Thoreau in this library of yours?

(At this point I led Curt—architect and bibliophile—to my Thoreau shelf and then rejoined the others while he looked for some passage he but half-recalled.)

MARC: No, in thunder. Sounds a little childish. In some infants No is the first understandable word to be pronounced. Negativism is social suggestibility in reverse. Which reminds me, Dy. Several studies have shown that college men of our day are much more inclined to say Yes than to say No to statements on a questionnaire, regardless of the content of the statements. And as a result of this great predominance of yea-sayers, many positive correlations among variables have been reported which, it now appears, do not indicate the relationships that they first appeared to indicate. The determining factor is yea-saying or nay-saying. Now, according to recent results obtained by Couch and Keniston, today's small minority of consistent nay-sayers are men of caution, deliberation, moderation, men who cannot subscribe to any extravagant or enthusiastic statement. Not one of them says No in thunder.

CURT: Excuse me, I didn't hear what you said. But let me interrupt a moment to read a couple of quotations from Thoreau which express, as in a parable, the essence of individuality as I envisage it. Listen to this: "The greater part of what my neighbors call good I believe in my soul to be bad, and if I repent of anything, it is very likely to be my good behavior. What daemon possessed me that I behaved so well?" Thus speaks the author of Gandhi's special inspiration, *Civic Disobedience*. The next one is even better:

In proportion as our inward life fails, we go more constantly and desperately to the post office. You may depend on it, that poor fellow who walks away with the greatest number of letters, proud of his extensive correspondence, has not heard from himself this long while.

MARC: Good enough. But we've been asked to talk about the individuality in our own time, to say whether we think it has been going up or going down these last decades.

CURT: Going down, going, going, gone. That's my point. There are no Thoreaus around. Nowadays, no one enjoys hearing from himself in solitude.

MARC: Come now, Curt. You have claimed—and I agree—that there is no generally agreeable definition of individuality, which means that we don't know what we're talking about; and, if we don't know what we're talking about, we can't measure its decline or be sure of its decease. Conceivably we might examine samples of the population of the United States and attempt to measure, in a multiplicity of ways, the range of spread of differences in respect to certain selected variables. Then we might compare our findings with the results obtained in 1900 and in 1925 and come to some tentative conclusions about recent trends. But no such estimates exist for 1900 or 1925, and the merit of a procedure of this sort is very dubious. Anyhow, it has not been undertaken in a systematic manner and, so far as I know, no social scientists are contemplating such a study. In short, it is quite impossible to say anything on this issue that deserves serious attention. Whoever speaks on it must base his opinion on an extremely small sample of impressions, most of them secondhand and, ten to one, he will be telling you more about himself—his predilections, the people that he sees, and the books that he has read—than he will about the health of individuality in these United States.

CURT: Oh, that wet blanket of social science methodology damping the fires of good talk! Glad I abandoned chemistry. Glad I'm now an architect suckled in a creed outworn. But here, as I see it, we are in accord. We agree that we are not talking about public facts, about anything that can be measured. We are merely communicating our impressions based, as you say, on certain predilections. But, then, when you come right down to it, what is healthier than gaily airing one's half-suffocated predilections? Is there anything better to be done?

MARC: Well, we don't have to go so far as to abandon all reference to reality and let reason acquiesce to an orgy of emotion. Surely, we are not talking in a complete vacuum of facts. There are numerous phenomena—actions of personalities and of types, events and classes of events—that can be roughly assessed along a continuum from sameness to novelty, or, as Dy has suggested, along a continuum from extreme post-socialized conventionality to extreme post-socialized individuality. Dy, if we took this as our criterion, what would you say? Has individuality been mounting or declining in America?

DY: Mounting, I would guess, in many areas, but declining appreciably in others. I have found that Riesman's perceptions are unusually astute and generally dependable. Anyhow, I agree with him. Some of the killers of individuality have already been convicted and their various stratagems exposed, by the editors of *Fortune*, for example. Do you want the textbook inventory? Urbanization, mechanization, structuralization, systematization, bureaucratization, departmentalization, special—

CURT: Skip it. Aren't all those "zations" pretty well accepted?

DY: Maybe. But still this happens to be one area for which some documentation is now available. Marc, of course, is familiar with Max Weber's analysis of bureaucracy and with Robert Merton's paper on the subject, which suggests that the degree of conformity imposed by bureaucratic structure so restricts individual resourcefulness and inventiveness that the full potentiality of the organization is never realized. Although there is no direct evidence to support this proposition, its reasonableness is certainly appealing.

CURT: I won't deny that bigness and social structure are important factors. But dig down a bit, go back to the plain language of Charles Peirce, language that is too unflattering to be tolerable to most people of our time. He said what we are either too polite or too ashamed to say without a euphemism, namely, that greed is the taproot from which this society gains its huge momentum. Charles Peirce, by the way, was an individualist of the first magnitude, of such magnitude that he was denied a professorship at Harvard. But I was speaking of greed. Combined with greed is the suspicion—despite contrary secret hopes and pious sentences—that there is no higher life in store for us in heaven, and, consequently, all desired upward locomotion must be achieved before death closes the account, some years before, in fact, so as to allow time for the enjoyment of whatever elevation one has been able to attain. Thus, speed is of the essence. The result is hectic greed embracing the machine as the quickest and surest means to a secular beatitude—a villa in Florida, let us say. The objects of greed's craving being imbedded in the earth—fertilities of all kinds, coal, oil, and minerals—this good earth, bountiful mother of us all, becomes the target of our importunate and aggressive zeal. We level her forests, despoil her soil of its fecundities, assail her abdomen with our bulldozers, tear her womb apart, and seize with frantic, lustful hands her stores and stores of substance, draw off her fluid energies, and then leave, in place of her fair skin, a covering of dust, ashes, slag, and devastation. Finally, in blasphemy, we cancel her incomparable beauty with the most hideous advertisements of her products fashioned to the public taste.

MARC: Greed is not limited to Americans. It is as old as the human race. And in this country it is balanced by an extraordinary generosity. But what has all this got to do with individuality?

CURT: I'm coming to that and it's nothing new to you. For everyone can see that in the course of this partnership between machines and men, the two become mutually influential and dependent: machines produce men in their own image and men produce machines in their own image, and pretty soon it is difficult to decide who's who in America —who deserves what credit in this great web of humanized mechanics and mechanized humanics. Anyhow, a requirement for this speed of greed is frictionless cooperation, cooperation which approaches the perfection of a fine engine—the ethics of bureaucracy, as Dy said. Here individuality is out of place—sand in the ball bearings—and so we get the sapless men whose souls and wives are bought and paid for by the giant corporation. When the successful pair eventually reach Florida or California, they find another giant mechanism arranged to deal out pleasure with merry-go-rounds of gaudy, barren entertainment. Being too tired and too automatized to find their own ways to joy, the two of them turn for stimulation to these paltry and expensive shows of culture. That's the gist of it.

MARC: Personally, I think you're way off base, dreaming a dream of a dream of a distemper. Is it the bourbon or have you become inebriated by your own mixed and blended metaphors?

CURT: It's your serious behavioral science face which instigates my mind to hop, skip, and jump this way. But don't be so stodgy as to think that your ponderous jargon can convey the palpable realities any better than my outdated rhetoric. Anyhow, didn't you rule that we should air our personal bents and biases?

MARC: Sure. But I also suggested that passion without reference to reality would get us nowhere fast.

DY: It seems to me that what Curt has been saying in an exaggerated way is informed by a large measure of truth, stale though it may be.

MARC: The materialism of American culture is a tiresome stereotype.

CURT: When people don't like a characterization of themselves, they call it a stereotype. If materialism is a stereotype, so also are energy, enterprise, individualism, pragmatism, ambition, competitiveness, humanitarianism, love of change, optimism, et cetera, et cetera. If materialism is not included, we will be disregarding what is the most harmfully consequential of current American assumptions, namely, that money can do pretty nearly anything—make friends, win a wife and hold her, carry a man up the ladder to the Social Register, achieve happiness and renown, and, to top it off, gain a conspicuous death notice, a coffin of the best mahogany, and an elegant, well-attended funeral. But more fatal than these is the assumption that the friendship of other nations can be bought, that peace can be bought, and, in the last extremity, that wars can be won with money. And as for my exaggerating a stale truth, Dy, my sketch of the condition of affairs is mild in comparison with Max Weber's. Luckily for my argument, our host subscribes to the *Partisan Review*, and the spring issue is here beside me. It contains an appreciation of *The Organization Man* by one of my favorite perceptors and evaluators of the American spectacle, Philip Rieff. Just let me read one short sentence selected by Rieff from the final paragraphs of the *Protestant Ethic*. Weber is writing of the possible or probable destiny of the Protestant who has pursued salvation and won wealth, of the moral athlete who has created a world of abundance, stripped of all religious or ethical significance, and then become complacent in it. Weber surmised that the last stage of this cultural development might be described as follows: "Specialists without spirit, sensualists without heart; this nullity imagines that it has attained a level of civilization never before achieved." No doubt you are both familiar with this indictment; but you may have forgotten, as I had, the word "nullity." It stuck in my gullet, and I found I could not cram it any further against the stomach of my humanity. The point I wish to make is that my own appraisal of bureaucratized Western man is far less contemptuous than Weber's and is to be viewed in relation to a profound hope that we Americans might compose and recompose a culture that would be, in Shelley's words, "an echo and a light unto eternity."

Dr: Maybe you are asking too much of human nature, too much of a culture that is sustained by an entire population rather than by a small elite of educated people with slaves, subjects, or domestic servants to carry on while they devote themselves to higher things. But let us return to individuality and conformity and consider how it comes about that the giant corporations find so many docile candidates for automation. How can we explain the susceptibility to regimentation which results in the Organization Man as William Whyte describes him—the sincere tie and the bribed wife? A good many of my psychiatric colleagues believe as I do that the preparation process starts in infancy. Mrs. Snooks is assured that a solitary child is an unpromising child. If he is not encouraged to be sociable he may fail to get along and get ahead. At the worst he may be heading for schizophrenia, or, if not that, alienation and a marginal existence. Kindergarten teachers are of the same mind. They take hold of Sammy Snooks and, after a season of tears and nay-saying, induce him to participate day after day in peer activity. Everything he does is judged in terms of its effect on the mood and harmony of the All. Pretty soon, Sammy will be announcing to his parents that all the boys are allowed to do this or that, and so he should be allowed to do it, too. Few parents have anything that will stand pat when faced by this announcement, false though it may be. Do they want to have their children suffer ostracism because of being different from their playmates? Are they equipped as parents to shoulder the responsibility for that amount of young humiliation? No. And so emancipation occurs much earlier than it did, say, fifty years ago. It occurs before the child has been able to establish a steady character of his own, and what he does with all the others of his age is to form a kind of personality which is responsive to every current of collective feeling, emanating, in most cases, from the more spontaneous, confident, and aggressive members of the gang. Lacking an inner guiding conscience, each becomes fearfully dependent on consensuality for direction, justification, and security; and, when, later on, after school and college, one of the more ambitious ones—possibly just married and in need of cash —goes to some corporation for a job, he has nothing in himself alone which is solid enough to keep him true when he meets the prescribed formulas and rituals. He succumbs step by step, as Marquand has so accurately portrayed for us, and in due course wakes up one morning to the fact that he has reached the point of no return. This, in brief, is the conclusion of those of us who go along with Riesman. But it should be added that the majority are conformists by definition; and where, pray, are conformists better placed than in giant corporations?

CURT: Dy, I believe you are in my camp. You have practically admitted that there are no real individuals today, one reason for this being that parents make their babies play with other babies as soon as they can toddle. Growing up in company, at school, and after school outside their homes, they remain amorphous—like interpenetrating colloids without membranes—no one knowing exactly where his self begins or ends and other selves leave off or start. No shells are built and so the heat of life becomes dispersed and, in accordance with the Second Law as I recall it, entropy increases; and eventually everyone begins to feel lukewarm and lonely, and hurries here and there in quest of warmth through social contacts. But there is no real warmth available, only bright shows of warmth—a hearty greeting, a synthetic smile, and a heartier farewell, with some talk of contacts in the future. Today the strategy of sociability is that of hit and run, a transit of rapid interactions. Differentiation is impossible without privacy, without solitude, without a heat-and-thought-retaining shell. One has to learn to stoke his own furnace, to keep the home fires burning, in cycles of excitement and quiescence, if individuality and creativity are to flourish. Colloidal men are running things today—a lot of good guys talking and laughing with each other, in factories, in lunchrooms, in committee rooms, around the cabinet table—everyone in conference with everyone but himself. These conferences are jolly because everyone has learned the art of reaching pseudo-agreements by avoiding basic issues. In this process, everything which is distinctive, sensitive, and excellent is leveled down and cheapened, and "mediocracy" takes over more oppressively than a tyrant; because it's everywhere at once and, therefore, cannot be attacked, and because it operates, as termites do, by gnawing away at one's foundations. I don't except myself. I engage in endless rounds of trivial exchanges. I suspect there is a fellow in me who likes to see and to be seen, to hear and to be heard—through any medium. Perhaps I am already more than half-seduced and am very near to being a superfluous, dispensable, and unnecessary duplicate. Why do most of us prefer large plate-glass windows, open doors, and open faces? Is it not, in part, because we are half-hollow and have so little in our depths to cherish and keep secret? Please stop me! So much catharsis may be enervating.

MARC: Let me speak! I've listened long enough. Curt, you're getting further and further from the plain facts. Who is blind around here? Don't you see what I see—a tremendous output of really vital variation in this country? Take Darwin's formula for evolution: "Multiply, vary, and be strong." Has any state or nation, weighed in these scales, ever equaled the United States of America today? We have an unprecedented rate of reproduction, unprecedented industrial and military strength, and an unprecedented degree of variation. The never equaled mixture of peoples in this country assures us of the maximal amount of genetical variation—the greatest differences, one might say, among the potential selves to be evolved and actualized. Also, our culture permits a rare degree of freedom of choice in respect to place of residence, marriage, vocation, clothes, mode of speech, and so forth, and our unprecedented level of family economics makes it possible for individuals in great numbers to take advantage of these opportunities. Finally, every American youth is presented with individuality as an ideal. He is both expected and encouraged to become self-reliant, self-sufficient, independent—to act on his own and take responsibility for the consequences. Thus genes, ideal, and opportunity are all favorable to the development of individual variations.

CURT: May I break in?

MARC: If you have to. But you have been ticking quite a bit this evening.

CURT: I just felt compelled to say before you went further, that if too much freedom, too much opportunity comes too young, children blow off steam in noisy, futile ways, and this short-circuits or cuts out the salty inner growth which is the very bone of individuation. Americans run after every opportunity to spend and to be spent; they are eager to go everywhere and see everything; they want to meet and to get along with everybody, and to know what everybody is doing or about to do. They are as keen to see the worst as they are to see the best—more drawn to the worst, in fact. The result is a hypertrophy of tolerance, loss of the ability to identify the meretricious, and, finally, the movement of all high and low values to a common level. If individuality means anything, it means the discovery of one's own peculiar, rooted preferences, the acceptance of the best of these, and enough aplomb to say: *that* thing, *that* person, *that* book, *that* play, *that* idea—whatever it may be—is not within my pale. Americans are defective in their power to refuse, to refuse the second-rate. They want everything and as much as they can get of it, and so come out with thousands of little bits and pieces out of which no coherent picture can be made. As Charles Morris has shown, Americans are not disposed to select for themselves any one of several self-consistent philosophies of life. They want to include in their careers something from them all, no matter how disparate. In short, what I am saying here is that numerous opportunities for free choice, provided at a very early age, combined with the ideal of independence, encourage superficial exhibitions of individuality and thereby check the evolution of more significant variations.

MARC: Curt, your eye is in your mind, and so it fails to catch and hold what's going on around you. I am less introverted and, as I look about, my eyes inform me of originality bubbling and brimming over from a thousand springs. It is most evident, of course, in science, technology, and business. The enormous acceleration of inventiveness presents a problem of the first order: our physical and material environment is being changed so rapidly that our natural capacity for adjustment is already seriously overstrained. If a social philosopher were asked to judge, he would have to say that today there is *too much* rather than too little creativity.

CURT: Come now, you can't rest your case for individuality on the march of technics, the triumphs of mass production. Give your awards to the machine, not to human personality. Individuality is the property of a few persons qua persons, but not of instruments. In your trips across the country, do you ever meet people who astonish you? People who give voice to tastes, ideas, beliefs that you have not heard a dozen times, a hundred times, before?

MARC: Certainly, I have. But now I am pointing to something else—

individuality of thought running into science and its applications. Take man's new artificial organs, servomechanical systems, information systems, logical thinking systems, transmission systems, et cetera, et cetera —products of a veritable epidemic of creativeness. The outcome is not a new biological man or a new social man, but a multiplicity of new sociomechanical units, each composed of a small group of specialists in harmony with a delicate and supremely intelligent, handsome instrument. These astonishing emergents are resultants of numerous individual flights of thought, more particularly of the mental processes that produced the science of cybernetics; and these particular mental processes, you can't deny, are part and parcel of a highly distinctive personality. It appears that we have reached an era when man's formative powers are going into works rather than into self. People seem to feel that each self must be trained and ready to respond from moment to moment—like a servomechanism—to the novel situations that result from all these novel works.

CURT: Marc, you are painting a picture that is more appalling than anything I have read in the Apocalypse. You are telling us that the agent of creative evolution is no longer a man of extraordinary worth, but a superb instrument serviced by a team of robots. May the best team win, and may the nation with the best system of best teams win! This time I surrender unconditionally. I'm going to buy myself a trailer capable of spontaneous locomotion and fill it with a complete complement of artificial organs—everything but heart and sex glands—then teach my wife to implant purposes, both immediate and ultimate, into the assemblage of organs, and see if we, as an emergent unity, cannot go places and see things in Tierra del Fuego. But where is individuality in all this? In the servomechanism with its distinctive final purpose?

MARC: Curt, you remind me of Miniver Cheevy, child of scorn, who loved the days of old and sighed for what was not. In your case it is a Walden Pond complex that engenders detestation of every technical invention since the steam engine. Your genes arranged themselves for living in another age. Bad timing, old boy. You were born too late, not made to appreciate the marvels of physical science. But how about the social sciences, psychology and sociology? Do you deny that creativity of a profound and revolutionary sort occurred in the minds of such individuals as Freud and Jung? Would you not admit that their thoughts and writings have radically changed our views of man and of society? I have often heard you use words that signify things which were undreamed of before their day.

CURT: I suppose I must admit all that. But I notice that you went to Europe for your illustrations of profound revolutionary thought. Can you imagine Freud in Pittsburgh or Jung in a suburb of St. Louis? My knowledge is limited to the odds and ends that I have snatched from you; but the impression I have gained is that the social sciences in America are acting in such a way as to obliterate the individual. What would you say, Dy?

DY: I see what you mean. Social science looks for uniformities in order to arrive at laws or general propositions, each of which is more or less true or probable. Thus in the last analysis it is a matter for statistics to decide. The biggest part an individual can play is to count one, either in confirming or in disconfirming some hypothesis to be tested. A disconfirmist is an annoyance, sometimes an intolerable frustration, to a behavioral scientist, the success of whose endeavor depends on the discovery of regularity. One might say that an unaccountable disconfirmist is to science what an unmanageable nonconformist is to Mrs. Grundy or to government. Laws, in both cases, are constructed to apply to all, but only a majority abide by them. The illegal personalities are generally excluded from science as they are from respectable society. Anyhow, the march of the behavioral sciences in America seems to be moving away from studies of differentiated individuals and toward the discovery of majority trends, dominant patterns, cultural norms, et cetera, et cetera. Numerous variant patterns are inevitably disregarded, and this means that excellence is disregarded, since this, by definition, is too rare to add up to an impressive figure. Thus quality disappears as quantity takes over. Furthermore, the publication of these findings, with their emphatic expositions of confirmist patterns, results in still more confirmity, because there are always thousands of people who want to go along with the majority. It is even conceivable that the mere announcement of a fictitious social law would be enough to make it true in a few years. Having never thought of this before, I am reminded of the young girl who said: "How do I know what I think until I have heard what I have said?" Anyhow, the sheer flow of words seems to have brought me to the notion that the social sciences—excluding psychoanalysis and personality psychology—may be one determinant of the decay of individuality.

MARC: Both of you have missed the point. My contention is that there is more variation and originality, more individuality than there ever has been in this country, but that many fail to recognize it because it is appearing in new and unfamiliar guises. In the first place, as I said before, it takes the form of creativity, inventiveness, ingenuity, going into works rather than into self. In the second place, it occurs quite frequently in groups, small congenial groups. For example, scientists have not only learned that cooperation is required for the solution of most problems, but they have also come upon a way of thinking fruitfully in company. There is still a great deal of individual, solitary contemplation; but it might be said that within the last twenty years, the group has become the carrier of life, the unit of variation, the spearhead of evolution. A group may have individuality. In the third place, today uniqueness is not limited to a few outstanding persons; it is more evenly distributed. Instead of a dozen isolated peaks rising from a flat plain of commonplaceness, we see a great number of hills and a few mountains, a quite admirable range of heights, something like the Alleghenies. When people recall the American past in this connection they are apt to think of a few rare wonders—Emerson, Thoreau, Melville, Whitman —and such tough veterans of self-assertion as John Brown of Osawatomie. But they forget the enormous incubus of conventionality that burdened the contemporaries of these men. Today we may have fewer snow-capped Matterhorns of individuation, but we have a multitude of Snowdons and Mt. Washingtons.

DY: Here I agree with Marc. Have either of you ever tried to push your way through the magazines and secondary literature of America from the Revolution to World War I? There is not one distinctive taste or scent from start to finish. Style is the acid test. For it is among writers that one expects to find the clearest symptoms of individuality, men who are free agents by profession, men whose very livelihood depends on originality. And if you say that nineteenth century authors of the second and third order curbed their imaginative powers because they knew that originality would not bring in bread, then my point is confirmed. In the nineteenth century even appreciators of individuality were scarce as black swans. Today, on the other hand, there are countless books, plays, magazines—even newspapers—in which one finds fresh, animating phrases and novel ways and modes of thought that are as wine to the spirit. Indeed, they come in such abundance that we forget that they were not there from the beginning.

MARC: Hurray, you're coming over to my side! By the way, have you read Russell Lynes's description of what he calls the "Upper Bohemians" of our time? No? I believe he would include you and Curt in this category. In A Surfeit of Honey, Lynes points out that the Upper Bohemians represent a new and unusually cohesive subculture in American society, dissociated in large measure from the race for material success. Pertinent to the present issue is the large scope of interests among these people, their relaxed tolerance of wide variations in styles of living, but more especially the fact that they prize individuality as much as anything so long as it does not savor of fanaticism. Upper Bohemians—publishers, writers, lawyers, architects, educators, and humanists generally—abound in our larger cities. There may be no Thoreaus or Emily Dickinsons among them; but they certainly include any number of unique characters, some, indeed, who are far more eccentric and far more iconoclastic in their judgments than either Thoreau or Emily Dickinson. And as for eccentricity, in what other country of the world could you find so many wacky religious sects, art colonies, and utopian communities as you do in California?

DY: Are you thinking of the hills around Los Angeles?

MARC: Yes, and other places. Carmel thirty years ago, for instance, and today, Big Sur. But now I am reminded I have some concrete data, a few more twigs of evidence to support my argument. Excuse me while I get my briefcase.

CURT: There is one image of individuality which comes to mind quite often. I received it from Samuel Butler, an individual in his own right: "Life is like playing a solo in public and making up the music as you go along."

DY: Yes, I like that one. Three or four centuries before Butler a man did not have to piece together his own music. He was content, yes, proud, to play as one member of an orchestra the sublimest music of the West, the music of the celestial choir transmitted to him by pope, priest, or pastor. But after the Age of Reason and of Revolutions, a man of mettle felt that it was up to him to make up something for a solo.

Today he is not called upon to make this effort. It is done by little groups in a condition of *participation mystique*, swaying as one body to the music of the mass media. By the way, when we were talking about groupism and peerism a little while back, we should have stressed the fact that most of our teen-age aggregates are, in large part, bound together by an anti-authoritarian, anti-father compact—like the G.I. culture of World War II. This is of profound significance, because, after World War I, in conjunction with anti-authoritarian and anti-father sentiments, came strong currents of antipathy against Puritan and Victorian morality, against God the Father, especially the Father-Son motif, and, indeed, against the expression of any of our world's once elevating and inspiring ideals. Within a few years scores of slang words were born —eyewash, baloney, and many cruder ones—which voiced the contempt of the younger generation of those days for all the shining statements which had heartened the endeavors of Americans since the founding of this country. The G.I.'s would not say that they were fighting to make the world safe for democracy or anything of the sort. To them, *that* was nothing but baloney. They fought because they were drafted and they fought for self-respect and for the respect of their company of buddies, and, generally speaking, with the minimum of manifest respect for the whole tribe of officers. Perhaps this may be attributed, in part, to the fact that first-generation children have had to repudiate, so far as possible, the authority—the old ways, modes of speech, discipline, religion, and so forth—of their un-American fathers in order to get along and get ahead in school. Anyhow, we have today a population of young people who are solidly individualistic in at least one sense: they are not disposed to see anything that deserves reverence, or to feel that there is anything higher than their own interests, or to respond to any statement which seems to call for selfless effort. Anaerobic organisms, I would say, for whom the oxygen of age-old inspiration is of no avail. But enough of that. Here is Marc with an armful of granite data.

MARC: Not much in the way of evidence, merely a few pebbles. I have been reading the autobiographies of college men for almost thirty years, more than a thousand of them. And I have gained the impression that individuality is more evident than it used to be at this age. I happened to be carrying home a few autobiographies which were handed to me today, and glancing at the section in which the student gives some account of his philosophy of life, I noted a good many statements that accord with my previous impression. Let me see now. O Lord, the first one illustrates the opposite—groupism, I suppose.

The greatest joy and the greatest meaning seem to be the results of interaction with other people—this existence in the group is the realest thing we know.

But that one is exceptional. Let me read a few others at random, each from a different student:

Real freedom only comes in divorcing oneself from others. In the group the individual tends to become an amalgam of many people, beliefs, wants.
There is no philosophy worth having save that which one arrives at himself.
The vilest thing that can happen to a person is the subjugation of his will to another person.
I do not consider my state of happiness, real or imagined, to be in any way dependent on or related to what I think of other people or what they think of me.
Whether I ever go to Alaska or not depends on whether or not I feel the Southwest has become too tame. Wherever I live, though, I shall always stand for complete freedom and self-sufficiency of the individual.
My philosophy of life, in general, is live and let live. That is, I'll do what I want and other people can do what they want, and neither of us should give unwanted interference to the other.
Independence shows that one has sufficient knowledge to pick with discrimination. Of course, I mean unpretentious independence, for it reflects imagination.
The only meaning that an individual can find in life is the meaning that he creates in his own separate existence.
There must be a solemn trust with the will, that no backsliding into outwardly determined values will occur.
I want to touch the solid ground of unvarnished reality and sheer stark existence, instead of wasting time on the tinny superstructure of society and perhaps adding an ornament to it.
The doctrine that I preach is of independence, independence from other people, places, institutions.

CURT: Of course your samples are not representative of the country at large. All of them are written by Harvard undergraduates. Furthermore, they are avowals of an ideal, part of a philosophy of life, and, as I have often heard you say, sentiment and action may be exactly opposite. In the United States we have had the myth of individuality from away back and also, in some measure, individuality in practice. But now only the myth remains.

MARC: You seem intent on reminding us that you were a pallbearer at a funeral, despite the fact that we have pretty much agreed that the features of individuality are not readily distinguishable. I suspect that the body you interred was that of your singularly favored type—the I-am-the-captain-of-my-soul type—and that you have overlooked other types, the types which are prevalent today. For example, one uniformity running through this last collection of autobiographies and philosophies is a high degree of self-centeredness. One can find no intimations of the prospect of deriving happiness through self-forgetful work or through dedication to a cause. Each writer is for himself, first and foremost; although a large proportion of them say that the greatest satisfactions come from interacting with their fellows. They do not think of themselves as citizens, as parts of a larger whole, as members of a world community, or as carriers of culture. Effort, as they see it, will be devoted to the satisfaction of their private needs. Isn't this one type or one index of individuality? All of them implicitly or explicitly affirm that the self, every self, is of supreme worth, and that each person is wholly responsible for his own self and only for his own.

CURT: That fits in quite well with what Dy was saying while you were looking for your papers. He called them anaerobic because they lived and preferred to live without the oxygen of edifying words and poetry, words implying reverence or sacrifice. But I wouldn't favor correlating individuality with egotism. Self-love is universal. Its great strength is taken for granted in the Second Commandment: Love thy neighbor as thyself. This would be a mean injunction if self-love were feeble or inconstant. But, anyhow, individuality is not mere self-centeredness in my books. It is not the insubordination of a child or the hell raising of an adolescent. That would be individuality of a lower order, the species we are disregarding. Higher-order individuality is a veritable accomplishment, closely related to the development of identity as Erikson describes it in his incomparable manner. Dy, what is your audit?

DY: To tell the truth, individuality as a value, as a boast, as a stead for pride, strikes me, in certain moods, as naive, shallow, and pretentious. It lacks the depth dimension. As an ideal it plays a strategic role, no doubt, during those years in a young man's life when he must discover his own nature, select a vocation appropriate to his talents, and, in so doing, grow in a differentiated way out of the family husk in which he was imbedded and out of the colloidal matrix—as Curt calls it—of his adolescent peer group. But beyond that, it is too apt to lead on to illusory self-inflation, false poses, and counterfeit aggrandizements—tumors of the self. The individualist says "I" with a special stress and accent. "*I* did this. *I* did that"—always "I," as if he had never come upon the fact that he could not do any of these things without the participation of Nature, and also, in most cases, of other people. It seems that he has never humbly acknowledged that he is pretty nearly powerless vis-à-vis his own body and vis-à-vis the greater part of his personality and mind. He is not able to decide that the heart shall keep on beating. He is not able to decide that a plentiful supply of energy and enthusiasm will be available next morning. He is not able to decide to fall in love. He is not able to decide that fresh and significant ideas shall spring to mind to enliven his conversation or to advance his thought. He cannot choose to choose what he will choose. From first to last he is utterly dependent for his being, for the capacity to sense, feel, think, and act, for the delight of living, upon the perfect orchestration of billions of uncontrollable, irreversible, and inscrutable goings on within him. And yet his objective knowledge of these facts does not bring him around to wisdom. He takes it all for granted: accepts it without reverence, without gratitude, and without grace. The fault, as I see it, lies in a kind of hydrocephalus of the self. The self shouts, "I am the master of my fate!" and a minute later one tiny embolus slits the thin-spun life and puts an end to all that nonsense.

MARC: I don't get the stroke of your thought. Are you saying anything less trite than the fact that the mind is dependent on the body: no brain, no consciousness?

DY: You blunt my point. I am saying, or trying to say, that one necessary experience on the path to a mature felicity is full acknowledgment of our utter and unutterable dependence upon nature, within us and without, the sun, the earth and all that it contains, and upon each other. Acknowledgment of this in one's very marrow gives rise to that cluster of feelings—wonder, awe, reverence, gratitude, prayerfulness, and hope—which constitute the passion center of religion, the passion center, I would say, of the best lives in their profounder workings. Here the myth of individuality is a hindrance. Its high place in the American scale of values may, indeed, be one determinant of our emotional retardation, our perpetual juvenility, and, more recently, of our deficiency of first-order admirations, our incapacity for high seriousness.

CURT: We've gone around the clock with our conception of individuality. All the individuals in my hall of fame were marked by an unusual capacity for reverence, for first-order admirations, and for high seriousness. This was the very thing which brought them forth. It was in the name of their admirations that they spoke out and held their ground against hell and high water. Now you are telling us that the ideal of individuality is an impediment to such loyalties.

DY: Yes. It seems that I have talked myself into a contradiction. How can we explain it? It might be due to the fact that in the old days individuality emerged as an ideal *after* a young man had acquired conscience, character, and the habits of reverence and seriousness; and so when he cried, "I will be heard," he was more likely to have something valuable to say and fight for. Nowadays, the idea of individuality comes up much earlier. It starts and gains momentum at the breakfast table when the boy of four, with nothing of great moment in his head, shouts, "I will be heard," and his father pipes down and listens to him. Later, the boy's so-called individuality is manifested as resistance—sometimes apathy and affectlessness—toward nearly everything parents or teachers may present to him as worthy of their devotion. Could we say, Curt, that, in the past, individuality was based on a commitment to an ideal bigger than itself; whereas today it is founded on the refusal to accept the yoke of any such commitment?

CURT: The distinction seems valid. But I would call today's thing egotism, as I said earlier, rather than individuality. I don't see anything commendable in apathy and listlessness, or in acts of arrogance and violence, or in boastful and boisterous displays. When the brash fellow finally gets the floor, nothing comes out of him that is worth attending to.

MARC: I must interrupt here, if you don't mind, to tell you the story of an undergraduate which illustrates your point—someone speaking from an empty mind. He told me that for ten years he had enjoyed a recurrent fantasy of his standing on a high hill and addressing a multitude of people. When I asked him what he said to them, he was abashed and replied that this had never occurred to him. His fantasy did not include ideas or spoken words but the multitude were spellbound nonetheless. But, Dy, please go on with what you were saying a while back.

DY: I was discussing the myth of individuality as a juvenile illusion which lacks the depth and time dimension, lacks imagination and perspective. Take, for example, the type of individualist who privately or publicly boasts of his maturity, his degree of self-development—much as if the newborn child, vaunting in its first thrill of dawning consciousness, cried, "Look at me! Look what I have done! Look at this body and this soul that I have formed and shaped!" I'll admit, of course, that every child and every adult is unique. But, to a far greater extent, he is acting out a part from birth to death which nature and society long ago composed for him. Probe down a layer. Is it not clear that in a very real sense, the growth, continuation, and decline of every one of us is a recurrence, a recapitulation, a repeat performance, of a drama that is ancient as the hills, ancient in its concatenations of basic thematic patterns, despite innumerable variations in the expression and execution of these patterns? Seen in this light, the individualist's belief that his dispositions and decisions are his own and that the course of his life is determined largely by the knowledge he acquires and the choices he makes among alternatives—this belief eventually loses its sustaining power and one comes to the far richer conception of an underlying myth—full of warmth and wonder—which one is living out as part of the evolutionary process. This realization is very rare today for obvious reasons, one of which being the absence of fitting symbolic sagas exemplifying roles. How many of us are capable of making up a widely relevant form of music for ourselves in progress? There are scores of new old myths waiting impatiently for poet-authors, as Keats half-knew when he spoke of soul making and of Shakespeare's life as allegory; but, unhappily, our poets are all engaged with chaos. In the meanwhile, many of us are starving without knowing it, living on half a lung and half a heart.

CURT: Are you wavering? You seem to be describing my notion of individuality, not its opposite. I thought your intention was to point out the limitations of individuality as an ideal.

DY: No and yes. By my lights, individuality is something to be built for the sake of something else. It is a structure of potential energies for expenditure in the service of an idea, a cultural endeavor, the betterment of man, an emergent value. I am proposing that an individual self is made only to be lost—that is, only to pledge itself to some enterprise that is in league with a good future, and thereby find itself once more; but this time as the actor of a living myth, an instrument of culture.

MARC: You admit that the thing you're talking about is very rare. Shouldn't we, then, omit it from our present survey?

DY: I suppose yes. But I would like to register a protest against the exclusion of everything which does not sum up to a big figure. If we adopted that policy we would be restricting ourselves to the most commonplace phenomena. For example, a survey that left out the artists of America—and by artists, I mean poets, novelists, playwrights, painters, and musicians—would, in my opinion, be seriously unbalanced. Destiny has brought us to the position of top power among the free nations of the world, and, heretofore, top power—top power for a century or more —has generally consisted not only of military strength and material resources but also of a high level of civilization, a germinating center of humanistic and artistic excellence to which people were drawn for refreshment, enchantment, and invigoration. Where do we stand in these respects in the eyes of those nations of whose friendship and respect we are not unreasonably desirous? Below normal expectations, I would say. We have painters, poets, and novelists whose works are popular in Europe and in Russia, too; but most of the best of them are spiritual isolates at odds with the temper of the country at large.

CURT: I agree. And I'll lay a small bet that none of the participants at the conference on American values will attempt an estimate of the values of American writers. No matter how much appreciation of art and literature they may have as individuals, the speakers will omit all this from their surveys of our culture. It is to the artists, poets, and dramatists that we turn for the best representations of the great cultures of the past, why not here and now? Because American artists aren't connected or aren't thought to be connected with the works.

DY: Yes. In this country, I would say, one can discern two opposite yet interdependent currents of endeavor. The first is the more obvious one described by Marc: a tremendous amount of energy and creativeness engaged in science, in technology, in industry, and in business generally. In these spheres of activity, cooperation is essential, and the variant individual, qua individual, is very apt to be a misfit. There are, however, abundant opportunities, in all parts of these enterprises, for individual thought, especially when directed toward technical innovations and improvements. But all this massive material productivity is peripheral to the good life, and its tremendous rate of growth, accelerated by a cynical, nerve wracking, and relentless barrage of advertising, its very success in supplying creature comforts, its penetration into every sphere of action, is canceling the possibilities of a good life. It is without heart and without taste. I call it peripheral, because it is concerned with means without definition of desirable final ends, with strategies in the absence of a vision, with tactics in a value vacuum. At the center, in the hearts of men, things are going in the opposite direction, or what appears to be the opposite direction. Here one finds—in place of zest, integration, and construction—anxiety, neurosis, apathy, alienation, distrust, regression, and despair. As always, it is the artists and the poets who set forth most accurately the inner human situation, a condition of which the rest of us may not become aware for two or three decades. But by now we are all familiar with the thesis which the great majority of our better writers have been steadily representing to us, namely, that things fall apart, as Yeats expressed it; the center cannot hold. In other words, Siva is dancing in the phase of dissolution and destruction, rather than in the formative phase; and artists in legions are devoting their talents to his service. And they are alone no longer. For nowadays, pretty nearly everybody is consumed with interest in discord, violence, and deterioration—in the Blackboard Jungle, teen-age crimes, gangster warfare, psychopathic personalities, idiots, the Mad Bomber, polymorphous sexuality, rape, suicide, infantile complexes, schizophrenia, the Snake Pit, cacophony in music, fragmentations of the human figure in painting, decorticated he-man heroes in works of fiction, four-letter words, alcoholics, dope fiends, and numberless other deviations from fruitful ways of life. And, peculiarly enough by some odd coincidence, physical scientists are concerned, in their own domain, with the decay of uranium nuclei, nuclear fissions, and explosions, asymmetry, and an endless succession of genocidal weapons.

MARC: You sound like one of Jehovah's Witnesses relishing the prospect of Armageddon in the offing. Aren't you drifting away from our objective?

DY: Possibly. But I am a physician, and physicians, by temperament and training, are perpetually alert to signs of present or potential illness.

No matter how ruddy the patient's complexion, how bright the eyes, how supple the muscles, a physician never fails to put his stethoscope to heart and lungs. And so when I examine society I always listen to the sounds that art makes, and the sounds I have been hearing over recent years inform me of a state that is the exact opposite of the outward appearance of that robust energetic giant named American materialism. It is a state of profound antipathy to the whole works—not to one or another aspect of the system, such as bureaucracy or regimentation, but to the basic assumptions and evaluations which underlie the entire show. One large determinant of the artist's repugnance and estrangement must be that the giant is oblivious of his existence and oblivious of his values, and that the spread of the giant's tentacles and the spread of uglification go hand in hand. Anyhow, admiration, which, according to Thomas–Mann, is art's most indispensable emotion, is all but absent in America. "Where it is not, where it withers, nothing more sprouts, all is arid and impoverished." And so our novelists and playwrights occupy themselves with exhibitions of derision and disgust, or in skillfully portraying for us the most sordid conditions and the most debased expressions of human impulse. Such are the works of the best artists—the truest and the most talented—and I find myself very largely in sympathy with their viewpoint and their purposes. What is ominous and lamentable is the abyss between them and the governing institutions of this country. Endless demonstrations and analyses of social pathology coming from the most prosperous nation in the world: what can others think of us? Since there are similar resonating dispositions in large numbers of the reading and theater-going public, some of these writers—though profoundly at odds with their world—have been abundantly remunerated, and a very few, such as T. S. Eliot, Eugene O'Neill, and William Faulkner, have won, in their own lifetimes, the highest laurels, and, in some quarters, a degree of esteem bordering on idolatry. What can we say about the kind of individuality that is manifested by these artists, as well as by many others of the same stamp, would-be artists, or appreciators—the disinherited and alienated Ishmaels and existentialists in our midst?

CURT: This is a problem by itself, too intricate to be dealt with in this context.

MARC: But wouldn't you say that the modern artist and writer in

America is highly individual? When Dy was talking of alienation I couldn't help thinking of several of the autobiographies I have in this collection here. Let me read you one excerpt from an undergraduate's account of his initiation into this zone of the spirit. He writes:

Life tripped along until my junior year in high school. Then I got to know a boy named George—cynical, profound, skeptical, sarcastic, highly intelligent, casual in his manner yet intense in his questioning. And he always questioned. His cynicism infected me, he became my very good, my best friend, the best and closest I ever had. What were we cynical about? Ourselves, our teachers, our world—cynical about the very act of existence. Or rather, the fact of existence, for with us it was a passive experience. We let time and values and actions pass over us like a wash, like a coating of wax. We both had been raised as agnostics, but it was a mild sort of agnosticism, an un-thought-about agnosticism. First of all we turned everybody's religion upside down, and we shouted. We were roundly condemned, but George more, since he shouted more, and louder. That went by the boards and we began on our contemporaries, and on our society. We attacked everything, every person, every institution, with a bitter tooth. Our long secret conversations were rank with contempt. We were full of a magnificent disdain, and we fed it with all the knowledge we could get (and what wouldn't fit we disregarded)—Kafka, D. H. Lawrence, Hume, Rousseau, Voltaire, Shaw, Jung, Freud, Marx.

CURT: There is nothing particularly individual about that. Wholesale romantic nihilism is a common phase or stage of development, which may or may not lead on to individuality. In this case, it is probably rooted in self-disgust.

MARC: Well, I find it very depressing just the same. In fact, I find the present trend of this conversation depressing. Dy, I never realized you were such a pessimist.

DY: I'm surprised to hear that word applied to me, because I don't feel any more pessimistic than a surgeon does when he makes a diagnosis of operable gastric ulcer. It is true that I see some kind of hell ahead of us, and I don't approve of pretending that its occurrence is improbable. But my belief in man's potentialities is not shaken. I know on my own pulses that life can be unutterably ecstatic as well as unutterably serene; and I take comfort in the faith that despite all the sordidness, monotony, defeats, horrors, humiliations, and vulgarities of civilized existence there will be perpetual rebirths of courage and imagination, and that somehow man will break out triumphantly as he has so often in the past. Among us there are just enough salty men and women of extraordinary talent who are responsive to the evolutionary gods within, the angelic orders—just enough of this merit and this genius in our world to come forth in its proper season and redeem an entire culture. Being an American, I am an incurable optimist at heart. My pessimism is superficial.

CURT: Well, it seems that we've anatomized as much of this matter as we can tonight. But, Dy, I *still* can't understand why you dispraise my type of individuality.

DY: Besides the reasons I have given, it is because your type of individuality on a national scale means either isolationism or imperialism, or, if not these, a degree of nationalism which is too possessive and too proud to relinquish enough sovereignty to allow for the effective operation of world law, world government, and world police force—the only possible enduring safeguard against a holocaust of mutual extermination. Of course, the huge paranoid obstacle to world fellowship is Communism, with its implacable ambitions and outrageous strategems; but our cause is greatly weakened by the absence of any announced plan of global unity. Furthermore, I conjecture that the next stage of spiritual development will be inaugurated by another trinity—the Holy Ghost uniting Man and Woman. Your type of individuality is an impediment to both of these saving consummations.

MARC: On the tip of my tongue for the last ten minutes has been the observation that we have talked for a whole evening without once referring to the larger half of our population. Surely, you can't deny that individuality among women has increased by leaps and bounds since World War I. I could cite scores of notable examples and, if need be, rest my whole case on them. But, before we break up, I would like to call attention to a little ground for Dy's surmise. We have collected hundreds of the wish-fulfilling fantasies of undergraduates, in an unsystematic way for over twenty years and in a systematic way since 1953; and we have noted that the three most prevalent positive fantasies today are those of perfect marriage, children, and sexual conquests, in that order. Next come self-sufficiency, benevolent power, public display of intellectual eminence, and athletic glory. These results are in accord with Allport's studies of students' imaginary autobiographies from the present to the year 2000. In striking contrast to students in a dozen other countries, Americans at different colleges do not imagine themselves participating in great enterprises or devoting their energies to some superpersonal goal, either political or cultural. They dream of economic security, a house and a plot of land in the country, a happy family, and peace for a lifetime.

(At this point it seemed to me that my friends had had enough and so I asked them for a summary.)

MARC: Although we have been talking in a vacuum of facts and definitions, my convictions remain unchanged, namely, that individuality of thought going into science, technology, and industry has never even approximated its present level; that America is seething with creativity of many sorts. Also that individuality among women is on the increase.

CURT: Much of what Marc is celebrating is not individuality in the proper sense. It is either cognitive originality, technical inventiveness, or blatant masquerades—a ceaseless flood of talk and clamor from a dozen media, a mammoth pageant of sensational performers, each with his novel stunt or offering. Men of sap and savor have gone out. Today there are no trans-evaluators of basic values.

DY: We have only touched the surface of the matter. Real individuality is an inner state—a continuous experience—which cannot be measured or even described from the outside. But, in any event, it is no longer a problem area in America. It is approximately of the kind and of the degree that our situation warrants. The way is being opened for something better.

THE NATIONAL STYLE

by W. W. Rostow

I speak of the American in the singular, as if there were not millions of them, north and south, east and west, of both sexes, of all ages, and of various races, professions, and religions. Of course the one American I speak of is mythical; but to speak in parables is inevitable in such a subject, and it is perhaps as well to do so frankly. There is a sort of poetic ineptitude in all human discourse when it tries to deal with natural and existing things. Practical men may not notice it, but in fact human discourse is intrinsically addressed not to natural existing things but to ideal essences, poetic or logical terms which thought may define and play with. When fortune or necessity diverts our attention from this congenial ideal sport to crude facts and pressing issues, we turn our frail poetic ideas into symbols for those terrible irruptive things. In that paper money of our own stamping, the legal tender of the mind, we are obliged to reckon all the movements and values of the world. The universal American I speak of is one of these symbols; and I should be still speaking in symbols and creating moral units and a false simplicity, if I spoke of classes pedantically subdivided, or individuals ideally integrated and defined. As it happens, the symbolic American can be made largely adequate to the facts; because, if there are immense differences between individual Americans—for some Americans are black—yet there is a great uniformity in their environment, customs, temper, and thoughts. They have all been uprooted from their several soils and ancestries and plunged together into one vortex, whirling irresistibly in a space otherwise quite empty. To be an American is of itself almost a moral condition, an education, and a career. Hence a single ideal figment can cover a large part of what each American is in his character, and almost the whole of what most Americans are in their social outlook and political judgments.

George Santayana, *Character and Opinion in the United States*

A man's temperament might, perhaps, be defined as the mode or modes of a man's feeling, the struck balance of his ruling desires, the worked-out sum of his habitual predispositions. In themselves, these elements were inscrutable. There were usually too many of them; they were often of irreducible complexity; you could observe only results. . . . The to-be-observed result was a total way of life. As far as the natural self-divisions in a human being would allow . . . this way of life, conditioned all knowledge, all emotion, all action.

James Gould Cozzens, *By Love Possessed*

Prefatory Note. The task of this paper is to make some observations which embrace the five themes around which the Conference is centered.[1] The problems considered by Messrs. Kaplan, Oppenheimer, and Kennan —the clash between good and evil in man as a social animal, between theory and fact, and between order and innovation in human organization—are, of course, common in one form or another to all cultures and societies. How men cope with these among other problems as they go about their business reflects what is here called a national style. If the study of national character is an effort to establish a collective personality, the examination of national style seeks to define how that collective personality reacts to and acts upon its environment. The method of this paper, then, is to link the various themes by relating them not to each other but to the common style which they reflect.

The text is developed in three parts. Part I treats what is here called the classic American style. This style, rooted in nonconformist Britain, emerged distinctively toward the end of the seventeenth century as the imperatives and opportunities of a wild but ample land began to assert themselves over various transplanted autocratic attitudes and institutions which proved inappropriate to the colonial scene. In the eighteenth century, America could produce a Benjamin Franklin, a Thomas Jefferson, an Eli Whitney; and foreign travelers could begin their catalog of American traits, many of which remain recognizable down to the present. In a sense, however, the classic American style came fully to life only as the surge to the West began in earnest after the War of 1812 and the passing from the scene of the generation of Founding Fathers. What Part I tries to establish is the manner in which Americans came to deal with their problems in, roughly, the century after the Battle of New Orleans, or, if you like, in the period between de Tocqueville and Turner.

Part II tries to give the concept of the classic American style a further concreteness by examining certain passages in American history relevant to each of the three initial themes.

Against the background of the latter-day themes—considered by Messrs. Kluckhohn and Murray—Part III considers how the direction and character of change may have altered the classic national style to a degree in recent decades. It poses, finally, the question of how the national style as a whole and recent changes in it strengthen or weaken the society's ability to deal with certain major problems it confronts and is likely to confront over the foreseeable future.

PART I: THE CLASSIC AMERICAN STYLE

The American Household. The classic American style is simply one way of coping with the inescapable dilemmas which are, universally, the substance of organized human life. Among the dilemmas which Americans, like others, have had to face are these: a consciousness of both good and evil in themselves and others, a compulsion to pursue individual advantage and a need to share the values and destiny of a larger community, an awareness of the uniqueness of particular circumstance and a compulsion to generalize, and an inborn instinct for order and continuity in social organization and the requirement of change and innovation in order to survive.

In finding the balances and compromises necessary to live with these dilemmas, men do not generally work out consistent institutions, values, or patterns of action. Neither individuals nor societies appear to be intrinsically well-integrated units. They somehow rock along, when they are viable, in patterns of apparently irrational balance.

In consequence, nations often appear to behave paradoxically when judged by arbitrary norms of consistency. In the case of the United States, we often appear simultaneously as among the most idealistic and the most materialistic of peoples. We are given simultaneously to extreme empiricism in dealing with reality and to applying peculiarly spacious abstractions to particular circumstances. We pride ourselves on efficient administration, while our most effective performances have been *ad hoc*, convulsive responses to acute crises. We elevate the individual uniquely in our social life and values and in our politics as well, but we maintain bureaucratic structures which weigh heavily on him, a political system peculiarly suspicious of personal power, and a set of social conventions which exact a high degree of conformity. The performance of other nations could be similarly evoked in terms of paradox.[2] It is the content rather than the fact of paradox in the American style which concerns us here.

A national style—like the performance of a unique human personality—is likely to be the product of a variety of different elements. W. H. Auden once described T. S. Eliot not as a man but as a household: a high church archdeacon, a wise and passionate old peasant grandmother, and a young boy given to slightly malicious practical jokes, all living somehow together.[3] The performance of nations is like that of individuals in that it combines discrete, fortuitous elements of heredity and environment, interacting, effectively coming to terms with problems (or failing to do so) in a recurrent fashion, building up over time relatively stable patterns of performance.

To understand the content of the American style we must, therefore, establish the nature of the American household. Out of what basic elements did a distinctive American style emerge? Essentially, the classic American style emerged from the interaction of three powerful and persistent elements in the nation's experience: a nationalism and sense of community achieved by explicit commitment to particular ideal concepts of social and political organization, a day-to-day life challenged and dominated by the extraordinarily rich material potentials of the American scene, and a sequence of national life whose continuity and success appeared progressively to validate the initial commitments in the nation's culture and values, permitting innovation to take the form of a sequence of relatively minor, piecemeal adaptations of a stable basic structure.

It is to an examination of each of these three basic components of the classic national style that we now turn.

The Unifying Function of American Ideals. Many great nations have linked their nationality to a sense of mission which transcended their borders: in different ways and at different times the Chinese, Russians, Germans, British, French, and Spanish. The various concepts of national mission have generally been associated with pride in race, culture, cumulative national achievement, effective power, and religion. For limited periods the nationalism of several powers has been associated with a set of abstract ideas about how societies should be organized; for example, that of France and Russia in their postrevolutionary phases. American nationalism is special—in degree at least—because for almost two centuries, in both its domestic and external manifestations, it has been strongly colored by the ideal principles on which American independence was asserted and toward which American society was subsequently committed to aspire.

In certain of the colonies the coming to America itself was associated with religious mission; down to the present, American nationalism has been suffused with a sense of higher sanction for the particular forms of social individualism, political democracy, and private enterprise which we have evolved. As Reinhold Niebuhr has pointed out, the Calvinist and deist traditions converged in this matter, permitting Americans to derive this higher sanction from either divine or natural law.[4] Our social rituals conventionally open with a prayer followed by the salute to the flag—and we have elevated the Plymouth colony, with its special sense of pilgrimage—to a place in our folklore quite disproportionate to its objective role in the making of New England and, ultimately, the nation.[5] In the minds of Americans—and throughout the world— the concept of the American nation retains a dimension of ideological experiment and of ideological leadership.

The "liberty and justice for all" toward which we were committed to aspire took on a special importance and power within the American continental community. These ideal national goals have been the essential device for unifying a society otherwise fragmented by acute individualism, regionalism, and race. We have lacked the cement of hierarchical political and social institutions, a long history, a common race, or even a common religion. But we fashioned national unity out of a mixture of seventeenth-century Protestant values, the dreams of the eighteenth-century Enlightenment, and then, as time moved on, the cumulative experiences and myths we built upon them.

The commitments to govern by methods which left maximum individual freedom and to organize social life on the principle of equality of opportunity have not only given content to American nationhood but, perhaps more important, they have served at all levels as the essential solvent, the source of compromise, the common meeting place in a society otherwise dedicated to the proposition that its affairs should be conducted by vigorous conflict and competition among individual, group, and regional interests.[6] The vagueness of conventional articulation of the national ideals has, in itself, served the important function of permitting a maximum sense of association with the national ethos by groups whose more immediate interests and cultures widely diverged. Historically, our values, like our political institutions, have been federalized; and, in the midst of the diversity of the continent, the narrow but exalted area of national consensus mattered greatly. From the addresses of the President to the after-dinner speech of the most narrowly focused special interest group, the articulation of the society's common values and an evocation of the drama of successful American growth within their orbit play a role which in older societies is covered by the rituals of ancient legitimized tradition.

The role of shared values and of participation in the special adventure of America has thus been more than a substitute for a conventional patriotism. It has played a local and intimate role as well. Americans, living with the heavy weight placed on the individual by Protestant theology, in a society denied (like most other Protestant societies) the cushioning effects of a mediaeval heritage, have had to fashion alternative ways of mitigating the burdens of isolation and personally answerable responsibility. There is some truth in D. H. Lawrence's designation of American democracy as a negative creed: "Henceforth be masterless." [7] Some truth but not the whole truth, for men are lonely and need connections beyond themselves. American individualism has meant, in a sense, merely that we have created a structure of masters different from the clans and the hierarchies, the clearly defined social rituals, the comforting familiar traditions of the Old World. Among our masters are a narrower but perhaps more intense family; a tendency overtly to conform to the will and manners of the political and social majority; a written Constitution elevated to a peculiar sanctity; a nationalism associated with an ambiguous but, in the end, meaningful idealism; a marvellously complex array of voluntary associations, built on the tradition of cooperation and compromise among like-minded equals, a variant of the English concept of liberty. And, as de Tocqueville perceived, the heroic image of the nation's adventure, and an identification with it, was a peculiarly important instrument for unifying a society of detached individuals:

I readily admit that the Americans have no poets; I cannot allow that they have no poetic ideas. In Europe people talk a great deal of the wilds of America, but the Americans themselves never think about them; they are insensible to the wonders of inanimate nature and they may be said not to perceive the mighty forests that surround them till they fall beneath the hatchet. Their eyes are fixed upon another sight: the American people views its own march across these wilds, draining swamps, turning the course of rivers, peopling solitudes, and subduing nature. This magnificent image of themselves does not meet the gaze of the Americans at intervals only; it may be said to haunt every one of them in his least as well as his most important actions and to be always flitting before his mind.[8]

Virtually all cultures create ideals of behavior to which the individual cannot fully or regularly conform. There is nothing unique about the commitment of the American to values which he must, to a degree, violate in order to live in the world as it is. In most societies, however, the political and social life of the community—and its diplomacy—are not so directly tied to explicit moral purposes. Despite the early defeat of theocracy in New England and the lack of an established national church, there remains a sense in which we have continued to identify church and state. This identification of nationhood with a commitment to strive for good purposes accounts for the "moral overstrain"[9] which, Gunnar Myrdal noted, remains a peculiarly powerful engine within American society. It had led a less friendly foreign observer to conclude:

Americanism is not merely a myth that clever propaganda stuffs into people's heads but something every American continually reinvents in his gropings. It is at one and the same time a great external reality rising up at the entrance to the port of New York across from the Statue of Liberty and the daily product of anxious liberties.[10]

The Operator's Way with Ideas. Counterpoised against the society's active commitment to great ideal goals was the character of American life in the classic period: a life of hard, absorbing, material pursuits, executed on the basis of individual initiative, conducted to individual advantage.

The nation has been extremely rich in land and other natural resources in relation to its population. It was enormous in scale relative to means of communication over the nation's formative period. It presented for more than two and one-half centuries the challenge and possibility of an open frontier; and, for a full three centuries, the American environment made economically attractive to many a virtually unobstructed flow of immigration. In this setting individual effort and competence yielded high returns in economic welfare, the attainment and expansion of which drew off the bulk of the society's talent and energies.

The attraction of economic life was, however, negative as well as positive. In the classic century—and notably after the Civil War—the society's internal structure and relations to the outside world were such that positions in neither church nor state represented roles of great national prestige and authority, let alone affluence. Men came to seek in the adventure of the American economy—in the test of the market— not only material advantage but also the sense of power, achievement, and status elsewhere granted by a less monolithic, more heterogeneous scale of values.

The mobility of American life, the lack of stable connection with family and place, heightened the attraction and psychological importance of individual achievement. The divorce of the individual from a sense of direct connection with a stable, structured community was further increased by the flow of immigrants. The problems and pace of adjustment varied, of course, with each wave and source of immigration and social class of immigrant as well as with the region and community within which the immigrant settled. Despite great variation, however, between the hungry forties and World War I each wave of immigration faced a pattern of adjustment to the prevalent values and culture of the nation which was, by and large, accomplished by generational stages. In this process of adjustment the demonstration by the individual of effective performance in economic and political markets played a substantial role. The man who could solve palpably urgent material problemss, organize and operate profitably a productive enterprise, deal effectively with the day-to-day compromises and accommodations of local social and political life thus rose in status; his operational cast of mind came to dominate the American scene, a cast of mind biased toward the assessment by individuals of concrete, particular problems, empirical in method, pragmatic in solutions.

But men have a need and instinct to generalize their experience, to organize, somehow, the chaos around them; and when Americans, busy with limited practical chores, building a new continental society, reached out for larger abstractions they tended to balloon out concepts derived from personal, practical experience. They generalized what they intimately knew. De Tocqueville described vividly how it came about that a nation of individualist empiricists were powerfully drawn to a particular use of highly abstract concepts:

The Americans are much more addicted to the use of general ideas than the English and entertain a much greater relish for them. . . . He who inhabits a democratic country sees around him on every hand men differing but little from one another; he cannot turn his mind to any one portion of mankind without expanding and dilating his thought till it embraces the whole. All the truths that are applicable to himself appear to him equally and similarly applicable to each of his fellow citizens and fellow men. Having contracted the habit of generalizing his ideas in the study which engages him most and interests him most, he transfers the same habit to all his pursuits; and thus it is that the craving to discover general laws in everything, to include a great number of objects under the same formula, and to explain a mass of facts by a single cause becomes an ardent and sometimes an undiscerning passion in the human mind. . . . When I repudiate the traditions of rank, professions, and birth, when I escape from the authority of example to seek out, by the single effort of my reason, the path to be followed, I am inclined to derive the motives of my opinions from human nature itself, and this leads me necessarily, and almost unconsciously, to adopt a great number of very general notions. . . . Men who live in ages of equality have a great deal of curiosity and little leisure; their life is so practical, so confused, so excited, so active, that but little time remains to them for thought. Such men are prone to general ideas because they are thereby spared the trouble of studying particulars; they contain, if I may so speak, a great deal in a little compass, and give, in a little time, a great return. If, then, on a brief and inattentive investigation, they think they discern a common relation between certain objects, inquiry is not pushed any further; and without examining in detail how far these several objects agree or differ, they are hastily arranged under one formula, in order to pass to another subject.[11]

The American mind, devoted to arduous practical tasks, came, then, also to be equipped with an arsenal of general concepts—often legitimate but partial insights—not rigorously related to each other or to the bodies of fact they were meant to illuminate.

On balance there was little in American life—its content and its values—that encouraged the care and contemplation required to array the intermediate structure of abstractions, test them for internal consistency, and make orderly patterns of thought. Regions, towns, and families did, it is true, exhibit something of the Buddenbrooks dynamics, that is, a third generation (symbolically or in fact) born to both money and social status turning to the life of the mind. But these enclaves of reflective leisure could not hold up for long against the vortex of American life. Even in the older, more stable sections of the East Coast the proportion of first-rate talent that could be drawn and held in intellectual pursuits—as against the claims of business and finance, railroads and the West, shipping, or the law—remained small, down to and beyond World War I.

The national style reinforced itself, moreover, by coming to suffuse the widening process of public education. The principle of free public education was fought through in the North during the pre-Civil War decades; and the new elementary schools reflected a bias toward practical, usable thought, as did the high schools which carried the educational revolution forward from about 1870. In a sense the gospel of education for explicitly practical purposes had been written into national law by the Morrill Act which, in itself, set in motion a self-reinforcing process in the land grant colleges. Toward the end of the classic period, the nation produced in Dewey a philosopher of education who challenged the *status quo*; his challenge was not to the gospel of teaching practical things but to how they were taught and to the cost of existing methods for the individual personality.

When American institutions of higher learning moved toward maturity at the close of the nineteenth century, the architects of the new graduate schools were instinctively drawn to German university models. The Germans—who had left an imprint on American education earlier in the century—placed a high premium on facts and their ordering by precise rules of evidence. Their concept of professional hard-working scholarship harmonized with the instincts of a nation of empiricists entering into an age of industrialism and specialization. The nineteenth-century Germans, when they came to generalize in the social sciences, were, like Americans, prone to broad concepts, only loosely linked to the bodies of fact they so painstakingly compiled. On the whole, Americans pulled up short of the cosmic level of German abstractions, mainly steering clear of universal systems; but a family resemblance remains. We have continued, in a substantial part of the nation's intellectual life, "to explain a mass of facts by a single cause."

American education and intellectual life generally have altered radically in the past several decades. Nevertheless, the dominant, if changing, mode of advanced education is a specialized empiricism whose fragmented results are bound into unity, if at all, by vague high-order generalizations. In the classic period American intellectual and scientific life produced many knowledgeable men; a number of creative insights; and, at its best, figures of wisdom with great sensibility about the nature of the physical world or about how human life is really conducted. But it yielded few general theoretical structures of distinction.

In both its dimensions—a devotion to the ordering of fact in terms of low-order abstraction and a certain vague disorder at high levels of abstraction—the classic American intellectual style has reflected the operator's biases and fitted his needs. Committed to do the best he can in terms of goals defined by the concrete task he has undertaken or the institutions of which he is a part, the operator desires to know in detail his field of action but wishes to be as eclectic as he need be and as unhampered as possible by considerations outside those implicit in his operations.

The classic American manner of dealing with ideas in relation to reality is by no means unique, but it is distinctive. We are evidently a part of the Western European intellectual and philosophical tradition. But cut loose from the surviving mediaeval traditions and institutions of Western Europe, devoted overwhelmingly to building a rich modern society out of an empty continent, we developed an empiricism more acute and energetic than that of our contemporaries.

Continuity, Success, and the Ad Hoc *Formula.* How was the gap bridged between a heightened reliance on idealism to define and maintain a sense of nation and community and a heightened reliance on the vigorous interplay of individual, regional, and group interests to do the day's work? How was the gap bridged between a concentration of effort on particular chores, perceived in terms of low-order abstractions, and the rich but somewhat disorderly kit bag of higher abstractions into which Americans reached for their general organizing principles? The answer appears to be that Americans built their style around the task of solving problems. They were content to leave implicit the moral and philosophic ambiguities which flowed from the method of compromise and experiment. Relatively little attention in formal thought or articulation was given to the common law formulae which emerged from these living processes because of two massive facts: the first is the extraordinary continuity of the American experience over the classic period, a continuity which persists in many domains down to the present; the second, that as a national society the United States was a distinct success. Men are more inclined to examine with intellectual refinement a complex system of which they are a part which is confronted with radically new problems or which is failing than a going concern. And when, toward the close of the classic century, some Americans became more reflective and articulate about their society they tended to elevate "life, experience, process, growth, context, function" over "logic, abstraction, deduction, mathematics, and mechanics." [12] Holmes' dictum embraced more of the national style than the law: "The life of the law has not been logic: it has been experience."

The continuity and success of the national experience had a number of distinct dimensions which converged to produce the result.

First, of course, was the frontier. From the earliest stages of the Massachusetts and Virginia colonies down to the twentieth century—for almost three centuries—the existence of an accessible and productive frontier gave a special reality to the individualistic values of the society, strongly coloring its institutions, from the family to politics, and its culture. The frontier was a long historical process, not a piece of real estate; and American economic, political, and social life consisted in good part of the interplay and balancing of interests between the frontier areas and the more stable communities and institutions that moved in behind the frontier. Certain political patterns (for example, the conflict of interest between soft money, indebted farmers, and hard-money urban property owners, between those who wanted the state to build "public improvements" and those who wanted to lower taxes) are continuous from one end of American history to the other; and Americans became expert at working with them in their many variants. More than that, the concept of the frontier, its existence somewhere to the West, imparted a continuing sense of promise, possibility, and adventure to those who lived their lives out in more ordered eastern settings.

Despite the expanding frontier, however, the task of maintaining unity was, in one sense, eased as time went on. The scale of the nation was roughly matched and then outmatched by the development of communications capable of binding the regions together and giving them unity. In terms of the central problem of achieving and maintaining nationhood among a group of regions with powerful distinctive interests and attitudes, the working techniques of federalism proved essentially viable with only incremental modification.

Similarly, the initial *tour de force* of generating effective (even if barely effective) national action from a dispersed and locally oriented population—in the 1770s and 1780s—has been somehow maintained despite the increase and physical spread of the population, the impact

of diverse immigrations, and the emergence or sharpening of class groupings as industrialization and urbanization proceeded. The attachment of
American nationalism to certain overriding principles of social and
political organization has served adequately as a rallying point for nationhood, surviving the brutal test of civil war. The structure of private social
groupings has continued to ramify and to weave a highly individualistic
and mobile population into a firm social fabric; these groupings have
come to share a widening area of common values. Above all, the canny
insights of the Founding Fathers yielded a constitutional structure
which, when supplemented by the intermediation of a two-party system,
a Supreme Court, and an Anglo-American system of law, has weathered
the gross changes in the scale and character of American society.

The maintenance of national unity was eased, of course, by the degree
of vertical mobility American society continued to offer. Although social
mobility in an urban, industrial setting is a quite different phenomenon
from social mobility in a setting where it consists mainly in the possibility of acquiring cheaply an agricultural homestead, Americans have
made the transition from one to the other without ceasing to envisage
as possible for themselves—and especially for their children—a marked
rise in social and economic status on the basis of individual capabilities
and performance. The nation's evolution has steadily confirmed and re-
confirmed the central unifying concept of equality of opportunity in a
sufficiently meaningful way to maintain loyalty to the nation's social
system.

Both the adjustment to conflicting regional and group interests within
our national society and the process of social mobility have been enormously aided by the sustained growth and high output per head which has
marked the history of the modern American economy. This not only
gave reality to the concept of progress but also permitted men to achieve
compromises in which they shared the increments to communal wealth
without the bitter, corrosive conflicts which come about when men feel
they can rise only at the expense of someone else's decline. In one sense,
it was precisely because the land to the west was not congenial to cotton
culture and could no longer be divided evenly between slave and free
states that the Civil War ensued: the South felt that the nation's extension to the West Coast could only be at the expense of decline or

loss of its way of life. In that sense, the great exception reinforces the general rule.

Above all, the cast of American values and institutions and the tendency to adapt them by cumulative experiment rather than to change them radically has been progressively strengthened by the image of the gathering success of the American adventure, whether it was judged on economic grounds, on grounds of political workability, or in terms, even, of international status. The nation, founded in defiance of a major power, living for a time at bay in both a military and a political sense, came early in its history to feel that its initial concept of a transcendent ideological destiny was justified by the turn of events in the world outside. Until well into the twentieth century there were grounds for believing that the American pattern was, indeed, the wave of the future; and, although somewhat chastened by the experience of recent decades, Americans have by no means wholly lost a sense of mission, based on confidence and pride in the success of a unique moral, political, economic, and social experiment.

We can now sum up briefly. The moral problem posed for Americans has been solved by an incessant process of compromise and conflict and evolutionary adaptation taking place within a continuous framework of institutions, hammered out of a colonial life and a revolution rooted in inherited British values. The philosophical problem posed for Americans has been solved by a dedication to the vigorous extension of economic, political, and social processes. With certain notable exceptions, the accidents of history and the American environment made it possible for these processes of extension to be conducted by incremental modification arrived at by widespread experiment after vigorous debate. The whole cacophony of American articulation about politics, social values, economics, and ethics has had a real importance in keeping alive the nation's unifying values; but more significant for how the nation actually worked have been the subtly balanced concepts left implicit in the working processes of a society blessed, for most of its life, by the possibility of solving its essential problems in relative continuity with its past experience.[13] American ideals have a living place within these working processes, but a place more compromised, less innocent than our conventional modes of articulation would allow.

But the intellectual content of a process is immensely complex. It involves many factors interacting over time. The normal forms of rigorous logical exposition can grip only elements within the process and are likely to give them a more rigid and static cast than, in fact, they have; the number of unknowns is likely to be greater than the number of equations that can usefully be formulated. Men successfully operate processes by accumulating experience, feel, judgment, by sensing recurrent patterns rather than isolating clean-cut logical connections of cause and effect. This is how good captains of sailing vessels have worked—good politicians, good businessmen. This has been the typical American style in operating and developing the nation's society.

Its success, however, is dependent on two conditions which are, to a degree, alternatives. First, the problems confronted must be, in their essence, relatively familiar and capable of solution by only moderately radical innovation on the basis of existing principles or institutions. Second, there must be sufficient time for the experimental exploration of possible solutions and the osmotic process of accepting change. The more time permitted, the greater the workability of a technique of problem solving by empirical experiment.

It is, therefore, in the less radical orders of innovation—in science, industry, and politics—that the nation has excelled. Or, put another way, the American style is least effective when it confronts issues which require radical innovation promptly.

The great vigor and relative success with which American society has thus far overcome crises should not conceal the fact that many of those crises represent failures in the workings of the society. But it is of the nature of crisis that action can no longer be postponed; and, in addition, crises transcend in their implications the immediate issues in contention and threaten more basic values and institutions. In the American case the basic values and institutions of the nation have, by and large, commanded the support of a substantial majority. The crisis thus becomes a concrete operational problem to whose immediate resolution a unified nation turns. And the need for action—in the American case, its success—often permits the underlying causes for the crisis to persist, unexamined and obscure.

In short, a gift for vigorous communal action in the face of crisis—invaluable as it is—should not be confused with a talent for prompt and radical innovation in the face of new circumstances. This is the essence of the danger which confronts contemporary America, notably in its military and political relations with the world where the pace of technological change and of revolutionary political transformation may give us neither the continuity of experience nor the time the classic American style inherently requires for success. Resolution of our current problems by the technique of crisis action may yield misdirected efforts or action undertaken too late to ensure the society's interests.

PART II: THE CLASSIC STYLE IN ACTION

The concept of the classic national style developed in Part I is meant to embrace the three themes of the Conference historically rooted in the American past. The most suitable device for considering their linkage appears to be a series of notes on historical cases, of which five are now briefly explored: the Constitution, Lincoln's articulation of the meaning of the Civil War, the concept of the national interest down to 1898, the reconciliation of industrialization with a continued commitment to the principles of political and social democracy, and the origins of the American technique of large-scale administration. These cases are meant both to illustrate the national style in operation and to note certain exceptional deviations from it.

The Constitution. The debates on the Constitution—at the Convention and in the states—were a unique occasion in American life. A whole generation of leaders in the American community—and, to a lesser degree, the whole electorate—were forced to consider explicitly and to reconcile formally the conflicting presuppositions of democratic political life.

In one sense this was no new experience for Anglo-Saxons or, indeed, for Americans who had been living with written constitutions in one form or another since the joint stock company left its stamp on certain of the colonial charters; who had been vigorously operating a colonial system which left considerable scope for the development of democratic politics; and whose system of law had been transplanted successfully from its already substantial British base. The conflicting imperatives of liberty and order, individual freedom and the protection of property, local and national loyalties were not new themes to Americans of the 1780s. The generation that made the American Constitution had been struggling actively to find an appropriate formula for government in America for at least thirty years, say, since the Albany Plan of 1754. From one perspective the Constitution can be regarded simply as a limited step forward in a typically American sequence of experimental development which flowed on with the evolution of the two-party system, the powers of the Supreme Court, and so forth.

On the whole, however, it is probably more illuminating to regard the making and acceptance of the Constitution as a radical innovation. In the backwash of a successful revolution, confronting a succession of internal and external problems which threatened the unity and viability of the new nation, the men at the Philadelphia Convention were forced to do more than conduct merely another pragmatic exercise in problem solving. The problem they faced could not be solved by the enunciation of high principle, by minor innovation in an ongoing system whose foundations could be left implicit, or by some combination of the two. They had to structure formally the relationship between political ideals and political reality. It is no wonder that their deliberations were marked by an almost total lack of conventional political rhetoric.

Conscious to a remarkable degree of their mission in the context of the world's political history, they examined explicitly the conflicts they aimed to reconcile: an irreversible commitment (willingly or grudgingly acknowledged) to the democratic process and fear for the unwisdom of the popular judgment and for its disrespect of property rights; a need to make a defensible nation, with a free trading market, and an awareness of the power of state interests and the concessions they could exact; a need to centralize executive power and an acute awareness of the inability of man to handle much power with grace; and so on. The American political leadership gathered at Philadelphia, a generation peculiarly comfortable with abstract thought, acknowledged the dilemmas implicit in the concept of unified democratic America and did not hesitate to reveal their compromises with the purity of democratic ideals. The Federalist Papers are nearly—if not quite—as frank as the Convention debates.

It was not their willingness to compromise that gave their deliberations a special character, for compromise was not new either in local politics or in the conduct of national affairs under the Articles of Confederation. It was, rather, the openness and clarity with which they acknowledged and articulated an American version of the general human dilemmas in the organization of society.

The Founding Fathers were not, of course, infallible. Although they were men acutely aware of sin and special interest, they were over-idealistic about the possibilities of choosing a president above party. But, by and large, their brief but thorough exposure of the roots of the American political problem yielded a remarkably secure and workable structure; and the day-to-day operation of American politics has continued to evolve in the spirit of reconciled idealism and special interest out of which the Constitution was made. American politicians have not been judged on an absolute moral scale. They have been judged and are judged today by their ability simultaneously to project the common values and goals of the community and to move toward them a little while building majority coalitions out of the special interests of their constituencies. On the domestic scene compromise is not judged appeasement unless it transcends a subtle and scarcely definable boundary in common law and behavior.

The immensely subtle business of politics has become one of the implicit common law processes by which the society does its work. The language of political oratory is not designed to expose the political process so much as it is to associate particular political figures and positions with the nation's powerful half-true unifying ideals. It is to the phrases of the Declaration of Independence rather than to those of the Constitution that our political orators habitually turn. Despite active debate on particulars and chronic re-interpretation by the courts, the Constitution—taken as a whole—was quickly placed on a pedestal at a distance and surrounded with a haze of sanctity and transcendent wisdom which has tended to conceal the doubts about humanity, some bordering on the verge of cynicism, which it incorporates and which have helped to make it workable. Similarly, the sharp-edged dilemma of an individualistic society, embracing the principles of both one man, one vote, and the sanctity of private property, has never since been examined with such cool clarity by professional politicians.[14]

In the 1780s, then, the United States needed to take a large step, markedly discontinuous with its current position. The framework of politics built up out of local, colonial, state, and national government under the Articles did not work, and probably could not be made to work with minor modification if unity were to be maintained against internal and external centripetal forces. The problem demanded gross innovation. And that innovation was successfully accomplished. The nation having survived by, say, 1815 the stormy first twelve years of the Constitution's operation; having accepted the inevitability of two-party strife, including the new dimension it gave to the already complex concept of the presidency; having accepted the role of the Supreme Court asserted by John Marshall; having come through the great European upheavals and the War of 1812 with an enhanced sense of nationhood; Americans turned away from their transient mood of intense political introversion and devoted themselves to operating vigorously within the new institutional framework. Its complex origins faded into the mists. Truly fundamental constitutional issues were raised only by the problems leading to the Civil War; and these were kept from dominating the national political scene until well along in the 1850s. The rest was piecemeal adaptation in common law or by formal amendment around a set of problems, many new in content but essentially familiar and recognizable in their essence.

Despite a continuity with developments before and after the Convention, the making of the Constitution was, on the whole, an exception to the classic American style—the product of a unique set of circumstances and, indeed, a unique generation of Americans. The subsequent canonization of the Constitution, the method of Constitutional adaptation, and, above all, the gradual development of continental politics within it on the basis of a two-party system, sustained by complex intra-party negotiation of grass-roots interests, reflect fully the national style.

Lincoln and the Civil War. In the conflict over slavery, the nation again faced a problem where even substantial modification of familiar processes could not work. The forces of geography, economics, and of American history in its widest sense decreed that the slave South would have to become a minority region as the nation extended to the West Coast. Feeling at stake the loss of a distinctive way of life, the South preferred to risk going down in the manner to which it had become accustomed rather than to accept the future it believed implicit in Lincoln's victory. There is, of course, all manner of ambiguity in the process leading to the Civil War which makes its inevitability still debatable. Could the North have made it psychologically and politically possible for the South to have accepted a limitation of slavery within its existing area? Could the South have better assessed the underlying attachment of the North to unity and the North's military potential when mobilized and thus assessed more accurately its likely fate in a military showdown? But however temperate the North might have been, however willing to continue to tolerate slavery within the Union, it was impossible to suppress the conflict between the principle of slavery and the principle of majority rule in the new territories; and, perhaps, it was impossible for any American, North or South, to predict persuasively how, in fact, the North would react when it confronted the brutal fact of national disunity at Fort Sumter. In any case, after a decade of typically American experiment with formulae, no one had defined in 1860 a politically viable extension of the process of compromise over slavery which had begun in the negotiation of language for the Declaration of Independence and run through the Constitutional Convention down to the Missouri Compromise and 1850.

Thus Lincoln, like the Founding Fathers, faced a problem of gross discontinuity, of radical innovation which could no longer be postponed. And, like them, he proved capable of articulating in powerful abstractions the dilemma which the nation confronted and the solution he proposed.

There were two issues: national unity and the status of the Negro in American society. Lincoln evolved and held with remarkable firmness a particular view of their connection. He was for national unity and against slavery, but he refused to permit himself the indulgence of identifying the two issues. He was prepared openly to compromise on the moral issue of slavery in the interests of national unity; and he did not let himself believe that the Negro's status in American life could be brought into conformity with American social values by the simple fact of victory in war. Abolition was, indeed, a by-product of the conduct of the war and its outcome; but Lincoln knew that the nation confronted a long and painful evolutionary process to which Northern victory in the war might contribute but which it did not guarantee. In short, Lincoln denied himself the emotional luxury of a crusade.

Since the Constitutional Convention there has been no major political figure other than Lincoln who manipulated and balanced with such clarity and self-discipline the conflicting abstract goals on which

American life has been built. And in all its consequences for his own time and later, in this lay his genius.

Among other things, Lincoln was from his youth a thoroughly professional and dedicated American politician. He rose to eminence and power on the slavery issue to which he brought every quality of his spirit, his perception, and his ambition. The position he devised was extremely powerful politically because it was his insistent separation of unity from abolition and the priority he gave the former which, essentially, held the border states in the Union and made victory vastly easier if, indeed, it did not make it possible.

The ultimate power of Lincoln's articulation of the meaning of the Civil War arose, however, not merely from his sturdy separation of the Constitutional issue of unity from the moral issue of slavery. His position gained its final stature from the special ideological dimension he gave to the concept of unity. He knew that in many parts of the nation the question of unity was tied up with special interests of great political power; for example, the new West's determination to keep the route to New Orleans within the Union. These interests and pressures he fully exploited. But he did not stop there. While exposing the national moral blemish implicit in the history and status of the Negro in America, from his first inaugural onward Lincoln reaffirmed the concept of the United States as a nation whose survival in unity had transcendent meaning. He recommitted the nation to continuity with its old sense of an ongoing mission, a special evolving process, imperfect but ultimately governed by moral and religious values.

The nation could not sustain the tension and balance of Lincoln's highly abstract position any more than it sustained the mood and terms of the Constitutional Convention. The conflicts briefly synthesized to produce a constitution fell back into the arena of national politics, to be refought and compromised again and again. Similarly the interests and passions briefly synthesized by Lincoln fell out into their component parts. The painful sequence of the Reconstruction and its failure was played out; and the status of the Negro in terms of ideal American values was left very slowly to evolve by typically ad hoc experimental American processes. Nevertheless, in each case the crisis of radical innovation was passed: viable rules for American political life were made and accepted; the Union was preserved; the nation could, without unacceptable cost, lapse in both cases back to its instinctive operating style.

The Concept of the National Interest to 1898. The special character of the United States as a national community raised, from earliest days, a problem in foreign policy rooted in the same dualism with which the Founding Fathers and Lincoln were forced to wrestle: how should the special sense of ideological mission built into American nationhood be related to the conventional concerns of a nation-state living in a world of competing national sovereignties?

The Revolution itself had been fought in part in terms of ideological principle, in part through a wholly conventional balance-of-power alliance with France. Against this background the nation had to orient itself after 1793 to the Revolutionary and Napoleonic Wars. Despite American remoteness from the major battlefields, these wars had a pervasive effect on the American economy and on American political life as well. They brought with them a series of disruptions—from Citizen Genêt and the Alien and Sedition Acts to the Embargo and the War of 1812.

What was the American interest in the outcome of those wars? Should that interest be determined by an assessment of its ideological content? By memories of past assistance from the French? By revulsion from the excesses of the French Revolution and a continued sense of racial and cultural connection with the British Isles? Or, was there a distinctive American national interest that transcended instinctive ties of ideology, gratitude, and memory—and, even, short-run economic advantage?

In his Farewell Address Washington spoke of these matters in the context of a general theme which embraced domestic as well as foreign policy. The early portion of his statement considered the dangers of party faction within the United States and, particularly, the danger of developing parties rooted in competing regional interests. He saw this danger compounded if domestic party strife, regionally oriented, were to converge with distinctive foreign policy positions, with each party tied in sentiment and interest to a major European power—a real enough danger in the 1790s. His objective was to strengthen the shaken sense of nationhood. His method was both to define on the domestic scene an area of national interest beyond region and party, and to define a distinctive American interest in relation to the world, independent of the national ideals. He sought to delimit the sphere in which Americans would act in terms of the essentially universal ideals out of which the nation was constructed.

His military assessment asserted that in the short run the American nation could be protected by its own strength combined, as opportunity required and offered, with that of other powers whose interests temporarily converged with ours; and he sensed that in the long run the rise in American military potential relative to others, if translated into a reasonably substantial defensive force at readiness, could cope with whatever threats might arise over the foreseeable future.

Washington did not deny or ignore the reality of the American commitment to a distinctive set of values in political and social life. He spoke movingly of the nation's attachment to liberty. But he counseled, essentially, that the nation's ideological commitment was likely to be fruitful to the extent that the nation exploited the military possibility of a security achieved and maintained without taking up fixed positions in the European power struggle, working out its ideological destiny within its expanding borders.

Washington's formulation of the national interest ranks with the making of the Constitution and Lincoln's position in the Civil War as one of the rare moments when the various complex strands in a major American problem were articulated in explicit relationship to one another at a high political level. And, by and large, his subtle injunction—both coarsened and elevated in popular thought—dominated American foreign policy for almost precisely a century; but over that period the inner structure of his thought and the assumptions which gave it a validity in the world arena of the nineteenth century were carefully reexamined by only a few. Accepting isolation in Washington's sense as a working formula, from Jefferson's administration forward, the nation devoted itself to the living process of building and consolidating a continental structure. The United States managed to acquire the requisite territory and to neutralize the hemisphere from any increase in major power influence at remarkably little diplomatic or military cost. And all this was done, step by step, with shrewdness and skill. The cumulative myth of American isolation was, however, a quite different affair from Washington's thoughtful prescription or the way our foreign policy evolved. A gap emerged between the concept of a virtuous, isolated America, uniquely free of enmeshment in wicked balance-of-power politics and the way American relations to the world were actually conducted. We practiced balance-of-power politics abroad just as we did at home in party politics conducted on a continental basis; but our ideal concept of ourselves made it difficult to articulate what, in fact, we did.

In the major issues of American diplomacy the world-wide interplay of force and potential force was, in fact, never far from the surface of things. Victory in the War of Independence itself hinged on an American alliance with France which was a by-product of Anglo-French power conflict. And, after the nation was formed, the success of its diplomacy continued to depend on a systematic exploitation of the continuing power struggle among the great European states. This was true, for example, of the whole series of Anglo-American negotiations which absorbed a considerable proportion of the nation's diplomatic energies from Jay's Treaty of 1794 to the Alaska boundary arbitration of 1903. Serious Anglo-American tension developed from time to time, even as late as the Venezuela Boundary Dispute of 1895–1896. But the underlying security interests of Britain and the military potential of the United States defined a fairly spacious working area for diplomats. After 1815—barring a tense passage during the Civil War—a virtually unarmed but rapidly growing United States could bargain on a basis of equality with a Britain controlling the seas, due to the vulnerability of Canada and the growing sense that, militarily as well as economically, the maintenance of the British world position required a United States that was, at the minimum, not hostile, and which was, potentially, a counterforce to Britain's continental rivals. Britain's military and diplomatic strength was sufficient to prevent any superior power or power bloc from crystallizing in Europe against it; but it was not sufficient to conduct a second active front in the Western Hemisphere. And, as the century wore on and the weight of Germany was progressively felt in the diplomacy of the Old World, Canning's concept of the New World's balancing role, enunciated during the Monroe Doctrine negotiations, took on a new vitality in British minds.

The United States benefited in other directions from the military preoccupations of European powers with what they regarded as higher-order business. As nearly as we can reconstruct Napoleon's thought, Jefferson was offered the Louisiana Territory by the French to avoid its occupation by the British when war was resumed in 1803 after the brief Peace of Amiens; and Seward was offered Alaska in part because the Russians, with memories of the Crimean War, wished an American buffer between Siberia and British Canada. The ease with which the American continent was consolidated (with substantial recourse to arms only in the Mexican War and against the Indians), the relatively easy acceptance by the world's powers of the Monroe Doctrine, and, even, the possibility of conducting the Civil War without dangerous interference from other nations all hinged on a fortunate relation between American interests and the interplay of military power on the world scene during the nineteenth century.

By and large, in a practical way, this was well understood by those charged with American foreign policy in the nineteenth century. The Presidents and Secretaries of State who consolidated the continental structure and made the Monroe Doctrine stick were not, by and large, naive men. Although by no means uniformly successful, the American Secretaries of State included some of the ablest and most professional political minds the nation produced: Jay, Jefferson, Marshall, Madison, Monroe, John Quincy Adams, Clay, Van Buren, Webster, Calhoun, Seward, Blaine, and Hamilton Fish. The specific issues of American diplomacy in the nineteenth century were often of first-rate domestic political importance, touching vital and self-evident national and regional interests, determining the geographical contours of the nation and its status in the Western Hemisphere. On the great continental and hemispheric issues the national diplomatic tradition was purposeful and thoroughly professional; and it was backed by a general sense of moral legitimacy, a sense that it was right to extend on this continent the American system and way of life. American diplomacy also exploited the possibilities opened up by power politics in the Far East. In China, where the nation developed considerable commercial interests after 1815, American diplomacy moved in behind the British victory in the Anglo-Chinese War of 1839–1842 to negotiate in the treaty of Wanghia (1844) a favorable commercial treaty including explicit extraterritorial rights. Caleb Cushing combined a degree of threat with his diplomacy; but, after their defeat by Britain, the Chinese, resigned to the disturbing fact of enlarged trade with the outside world across the seas, were mainly concerned to avoid excessive unilateral rights accruing to any one power.

In Japan Commodore Perry's show of force initiated the opening of Japan to trade in the treaty of 1854; but the opening was extremely narrow until Townsend Harris, in the wake of the major European powers, negotiated the commercial treaty and convention (1857–1858), arguing pointedly the advantages of interposing nonimperialistic America to soften the impact on Japan of the Russo-British rivalry.

From its initial exploitation of Anglo-French rivalry in the War of Independence down to the end of the nineteenth century, American diplomacy, with economy of force, thus exploited the cross-purposes and the forces set in motion by the rivalries of the major European powers to advance its own various national interests. We were engaged in the balance-of-power business to just about the extent and in the manner Washington had envisaged. But we went about that business from day to day without acknowledging what it was. And we maintained popular myths of both special virtue and invulnerability which reality has since sharply challenged.

The challenge arose for a simple reason: the course of events in Eurasia, notably the rise of Germany, Russia, and Japan, produced a sequence of threats to the Eurasian balance of power. A policy of exploiting in the American interest the consequences of an indecisive Eurasian power struggle no longer sufficed. We could no longer assume that no single power or power grouping would dominate Eurasia; and we had to face the fact, long implicit in our position, that the nation's security was endangered if Eurasia were to be dominated by a single power or power coalition.

In intervening, as in the end we did, in the major Eurasian affairs of this century we confronted two new circumstances. First, the United States met other major powers on issues where they judged to be at stake interests of first importance to them. American diplomatic victories could not be achieved simply as a by-product of major power clashes. An American diplomacy not backed by force was thus unlikely to be effective. Second, American diplomacy faced issues where the nation's own interest in the outcome was not embraced in Washington's formula; and he has had no successor capable of imprinting the nation's mind and its day-to-day working relationships to the world with a concept of the national interest which held in balance and relationship to one another the nation's legitimate and abiding ideological and power interests. Lacking this new synthesis we have rocked along from crisis to crisis, bringing to bear a succession of partial images of our interests and purposes in the world: the Mahan-inspired "large view" of the early days of the century; Wilson's inadequately based projection on the world of our domestic political system and values; the limited withdrawal of the 1920s; the pathological isolationist retreat of the 1930s; the ad hoc synthesis of Mahan and Wilson by which Franklin Roosevelt took us through the Second World War; Truman's vigorous, successful, but again ad hoc duel with Stalin; and the effort to maintain a (rapidly changing) status quo which marked Eisenhower's first administration. Over half a century we have, indeed, come to accept de facto status as a world power. And, in 1917, 1941, 1947, and 1950 we have behaved, in the face of acute crisis, as if the nation understood its abiding interest in avoiding the passage of the Eurasian power balance into the hands of a single power or effective coalition we could not strongly influence or dominate. And through this series of convulsive reactions to crisis we have managed to survive and to maintain a domestic society incorporating, more or less, the values of our past.

But, in the face of the rapid series of changes in our external environment and the sequence of radical innovations they have required of us, we have not been able to formulate concepts of our interest and policies based upon them which were sufficiently at grips with the forces playing around to anticipate and to avoid costly crises. We have, in short, not been able to translate into a successful working process the task of protecting the national interest under twentieth-century conditions. And to this result the gap between our actual position in the nineteenth century and the powerful myths we permitted to generate about it have contributed.

Industrialization and an Individualist Society. If the American military and foreign policy performance in the first half of the twentieth century is judged to be a relative failure of the national style, the accommodation of the society to industrialization must be judged a relative success.

The problems posed by industrialization were, in fact, new and heightened versions of conflicts built into the foundations of an individualist society. The religious concept that each man, a unique soul, sovereign in taste and preference, stands equal before God and the law immediately sets up conflicting touchstones for public policy.

On the one hand the individualist-utilitarian creed sets up a strong presumption in favor of a competitive economy guided by consumers' preference, allocating monetary reward on the basis of individual performance in the market, guaranteeing the stability of private property—in short, a presumption in favor of private capitalism as the dominant mode for maximizing the general welfare in a community of unique and sovereign individuals.

On the other hand four questions are immediately raised by the same premises:

1. To what extent is it legitimate to interfere with a free market economy in order to maintain equality of opportunity—negatively through inheritance taxes and the control of monopoly; positively by mobilizing income in the hands of the state for purposes of education, public health, etc.?

2. To what extent should the state act in order to perform those economic functions necessary for the general welfare which the incentives of a private economy do not necessarily induce on a proper scale and at the proper time; for example, the building of roads, canals, railroads?

3. To what extent should the state interfere in private markets to accelerate or to cushion processes of structural change judged either necessary or harmful to the general welfare; for example, by tariff protection, by efforts to control the general level of prices, by a counter-cyclical policy to deal with excessive unemployment?

4. To what extent should the state recognize that the most natural (if psychologically ambiguous) assumption is that inter-personal comparison is possible; that the law of diminishing relative marginal utility applies; that a dollar of income means less to a rich man than to a poor man; and that, therefore, the general welfare may be increased by the transfer of income, through progressive taxation, from those relatively rich to those relatively poor? [15]

In coming to accept during the classic century a version of the individualist-utilitarian premises, the United States committed itself to an extremely complex problem in balance. Despite the emotionally charged slogans in terms of which the content of the balance has been fought out, no simple formulae derive from our ideology except that a compromise balance should be sought which approximately maximizes the general welfare by a mixture of free-market and other methods.

In certain matters the problem of balance was already familiar in pre-revolutionary times; for example, the inflationist bias of back-country farmers set off against the hard-money interest of their urban creditors. And key elements in the problem were, of course, at the center of thought and controversy over the American Constitution which sought both to preserve a stable legal environment for private capitalism and to give acceptable meaning to an individualist political system. From that time forward reconciliation by compromise remained the central theme of American politics, moving on from one range of concrete issues to the next as the scale and technical method of the society gradually altered, solutions being found after protracted debate and experiment and struggle on an *ad hoc* basis.

Americans made no major contribution to the nineteenth century literature of classic economics which dealt at great length with the problem of balance at a high level of abstraction. Contrary to popular myth the British classical economists were not united in their view; they did not simply press *laissez-faire* to its utmost limit. They explored the difficult choices posed for a society committed to the individualist-utilitarian principle and prescribed policy over a wide range, depending on their private sense of where an appropriate balance should be struck.[16] The American literature on the problem tended, in general, to be closer to the arena of politics, more explicitly in a pamphleteering tradition than the British; where it was couched in more abstract terms it tended to inflate to the level of general principle one side of the balance or one problem of balance—as, for example, the college presidents and clerics who articulated the gospel of wealth in the Guilded Age, and Henry George.[17]

In politics Jefferson's turn-of-the-century acceptance of the essential Hamiltonian institutions set the initial frame of national compromise which soon embraced Marshall's concept of judicial review as well. And down to the period of accelerated industrialization that settlement left only three major areas of conflict: the tariff, the National Bank, and the role of the state in financing "public improvements" or overhead capital as we now call it. These were good, big political issues capable of generating strong feeling; and, in the case of South Carolina and the tariff there was a touch of danger to the unity of the nation. But conflicting regional interests, which by and large lay behind them, were an old American story in the second quarter of the century and, excepting slavery, clearly compatible with the society's basic presuppositions. By and large, the Jeffersonian vision remained valid until the society moved into accelerated industrialization in the two decades just before the Civil War; that is, the vision of a nation avoiding acute conflict between an atomistic electorate and concentrated economic power by remaining predominantly a society of landowning farmers.

With the surge into mature industrial status after the Civil War the problem Jefferson feared came vigorously to life. A whole range of major issues of imbalance emerged and were increasingly recognized, from the level of poetry to journalism. The new concentrations of wealth and power constituted, evidently, a major shift in balance, reaching out not merely into the market place and the price system but also into politics and the courts. By the time of the entrance of the United States into the First World War, however, the grinding processes of American politics had begun to put the system back into a state of moving equilibrium more nearly in accord with the nation's fundamental value commitments.

One major problem disappeared, as it were, on its own. The post-Civil War decline of farm prices had yielded, down to the mid-1890s, extended agitation for some monetary device that would reverse a price trend that bore with special weight on the agricultural community. This problem was eliminated (down to 1920) by the world's economic history rather than by public policy. But for the rest, much was done legislatively, by institutional change, and by change in prevailing attitudes toward the economy. The problem of monopoly was brought under law and (in the case of the railways and utilities) administrative surveillance and rate controls. The labor unions were by 1916 excepted. These shifts permitted processes of better balance to operate through the courts, in the market place, and, perhaps most powerfully, in the minds of businessmen whose natural inclination to inhibit competition came increasingly to be restrained by the concept that monopolistic negotiations were dangerous, inappropriate, or wrong. The tariff, pushed progressively to extreme levels by 1909, was mitigated under Wilson.

The central banking function was placed explicitly, if somewhat obliquely, within the orbit of public policy in the Federal Reserve System. And the most revolutionary of all devices derived from the individualist-utilitarian creed—the income tax—was quietly accepted in 1909 by a coalition of both parties (ratified in the states, 1913) after rejection as unconstitutional in 1894.

The whole of this balancing process was conducted against the background of the rich literature of the progressive movement, ranging from Lord Bryce's classic and Herbert Croly's elevated essay on American life to the ardent and vivid exposure of specific outrages in the muckraking literature. Except, perhaps, for Debs and the Socialists on the periphery, what was proposed was a set of concrete reforms.[18] The progressive movement did not press for the end of industrial capitalism. It insisted that the nation acknowledge the reality of the problem of reconciling an industrial society with the essential values of political and social democracy. And what emerged out of the investigations, polemics, debates, compromises, and experiments was a series of limited innovations in national policy. The vagueness and ambiguity of such political banners as the Square Deal and the New Freedom did not represent an inability of Americans to formulate or to understand more intellectually rigorous ideologies, but, rather, a continuing commitment to the process of achieving progressive balances within the complex ideology of individualist-utilitarianism. Despite the inflamed rhetoric of debate, these matters were fought out in the framework of an underlying consensus that the nation would remain loyal to private capitalism as the primary but not exclusive agent for maintaining an individualist society, with approximately equal opportunity for individuals, seeking to maximize the general welfare.

The process of readjusting the balance was resumed when, after the hiatus of the 1920s, the nation faced the Great Depression and political power shifted hands. The action of the government (except for the problem of dealing with massive unemployment) took, essentially, the form of limited specific innovations, each with a substantial history of prior thought, debate, and (in some cases) experiment behind it. This was so with respect to farm policy, social security legislation, banking and securities legislation, the TVA, and even the enlargement of labor's rights to organize and bargain collectively. In these dimensions of the New Deal the shift in political power simply released energies and made possible legislative and institutional change on the basis of at least partially developed concepts and plans, each with a considerable history. For that reason so much of the legislation jammed through in the vigorous chaos of the first New Deal phase has proved permanently acceptable. The nation was moving forward on paths which had been reasonably well prospected, by techniques of balance rooted authentically in its ideology, under slogans with evident resonance all the way back to Jefferson at least.

On the other hand, the nation was neither intellectually nor politically prepared to formulate a national policy to deal with extreme unemployment. Still, in 1933, after three and a half years of progressive economic decline, it faced an urgent problem requiring radical innovation. The business cycle had been accepted over the whole of the nation's life as, by and large, a rhythm outside the scope of public policy to correct, even though the fortunes of politicians were intimately tied to that rhythm. From the first decade of the century an increasing amount of research on the business cycle had been proceeding on an orderly academic basis with suggestive, if occasionally odd, proposals from the nonprofessional wings; but it had yielded no coherent general view of the dynamics of the economy and no persuasive concepts for public policy.[19] There was no implicit consensus, no framework of accepted ideas and institutions within which Americans could bring the national gift for operational vigor effectively to bear. The theories that were brought to bear within the New Deal on the problem of recovery were an extremely confused mixture.

Under these circumstances Roosevelt's stance in March 1933 was, simply, that he recognized the existence of a major national crisis and that he proposed to act with vigor and confidence in the face of it. So far as unemployment was concerned, he lacked a program, notably since he had campaigned on the principle of a balanced budget. In this mood of mixed determination and profound intellectual uncertainty Roosevelt reached back to the last great national crisis the nation had faced, the First World War, and created the NRA on analogy with the War Industries Board.[20] The NRA absorbed and dissipated in the course of 1933 a good deal of the nation's initial emotional response to the new president's mood and, in the end, slowed down the process of recovery.

It was removed from the scene by the Supreme Court in 1935, leaving behind the Wagner Act and various other contributions to institutional reform, but widespread confusion on the cause and cure of large-scale unemployment. Gradually, however, out of the maze of debate and experiment it did emerge that the central task was to increase effective demand. The national budget was used in various ways to this end. It was never used, however, on a scale and with a conviction capable of bringing the economy back to full employment; well over 10 per cent of the working force remained unemployed until the rearmament boom took full grip on the economy in 1941–1942.

The New Deal exercise in employment policy—a classic problem requiring radical innovation in a short period of time—thus saw the American style yield a quite mediocre result.

American society was, however, sufficiently unified on essentials and sufficiently resilient to carry the burden of chronic unemployment without fracture; and if one were to apply merely the criteria of domestic performance to the American experience of the Great Depression, one might say that this shocking affair was successfully weathered and the American style vindicated. For out of the New Deal experience, the Second World War, the growth of knowledge (based, in good part, on Keynes' *General Theory*), and popular conviction a remarkable postwar consensus emerged both as to the character of the employment problem and the techniques for dealing with it by public policy in a political democracy.

From 1917 forward an assessment of American domestic policy has an extra dimension. One must ask to what extent the manner of solving or failing to solve our domestic problems affects the world environment of American society and, ultimately, the American national interest. From this perspective, in all its many ramified consequences throughout the world, the confusions of the Hoover and Roosevelt administrations in dealing with the problem of unemployment must be rated a major failure of the national style.

The Historical Origins of the National Style in Large-Scale Administration. American industrialization has brought with it a remarkable growth of large-scale units which now embrace, directly or indirectly, an extremely high proportion of the nation's life—business, governmental, intellectual, and, even, artistic. Bureaucracies are, of course, by no means

a uniquely American phenomenon or even a phenomenon of industrialization; and in many other societies the traditions and methods of
bureaucracy are still based on models which antedate the Industrial
Revolution.

Lacking a national history which stretched back to the Middle Ages,
American society began without substantial bureaucratic elements. In
the early decades of national life continuity with European forms of
organization existed only in the professional military establishments, in
the General Land Office, and in such minimum essential parts of government as tax collection and the post office. In the nineteenth century,
units within the national and state governments were generally small;
and the problem of relating staff to line, policy to operations could
generally be overcome by the presence of a single politically responsible
figure.

American industry confronted the problem of scale somewhat sooner
than American government, and it exhibited early a tendency which has
persisted to the present day; that is, a combination of abundant use of
capital and acute specialization of labor. Americans took with special
vigor to Adam Smith's propositions about pin manufacture. There is a
continuity from Eli Whitney's innovations in mass production down
through Taylorism and beyond, stemming from the fact that the
population-resources balance in the United States made labor relatively
expensive and capital-intensive methods profitable. At the operating
level—of a machine tool layout or an assembly line—we have steadily
exhibited a gift for economy and efficiency.

When industry began to take a firm grip on the textile towns of New
England in the 1820s and 1830s, a classic pattern of development and
administration began to emerge which, in many sectors of the American
economy, has continued until very recent times; it is still to be observed
in certain young industries.

The key to the industrial development of New England was the perception of Francis Cabot Lowell that the problem of costs on the New
England scene could be solved in such a way as to meet British competition, at least in certain grades of cotton textiles. Basic technology
he could import illegally and find here the ingenuity to manufacture
the machines, conduct maintenance, and make the necessary modifications; power he could find in the flow of New England streams; and a

labor force he could develop by giving to the unmarried daughters of
New Hampshire and Massachusetts farmers a decent human setting in
the Lowell dormitories. On the basis of these initial insights, he and his
successors created a viable industry which, decade by decade, continued
in a process of extension. Problems of innovation did not cease. Machinery had to be improved, cyclical fluctuations weathered, the labor
force shifted on to an immigrant labor basis, adjustments made to
changing tastes. But with a market initially large in scale, expanding in
both population and in real income per head, the task of American
industrial growth remained, classically, one of vigorous extensive exploitation of an initial perception about how profit could be made. So
it was, for example, with Rockefeller's insights into how the national
petroleum market could be corralled; with Henry Ford's concept of the
cheap, mass-produced automobile; with Eastman's Kodak.

In short, the creative insights out of which various key sectors of the
American economy took their start were not, historically, the product
of large-scale staff organizations. On the contrary, they arose from the
head of a single man or from the consensus of an exceedingly small
group. Large-scale units emerged in consequence of the correctness of
the initial insight, the vigor with which it was translated into reasonably
efficient process, and the powerful upward lift of the American economic
environment.

This does not mean, of course, that American business units have
faced no important problems of innovation after large-scale status was
attained. They constantly faced change and readjustment, as, for example, Sears, Roebuck, progressively shifted its market focus from the
farm to the city to the suburbs, to Latin American markets, changing
the while, year by year, the contents of its catalog. In a larger sense,
however, down to quite recent times the really substantial innovations in
industry could originate in the mind of one man or in a small group;
they could be pioneered on a small scale; and they could yield massive
institutions operating subsequently—at least for some time—by processes
requiring relatively minor innovation.

From one perspective, the central contemporary problem of American
organization is how to perpetuate the creative process of innovation
when innovation must occur within large-scale bureaucracies whose
initial underlying concepts have lost vitality and relevance.

Like American politics, American industry relied historically, then, on the ability of an individualistic society to throw up a succession of innovating leaders. In government these men united functions of staff and line; in industry, ownership and management. This did not mean, however, that all administrative processes could be solved by the orderly use of specialized machinery and efficient plant layouts.

Serious problems of American administration arose, for example, just before the Civil War, when the railway networks stretched out from the East to consolidate half a continent; and these problems produced the perceptive observations of Henry Varnum Poor.[21] He saw clearly that the separation of ownership from management and the obsession of management with profit possibilities arising from railway extension, financial manipulations, and the monopolist's relative freedom to raise rates left management grossly inefficient, the ablest operating men profoundly frustrated, the run-of-the-mill operations reduced to meaningless routine jobs. In examining the problems of morale and leadership in large-scale units, the requirements for systematic organization, efficient internal communication, and public information, Poor anticipated much of the approach as well as the substance of latter-day American administration experts.

The question Americans have come to pose is: How shall we make an existing large-scale operation, faced with fixed or slowly changing problems, work efficiently? This remains the central focus of thought on administration down to Herbert Simon's sophisticated treatment of administrative process:

The theory of administration is concerned with how an organization should be constructed and operated in order to accomplish its work efficiently. A fundamental principle of administration, which follows almost immediately from the rational character of "good" administration, is that among several alternatives involving the same expenditure the one should always be selected which leads to the greatest accomplishment of administrative objectives; and among several alternatives that lead to the same accomplishment the one should be selected which involves the least expenditure. Since this "principle of efficiency" is characteristic of any activity that attempts rationally to maximize the attainment of certain ends with the use of scarce means, it is as characteristic of economic theory as it is of administrative theory. The "administrative man" takes his place alongside the classical "economic man." [22]

The virtues and deficiencies of Simon's view are precisely those of the neat formulations of classical economic theory: they illuminate the efficiency conditions in static processes, but growth and major structural change are assumed to occur as the result of forces outside the analytic system. And the great question is never posed: To what extent do the short-run imperatives of administrative order clash with the innovational requirements of long-run survival? Once established, large-scale units face the problem of generating out of their own structures new innovations capable of maintaining their vitality. As a basic point of departure modern administrative theory is no more appropriate to the process of innovation than short-run Keynesian income analysis is to the process of economic growth.

The problem of innovation and change is, indeed, treated to a degree by American administrative analysts; but it is subsumed in a rather abstract way in the concept of "the choice among alternatives," just as modern economic theory assumes that entrepreneurs choose the most profitable techniques available from a given "state of the arts." This is a gross evasion; for the heart of the decision-making process is the posing of the alternatives. Innovation—creativeness—consists in thinking up an alternative which has not been thought of before. The good executive knows that one of his major tasks is to ensure that all the conceivable alternatives are explored and available to him, not merely those which his operating subordinates or staff men think up, agree upon, and regard as appropriate to place before the old man.

By making the act of decision the center of the job—and deflating the problem of formulating alternatives—we develop concepts of the administrative process attuned, at best, to modest, slow moving innovation. When, for example, Simon and his colleagues treat such issues as "the growth of administration," "how problems give rise to administrations," and "the strategy of planning," their examples derive from American domestic life in which innovations are seen to arise from a slowly accumulating sense of an unresolved problem, gathering popular momentum until a political consensus is reached and action is taken.[23] Subsequently, the planning process is seen as the projection out to the future of familiar ongoing processes and trends.

It is not unfair to say that the bulk of even the best formal American thought about administration is concerned with how to make relatively static processes operate efficiently, not with the question of how to solve radically new problems. Our administrative experts are the intellectual grandchildren of Henry Poor, puzzled by the inefficiency of the large-scale institutions that emerged in the wake of the railway innovations of the three pre-Civil War decades. The question of how railways were brought to life is left, as it were, outside the administrative expert's purview. His concept of orderly administration at the staff level is, essentially, an extension to staff work of Taylorism; that is, we have applied to staff structures the same rules of coordinated specialization on which efficient assembly lines have been built. The classic American table of organization for staff work consists in a hierarchy of specialized experts, each surveying a sector of operations, passing upward his recommendations for marginal change to be considered by the responsible executive in his "choice among alternatives." There has been no perception—until very recent years—that the definition of alternatives in a rapidly changing field for action is, in itself, a powerful creative act most unlikely to be generated by specialized bureaucrats.[24]

In government as in industry, for the bulk of our history, innovation could be centered in the hands of a relatively few individuals or in small homogeneous groups. Until well into the twentieth century, for example, the pace and content of diplomatic life allowed the President, the Secretary of State, or both together to handle personally all major issues. More than that, the scale of government permitted day-to-day administration to be in fairly direct control of the same men who made policy. At the turn of the century the Department of State had a staff of less than one hundred, its routine operations under the direction of a chief clerk with direct access to the Secretary. Excepting the Civil War period, the other Cabinet departments were also small and staff work could be centered in the hands of a man or a few men. Government bureaus and commissions did emerge in the latter years of the nineteenth century with regular, recurring tasks, military and civil, but these were relatively small in scale and limited in authority; and they settled down to the quiet life of well-entrenched bureaucracy. The permanent officer corps in the Army and Navy were, in effect, moderate-sized clubs of men and their families, bound together by ties of personal intimacy, common academy backgrounds, and a common unfolding experience.

In the early years of the twentieth century, however, at just about the time when American industry was beginning to face on a wider front the kind of administrative problems the railways had already confronted for some decades, the national government also came face-to-face with the question of large-scale administration. In the aftermath of the Spanish-American War, for example, the size of the permanent Army and Navy roughly quadrupled, as compared to its average post-Civil War level. And the trend toward increase in scale within the government continued as a powerful trend down to the present, almost irrespective of the policies of the various administrations.

Like modern American industry, then, American government has been confronted with this central question: How shall change be instituted to meet new circumstances in large-scale units which, of their very nature, and, especially of their commitment to relatively static standards of efficiency, limit the capacity of those relatively few creative men capable of innovation and leadership? [25] In dealing with this problem we have been inhibited in both industry and government by the following fundamental characteristics of the national style:

1. An empirical approach that tends to discount the reality of problems, defined by imaginative projection of trends, until they have reached a stage so acute that they obtrude on the field of vision of responsible operators: in government, over the incoming cables or voting shifts in the electorate; in business, on current cables or voting shifts in the electorate; in business, on current income accounts; in war, by initial defeat in the field.

2. A related tendency to organize staff work on highly specialized lines which make difficult the development of an overall view of the problems confronted by any major institution.

3. In consequence of over-specialization, the tendency to over-man staff work units in such a way as to minimize the amount of time available to any responsible figure for coherent thought and reflection, and to dilute the insights and views of knowledgeable specialists as they pass upward through bureaucratic hierarchies.

4. A tendency to accord all units in an organization a voice in major decisions touching their area of operation, in the interests of organizational cohesion.

5. As a result, fundamental policy decisions take the form of compromise among responsible operators.

The concept of a high executive, under these circumstances, has ceased to be that of the creative innovator or forceful leader and has become that of the negotiator of successful compromise.[26]

In domestic policy the whole process is powerfully checked and governed by the sensitive market of the polling booths, and in business by the equally powerful pressures of competition and profit margin shifts. In both areas, the rate of innovation required may be increasing, but it can be handled tolerably well by the processes of institutionalized innovation we have constructed when souped up by outside trouble-shooters, efficiency experts, and idea men.

In military and foreign policy, however, neither the domestic political process nor the competitive market place of power operate sensitively until acute crises have arisen; and the character of innovation required to deal with reality is more radical. Here we have trouble.

Our two great institutions designed to synthesize a view of our national problems of security and foreign policy—the National Security Council and the Joint Chiefs of Staff—are, for example, essentially committees of operators, bureaucratic departmental chieftains, each freighted with large vested interests to protect, each biased heavily toward the *status quo*, as, indeed, operators must be. They cannot, under these circumstances, survey in a systematic way the horizons of our national position and formulate policies which effectively unify day-to-day operations.

High-level policy tends to emerge in one of two forms: either as general statements so broad that operators can go on doing what they are doing, interpreting policy statements as they will; or as tough, practical compromises, allocating money or other scarce resources, in which the pattern of policy is much less important to the outcome than the bargaining weight of the negotiators. First-class ideas cannot emerge from a committee of hard-pressed bureaucrats any more than a first-class book can be written by a committee of professors.

What is the result? Policy making consists in a progression of reactions to major crises. Having failed to define, to anticipate, and to deal with forces loose in the world, having tried merely to keep the great machine of government ticking over from day to day, in the face of issues even operators cannot ignore, the problems swept under the rug or never recognized at last come ticking in over the incoming cables. Then, as a nation of operators, we respect the reality of the matter and—

in the past at least—we have turned to with vigor. We rig up an ad hoc effort—often by-passing all the bureaucratic machinery created to deal with our affairs—launch hastily some new courses of action; and these become the working norms of policy until the next crisis comes along. At a first approximation it is quite accurate to say of any moment over the past fifteen years that current military and foreign policy has been a bureaucratic version of that created ad hoc to deal with the last crisis.

We have been saved because we do not respect our tables of organization nearly so much as would appear. A battalion in the field, a firm in trouble, the White House at a moment of national crisis has its decisions made for it by the few men who really matter, rallied around for the occasion by the responsible officer who seizes personal command. Everyone knows that the vitality of even the largest of institutions hinges, in fact, on a few key men. Somehow, for example, the character and personal operating style of the President manage to suffuse the most humble office in Washington. But we find it difficult to acknowledge that the qualities of a few men matter so much when we set up our institutions.

We have thus applied an acutely pragmatic style, created out of a remarkable continuous national experience, to the structure of our large-scale institutions, even those responsible for the nation's security. Their normal method of operation sets up major barriers to a successful process of innovation. The nation has come to rely on convulsive reactions to crises as the form of closing the gap between policy and reality. But we live in a world where it is altogether possible that crisis may take the form of situations where even the most vigorous ad hoc effort by the nation could come too late to retrieve our abiding intrests.

PART III. RECENT CHANGES AND SOME CURRENT PROBLEMS

Introduction. This final section seeks to define and to illustrate the extent to which recent changes in American society have tended to alter the classic national style. The contemporary institutions and texture of American life reflect both the dynamics of American development as a domestic society and the forces impinging on us from a sustained involvement on the world scene since about 1941. An initial effort is made, therefore, to array the two sets of factors which sometimes converge, sometimes diverge in their consequences. Against the background of this array the paper returns to the elements in the national household isolated in Part I and considers the changing function of American idealism, the choices newly opened up or denied by contemporary American society, and the adequacy of the contemporary operating style to solve the problems the nation confronts.

Continuity and Change in the Setting of American Domestic Society. The physical and institutional environment of American life has, of course, altered radically in the last fifty years and has been subject to rapid change in the postwar decade. Most recent developments, however, have a considerable history. Change has not been continuous, as, indeed, it could not be in a half century which included two World Wars and a unique world depression. Nevertheless, six major, persistent trends can be identified as operating since the beginning of the century, which may now have achieved such scale as to require some redefinition of the context within which American citizens live and make their value choices.

1. *Urbanization and suburbanization.*[27] In 1900, 40 per cent of the American population was classified as urban; in 1950, 56 per cent. In 1910, of those living in metropolitan areas, 23 per cent were located in satellite districts; thirty years later the figure had moved forward modestly to 32 per cent; in the next decade, however, suburbia expanded to embrace about 42 per cent of the population of metropolitan districts. And this was, evidently, not the end of the matter.

The average American is increasingly a resident of a satellite district within a metropolitan area. More than that, radical improvements in means of communication and transport have tended to break down the isolation of rural and small town life, extending the suburban character of the nation.

2. *Bureaucratization.* The proportion of the total working force employed within large-scale units has increased. So far as the economy as a whole is concerned, this phenomenon turns out to be a consequence mainly of the shift of labor out of agriculture rather than of any marked tendency toward increased concentration in American business. Since 1929 the proportion of agricultural to nonagricultural employment has fallen from more than 25 per cent to less than 10 per cent.

So far as industry is concerned, such comparable statistics as are available indicate that the proportion of wage earners in the largest 5 per cent of manufacturing establishments has risen modestly, from 55 per cent in 1914 to 62 per cent in 1947.[28] But the trend in manufacturing does not apply to business as a whole because of the vitality of small business units in other sectors, notably retail trade and services where the proportion of the total working force engaged had increased. The independence of these small units is, however, often compromised by their links to great corporate units, e.g., automobile dealers.

Government, of course, has greatly expanded. The Civil Service rolls of the federal government rose from about 600,000 in 1930 to about 2,400,000 in 1955; and the armed forces still remain mobilized at something like ten times their level of the 1930s. Cumulatively, about 20 million American men have known the round of military life.

By and large, then, the experience of life and work within a large-scale organization is increasingly typical of American society; and the white-collar experience of the office is increasingly more typical than factory or farm.

3. *The increase and stability of real income.* The Second World War and the postwar years have seen about fifteen years of full employment and more or less regular growth in output per head. Mainly because the United States entered the Second World War with heavy unemployment, the nation was able to conduct not merely a major war effort but also to sustain or even slightly to increase real income per head. Since 1945 the rise in income per head has continued. Between 1948 and 1954, for example, the proportion of American families with incomes over $5000 (at 1948 prices) rose from 21 per cent to 30 per cent. This upward shift in welfare was accompanied by institutional and political changes which appeared increasingly to guarantee that a major depression would not recur without effective compensatory action by the government. Under these circumstances the nation resumed in the postwar years trends already strong in the 1920s; that is, to allocate increases in real income to improved housing and, in general, to expand the proportion of consumption outlays on durable consumer goods, financed increasingly by means of consumer's credit.

4. *The acceptance of the welfare state.* The alterations in the role of government in relation to the nation's industrial economy, begun with the Progressive Movement more than a half century ago, have now yielded a consensus among a substantial majority of the population that

the government should continue to perform a wide range of economic functions. These functions are designed to guarantee equality of opportunity, economic security, and to provide important margins of social overhead capital for the society. If these commitments in principle are maintained for the rapidly expanding and migrating American population, the prospect is that the role of government will expand rather than contract over, say, the next several decades. This expansion will be required to build roads and schools, to restructure the centers of old cities, and to meet enlarged commitments to social security, the aged, and public health. The process of balancing the requirements of a society committed both to private capitalism and to other elements in the individualist-utilitarian creed has thus produced as a permanent feature an enlargement in the scale and functions of both federal and state governments, raising a whole range of unresolved problems for public finance and fiscal policy, making more acute, as well, the problem of avoiding chronic inflation in a democratic society committed to relatively full employment.

5. *The rising intellectual level.* The dynamics of the national commitment to popular education extended rapidly toward the end of the nineteenth century into secondary and higher education. Its broad consequence can be seen in the relative educational status of enlisted men in the First and Second World Wars.[29]

Years of Schooling	Percentage in World War I	World War II
Total	100.0	100.0
Grade school	76.7	30.9
High school		
4 years	4.1	23.3
3 years	2.7	11.2
2 years	4.8	10.9
1 year	6.3	7.8
College		
4 years	1.2	3.6
3 years	0.9	2.0
2 years	1.5	4.0
1 year	1.8	6.3

Veterans' benefits and the high level of postwar incomes have carried this process forward with wide-ranging consequences covering the whole realm of public taste, opinion, and manners.[30]

There has been a parallel maturing of American intellectual life marked, for example, by a sharp increase in the American contribution to theoretical concepts in both the physical and the social sciences. This trend toward virtuosity in theory was certainly accelerated by the intellectual immigration from the European continent of the 1930s and probably, even, by the intrusion on American academic life of certain war and postwar problems where theory and theorists proved useful and effective. But the development appears to have been implicit in the aspirations and intellectual values of the generation of American scientists which came of age between the wars and which reacted along a broad front against the extreme empirical bias of its elders.

6. *Increased social homogeneity.* In the pre-1914 years immigration to the United States was running at the rate of about one million per year. It fell away in the 1920s and became a thin trickle in the 1930s. The process of adjustment to the predominant values of American life and culture has steadily proceeded, generation by generation; and it has broken down or strongly diluted those groupings in American life based on racial or national origin who lived for a time predominantly within non-American cultures. To this process has been added the industrial revolution of the past two decades in the South which is again producing changes in the direction of national uniformity, as is the general acceleration in physical mobility since 1941. There has thus been a marked increase in the social homogeneity of the American population. This broad trend leaves, however, the problem of the social status of the Negro in a special category, felt, perhaps, with a special acuteness as other minority problems have become less sharp, as the average economic and educational level of the Negro has risen, as his level of aspiration has risen, and as the nation's position in the world arena makes it newly self-conscious of the residues of the "peculiar institution."

Abstracting, then, from the Second World War and the international involvements of the post-1945 years, American society appears to have found a distinctive moving equilibrium in which certain of the old processes—notably the open frontier and a large flow of immigration—

have been supplanted by the dynamics of an industrial growth oriented increasingly to durable consumer goods and to the migration to the suburbs. Having gradually thrashed out a resolution which narrowed the conflicts between industrial private capitalism and the other values of political and social democracy, Americans have found themselves in the mid-1950s a suburbanizing nation, increasingly at work in large bureaucracies, with a new security of employment, rising levels of welfare, rising standards of education and of intellectual sophistication, and an increased social and political homogeneity.

This setting—at once different, more restricted, and less inhibited than the past—has posed new value choices for Americans in ordering their lives; but the setting of contemporary American life is a product not merely of the working out of parameters implicit in the sweep of our domestic history but also of their interplay with forces arising from our protracted engagement in the world arena of power since 1941.

The Impact of World Power Status. For the better part of the past two decades the United States has been steadily caught up in world affairs on a scale never before known in our history. Although the Second World War was the largest and most prolonged of the nation's external military ventures, it is the twelve years of post-1945 involvement which are probably more significant for the contours of our society. If there had been no Cold War in the wake of the Second World War, that war, like the other military engagements in our history, might have receded into a status as another *ad hoc* national drama with relatively few long-run consequences for the character of American domestic life.

What the United States has had to face and to accept for the first time in its history is an environment of chronic insecurity, with a substantial proportion of the national income steadily allocated to military purposes and with a large military establishment not only drafting young manpower but also reaching deeply into the industrial and intellectual life of the community, imparting a strand of garrison life to the society as a whole. All of this was familiar to the societies of the major powers of Eurasia which had evolved into nationhood over centuries when war or the threat of war was the normal state. Given our history and the way we looked at that history, it was not easy for Americans to accept chronic insecurity and the allocation of a substantial proportion of national resources to military affairs at a time when American troops were

not actively engaged in the field. And this newness was enhanced by the
character of the only important American military engagement of the
postwar years—the Korean war. The United States was unprepared—by
its view of its history and by grave ambiguities in prevailing concepts of
the national interest—to see its men killed in a war which yielded something short of what appeared to be clean-cut victory. Nevertheless, in
one way or another, the nation has maintained the commitment made
during the Second World War to undo what it regarded as its failure
to stay in the world after 1918. Broadly speaking, we have remained
internationalist and have accepted, grudgingly or with grace, with
insight or obtuseness, the consequences of major power status.

The American role as a major power in the post-1945 world has, of
course, had many consequences for the domestic society. In a fundamental sense our international status set in motion forces which ran
directly counter to the directions decreed by the dynamics of our domestic society. We emerged after the Second World War in a position (and
with the evident desire) to cultivate a rather attractive domestic garden.
And we had reached a stage of economic, social, and political development where a uniquely comfortable life under conditions of relatively
low political and social tension was probably possible. We were struck at
just this stage with the need to take large and active measures to protect
the security of the society against forces and methods for which we were
not well prepared. We have had to allocate not only large resources to
this end but also a high proportion of the energy and talents of the
nation. An America come to terms with the welfare state at high and
rising levels of real income and America the fortress base of the West in
an intense Cold War is, indeed, a curious mix.

Nevertheless, in its impact on American society the Cold War has
converged with many of the trends built into our domestic dynamics,
imposing, as well, important counter-trends.

Specifically:

1. The scale of the military budget has made it easier to maintain full
employment but posed more sharply than would otherwise have been
the case the problem of inflation control in a democracy.

2. The scale and the ramified industrial and intellectual activities of
the military establishment have accentuated the trend toward bureaucratization.

3. The workings of Selective Service, combined with the social values built into our military establishments and veterans' benefit legislation, have accelerated the trend toward social homogeneity, toward higher average levels of education, and (via veterans' housing) toward suburbanization.

4. The imperatives of the arms race in new weapons and, to a degree, the problems of policy making in relation to societies which do not share instinctive American value norms and institutions have stimulated the development of both the natural and the social sciences, encouraging the use of higher order abstractions than would have been demanded if American science had continued to be oriented toward the concerns of a more isolated domestic society.

5. The cumulative effect of overseas experience during the Second World War, of occupation duties, of the Korean war as well as the narrower but powerful experience of work by Americans in overseas aid and information programs have radically increased the knowledge and awareness of the world outside the United States; and the flow of international news, punctuated by a series of major crises, has carried this awareness deep into the society in all regions of the country. Although knowledge and awareness are by no means to be equated with sympathy and a sense of common interest, isolationism has been diluted by these intrusions of the world on American life.

6. The existence of chronic national emergency has led to the development of an elaborate system of personnel security by the federal government. Given the scale of the national security effort and the administrative techniques of the personnel security program, the lives of millions of Americans have been touched in one way or another by this dimension of national policy, quite aside from that phase of the postwar experience when personnel security issues became embroiled in national politics.

The Upshot for the National Household. To what extent have the components of the classic national style been altered by this interweaving of welfare and garrison states?

Is American nationalism still rooted in some form of meaningful attachment to the old set of individualistic values and ideals? Is the round of day-to-day life—and the choices made by Americans among the alternatives open to them—still dominated by the rich material potentials of the environment? Are the problems which the nation confronts still susceptible of solution by piecemeal compromise or adaptation, by slow-moving processes involving only modest innovation at each stage? To what extent has the national style altered to permit more prompt and radical innovation where such is required?

The Contemporary Role of the Classic American Idealism. The national commitment to its traditional ideals has, in some meaningful sense, persisted; but the contemporary setting of American society has altered significantly the areas where these ideals have been forced to contest against other interests and motives. The wholesome burden of dilemma imposed by a communal commitment to ideals has not been lifted; but the content of our major moral dilemmas has changed. In general, the value dilemmas arising from domestic life have become less sharp, and they have shifted somewhat in character; but they have been superseded by two major dilemmas arising from our status as a world power in a period of protracted tension.

The great debate over the appropriate balance between the interests of private property and the interests of the private citizen has by no means ended. The heirs of Cotton Mather, Hamilton, McKinley, and Coolidge can still be detected as well as the heirs of Roger Williams, Jefferson, Jackson, Wilson, and Franklin Roosevelt. Nevertheless, the degree to which our national life is challenged by the clashing imperatives of the individualist-utilitarian creed has diminished.

What believer in the classic virtues of private capitalism can take comfort from the well-behaved committees of professional administrators who now run our major business firms on behalf of the insurance companies and the other agglomerations of small savings which, increasingly, own them? What believer in the cause of the underdog can identify himself with the problems of Dave Beck or even of that professional administrator, David J. McDonald? There are still issues which can make the old fire horses paw the ground—on the one hand, a $72 billion budget; on the other, Hell's Canyon or Dixon-Yates. And there will certainly be others. But the great affairs of domestic policy—education, health, water supply, the rebuilding of cities, the control of inflation, the provision of adequate social overhead capital for a bulging population—are, in a curious way, community rather than special interest or regional issues, evoking somewhat different alignments than those we have lived with since the Civil War. Segregation is, in one sense, a special case—a stage in a long, slow, familiar, ongoing process. But its solution—like the solution to the other major domestic issues—requires an extraordinary concert of effort by the majority in each community, an effort which could not be conceived of as realistic until quite recent times.

On the other hand, the society is confronted with the clash between the interests of national security in a period of acute danger and the values of individual freedom. This is not a new issue for Americans who have survived the Alien and Sedition Acts, the Palmer raids, the treatment of Japanese-Americans in the Second World War. At all stages in our history individual freedom faced limits set by the common interest; indeed, the Constitution, in its essence, acknowledges and seeks to compromise the inevitable conflict. But our recent experience is unique because it is the most protracted passage of national crisis we have ever faced. The McCarthy phase was evidently its most extreme expression when, for the better part of four years, a number of forces converged to permit McCarthy to throw the nation off its natural political balance. But the problem has continuing, if less flagrant, ramifications which distort the society away from the traditional norms of an open society at peace; e.g., a national budget regularly more than 15 per cent of gross national product, the draft, substantial areas of secrecy in scientific research, the reinforcement of the apparently instinctive conservatism of contemporary undergraduates by the desire to protect future job opportunities.

At first glance one might conclude that the increasing homogeneity of the society as well as the experience of protracted national tension have yielded a more conventional national patriotism than we have known before; and in a number of directions this kind of nationalism—which was hitherto associated with short periods of intense military engagement—has, indeed, clashed with the concept of the nation as the repository of certain fundamental values which transcend nationhood. But the sense of dedication to some version of these transcendent values has by no means disappeared. It would be quite incorrect to conclude that under the strain of Cold War the American community had abandoned the old link between nationhood and ideal values. Virtually without exception, Americans feel impelled, in the end, to justify their positions by an identification of the national interest with some version of these old values, be it in a McCarthyite crusade against materialistic Communism; a Humphreyite [31] effort to protect the United States as an effectively functioning capitalist island; or a Trumanite effort to build and sustain a viable coalition not merely capable of holding the military balance of power but also reflecting in some meaningful sense the notion of a Free World. More than that, the effort to find formulae which would reconcile the exigencies of Cold War with the traditional values of a democratic society has been pursued with increasing vigor, as the character of the problem came to define itself and the diffused but powerful institutions of a free society came to grips with one specific consequence or another of the clash between security and individual freedom.

In short, American law, politics, intellectual life, industry, and the government bureaucracies have been affected by the conflict between the instinctive values and habits of an open society and the inescapable problems of survival in the face of potentially mortal challenge. Where full reconciliation has proved impossible, the older individualistic values have, to a degree, given way to overriding communal values, sometimes in acts of fear and confusion which saw the nation at its worst; but, as time and the national gifts for process have operated, the area of loss—where it was not irretrievable in human and institutional terms—was diminished. It is not the task of this paper to measure the extent of the loss or to judge whether or to what degree it was inevitable. This argument would simply assert that the nation became seized of a new major problem involving its basic value commitments; and its performance in the face of it reflected the continued active presence of the old values in the working processes of the society.

The greatest of the problems posed for the nation's traditional identification with a set of explicit ideals has been in fashioning a military and foreign policy abroad capable of dealing with the threat posed by modern communism. Here, on a world basis, the nation has faced something like the problem it once confronted during the Civil War. Communism (like slavery in the South) has posed two distinct but related threats to the nation's interest: a direct threat to the national military security and an ideological threat with implications for both the nation's military security and for its survival as an open society. The balance of power in Eurasia could be lost to the United States by the movement of

Soviet or Chinese Communist ground forces; and, equally, it could be lost if, in hope or despair, men and women in the decisive regions of Eurasia should turn to communism—or, in apathy, let the Communists take over—as a believed solution to problems which could not be solved within the orbit of the democratic process and the alliances of the non-Communist world. Quite apart from the military threat of Communist victory in Eurasia, the survival of the United States as a free society, under conditions of mid-twentieth century communications, would be in jeopardy if we were to become a democratic island in a totalitarian sea.

The conduct of American military and foreign policy has thus required related but distinctive courses of action designed both to deter Communist military strength and to defeat the Communist challenge as an ideology. The task has been complicated because the techniques and attitudes of mind necessary to deal with the threat of military aggression did not neatly converge. Indeed, they have often clashed with those necessary to deal with the ideological threat of communism. We have had no Lincoln to pose the problem of balance and relationship clearly. We have, nevertheless, sought a balance, but have had chronic difficulties in articulating it in words or in action, right down to the awkwardness of the two (fundamentally legitimate) strands in the Eisenhower Doctrine.

In general, when Americans could in a single act move in conformity both to patent national interest and to familiar ideological principles the nation has been effective; for example, in European policy over the period 1947–1952, embracing the Truman Doctrine, the Marshall Plan, and the early buildup of NATO. Thus, also, in the early stages of the Korean war there was a convergence of military interest and more abstract loyalty to collective security and the United Nations.

Where our interests, as we saw them, clashed with our ideal values we had difficulty. We were inhibited from moving effectively against the Viet Minh in 1953–1954 by (among other factors) a reluctance to risk American lives in a cause tainted with colonialism. Obversely, where our ideological instincts could be satisfied only at excessive cost or risk—as in the liberation of Communist China, Korea, or Eastern Europe—we adopted awkward postures and ineffective policies.

In general the character of the Cold War, as decreed by Communist strategy and method, has denied us the opportunity to react to national

threat in the style with which we were most comfortable; that is, a clean
and total switch from peace to a war which could be fought with the
widespread conviction that both our interests and our ideals were at
stake. We have been forbidden a convulsive once-and-for-all resolution;
the nature of modern weapons and the strength of the enemy, in the
end, eliminated total crusade as unrealistic, despite its evident and understandable temptation as a method. In consequence, we have faced a
sequence of dangerous but not definitive crises which force us to explore
the character of our abiding interests, the limits of our power, and the
limits of our idealism.

We have been confronted, then, in foreign and military policy by
delicate and troubling problems of balance which we can no longer
ignore or conceal in comforting myths. At their core, these problems link
directly to the general issue: How should American ideals be weighed
relative to more conventional interests? From the first reserved response
to the Truman Doctrine in 1947—as too militaristic and bypassing the
United Nations—down to the current foreign aid debate, a decade later,
Americans have wrestled honestly if indecisively with many versions of
this question which is no more or less than the nature of the national
interest. To what extent is the American interest in the world to protect
the handsome real estate of this island continent? To what extent is the
American interest to maintain a world environment for this society
which will permit it to maintain its abiding values? If both are judged
legitimate (for the second concept embraces the first and the first may
require the second for its fulfillment), how shall the pursuit of the two
interests be related and balanced? These great issues have been explicitly
on the nation's agenda since Mahan began to influence some Americans
in positions of authority more than a half century ago; and they were
sharply posed, in quite different ways, by the First and Second World
Wars. But it is only in the postwar decade that they have been thrust,
day after day, year after year, upon the nation in contexts that make
evasion difficult.

Thus at home and abroad the image of the United States as a national community dedicated to strive toward the values of the Enlightenment has not lost its relevance; but the major problems raised by
this commitment have altered and, above all, the nation has been forced

to wrestle with its values before the world as it exercised major power status in a decade's protracted Cold War.

Changing Incentives and Alternatives in Contemporary American Life. It will be recalled that the second component of the classic American style was taken to be the fact that the setting of American society both required and made attractive a peculiarly vigorous pursuit of material advantage through individual enterprise. The rewards of power, social status, adventure, and material satisfaction tended all to derive from personal performance in the market place, notably after (about) 1830, when the initial generation of political leaders passed from the scene and the surge to the West and into industrialization gathered momentum. Contemporary Americans, faced with a somewhat different range of realistic alternatives than Americans of earlier generations, have, to a degree, shifted their scale of effective values. The reasons for this shift (the character of which is dealt with in Mr. Kluckhohn's paper) are complex; and I, for one, am not prepared to offer anything like a full explanation. What can be said is that American society—the terrain within which individual human beings must choose to fulfill alternative values and aspirations—has altered; and that the change of terrain is part of an interacting process which has brought about the shift in values.

There are, perhaps, four major specific respects in which the alternatives offered to the individual by the American environment have shifted.

1. The level and apparent security of real income has diminished the scale of effort required to meet expected levels of welfare; and, among other things, it has permitted the option of increased leisure, earlier marriages, and more children, with diminished felt sacrifice in material income. In short, if we assume that the economists' concept of diminishing relative marginal utility is generally applicable, one could say that the rise in the level and the security of material welfare has diminished the marginal utility of money as against the private values of marriage, babies, leisure.

2. The urbanization and bureaucratization of American life have, in both fact and prevalent image, altered the setting in which Americans work and must seek to fulfill their talents. The shift is, broadly, from individual or small-scale enterprises to group and large-scale institutions. This shift to bureaucracy may have encoureged men increasingly to

express their individuality in areas outside the market place and to alter their norms of behavior on the job to conform to the requirements of large-scale institutions.

3. The rise in the scale and scope of government has shifted a number of the places of power and prestige out of the economy into the service of the state. And a higher proportion of the talents of the society than in earlier times is now—full time or part time—in the state's service. The convergence of power, adventure, status, and material reward no longer exists to the degree that it classically did in the private sector of the economy.

4. The threat of a third World War and the shadow of the new weapons may, to a degree, have altered the older American optimism and sense of confidence in the progressive and successful unfolding of a long future. The insecurity of the postwar world may have helped reduce the premium Americans attached to the economic future over the present, while increasing their concern with values which transcend the vicissitudes of a life span—notably, family and religion.

In these respects the interweaving of facets of the welfare and the garrison states may help to account for those shifts in national values—reflected in phenomena as palpable as the birth rate and as elusive as the hopes and fears of the young—which, we all sense, require some revision in the classic view of the dominant cultural values of American society.

Can the Nation Solve Its Problems? The third component of the classic national style was judged to be its continuity of experience and setting. This continuity permitted the nation to resolve conflicts between public idealism and special interests through relatively stable processes of political and social compromise and to adjust to a changing reality by processes of vigorous experiment and incremental innovation. Two questions now arise. Has the American method for handling its problems significantly changed? Are the problems confronting the nation—now and over the foreseeable future—capable of being dealt with by means of its contemporary operating style?

On domestic matters, the classic style still operates. And, over a wide range of issues, it operates with a heightened effectiveness. The two major political parties continue to work as intermediate instruments of compromise and reconciliation on a continental basis. The private voluntary associations within American communities have never been more active, more devoted to commonly shared objectives, or equipped with a longer agenda of communal good works. And when one examines the classic sources of conflict within the national community—labor and capital, the farm and the city, regional interests, racial and minority groups—one finds each conflict has been softened—not eliminated, but softened—by the increased physical and social homogeneity of the society as well as by the persistence of high levels of employment and rising standards of welfare—excepting, as before, the desegregation issue.

Nevertheless, a group of major domestic problems remains. These are awkward because they do not lend themselves to the most familiar forms of political resolution. The process of solving national problems has, in the past, been accelerated by the fact that the major issues involved urgent and direct special interests of particular groups within the nation. These groups were articulate; they pressed hard on politicians anxious to pick up marginal votes; and the interplay of unambiguous special interests drove the political process forward. But the agenda of American domestic life for the next decade—as nearly as we can perceive it—consists in large part of issues where the problem is not so much to compromise conflicting group interests as it is for the community to act (or fail to act) as a collectivity on an expanded range of common interests. This is the case with the problem of inflation; with school buildings and teachers' salaries; with enlarged road building programs; with the rebuilding of the old cities, including the clearance of slums; with public health; with the care of the aged. If this agenda is to be dealt with, the community must decide that extra dollars spent on communal purposes outweigh the value of marginal dollars spent within the private budget. The struggle must take place to a substantial degree within the mind of the individual citizen rather than as among different groups of citizens, each motivated by overriding special interests. American national politics is shifting, in a sense, toward the long familiar patterns and issues of small town politics—the roads, the schools, and all the rest.

These communal problems must be faced at a time when the public budget is strained by security outlays and by the unavoidable consequences of providing minimum public services for a rapidly expanding population. They cannot be resolved by "soaking the rich." They confront the community with either inflation or some alternate form of sacrifice. The nation will have to judge as among degrees of risk in the missiles race, the quality of education for the young, and the horsepower of its automobiles.

It is by no means clear that the American community is incapable of making the calculus intelligently, i.e., in such a way as to preserve the society's fundamental values and its physical security. The communal trend of national life and experience should make sound decision on these problems easier than it would have been in, say, the 1920s. Nevertheless, how the community decides to dispose of its annual increment in real income as among security outlays abroad, communal outlays at home, and the private budget will prove a searching and, in some respects, a new form of challenge to the political and social process at the national level.

In short, American politics is shifting away from its classic task of compromising special interests to the task of harmonizing private and public values. And within the area of public values there is a clash between the imperatives of a welfare state (with a rapidly expanding population) and the imperatives of American survival on the world scene. There is a clear and basic continuity in our political processes; but they must be adjusted to deal with a problem familiar enough in kind but new in its scale.

With respect to techniques of innovation outside of politics the national style is now less empirical than it once was, and the major institutions of the nation, both private and public, are increasingly sensitive to the problem of how innovation can be induced in large bureaucratic institutions.

In industry there has been an enormous enlargement of funds available for research; a new high status is accorded not merely the natural scientist and engineer but also the economist, the psychologist as personnel expert, the sociologist or social psychologist willing to apply his skills to market research, and so on. American business has come to take an increasingly explicit view of its relation to the economy and to the whole society of which it is a part. Industrial economists examine longperiod trends in population and income, seeking to deduce the trend in demand for their firm's products and thus the appropriate rate of investment. They study their firm's relations to the public and to the political process in much the same way. In addition to their expanded staffs of assorted experts, the large American firms draw in all manner of expert consultants, freed of bureaucratic responsibilities and the operator's vested interests, to help them identify their problems and to propose innovational solutions. The vogue of the outside expert (as well as the brainstorming session) indicates that Americans are not settling for the values of Kafka-like bureaucracy without a struggle.

The American business firm, then, is no longer an atomistic unit concentrated on the current behavior of its prices and its costs, guessing as shrewdly as it can its future prospects, making relatively simple profit-maximizing decisions, the only communal concern of which is to ensure that its officers keep out of jail. It is a self-conscious unit in a complex, interacting society, trying to understand as well as to exploit its environment, trying to influence (if not fully to determine) its own technological, social, and political setting.

There has been a parallel revolution in the institutions and attitudes of the national government, notably in national security policy where, in a sense, we are committed to try to influence world history in our own interest. During the Second World War (quite aside from the atomic bomb) all three military services found that the natural scientist, the economist, the psychologist, and the psychiatrist had important uses. And in the postwar period a relatively elevated status for the staff man was institutionalized in new planning machinery, both within the major bureaucracies and among them, notably, in the Joint Chiefs of Staff and the National Security Council. Like modern business, modern government bureaucracy has sought out and used the occasional consultant with great vigor. The post-1945 soldier remains respectful of the academic and the intellectual. There is, for example, no more radical and significant shift in the institutions of American life than the wide scope of the training now given to the professional military at the various war colleges, as compared to the narrow prewar curricula, and the altered character of the roster of lecturers.

So far as the direction of change is concerned, American society has, then, responded to the innovational challenges it has faced at home and abroad; and it has begun to restructure its attitudes and institutions in the directions required to meet them. The operative question is, however, whether these changes are likely to prove sufficient in scale and appropriate in direction to protect the nation's interests in a peculiarly treacherous world arena of power.

In the fields of military and foreign policy there is room for doubt that we have yet found an adequate balance between staff and line, between reflection and operational vigor. We have been unable, for example, in the postwar years to bring the three military services within the orbit of any coherent pattern of national security strategy. The directions and priorities in staff work are largely geared to a competitive struggle for survival (if not hegemony) among the three services. There are, indeed, advantages in competition; and no single man is likely to know the correct solution at any period of time in a world of extremely rapid change. Nevertheless, on balance, our failure to unify the three services is a major unresolved national problem. It has led not only to waste but also to misallocation of effort. For example, the problems of deterring limited war have been grossly underestimated as an element in the national security problem, due, in part, to the competition of the services for function and funds in the dramatic area of all-out nuclear war.

Our difficulties have been compounded to a degree because we have brought to the Pentagon administrative concepts geared to a much slower pace of innovation than that we now confront. It is an interesting symbolic fact that the present structure of the Office of the Secretary of Defense is patterned explicitly on that of General Motors. The year-to-year competition between General Motors and (say) Ford in models, procurement, and marketing resembles only remotely the arms race between the United States and the Soviet Union. Although in a matter of this kind no one man's testimony is to be taken as definitive, there is an evident element of truth in the observations of Trevor Gardner on the missiles research and development position early in 1956.

Here is what is wrong:

1. The Army, the Navy and the Air Force, each working on its own parochial guided-missiles program, are vying with each other in an intolerable rivalry.
2. The over-all missiles program is smothering in an administrative nightmare of committees and subcommittees competing with each other for influence and appropriations.
3. The ICBM project, which two and a half years ago was given a top-priority status, now shares top priority with many subsidiary missiles projects and the result is that there is no such thing as top priority.

4. The executive personnel of the missiles program is notable for its preponderance of management experts recruited from private business, and for its poverty of full-time scientists who qualify as missiles experts and know what they're talking about.[32]

The imperatives of bureaucratic order and consensus, which we have come greatly to value, evidently clash with the requirements of pace in innovation. It is altogether typical that we tend to talk about the arms race in terms of the relative size of the total pool of Soviet and American engineers—a new form of "numbers racket." We like quantitative forms for our problems and shy away from the hard fact that the technological arms race is a problem in quality and priority where the criteria of mass production industry do not automatically give the right answer. It is not the number of Soviet engineers that threatens us; it is the sharpness of Soviet priorities and their ability to concentrate their best talents around them which permit a nation with a third our real income to close on us.

In foreign policy a different aspect of the national style gives us chronic difficulty—the relative ease and continuity of our political and social experience. We had to fight for independence, but from early colonial days the basic presuppositions of American life were those of an individualist society. We never had to struggle to free ourselves from a feudal social and political past. Certain initial feudal carry-overs—like primogeniture—dropped away quickly in the face of American reality. As Hartz emphasizes from de Tocqueville, essentially we were "born free" as a nation, taking for granted concepts and conditions which elsewhere could be approximated only after bloody struggle. Economically, moreover (with the exception of parts of the South), we have never known the pressure of overpopulation on the land leading to conditions which tend to perpetuate poverty. For the nation as a whole there was no vicious circle to be broken before economic progress became the normal condition of life.

Thus, as we face a world where something like a billion and a half human beings are caught up in one version or another of an effort to break old, static molds and to modernize their societies, we can find little instinctive in our history or in our political or economic processes which fully meets their case. In a broad sense, of course, their struggles for freedom and independence appeal to us, as does their aspiration for material progress. Moreover, if we are prepared to reflect on the meaning of Washington's Farewell Address, it is not very difficult to understand their instinct for neutralism. Nevertheless, from our wartime relationship with the Chinese Nationalists down to the Middle East crisis and the foreign aid bill debate, we have had difficulty in understanding the complex processes at work in the underdeveloped areas and in harmonizing our efforts with those of the men and women caught up in the great nationalist revolutions now going forward in strategically decisive areas of the world. We have, to our cost, been excessively culture bound in facing this mammoth fact of the twentieth century.

It will take more reflection and imagination—more application of vicarious rather than instinctive knowledge—than we have thus far brought to bear on national policy to protect the national interest as these revolutions evolve over the coming decades; for good or ill, geography, communications, and the facts of twentieth-century power make it dangerous if not impossible to adopt toward Asia, the Middle East, and Africa the distant and skeptical stance of John Quincy Adams toward the new Latin American republics more than a century and a quarter ago.[33]

The nation faces similar problems of comprehension in other directions. In Western Europe, Japan, and other regions where we have come to believe that a firm basis of common understanding and common objectives had been established, we have been affronted from time to time by behavior and moods which in no way fit the American image of the Free World alliance. While diplomacy is hard at work restoring the semblance of the Atlantic Alliance after Suez, the occurrence of that crisis and its consequences have revealed a gap between the reality of the transatlantic relationship and our conception of it.

And, perhaps, above all, we have been forced to reach out beyond our instinctive concepts to understand the forces at work within the Communist Bloc. Since we could not in any rational way undertake a definitive military crusade against Moscow and Peking, we have had to peer across the Iron and Bamboo Curtains and try to understand the grossly unfamiliar forces which have determined the patterns of change within the Communist Bloc, with which our own destiny is now inextricably entangled.

In every major dimension the nature of our interaction with the world environment forces us to look at ourselves and the world in terms of a set of abstractions new to American thought and history. The automatic transfer of concepts from our own round of life no longer suffices.

A Conclusion. How, finally, shall we assess the national style?

The relevant criterion is, surely, this: to what extent does it permit us to preserve our chosen values while protecting our common interests? In one way or another this question has been central to American life since the nation was formed under the Constitution; and it is not to be expected that we could now render a definitive judgment. As befits living men and a lively culture we are in the midst of an unresolved, active process.

We are trying to reconcile a commitment to the unique, responsible individual with two sets of forces: those set in motion by the maturing of an industrial welfare state, and those impinging on us from a world caught up in a struggle for power and in massive revolutionary change. Since nations, like people, live in a context of uncertainty, we cannot know the outcome of the process. We cannot be sure that the concept of the individual in a democratic society, as we have defined it historically, will survive in some recognizable form the blandishments and pressures of welfare and garrison states. We cannot assert with confidence that we shall achieve tolerable solutions to the problems thrown up by an age of fusion weapons and world-wide nationalist revolutions. What we can do is to observe the national style grappling with the contemporary agenda; and we can prescribe as we are moved to do.

Surveying a scene where the individual appears hard pressed, many of our wisest and most perceptive men have ended by reaffirming the continued legitimacy and sanctity of the concept of the unique human personality. Riesman, for example, closes *The Lonely Crowd* with: "On one thing I am quite sure . . . men are created different; they lose their social freedom and their individual autonomy in seeking to become like each other." Such reaffirmations—notably those of our novelists—are often colored, however, by a kind of defeatism, by an explicit or implicit judgment that the requirements of large-scale organization or the requirements of an effective communal effort require the individual to surrender to the alleged needs of the group and to work out his private destiny by some Hegelian sublimation or by enlarging the private area of withdrawal. The argument of this paper would, to a degree, challenge such pessimism. A reassertion of the importance of the unique individual may not only be good for our souls but also essential to a more effective communal and national performance.

We are caught up in an age of radical innovation. Innovation requires ideas and that special kind of answerable courage in which men lead others in taking steps in the dark.[34] Ideas and courage are the gifts of lonely individuals, not of committees or bureaucracies. If the national style accommodates itself to the problems we face there should emerge a new respect and status for the individual loyal to his private vision.

So far as administration is concerned neither in nor out of government are there grounds for complacency. We have evidently not yet solved the problem of efficient large-scale organization in an age of radical innovation. It may emerge that we are now merely in an awkward transition, having carried over too hastily the patterns of large-scale mass production into large-scale organization. Our present steep organizational pyramids may give way to shallower structures with increasing degrees of autonomy for the individual, fewer layers of command, fewer decisions negotiated by committees. It may well be that, as we take the measure of the requirements of organized life in the twentieth century and especially when we weigh the claims of innovation over static order in our bureaucracies, we shall find that we can do our business with smaller staffs, with higher degrees of personal responsibility, acknowledging more openly than we now do that the success of our common enterprises hinges on strong-minded, responsible, and creative men. We may, in short, learn how to institutionalize the insights we display only at moments of crisis.

Something parallel to this restructuring of our bureaucracies may be demanded of our intellectual life. If our universities are to make the contribution to society they should in an age requiring radical innovation, they must look beyond Ranke's rule of sources and develop more general concepts of man and the world. Out of the intermediate and higher ranges of abstraction new ways of looking at things emerge; and it is from new ways of looking at things that solutions are found to new problems. Without losing our grip on facts and our respect for their hard reality we must begin to transcend the pre-1914 German patterns on which our intellectual trade schools are still largely based. With all due respect for James and Dewey it takes more than a common sense instinctive to the round of American life to deal with the age of guided missiles; the age of revolution in Asia, the Middle East, and Africa; and with that exciting but dangerous passage of history in which communism as we have known it discovers that it is not historically viable. To bring to bear what understanding the human mind can generate demands more than shelves of specialized monographs. We must come to give as much systematic thought to the problem of unifying knowledge as we now give to the more familiar process of extending its factual range. And this can come about only if we encourage the individual to strike out boldly on his own; for intellectual synthesis is an event that takes place in a single mind.

Somehow, finally, we must, if we are to succeed, find ways of suffusing the national government with a sense of private adventure, for a high proportion of the society's tasks of innovation must, in the end, be carried out in Washington. The individual human beings in the great bureaucracies must be encouraged to think, to throw up new ideas, to debate. The illusion that our affairs can successfully be handled by negotiating minimum consensus in layer after layer of inter-departmental committees must be broken. The government must recapture a sense that creation is something we badly need; that creation is a job for men backing their play with integrity; and this spirit must suffuse the whole apparatus, from the office of the president to the lower GS-5. The inter-departmental machinery of negotiation and consensus will, of course, continue to grind along. Certain heavy imperatives of order must, of course, continue to be respected. The age-old patterns of bureaucratic life will not suddenly be broken. But the bureaucratic processes must be made to grind on something other than departmental vested interests and the pre-compromised views of men anxious, above all, to avoid controversy or trouble.

One can assert with confidence that these are the directions in which our society must move if it is to maximize the chance that it deal successfully with its problems. It is quite another matter to predict with confidence that we shall, in fact, learn how to suffuse our national life and institutions with a new individualism. The sceptic's case is easy to make. The image of vast institutions, apparently beyond the control or even the comprehension of any individual, with a logic and momentum of their own, is strong in all our minds. The expertise which they absorb and use is increasingly specialized. Individual men appear to know only a diminishing part of the total information on which action must be based. But we must be careful not to be taken in by images of our own creation. The truly important policies of our great institutions and even of the national government are, in the end, still made by a few men; for there is no other way. It is difficult to bring to bear the insights of many specialized areas of knowledge on a particular problem; but it is done every day, better or worse, by those who must act.

It is, in short, too soon to despair. Our children are still born into the world with very strong egos; and the long lesson of the past is that history is tolerant of the individual if he avoids the larger illusions of grandeur.

NOTES

1 This effort at synthesis was initially drafted without reference to the other papers prepared for the Dedham Conference which arrived as this essay neared completion. The present version remains essentially unaltered except for some extremely helpful suggestions of A. M. Schlesinger, Sr., and A. M. Schlesinger, Jr. I am grateful to my colleagues at the Center for International Studies who read and criticized an early version as well as to John Blum, A. D. Chandler, Jr., Clyde Kluckhohn, and Gregory Rochlin. My most substantial debt, however, is to Elspeth Davies Rostow whose views and judgments are reflected at many points in this text.

2 For a recent exploration of the content of contemporary French paradoxes, see David Schoenbrun, "Manners and Morals of the French." "A Frenchman is rarely seen drunk in public or in private but France has the highest rate of alcoholism in the world. Frenchmen are fervent patriots but they invest their money abroad. A Frenchman is thrifty to the point of miserliness in his private family affairs but will cheerfully raid the public Treasury and laugh at constantly mounting national deficits. A Frenchman prides himself on his logic but turns off the heating system exactly on March 21, the first official day of spring, even though it may be snowing outside. A French deputy delivers fiery speeches in Parliament about the vital importance of putting down the rebellion in Algeria and then votes against the government's bill for increased taxes to pay the cost of putting down the Algerian revolt. All the French want is to be allowed to live in peace—yet France has been at war longer than any other country." Harpers Magazine, March 1957. For further reference, see D. Schoenbrun, As France Goes (New York: Harper, 1957).

3 New Yorker, April 23, 1949.

4 R. Niebuhr, The Irony of American History (New York: Scribners', 1954), chapter 2, especially pp. 23–24. "It is particularly remarkable that the two great religious-moral traditions which informed our early life—New England Calvinism and Virginia Deism and Jeffersonianism—arrive at remarkably similar conclusions about the meaning of our national character and destiny. Calvinism may have held too pessimistic views of human nature and too mechanical views of the providential ordering of human life. But when it assessed the significance of the American experiment both its conceptions of American destiny and its appreciation of American virtue finally arrived at conclusions strikingly similar to those of Deism. Whether our nation interprets its spiritual heritage through Massachusetts or Virginia, we came into exist-

ence with the sense of being a 'separated' nation, which God was using to make a new beginning for mankind. We had renounced the evils of European feudalism. We had escaped from the evils of European religious bigotry. We had found broad spaces for the satisfaction of human desires in place of the crowded Europe. Whether, as in the case of the New England theocrats, our forefathers thought of our 'experiment' as primarily the creation of a new and purer church, or, as in the case of Jefferson and his coterie, they thought primarily of a new political community, they believed in either case that we had been called out by God to create a new humanity. We were God's 'American Israel.' "

5 S. E. Morison, *By Land and by Sea* (New York: Knopf, 1953), chapter 10.

6 The cast of this essay is designed to dramatize the role in the American experience of certain unifying concepts and institutions. Its themes should not obscure the equally fundamental fact that, within the framework of consensus, implicit or explicit, conflict and debate have been the engine which has driven us forward—a fact forcefully emphasized by A. S. Schlesinger, Jr. in a criticism of this essay's final draft. In this connection, Charles Curtis has recently written:

"I suggest that things get done gradually only between opposing forces. There is no such thing as self-restraint in a people. What looks like it is indecision. . . . It may be that truth is best sought in the market of free speech, but the best decisions are neither bought nor sold. They are the result of disagreement, where the last word is not 'I admit you're right,' but 'I've got to live with the son of a bitch, haven't I?' " *A Commonplace Book* (New York: Simon & Schuster, 1957), pp. 112–113. The present analysis would accept the fact that the nation's consensus has been the product of clash and debate. But it is designed also to establish why Americans have chosen in the end to live with one another—a result by no means foreordained in all societies and, in itself, a matter of substance.

7 *Studies in Classic American Literature* (New York: Anchor, 1955), p. 18.

8 P. Bradley, ed., *Democracy in America* (New York: Vintage, 1954), vol. 2, pp. 78–79.

9 G. Myrdal, *An American Dilemma* (New York: Harper, 1944), vol. 1, p. 21.

10 Jean-Paul Sartre, "Americans and Their Myths," *The Nation*, Vol. 165 (October 18, 1947), pp. 402–403, quoted in K. Davis, H. Bredemeir, M. Levy, *Modern American Society* (New York: Rinehart, 1949), p. 48.

11 Bradley, ed., *op. cit.*, vol. 2, pp. 15–18.

12 Morton White, *Social Thought in America* (Boston: Beacon, 1957), pp. 12–13.

13 This conclusion should be compared with the related judgments of three recent commentators: Louis Hartz, *The Liberal Tradition in America* (New York: Harcourt Brace, 1955); John Kouwenhoven, "What is American About America," *Colorado Quarterly*, June 1956; and D. J. Boorstin, "The Place of Thought in American Life," *The American Scholar*, Spring 1956. Dealing respectively, with American political, cultural, and philosophic patterns, each makes central to his analysis the notion that American life has concentrated on the extension of relatively continuous processes embedded in circumstances special to American history and its environment. Hartz poses the question of how a society "born to freedom," having lived its life without knowing fully the uniqueness of the stable, implicit assumptions within which it has evolved, can deal with a world moved by forces unfamiliar to the American experience. Kouwenhoven isolates the uniqueness of American culture in its invention of ongoing processes—from the Manhattan skyline to Mark Twain's storytelling, from Whitman's *Leaves of Grass* to jazz. He concludes: "Without childishly denying the relevance of the past, can we not recognize that the American past does not, like the past of many other peoples, extend downward into the soil on which we at any moment stand. Our past, by and large, extends laterally backward across the mountains or plains, or across the sea, to somewhere else. Our history is the process of

westering and the counter process of return; of motion into and out of cities; of motion up and down the social ladder—a long, complex, and sometimes rapid sequence of consecutive change. America is not an artifact. It is not a fixed and immutable ideal. It has not order and proportion. And yet neither is it chaos, except as that is chaotic which no single mind can comprehend or control. America is process, and in so far as we are American, the work of our heads and hands and hearts inevitably reflects that fact."

Boorstin isolates five distinctive characteristics of the national culture: "Interest in institutions rather than ideologies, in process rather than product; the success criterion; the importance of context: the implicitness of ideas; the nirvana of success: self-annihilation through mastery and adaptation; and continuity and conservatism of ways of thought." He concludes: "American empiricism has tied our thinking to the slow, organic growth of institutions. By rejecting ideologies, we reject the sharp angles, the sudden turns, the steep up-and-down grades, which mark political life in many parts of the world, in favor of the slow curves, the imperceptible slopes of institutional life. If ever the circumstances of a culture have suited a people to think 'institutionally,' American history has done so. For us, fortunately, it is impossible to distinguish the history of our thought from the history of our institutions."

[14] Universal manhood suffrage did not, of course, apply throughout the American states in the 1780s. The problem posed by the unpropertied voter was, nevertheless, real enough in the minds of the Founding Fathers.

[15] In addition, other values within the common Western creed counsel simple human compassion, raising the real, but quantitatively lesser question of the extent to which the state (as opposed to individual charity) should allocate resources to the poor, the aged, the overworked, the insane, and to others in need.

[16] For an excellent review of the classical literature in these terms see L. Robbins, The Theory of Economic Policy (New York: Macmillan, 1952).

[17] See, notably, R. H. Gabriel, The Course of American Democratic Thought (New York: Ronald Press, 1940).

[18] It is not wholly clear whether the pre-1914 American socialist movement is most accurately to be regarded as distinctively different from the progressive movement in its fundamentals or, merely, as a sect with a somewhat longer list of limited reforms and a special set of banners.

[19] For a review of the various strands of thought which were ultimately brought to bear in New Deal policy see A. Schlesinger, Jr., The Crisis of the Old Order (Boston: Houghton Mifflin, 1957), chapter 23.

[20] The other major early recovery move under the New Deal consisted in altering the dollar value of gold—a move which also had historical resonance, going back to the bimetallist agitation of the 1880s and 1890s.

[21] This passage is based directly on the work of A. D. Chandler, Jr. See, especially, "Henry Varnum Poor, Philosopher of Management, 1812–1905," in Men in Business, W. Miller, ed. (Cambridge, Mass.: Harvard University Press, 1952); and Henry Varnum Poor (Cambridge, Mass.: Harvard University Press, 1956), especially chapters 6 and 7.

[22] Administrative Behavior (New York: Macmillan, 1948), pp. 38–39.

[23] Herbert A. Simon, Donald W. Smithburg, Victor A. Thompson, Public Administration (New York: Knopf, 1950).

[24] Poor himself, examining intensively a single case which happened to forecast a problem which was to emerge generally, was fully sensitive to the creative problems of management. He considered the requirements of human quality and motivation in business leadership and administration in terms which only the most current American literature can match. Compare, for example, Chandler, op. cit., pp. 156–158, and

M. Newcomber, *The Big Business Executive* (New York: Columbia University Press, 1955), chapter 2.

25 For a classic exploration of this problem see E. E. Morison, "A Case Study of Innovation," *Engineering and Science Monthly*, April 1950.

26 Compare, for example, D. Eisenhower, *Crusade in Europe* (New York: Doubleday, 1948), pp. 74–76, on the task of a modern military commander and M. Newcomber, *op. cit.*, pp. 20–23, on the functions of a modern business executive.

27 For essential measurements of this phenomenon see A. Hawley, *The Changing Shape of Metropolitan America* (Glencoe, Ill.: Free Press, 1956).

28 A. D. H. Kaplan, *Big Enterprise in a Competitive System* (Washington: Brookings Institution, 1954), p. 70; and, in general, chapter 3, for a survey of evidence on changing business scale.

29 J. F. Dewhurst and asociates, *America's Needs and Resources: A New Survey* (New York: Twentieth Century Fund, 1947), p. 380.

30 See S. Stouffer, *Communism, Conformity, and Civil Liberties* (New York: Doubleday, 1955), on the correlation between "tolerance" and level of education, especially chapter 4 (pp. 89–108) and the conclusion on p. 236. Stouffer (p. 92) presents the following data on education by age group in a national sample.

*Percentage Distribution of Education
Within Each Age Group*

National Cross Section	21–29	30–39	40–49	50–59	60 and over
College graduates	8	10	9	7	4
Some college	14	10	9	9	6
High school graduates	40	33	20	14	13
Some high school	24	23	24	20	13
Grade school	14	24	38	50	64

31 The reference is to a former Secretary of the Treasury.

32 *Look*, May 15, 1956.

33 *The Selected Writings of John and John Quincy Adams*, A. Koch and W. Peden, eds. (New York: Knopf, 1946), p. 319: "So far as they were contending for independence, I wished well to their cause; but I had seen and yet see no prospect that they would establish free or liberal institutions of government. They are not likely to promote the spirit either of freedom or order by their example. They have not the first element of good or free government. Arbitrary power, military and ecclesiastical, was stamped upon their education, upon their habits, and upon all their institutions. Civil dissension was infused into all their seminal principles. War and mutual destruction was in every member of their organization, moral, political, and physical. I had little expectation of any beneficial result to this country from any future connection with them, political or commercial. We should derive no improvement to our own institutions by any communion with theirs. Nor was there any appearance of a disposition in them to take any political lesson from us. . . ." As with many "realistic" judgments, Adams' view of prospects in Latin America proved a shade too pessimistic.

34 ". . . all great and honorable actions are accompanied with great difficulties and must be both enterprised and overcome with answerable courages." *William Bradford, of Plymouth Plantation*, S. E. Morison, ed. (New York: Knopf, 1952).

PART II

List of Participants

Alfred H. Barr, Jr., Director, The Museum of Modern Art
Richard M. Bissell, Jr., Economist, United States Government
Lyman Bryson, The Institute for Religious and Social Studies, Jewish Theological Seminary of America
McGeorge Bundy, Faculty of Arts and Sciences, Harvard University
Joseph I. Coffey, Colonel, United States Army
Paul A. Freund, Harvard Law School
John W. Gardner, President, The Carnegie Corporation
David B. Gleicher, Center for International Studies, M.I.T.
Richard W. Hatch, Center for International Studies, M.I.T.
Richard Hofstadter, Department of History, Columbia University
Carl Jonas, novelist
Abraham Kaplan, Department of Philosophy, University of California
Carl Kaysen, Department of Economics, Harvard University
George F. Kennan, Institute for Advanced Study, Princeton University
James R. Killian, Jr., President, Massachusetts Institute of Technology
Clyde Kluckhohn, Department of Anthropology, Harvard University
Max F. Millikan, Director, Center for International Studies, M.I.T.
Elting E. Morison, School of Industrial Management, M.I.T.
Henry A. Murray, Department of Social Relations, Harvard University
Duncan Norton-Taylor, Assistant Managing Editor, *Fortune Magazine*
J. Robert Oppenheimer, Director, Institute for Advanced Study, Princeton University
David M. Potter, Department of History, Yale University
David Riesman, Department of Sociology, University of Chicago
W. W. Rostow, Department of Economics, M.I.T.
Paul A. Samuelson, Department of Economics, M.I.T.
Arthur M. Schlesinger, Sr., Department of History, Harvard University
Julius A. Stratton, Chancellor, Massachusetts Institute of Technology
Morton White, Department of Philosophy, Harvard University
William S. White, *The New York Times*
A. T. M. Wilson, Director, The Tavistock Institute of Human Relations

Donald L. M. Blackmer, Assistant to the Director, Center for International Studies, M.I.T.
Arthur L. Singer, Jr., Administrative Officer, Center for International Studies, M.I.T.
Carol F. Anderson
Patricia E. Coughlin
Mrs. Gertrude Winquist, Hostess, Endicott House

COMMENTARY: AMERICAN ETHICS AND PUBLIC POLICY

by Elting E. Morison

IF I SEEM to have been led far afield at times, remember Mr. Kaplan put me on these trails. Actually this paper is no more than a set of variations on a theme—or set of themes—by Mr. Kaplan.

You will recall from these collected papers a remark to the effect that T. S. Eliot was a household and that a personality, in Harry Murray's words, was a full congress. You will also notice how often the prevailing antitheses of American life are raised for inspection—Kaplan's dualities; Kluckhohn's extended list of contradictions; Rostow's paradoxes.

It is no profound observation to suggest that the different voices within one and these larger antitheses are not the special properties of a peculiar national character. Everyone, everywhere, always is tugged by rival urges: to be alone and to be together; to hold fire and ice in the same hand. These opposing urges, it is to be supposed, are the essential nature of lives that begin with birth and end in death.

Their existence, if man were left wholly free to meditate, could give only difference and depth and attractive irony to existence. But since things do find their opposites, against the desire to meditate runs the desire to act. And it is in the realm of action that the antitheses cause trouble—how to reach unanimous or even majority opinion out of the continual debate within the personal congress; how to fashion sensible decision out of contrasting objectives.

It is possible, of course, to avoid action—to be caught on dead center between the conflicting interests—but that, as in Hamlet, is understood to be tragedy. It is also possible, in the interest of action, to split the antitheses—as Ecclesiastes proposed in his timetable for building up and breaking down or for sewing and rending. But, as Ecclesiastes discovered, it isn't as simple as that. For one thing, there is trouble in the timing;

319

it is hard to get a nice match between the moment and the feeling. For another, it turns out that men go on harboring joint desires. At the moment they refrain from embracing, they can think up good reasons to embrace. At the same instant they want some part of the satisfaction that comes, for example, in the time to love and also some part of the satisfaction that comes in the time to hate.

This seems to me to be the principal thing that anyone charged with responsibility for a family, a factory, a state—or for himself—has to have in mind. The disorder caused by the turmoil of rival urges is not, of course, ordinarily paralyzing. More often than not, some of the debaters in the interior congress speak with greater authority than others; and more often than not one end of a paradox is heavier than another. So ordinarily a personality in good order can act at least as a satisfied majority in pursuit of a preferred objective. But as conditions change, as they always do, a minority voice in the congress may emerge as the leader of a new coalition; or the balance along the line of the paradox may shift. These changes may occur any time and bring with them changes of policy—a reorganization of energies within the person or the body politic.

Thus, I assume, the conduct of human affairs—if the alternating harmonies of inner voices and the adequate satisfaction of antithetic desires are to be taken into account—demands the free play of diverse elements in unstable equilibrium. To endure the free play requires a tolerance for waste and lost motion, the acceptance of acute anxiety while one waits to see what is going to happen next. It requires also a concern for how things illogically work themselves out that is greater than the concern to pursue a particular logical end. It requires a heavier commitment to the general process of living than to any special product to be derived from man's endeavor.

The load on any man or society that takes this view is obviously immense; historically it has often been rejected. Out of fear, or in the interests of symmetry or for a rational conclusion, men have often tried to establish sound policy simply by cutting off one end of the presenting paradox. By such means they have been momentarily freed to announce that they are in earnest, that they will not equivocate, that they will not excuse, and that they will not retreat. They have been momentarily freed to subjugate, like Alva, a territory; or to build, like Henry Ford,

more automobiles cheaper in a season than anybody else. This is all, or
at least almost all, to the good; and at the end you have something accomplished, something done. But if you have achieved these things
without equivocatings, excusings, and retreatings, you have probably
done so in an environment that has precluded the legitimate exercise
of human confusion. The case study here is the Book of Job. Because it
was inconceivable to either the Devil or Jehovah that a man who cursed
God could also love Him, Job was worked over until all the paradox was
scared out of him. Then he was the desirable end product, perfect and
upright, as defined by those who had laid down a policy about the upright and the perfect.

Mr. Millikan and Mr. Rostow have asked us to talk about good and
evil. My own view of evil is this: it consists of the effort to maintain a
particular end—for reasons of order, logic, aesthetics, decency, for any
reason at all—by means that deny men the opportunity to take into
account the inevitable alternatives posed by the diversity and paradox
in their own natures. The ends may be perverted—as to put Deutschland
over all; or ideal—as to make men noble; the means may be base—as with
rack, pinion, or castor oil, or benign—as to withhold from children the
fact that gods got drunk and told ribald anecdotes on Olympus. It
makes no difference.

This is no original view. For our civilization we have agreed it was
most memorably stated in the New Testament—with its intense concern
for the relationship of a man to himself and the next man to him, with
its distrust of logical system and uniform solutions, its parables radiating
off their ambiguous meanings, its biting conflicting admonitions, and its
insistence that wisdom is only wise if, as situations change, what is wise
also changes. Such a view of things appears to have been in the minds of
those who invented democracy—which is a method that in its looseness
and disorder permits conflicting urges to work themselves out, and the
ends of paradox to be held in tolerable but changing resolution. It does
not prefigure the ends or final result. It awaits the arrival of the new
occasions before supplying the new duties. That is why, it seems to me,
this country so often proceeds, as Robert Oppenheimer suggested, from
astonishment to surprise.

The virtue of such a method is well revealed in the history of our effort
to deal with the most interesting and dangerous internal problem of the

last eighty years—the organization of our industrial energy. Near the beginning of this history lies the Sherman Act—the early definition of a clear and present danger which conveniently did not include any very precise solution to the problem it defined. Thus it served as a proposition for debate and an instrument for public education. The debate which followed and still continues has produced an extensive range of argument and a striking array of shifting, proximate solutions. From the early simplicities of distinction between good and bad trusts the discussion went on to analyze the meaning of bigness, the difference between regulation within a frame of legislation and control by executive action, the invocation of the rule of reason and consent decrees. It is worth noticing that whenever specific and limited points were settled in debate they were forthwith translated into law—as in the Elkins and Clayton Acts. It is also worth noticing that because no single, final, total solution was reached the public went on educating itself about a changing problem.

The history of this experience throws some light on two subjects raised by Mr. Kaplan: first, the relation between power and policy. Here the relationship established was entirely satisfying. Theodore Roosevelt set a precedent in his sporadic skillfully selected prosecutions, using his power not so much to impose a program as to define a difficulty, to suggest possible limits, to propose directions, and to excite the entire community into thinking about the difficulty. By small executive means he achieved very great democratic effects. The other subject raised by Mr. Kaplan was the transfer between our moral intent and our policy. In this instance the transfer seems to me almost total. Our purpose, as I have suggested, has been with the evolving process and not the prefigured end. Confronted by the dangers of industrial energy, the extreme and obvious solutions were avoided. Those who pined for the Jeffersonian days were not permitted to cut up the economy into little pieces. Those seduced by the terrible temptations that lurk in the organization of industrial energy were not permitted, as in Germany, to put it together in ways that would satisfy only the logical or aesthetic desire for efficiency or unity. For over eighty years we have borne the pain of leaving the question of the corporation open for periodic review and modification while still holding the explosive energies, on the whole, within tolerable limits.

In solving our internal problems, our methods—as the above example is designed to show—have served us on the whole well. But there have been curious side effects. Our full engagement in the immediate process has damaged our sense of time. It has left us, to a ponderable extent, regardless of the past and thoughtless for the future. We remain, too often for our own good, marooned in the present. More important, our method has seriously limited our capacity to explain to others what we are up to. The free, open, experimental society can no more define its ultimate intent than could the protozoa explain that it hoped to end as a man. Lacking more useful definitions, we have had to resort to massive equivocations—idiomatic equivalents of the grain of mustard seed—like the American way of life or the American dream, as Mr. Kaplan points out. Unable to understand or at least say much more than this, we have often found it difficult to relate ourselves usefully or intelligibly to external situations; we can only wish the world were safe for democracy.

All this is revealed in a letter Elihu Root prepared for the Second Philippine Commission in 1900. The new government, he explained, had not been created for our own satisfaction but for peace, prosperity, and happiness of the Philippines. "Such measures as are taken," he went on, "should conform to the furthest extent possible to the customs, habits, and even prejudices of the Filipinos." But fundamental to the rule of law and the maintenance of individual freedom he said are certain principles of government that must be established and maintained even though they conflict with the laws of procedure and the customs with which the Filipinos are acquainted. No person should be deprived of life, liberty, or property without due process of law; private property cannot be taken for public use without just compensation; and an accused person shall enjoy the right of speedy public trial.

This seems to me the voice of America whether it speaks to an overseas possession in 1900, or at Versailles in 1919, or on a transmitter to those behind the Iron Curtain in 1957. It says, in effect, that we have nothing to propose but the means we have found useful. If we impose these means or if you accept them, you will work your way toward peace, prosperity, and happiness. Historically, as Mr. Kaplan says, we have found it difficult to give more body to the conduct of our foreign affairs—to reduce our objectives to more precise, if more mundane, policies. Nor can we predict more precise results from the use of our procedures—which, in fact, are likely to lead anywhere from astonishment

to surprise and even to revolution. As the London *Times* said some time
ago, "We [the English] know or think we know who or what we are.
The Americans do not yet know. . . ."

Perhaps, if we were infinitely wise or infinitely courageous, we would,
as in the chapter on the Grand Inquisitor from *The Brothers Kara-
mazov*, meet the powerful agencies on the outside by silent embrace and
withdraw until others had profited by our example. This might be called
the higher as opposed to the provincial isolation. We are sufficiently
human or insufficiently divine, whichever way you wish to put it, so that
we will not wittingly take this course.

Instead we shall go on as we have recently begun, meeting the new
contingencies, which are so different from past contingencies in what we
take to be a reasonably statesmanlike way. Impressed by the delicacy as
well as the power of our intricately interdependent society, bolstered by
the amazing new information about our environment supplied by
physical scientists, economists, and psychologists, we shall endeavor to
set up sound programs intelligently connected to the available data—all
this to direct the environment lest it shake itself apart. Awed by the
threat of Communism, fearful of the armed might of Russia, we shall set
ourselves to think up wise policies and reasonable objectives around the
world.

These endeavors will be useful as indicating our real concern with
the most important issues of our time; they will indicate to others more
about ourselves than we have communicated before perhaps; they may
force us to think through what we really mean by free enterprise or
what we really expect out of the men on Formosa. But I trust we do not
completely succeed in these reasonable endeavors. Any policy however
sage, any objective however limited, tends naturally in time to restrict
alternatives; and, if long continued, tends, by extinguishing the free
play of diversity and paradox, to foreclose the future. The greater the
control we achieve over our destiny at home and abroad, the greater the
temptation to kill off the energies that introduce a saving disorder and
uncertainty in the control.

If we ever really yield to this temptation, we shall have no doubt ap-
proached the enervating conformity and narrowing of opportunity that
Mr. Kaplan points to as present dangers. I disagree with him only about
the present. True, the opportunity for extreme vertical rise has dimin-

ished. No man can go from a small house in Hartford to the single-handed control of the financial stability of the country as J. P. Morgan did. But the opportunity for the average boy in Hartford or anywhere is far greater it seems to me—the opportunity to be educated, to select from a wide array of alternatives a place where he can be gainfully and humanely employed; the opportunity to engage himself in exciting work in the beginning industrial, intellectual, or political situations; the opportunity to expose himself to an incredible range of stimuli and experience. And as for conformity, fond as I am of David Riesman, I wish he had never thought up the inner-directed man to serve as a magnet for all the filings of our wistfulness and nostalgia. That "man" has become the noble savage for our generation. For instance, in little things, the concern over the gray flannel suit and loafers has diverted attention from the fact that some of the best representatives of the older breed wore— every day—bowler hats, black waistcoats, and high buttoned shoes; the preoccupation with ranch houses in Park Forest and Drexelbrook has blotted out the memory of the seamless web of red brick on Beacon Street and brownstone on the east 30s, 40s, and 50s. And these surface conformities reflect to a considerable extent the interior situation. That gyroscope was, in fact, mass produced—designed to maintain a kind of standardized stability in the normal disturbances of life.

On the place of thrift, charity, the nature of women, the meaning of art, the ways to make a living, the relative merits of power and negotiation in settling domestic problems, you will find, I think, that the inner-directed man did indeed hold elaborate conversation with himself but emerged surprisingly often with views identical to those of his neighbor in the next brownstone. So rigid was the conformity, indeed, that black sheep were cut off without a penny and a divorce ended not only one marriage but many attendant friendships. So rigid was the stress of conformity that it often precluded the possibility of receiving any signals that would create a disturbance beyond the capacity of the gyroscope to deal with. It often precluded also the possibility of making useful exceptions to conventional rules—as the death of the folk hero Casabianca so well demonstrates.

The inner-directed man has a hard time living with uncertainty, ambiguity, and irony. His survival on the burning decks of the twentieth century would be open to question.

The degree and nature of the conformity we have today is far less dangerous. It seems little more than the saving agreements on certain things men have to make to save themselves the anxiety of a repeating series of individual decisions in conflicting circumstances. It also serves, as the conformity of the nineteenth century did not, as a useful network of information about what is going on throughout the society. Today it is not only possible, it is inevitable that we will know how the other half lives. Where the conformity of the nineteenth century man to his own interior pattern tended to exclude the communications one needs to live with his fellows, our present other-directedness gives us at least an opportunity to live more satisfyingly with them as political animals should!

The future is perhaps not so satisfying to contemplate; but my hope is that we can continue as we began—a little careless of exact transfer between theory and practice, a little innocent about the precise relation between power and policy. It will do no harm to have a slightly mis-understood, crude, experimental, graceless energy upon the major scenes of action in the coming world if that energy retains its zest in life, liberty, and the pursuit of happiness. There is some ground for this hope. The information we are acquiring about our environment is of necessity so divided among so many different sections of society that the likelihood of any single sector achieving the tremendous power that comes from putting all knowledge together is small. The continuous spasms of technological change shake up the whole society, dislocating vested interests, opening up new zones of opportunity, and steadily modifying the shape of the civilization. Then too there is the heritage. It may be that simple smugness, produced by rising standards of living, or paralysis, produced by the fear of a persistent adversary, will wear down the attractive power of this heritage. But we have lived a long time with the anxiety and excitement of not knowing quite where we were going and this should stand us in good stead as we continue on our way. There is exhilaration in trying to find out who we are, and the search should remain exhilarating as long as we are prepared to remain unsatisfied with any particular, precise definition.

COMMENTARY: THEORY VERSUS PRACTICE IN AMERICAN VALUES AND PERFORMANCE

by David M. Potter

MY FUNCTION as a commentator is to focus attention upon some of the relationships between the theme of Mr. Oppenheimer's paper and other themes that have emerged or are likely to emerge in this conference. One of the basic problems which we have to consider is the reluctance of the American people to accept responsibility for making grave decisions of policy. Historically, this attitude is linked with a distrust of authority and a consequent unwillingness to face up to the burdens and the consequences of authority, even when the exercise of power cannot be escaped. It is an attitude which has influenced American thought and policy profoundly. It has been an important factor in shaping American ideas of morality, as we see in Mr. Kaplan's paper. By invoking a morality of principle rather than a morality of responsibility, we have, in effect, abdicated our duty to decide questions on their merits or with reference to their consequences. When we say that we will do what is right and leave the event in the hand of God, we are really contriving to make the deity responsible for the way our decisions turn out and are indulging ourselves in the pretense that we are not answerable for the results of our acts. We invoke what purports to be an automatice process—the application of fixed moral law—to avoid the obligations of power and the responsibility for consequences.

This same propensity toward automatic solutions has also inclined us to political processes of diffused responsibility—with decision residing in millions of separate voters or in a document written in 1787—and to an economic system of self-operating controls. In seeking to justify these arrangements, we have attributed crucial virtues to them, assuming, for instance, that self-operating controls are uniquely conducive to the generation of incentives, or that the electorate is a repository of sound answers to difficult political questions. It is in part, and only in part, our addiction to this attitude which has prevented us from perceiving more clearly that "rather deep, refractory, and quite unprecedented cultural crisis" of which Mr. Oppenheimer speaks. But to say that the angle of our thought may have prevented us from facing the problems which he discusses is also to imply not only that we are in danger of mistaking our future but also that we may have already been mistaken in some of our interpretations of our past.

One of these interpretations which has appeared as a major theme, heavily emphasized, is the idea that American society is more flexible, more adjustable, more adaptable to change than more authoritarian societies. Liberty, it has been assumed, is conducive to flexibility, just as authority is conducive to rigidity. According to the same formula, freedom is dynamic, while institutionalized power, solidifying in bureaucratic molds, is static. It was but a corollary of this doctrine to hold that freedom releases incentives and incentives release energy, while authority inhibits incentives and therefore diminishes energy. Historically, Americans have certainly been a most energetic people, and we have taken this daemonic activity as a form of proof, validating the doctrine that the system of incentives is a generative factor in the experience of rapid American growth and, therefore, is the one intrinsic element which gives validity to the so-called capitalist system, or competitive system, or free enterprise system. Many critics who have deplored the inequitable distribution of income under nineteenth-century capitalism, or the brutality of a system that preserves efficiency by driving weak producers to bankruptcy, have nevertheless held to the free enterprise economy because they believed that the system of incentives inherent in it held unique value not only in terms of human progress but also in maintaining the vigor and dynamic quality of the society.

All of us have been acquainted with these widespread ideas for most of our lives. Most of us are, perhaps, skeptical of them in their more primitive or popular forms. Most of us, also, very likely, give some weight to them when they are articulated at a more advanced level.

Without addressing itself directly to these ideas, Mr. Oppenheimer's paper requires us, in a sense, to reconsider them, for it shows that there are some very important factors which the theoretical formulation has never taken into account.

The theory of the incentive system, as we all know it, holds that the different priorities in the needs of society will make themselves felt in differentials in the material rewards which individuals receive for helping to meet those needs. The differences in rewards will manifest themselves as differentials in stimulus to potential workers or enterprisers, and the relatively greater force of one stimulus over the other will constitute an incentive to the individual to engage in the activity which is most needful for society. Thus the causes of progress and of efficiency will be served simultaneously.

As theory this would be difficult to undercut. But in our application of the theory, we often make one rather basic and wholly gratuitous assumption—namely, that a system of differentials can exist only in a wholly free and unregulated economy. We were encouraged in this assumption by the facts that the free price system which lies at the heart of the unregulated economy does inevitably produce differentials of the kind assumed, and that the principal adversaries of the unregulated economy—namely the Socialists—were for a long time so strongly committed to the doctrine of rewarding each man according to his needs that it seemed inconceivable that they could ever sanction a system of income distribution which would discriminate sharply in favor of some workers and to the disadvantage of others.

Now, however, we face the general fact that the differentials on income in the Soviet Union range through an even wider scale than those in the United States, and we face the specific fact stated in the paper under consideration that the Soviet system is gaining upon us in its development of science by a technique of offering "formidable and rare incentives" for achievement in that area. These facts bring us to a simple and somewhat shattering conclusion: the qualities of an incentive system are in no sense peculiar to free enterprise, and the possession of such a system does not in any essential way distinguish the United States from the Soviet Union.

Certainly this does not mean that the American incentive system is indistinguishable from the Russian one. But it does mean certainly that the distinction lies in something other than the existence and operation of incentives. More precisely, the difference would seem to consist in the fact that the American incentive system is basically an automatic, un-regulated, or uncontrolled system, while the Soviet one regulates, controls, or, if you will, manipulates the incentives. The real distinction, then, lies in the fact that we have traditionally depended primarily upon consumer demand to control the incentives, with only secondary government intervention, while the Soviets hold that public goals, as defined by government, should fix the incentives.

We have placed our trust, economically, in a system of automatic incentives because the force which controlled them was in fact the aggregate of needs felt by the totality of our people, as expressed through consumer demand. It has been axiomatic in most of our thought, political as well as economic, that the needs of the people should be the determinants of public policy, and that, since the people are themselves the most sensitive instruments for reflecting their own needs, it should be left to them to determine the workings of the economic process through the operation of the price system or to determine the workings of the political process through the system of elections, parties, and pressure groups.

Spokesmen of this democratic theory have defended it on the ground that the citizens are, on the whole, competent judges of their own best interest, and critics have assailed it with the contention that the voters cannot really cope with public issues. In fact, there are some issues which the mass public can deal with effectively—namely, the issues involving their own directly felt needs—and others on which they will consistently give a poor account of themselves—namely, issues which lie outside the orbit of their felt needs. Although this may seem obvious to the point of banality when stated, it carries a further implication frequently overlooked: that democracy is neither effective nor ineffective in any absolute sense, but that the degree of its effectiveness at any given time will depend upon the extent to which its important concerns relate to the felt needs of the people; that the criterion of effectiveness of a democracy is not only the capacity of the electorate but also the nature of the problems with which the electorate must deal. Insofar as the public welfare is identified with issues which lie beyond the point at which important segments of the population feel them personally and directly, the effectiveness of a democracy in dealing with them is likely to diminish.

Historically, it has been our good fortune during most of our experience to confront problems which did reflect directly felt needs. Public land legislation, for instance, tariff legislation, labor legislation, wages and hour laws lie in an area where the vital interests of specific parties will prompt them to carry their case forcibly to the court of public opinion. This is what Mr. Oppenheimer means, in a sense, when he says that

if . . . the executive and legislative branches of the government have erred in their assessment of the problems of northwestern lumbermen, or of maritime labor, or of Marine recruits, there is an opportunity for those who are specialists in those ways, because they live in them, to be heard: and there is an underlying tolerance, sometimes violated, sometimes ignored, which yet gives to the voice of those most deeply concerned and most intimately and immediately knowledgeable the grave weight of the doctrine of the concurrent majority.

But, as he also shows, in areas where we have no significant groups who are "deeply concerned and intimately knowledgeable" democracy is capable of some distressing performances. Thus he finds grave defects in the public awareness of the need to train and recruit scientists and technical people, of the need to avoid wantonness with our country's resources, of the need to maintain an educational system with standards that are more than a half-empty mockery, and of the need to deal thoughtfully with matters affecting other lands and peoples. These shortcomings, which he regards as the most serious factors in the deep and refractory crises of which he warns us, are all precisely factors in which the directly felt needs of important elements in our population do not operate to guide and galvanize the political process.

Two quotations occur to me in this connection. One appeared in an editorial in *PM* during a presidential campaign many years ago, and it was a defense of our system of mass voting. Stating its point deliberately in terms of exaggerated simplicity, it said that every citizen should vote because "he is the best judge of whether his pants are torn." This might be true in elections where the primary task is to assign responsibility for past mistakes, for the citizen certainly knows when he has been made to suffer. But in some elections, I would argue, the problem of the voter is to foresee what subtle and indirect forces may be at work to tear his pants at some future time. His capacity to foresee and forestall those forces has never been conspicuous, and, in proportion as issues of this kind assume greater importance, it must be expected that democratic procedure will prove less satisfying in its results.

The other quotation is Woodrow Wilson's oft-repeated, and, I think, much misunderstood, proposal "to make the world safe for democracy." Although often charged with an unrealistic desire to impose democracy everywhere, Wilson had adopted no such ambitious plan. He only wished to make democracy safe where it already existed. But he was realistic enough to sense that democracy requires especial conditions for its safety. Two of these conditions might be, first, an absence of the concentration of power that can be achieved by authoritarian states but seldom by democratic ones; and, second, an absence of issues of a kind which require decisions that cannot be based upon the directly felt needs of the community.

While calling our attention to some of our own shortcomings, and of the formidable power of our adversary, Mr. Oppenheimer also adds that even if the adversary has solved certain problems more effectively than we have, "it can hardly be healthy for us to adopt his means," and that we must find "the solution of our problems on our own terms, in our own way, in our own good time." This injunction to stand steady in the face of a deep crisis serves to remind us that our own solutions must be in terms of our own genius. But when we come to solutions, it would seem that they must be drastic ones. For we are confronted with questions like these: Can an incentive system in which public policy abdicates control of the incentives compete successfully with one in which the incentives are planned by the state? Can our republic ever move back into the unmolested days when the chief business of government was to referee a distribution by the people themselves of a plentiful supply of loaves and fishes—a situation which sanctioned democracy by assigning to it precisely the function which it can perform best? If we have arrived at a point where the immediate felt needs of consumers no longer serve as sound controls upon our system of incentives because they no longer coincide with the ultimate, long-range needs of the national economy, and when the immediate felt needs of the voters no longer serve as sound controls upon the process of political decision because they no longer coincide with the ultimate long-range needs of public policy, then we are certainly confronted with a fundamental problem. One way of stating this problem is to say that we are faced with the question whether we can advance our democracy to a level which it has never previously needed to attain—a stage at which the machinery of policy formation can be made to operate effectively even in areas where we do not have the motive force of felt personal needs on the part of our people to propel it.

COMMENTARY: AMERICA'S ADMINISTRATIVE RESPONSE TO ITS WORLD PROBLEMS

by Richard M. Bissell, Jr.

IT IS tempting to limit a commentary on Mr. Kennan's paper to an expression of agreement with his eloquent and penetrating criticism of the cumbersome governmental machinery that has become so much larger and more complex in the last twenty years. Nevertheless, an effort is in order to probe into the circumstances that have brought about the state of affairs he describes, for the greatest difficulty with his paper is that, in a curious manner, it evades the very issue that is its principal theme. It describes an organization with decision-making faculties so paralyzed that flexibility, quickness of response, and purposeful action are almost impossible. Yet no explanation is offered as to why this degeneration has occurred, unless it be the implication that bureaucratic empire building or bad management is responsible or that excessive size is a first cause (rather than a symptom or consequence) of inefficiency.

Mr. Kennan goes through the form of presenting arguments for and against bigness and complexity in the government. But, in so doing, he is setting up a straw man. The truth, of course, is that everyone is against the slow-moving inefficiency he describes just as everyone is against war, poverty, and disease. Moreover, there are few so fatalistic as to believe that bad organization is an unavoidable human ill. The really interesting questions, then, are how and why an admittedly deplorable condition came into being and whether a better method of doing business can be evolved. Although Mr. Kennan does not address himself to these questions explicitly, he does give a hint of his views, which (it will be argued below) are not very helpful, precisely because they do not seem to reflect an appreciation of why the government is as it is.

Nostalgia for the days when foreign policy was the responsibility (and almost the monopoly) of a small and intimate group of highly qualified individuals is of no help in answering these questions. Everyone who labors in Washington yearns for such a happier world. Yet everyone is aware that our fall from grace was not the result merely of wrongheadedness but was a response, however unsatisfactory, to real pressures generated by largely irreversible historical developments. To remake the Executive Branch (or even the part of it that deals with external affairs) into a truly effective organization will require the solving of real and difficult problems and could not be accomplished by a mere corporate act of will even if such were politically possible.

The basic defect which it would be desirable to remedy is gross inefficiency in the process of decision making. The discussion that follows is, therefore, focused on decision making as such, on the quality of decisions, and the speed with which they are made. Decision making in and by large organizations rather than the psychology of individual action is of interest here. An individual may be too stupid to perceive the alternatives among which a choice may be made, too timid to make the choice cleanly if he does perceive the alternatives, or so nonrational that his choice of a course of action is in reality dictated by nonrational considerations obscure to the observer and to himself. Such an individual will make bad decisions, that is, decisions which do not represent well-informed and logical choices of courses of action which are optimal with respect to clearly and explicitly defined ends. Decisions that are bad in this sense will render the individual less effective whether he is handling his personal affairs, is the officer of a private corporation, or is acting as a public official. But this is not the kind of inefficiency that is the subject of Mr. Kennan's remarks or of any discussion of organization. The central question is not why individuals behave as they do given their environment but, rather, why certain organizational environments cause individuals collectively to be far less effective than one has every right to believe them to be individually.

What really distinguishes corporate and governmental from private individual decisions is that the former are inevitably collective. The corporate or public official has to cooperate in a complex manner with other individuals in the making of decisions. It is worth emphasizing at the outset, however, that devices do exist whereby a group of individuals may make a collective decision with only a negligible penalty in the form of friction and delay. For instance, there is no reason why the individual member of a board of directors should not be able to make his good or bad choices almost as quickly as if he were operating with sole authority in the conduct of his own private affairs. Issues are usually debated in a board before the members are called on for their votes, and the debate may be profitless and time consuming. But in the end, each individual makes his choice of a course of action, heads are counted, and a group decision has been made. Given a good chairman supported by rules that foreclose endless and unprofitable debate, and given above all the device of voting which defines each individual's part in the decision-making process, collective decisions can be made quite efficiently.

Most collective decision making, however, takes place not in legislatures or boards of directors but in large hierarchic organizations in which, at least in theory, all authority resides at the top and is exercised at lower levels only by delegation. The individual official is not one member of a group of equals with a legally defined authority measured by his (single or weighted) vote. Instead he is one cell in a many-celled organism; his influence on action depends on a variety of subtle relationships with superiors, colleagues, and subordinates. He is typically prevented by two types of constraints from making decisions as promptly and cleanly as if he were managing his own affairs.

One constraint is the obvious one that the delegation of authority to him is limited and that many major decisions must have the concurrence of his superior in the line of command. This limitation on his freedom of action is inevitable, but it is essentially harmless. It can, of course, be burdensome if the subordinate is timid or if the superior is incapable of delegation. As a practical matter, however, a faulty vertical distribution of authority is usually a consequence of a more fundamental trouble and by itself accounts for only a minor part of what is wrong.

The other constraint is that the individual decision maker is required, in the current Washington phraseology, to coordinate decisions, that is, to obtain the concurrence of colleagues in his choice of a course of action. In this context the term colleague is used to denote an individual who is in a parallel position in the chain of command, that is, who is neither the decision maker's direct superior nor his direct subordinate. Typically in any large organization the colleagues in question are not consulted as individuals but act as the ambassadors of other departments, each of which for some reason or other has an interest in the decision that is being made. Typically, too, the several ambassadors and the departments or components they represent are subject to no common superior authority except that of the chief of the organization several echelons higher in the chain of command. The actual or alleged interests of these several organizations in the decision are deemed to give the ambassador of each what amounts to a power of veto. To be sure, the veto power is not formally recognized nor is it absolute. The precise degree to which a particular organization can intervene in any given decision depends on such considerations as its power position in the whole federal establishment, the extent to which its vital interests are involved, and often the personalities of the individuals involved. Nevertheless, unilateral action in the face of the strong opposition of an important department is rarely taken. When, as they so often do, representatives of the interested departments assemble in a meeting or committee to arrive at a decision, they constitute (with only one important difference discussed below) the precise equivalent of an international conference of sovereign states animated by divergent national interests.

As a device for making collective decisions such a conference is far inferior to a board of directors' meeting or even a legislative assembly with all the opportunities for log rolling that exist. The reason, obviously enough, is that when all the private negotiation and public oratory are finished a board of legislators acts by majority vote, whereas an interdepartmental conference (like the United Nations Security Council) does not. And it is, of course, unthinkable that the policies of a corporation or of the Executive Branch should be determined by the votes of separate departments. Departments, like sovereign states, are not equal nor are they equally interested in or competent with respect to any given situation. They could not be given equal votes in all decisions. Aside from these practical considerations, moreover, the separate departments have authority (in theory) only by delegation from the Chief Executive, and differences can be constitutionally resolved only by an exercise of his authority. The ironic result is that there can be found at the heart of many a large organization which is designed for swift and effective executive action rather than for careful and protracted deliberation a decision-making institution with less ability to make up its mind than the French Assembly.

How does it come about that the participation of several departments or decisions of a large organization is needed (or permitted) in so many decisions, each of which presumably is or ought to be the primary business of some one of them? What is the origin of the widespread de facto veto power exercised by the subdivisions of a single organization upon one another? The existence of this state of affairs reflects a failure to divide up the voluminous work and multiple responsibilities of the whole organization in such a way that each department has a clear-cut job to do, which it is empowered and authorized to do in comparative independence of other departments. For example, the United States government has a program of economic support to India. A major element of this program is the sale of surplus wheat on terms advantageous to India. Are decisions concerning these wheat shipments to be made as if they were part of a world-wide operation to dispose of wheat or as if they were part of an Indian program embracing many types of goods and services? Obviously, the transactions are in fact serving both of these quite different purposes and there is no way in which a decision can be made about the sale of surplus wheat to India that does not have the concurrence of both the Department of Agriculture and the Department of State. Or, to take a very different case, assume that the continued military support of the Chinese Nationalists on Taiwan strengthens the strategic position of the United States in the Western Pacific. Assume also that support of this regime by the United States is deeply distasteful to the governments and peoples of India, Burma, and Indonesia. How is a decision to be made about this program in which these quite dissimilar costs and benefits must be weighed and offset against one another? The substantive problem would be difficult enough without organization complications, but there is plainly no way in which a course of action can be adopted that does not have the concurrence of the State Department and the Pentagon. In this particular example, just to make matters worse, the same decision is of great interest also to those responsible for economic aid and to the United States Information Agency.

These are two of the most difficult examples that could have been cited, and it is highly doubtful whether any pattern of organization in the Executive Branch would yield a sufficiently clear delineation of functions to make either one the business of only a single department. Nevertheless, a widespread failure of delineation and overlapping of responsibilities creates a situation in which the typical official cannot proceed rationally to inform himself about a matter under consideration, arrive at a judgment as to what should be done, and then take action either by making a decision on his own authority or by casting his vote. Instead, after making up his own mind, he must devote his skill and energy to negotiation, log rolling, and finally to skillful compromise with colleagues whose assent must somehow be secured before any action can be taken.

This process imposes the endless delays so familiar in Washington and multiplies the bureaucracy. Even worse, it ruins the quality of the decisions that finally emerge. The course of action that results from protracted arms-length negotiation between sovereign departments is typically a nonrational compromise which reflects their various separate and special interests, weighted in accordance with their power positions. One of the worst features of this process is its powerful bias in the direction of ambiguity. Except when an inherently quantitative decision is being made (for instance, with respect to sums of money or numbers of people), the inevitable compromise is apt to take the form of the adoption of language which makes possible the pretense and appearance of agreement but which leaves each department free to safeguard its vital interests. Thus, after much blood, sweat, and tears have been shed around the conference table, the ritual of making a decision is solemnly gone through while the unresolved disagreement is merely swept under the carpet. Either the decision is in effect postponed or else a course of action is in fact chosen by default which is quite different from that described in the ambiguous formal decision.

It will be said at once that this is a caricature of what happens inside every large organization since, after all, separate departments are ultimately subject in the line of command to a superior authority. It will be pointed out that the whole purpose of a pyramidal structure is to provide, at successively higher levels, officers with successively wider jurisdictions, bridging subordinate departmental gaps, who can reconcile conflicting views and conflicting considerations. For the individual decision maker this has the consequence, at least in theory, of providing an alternative to the process of negotiation and ultimate compromise, which is to refer the unresolved disagreement to higher authority and obtain a command decision. If the issue can be presented sharply, there is always the hope that a clean-cut choice will be made and the quality of the decision preserved.

In practice, however, the hope is rarely fulfilled. The same circumstance that compels so much coordination between subordinates, namely, the fact that it has been impossible to achieve a clean delineation of responsibilities, forces far too many decisions up to senior officers for resolution and thereby clogs the appeals machinery. In effect, the failure of delineation frustrates and nullifies the downward delegation of authority and decentralization of decision making which is commonly advised as the cure for bureaucracy. The superior officer who delegates a part of his responsibility to A and another part to B, but who does so in such a way that A must clear his every act with B and vice versa, has placed his subordinates in a position where they must either make their decision by compromising (that is, as if he did not exist) or pass them back up to him and thus undo his delegation of authority to them. When they elect the latter, the command decision he delivers is usually no better than, and little different from, the compromise they would have reached by negotiation. The subordinates find that their superior officer, precisely because of the failure of delegation, is overburdened and inaccessible, cannot take the time to comprehend the issues presented to him, and is preoccupied as much with keeping the peace and preserving balance among his warring subordinates as with getting the proper substantive decision made.

That the appeals procedure should be so unsatisfactory and command decisions often as poor in quality as bureaucratic compromises is merely another demonstration that effective delegation of authority and the decentralization of decision making thereby made possible are indeed essential to efficiency in a large hierarchic organization. The whole purpose of delegation and decentralization is to take all but the most important work and all but the most vital decisions off the superior officer's desk. It is to break up his job into smaller pieces so that a number of individuals can join with him in getting his work done, so that each piece will be more manageable in size and scope, and so that each can be performed by a subordinate who will bring to it more time and a narrower more expert knowledge than could the superior officer himself. It is only in this way that the impossibly large job of the President of the United States, the head of a federal department, or the chief executive of a large corporation can be performed. Yet this whole concept of organization collapses unless the work and the decisions that are delegated downward stay delegated. If it is impossible for one subordinate to act (in most matters at least) with reasonable independence of the others, there can be only two results: Either the decisions keep being referred back up to the top or they are made at the proper level but by the process of negotiation and compromise described above. Either too many decisions must ultimately be made by harassed and impossibly overburdened senior officers or reliance must be placed on the notoriously ineffective decision-making procedure of the international conference. Therefore, where delineation of responsibilities cannot be, or is not, achieved, almost all decisions are slow and difficult to come by, a majority of decisions are weak and irrational compromises, and many are so unclear and so incapable of enforcement upon those that disagree with them that they are practically meaningless.

This characterization was not intended as a rival to Mr. Kennan's more eloquent and colorful denunciation of the manner in which decisions are made in the federal government. Rather, its purpose was to focus attention on the failure to define and delineate the functions of the different parts of an organization as the proximate cause of the trouble. If the analysis is correct, the next question that arises is whether, in the particular case of the federal government's handling of the external affairs of the United States, a clearer definition and delineation could be achieved. The asking of this question leads one to wonder what has happened in the last twenty years to make this problem so much more acute. Both Parkinson's Law and Mr. Kennan's paper assert and describe the close relationship between bigness and inefficiency, and it is argued above that a major cause (if not the major cause) of inefficiency is the overlapping of responsibilities and jurisdictions. Is it to be inferred, then, that the reason the government (at least in the field of external affairs) has been growing far more rapidly than the mere volume of business would appear to require is that the overlapping has been getting worse? Has there been an important change in the structure and functions of the government which has increased the difficulty of dividing up responsibilities between the several departments in a tidy fashion so that each could be free to do its job without so much help or hindrance from others?

It will be argued below that the answer to these questions is in the affirmative and that there are real, though not necessarily insuperable, obstacles in the way of a return to the good old days. Before developing this thesis, however, it may be helpful to note, by way of background, that it has been possible to devise arrangements for efficient decision making in many corporations and that these arrangements involve an extensive delegation of authority downward to the chiefs of different divisions, coupled with a remarkably clean-cut definition of the authority delegated to each. Each of the large automobile companies, for instance, has divisions that sell different cars in competition with one another and also has divisions that produce components used in all of its cars. Obviously the decisions of, say, the Buick division manager impinge directly upon the Pontiac and Oldsmobile divisions and must be intimately coordinated also with those of his suppliers that are also within the company. In Washington one suspects these decisions would all be handled in committees and one suspects, also, that more time is wasted in committee meetings in Detroit than the general public realizes. Nevertheless, the division manager in many companies is given great freedom to produce, style, price, and sell his own product as he thinks best without regard to those of his colleagues who are also his competitors. And he may also be told that if he can buy components better from an outside supplier than from a division of the same company, he may do so. No doubt such praiseworthy flexibility is the exception rather than the rule in corporate business. But, however widely or narrowly such techniques are in fact used, there is no denying that this is one way of decentralizing decisions in a large corporation without compelling each subordinate to secure the concurrence of half a dozen independent colleagues before he takes any action.

Innumerable less extreme and dramatic examples could be picked from corporate business. For instance, it is typical to make a rather sharp functional separation between sales (including pricing), production, and purchasing. Even though these three types of activities are intertwined with one another in such a way that the most intimate technical coordination is called for between them, the three sets of decisions to which they give rise can be cleanly distinguished despite the fact that, say, a sales department decision may directly and immediately affect production and purchasing. If the sales manager of a steel company closes a contract by shaving his price, this will affect production schedules at the mill. Production schedules at the mill will necessitate changes in the procurement of raw materials and components. Nevertheless, the intimately related decisions of seller, producer, and buyer of inputs can be made day after day and week after week without each vice president having to secure the concurrence of others in his decisions. It is none of the mill superintendent's business to decide whether a price will be cut to get an order. If the order is obtained it is his business to produce the tonnage called for. His decision to produce the additional tonnage obviously does not require the concurrence (in the sense of policy approval) of the other vice presidents. Likewise, the purchasing agent's behavior is a response to requirements from the mill, and if he is kept advised of changes in those requirements he does not need any other officer to tell him how or where to buy supplies.

To make so simple a point at such great length would be to belabor the obvious were it not for the fact that the type of organizational relationship here characterized is almost unheard of in the federal government except in those agencies and with respect to those activities (such as, say, the operation of ships and transport aircraft) which are analogous to the productive activity of a corporation. Least of all is this type of relationship evident in that part of the federal government which deals with external affairs. For some reason, productive and other narrowly operational activities seem to lend themselves to a clean-cut division of labor and of responsibility along functional and often geographical lines. Relatively simple mechanisms suffice to achieve the necessary degree of coordination between different functional or geographical subdivisions of an organization, even when (as noted above) intimate coordination is called for. One circumstance which may go far to explain this fact is that the ultimate purpose of productive and operational activities is usually susceptible of clear definition, well understood by all of the participants in the activity, and accepted by all of the decision makers concerned.

By contrast, in such a vast and complex area of policy making as the domestic economic policies of the federal government the purpose in view is neither clearly defined nor understood in the same terms by the contending parties. The Departments of Agriculture, Commerce, Labor, and the Treasury no doubt could be induced to agree that prosperity is a good thing, but their agreement would last only so long as no attempt were made to state very clearly what is meant by prosperity or how it is to be achieved. It is notorious that these organizations speak for major arrays of pressure groups whose interests rarely coincide. They are not partners seeking a common purpose and separated only to achieve a division of labor and a functional delegation of authority. Their activities require not so much to be coordinated as to be refereed.

When it deals with the rest of the world, the Executive Branch should be able to operate less like a law court, i.e., less like an arena within which conflict takes place and more like an organized hierarchy with a reasonably well-defined purpose in view. Social pressures, especially in the field of foreign economic policy, are powerful but they leave considerably greater freedom of action and are far less divisive of the Executive Branch of the government than are the similar pressures in the domestic field. On the other hand, it is this realm of governmental activity that exhibits in its most extreme form the failure of delineation. Nor can any major part of this structural defect be blamed on pressures from outside of the government. (It can be blamed in appreciable degree on Congressional prejudices but the divisive weaknesses do not appear to be of legislative origin.)

The root of the trouble is this: For the purpose of dealing with and operating in the rest of the world, the federal government is organized along functional lines; yet few of the important decisions that are made relate only or even predominantly to a single functional arm. A catalog of more important functions illustrates the point. The military establishment prepares for war, stations troops abroad, administers military aid. At least two quasi-independent organizations make grants and loans abroad. Upward of ten departments, agencies, and committees act on commercial policy within the broadest limits they can persuade the Congress to accept. There is a separate information (propaganda) agency. And even the Atomic Energy Commission is coming to have a foreign policy of its own. Finally, the State Department both acts as a major policy maker in its own right and presides over this community of foreign policy makers (at least when the Secretary of State is a powerful man as Marshall, Acheson, and Dulles all have been).

Few of these activities are really new, but twenty years ago the various federal departments responsible for them could conduct their business in much greater independence from one another than is possible today. The military departments were then engaged almost exclusively in the business of preparing for war (within the limits of their then meager budgets). There were occasional visits of warships to foreign ports but no forces of any magnitude deployed outside of United States territories. The United States maintained crippling and outrageous tariffs, but there were no decisions to be made about them by anyone except on the periodic occasion of new tariff legislation. The United States made foreign loans in the 1920s and again in the 1930s. But these were treated as very much the business of the Treasury and the Federal Reserve Bank of New York. With many fewer and less critical decisions to make, more time to make them, and with an inclination to treat finance, commerce, and diplomacy as three largely unrelated activities, governmental organization appeared more adequate to its task.

Today one has only to review the above catalog of governmental activities to realize how much more intimately they are intertwined. The change in the state of the world has altered the character of the decisions to be made at the same time that it has expanded enormously the sheer volume of the government's international business. The United States is trying to accomplish more things and different kinds of things than ever before outside its own borders. The world-wide struggle between two major blocs, the revolution that is in progress in the uncommitted nations, and the position of the United States as leader of one of them have compelled the most strenuous efforts to influence the course of events in the outside world in order to maintain an environment in which this society can develop. Accordingly it is committed to the arms race, to the support of alliances, to an effort to guide the development of the uncommitted nations into constructive channels, and to a world-wide ideological rivalry. In this situation such familiar government activities as the maintenance of our own military establishment and the making of foreign loans have not only grown greatly in magnitude but also acquired a significance as elements in a major national struggle that they totally lacked twenty years ago.

These externally directed activities of the federal government absorb a larger proportion of the nation's resources and personnel, impinge more drastically upon the national life, and require far more of the time, attention, and energy of the senior officers of the Executive Branch. As a consequence, what might in an earlier age have been called foreign policy today largely determines the size of the federal budget, decisively influences the direction and composition of foreign trade, dominates international finance, and exercises a growing influence on such matters as the location of industry, the use of the nation's scientific resources, and the whole development of the culture.

From the standpoint of government organization the most significant aspect of these developments has been the shift in the relative importance of the various instrumentalities used by the United States to project its power beyond its borders and to pursue its objectives in the world community. The most dramatic feature of this revolution is the nation's greater reliance on the increase of its own military strength, the maintenance of military forces abroad, and the promotion and support of military alliances. Almost as great a departure from the past is the current heavy reliance on government channeled and directed export of capital and other forms of economic aid as a means of strengthening allied and friendly neutral nations. The increased use of propaganda and information services is a third innovation. These activities are not only more prominent but also recognized to be the means to ends which transcend any one of the fields of activity. Thus military and economic means are increasingly used to achieve essentially political ends. There is no place for military decisions made with only strategic considerations in view or economic decisions based only on classic economic criteria.

These changes have made it inescapably clear that there is no separable body of policy and actions that can be called foreign policy. Rather, there is a foreign policy aspect to most major governmental decisions. The great decisions on the scale and character of our military and foreign economic programs and on the political posture of the United States are inevitably of deep interest to every major government department and Cabinet Member. The maintenance of the nation's world position and the pursuit of objectives outside of our borders is the sole preoccupation of the State Department, the Pentagon, and three major independent (or at least autonomous) agencies. At the same time, as crisis succeeds crisis, the tempo of decision making is much faster and the stakes are vastly greater than anything we were used to before World War II.

Today almost any foreign policy decision requires the weighing of costs and benefits not only by an officer expert in foreign policy but also by various more specialized officials each of whom brings to the problem knowledge of a limited but vital set of considerations. Since the federal government (like most other governments) is organized along functional lines, each specialist is also a departmental ambassador and each separate set of considerations that requires to be weighed is the special province and the special interest of a separate department. To be sure, a leading part in the making of such decisions as those instanced above is supposed to be played by the political officer, drawn from the regular State Department, who is supposed to be a generalist. And at the Cabinet level the Secretary of State claims, and is accorded by his colleagues, the responsibility for making policy decisions. The activities of the other agencies most deeply involved in international affairs are often described as operations, presumably undertaken pursuant to and in support of policy established by the Secretary of State. But anyone familiar with the actual day-to-day workings of the federal establishment realizes that this distinction between policy and operations is highly metaphysical. By and large, the situations and crises that provoke important decisions are nonrepetitive. The notion that there can be some kind of generalized rule of conduct dignified as a policy which can guide operators from month to month is a myth.

Despite the acknowledged primacy of the Secretary of State with respect to most international affairs, other senior officers of the government jealously guard their broad overlapping domains within which they too make policy. As a matter of policy the Treasury opposes any new expenditure of federal funds for practically any purpose. The Export-Import Bank favors only hard loans. The International Cooperation Administration (like its predecessor organizations) is apt to regard economic soundness and progress as ends in themselves and generally opposes the use of economic resources for political bribery. In the ad-

ministration of military aid the Pentagon appears to be concerned only
to arm American allies for a possible world war with Russia. The soldiers professionally insist on disregarding the evident fact that what is
mainly important is the internal political impact of military aid in many
Latin American and Asian nations. It is apparent that the Department
of State has no monopoly in the production of that elusive commodity
called policy and indeed that the distinction between policy and operations has little meaning.

If the Secretary of State has a strong personality and the full backing
of the President, he can exercise a certain degree of control over the
more important externally directed activities of the government. Nevertheless, the diffusion of authority at the top cannot help but produce
the situation described in the earlier part of this paper in which what
used to be called foreign policy is the business of many departments with
overlapping jurisdictions. Is there any way in which cleaner delineation
and therefore more efficient decision making could be achieved?

By way of clearing the ground, several approaches may be pointed out
as totally unworkable. To begin with, it would be quite hopeless to try
to put all of the government that deals with the world position and
external relationships of the United States in one department. There is
the practical consideration that no President in his right mind would
propose, and no member of Congress would favor, putting either the
Pentagon in the State Department or vice versa. Aside from this insuperable objection there is the more fundamental point made above that
foreign policy is an aspect of all policy, not a separate realm, so the
Secretary of State cannot be given direct authority over everyone concerned with foreign policy unless he becomes Prime Minister with authority over virtually the whole Executive Branch. Finally, experience
suggests that extension of the authority of the Secretary of State does
not strike at the root of the problem. Already the economic aid organization is, and the United States Information Agency used to be, a part
of the State Department. Yet decisions involving these autonomous
functional organizations are made no more smoothly, amicably, or efficiently inside the State Department than in the Executive Branch as a
whole. In short, an attempt to extend the authority of the Secretary of
State to the point where he would have a real monopoly of foreign policy

decisions is not only impractical but would merely transfer the real problem of the division of labor inside the State Department.

Another approach, which is both more modest and better designed to cure the real disease, would be to bring about a considerable functional reconcentration of authority further down the line in the hierarchy. In terms of the changes that would appear on organization charts, this might involve a real merger of the foreign economic policy agencies and the information agency with the State Department, and the cutting up of the resulting pie into geographical instead of functional slices. A less drastic way of accomplishing the same result would be to forgo actual transfers and simply arm the Assistant Secretaries of State with stronger directive powers. The purpose in any case should be to push this reorganization to the point where, say, the Assistant Secretary for European Affairs would be in real charge of at least the major nonmilitary activities of the government directed toward his area. Probably he should have a fairly senior military adviser and possibly his authority should cover the appropriate geographical desk from what is now the Office of International Security Affairs in the Pentagon. To round out the scheme, a parallel reconcentration of what are now functionally disbursed responsibilities should be accomplished at lower echelons, notably at the level of the country desks that are the basic building blocks of so many federal organizations.

There are other things that could be done to foster a reconcentration of authority and thus a cleaner delineation of responsibility. A long overdue reform would be to get the United States Treasury completely out of the foreign policy business. To be sure, it has a legitimate interest in tariff policy but there is no reason why the Treasury could not perform its classic functions of tax collection and debt management without having a major voice in either military or political affairs or in the larger aspects of foreign economic programs. This piece of surgery would slightly reduce the babble of voices in many a committee and might make it easier for the economic, military, and political officers to concentrate on the job of maintaining this country's world position without repeated flank attacks from the corner of New York and Pennsylvania Avenues. Similar surgery might be performed with profit on other departments whose stake in military and foreign policies is small in relation to the primarily domestic concerns.

Perhaps a reform of this magnitude would create an opportunity for the Assistant Secretary for European Affairs to assume a comprehensive responsibility for United States relations with Europe and the officer in charge of, say, the French desk an equally broad responsibility for United States relations with France. Hopefully these officers would have sufficient authority (by delegation from above) themselves to act, or secure action, on the many issues that are complex enough to cross functional lines but not of such moment as to require the attention of the Secretary. They would still lack real and final authority with respect to the many decisions involving the Pentagon or such agencies as the Department of Agriculture. But at least there would be fewer independent ambassadors in the meetings. There would be larger areas within which negotiation and compromise would be unnecessary and within which a generalist would possess the authority to use the economist, the soldier, and the other specialists without having constantly to engage in arms-length negotiation with them.

But even as one describes this vision of reform one is assailed by doubts. The frustrating process of coordinating would still slow the wheels of action and consume the best energies of officials. If all worked well, there would be less coordination as between functional specialists but there might be even more between one country desk and another or one regional Assistant Secretary and his colleagues. The hard fact is that the state of the world compels the use of many instrumentalities and this in turn requires the participation of many kinds of specialists in policy making and of many parts of the government in its execution. In this kind of a world the delineation of responsibilities and authorities in the executive branch will always be messy. The most that can be said is that, if ideal arrangements devised on paper could be made effective in practice, it need not be nearly so messy as it is today. And this would be no trivial result.

This proviso is, however, of crucial importance and requires a final remark. What has been suggested here is in effect a subordination of functional special interests and a reconcentration of authority in the hands of generalists. This is all very well but who are the generalists to be? In this kind of discussion it is always assumed that they would be political officers, or the members of a revivified Foreign Service, and that such persons would be competent to exercise the greater authority which would be placed in their hands. This assumption implies a great deal, however, about the qualifications of Foreign Service officers past, present, and future, and its validity cannot be taken for granted.

There is no intention here of reviving the childish criticism that the diplomat has the foreigner's interests more at heart than those of his own country. Nor is it germane to this discussion that a reorganization which increases the authority of one department and one group of officers is resented and opposed by others. The real issue is whether the typical political officer or Foreign Service officer regards himself as a generalist, interests himself in all the instrumentalities employed by the federal government, and is animated by a really broad concept and understanding of the national interest.

It has been emphasized above that the economist from the International Cooperation Administration, the banker from the Export-Import Bank, the financial expert from the Treasury, and perhaps above all the military officer from the Pentagon are in a sense special pleaders. Inevitably their several concepts of the national interest are weighted heavily in the direction of their several primary interests: sound economics, sound finance, or sound military strategy. Much of the inefficiency of decision making, the compromising and negotiation, is associated with the difficult process of reconciling their views and subordinating these special interests to broader but inclusive national interests. If this is to be done by giving the generalist the authority to make decisions swiftly and efficiently, the individual who wields the authority must not himself be a special pleader.

It is a hard fact of life, however, that the political officers are believed to be just that by members of the other professions that staff the federal government. Many of the latter will not submit to the arbitral control of Foreign Service officers without the bitterest resistance. The feeling is widespread that the Foreign Service has, in some measure, been left behind by the changes in the world situation that have been referred to here and that these have converted its members into a group of specialists with as narrow an outlook as any other group in Washington. If challenged to describe the political officer's vested interest, the answer would be that it is in the maintenance of smooth and friendly diplomatic relationships with other governments and the avoidance of actions that would cause serious friction with them, sometimes at the sacrifice of more solid or longer-term advantages. Perhaps this is an unfair characterization that smacks of caricature, but a more solid case could be made. The political officer's preoccupation is with the processes of diplomacy and with political situations and objectives. Although the instinct that leads him to subordinate so-called economic ends and to regard economic policy as a means to political ends is a sound one, there is bound to be a suspicion that this will be carried too far. In the area of military affairs, in which he ought to be more at home, the same tendency toward excessive subordination to political ends is suspected, and it can be far more dangerous. There is good reason to wonder how many political officers have a real grasp of the realities of power in the contemporary world.

Remarks like these are merely the speculations of one individual. On a less personal level, it can be said with confidence, however, that if the processes of government are to be made more efficient by concentrating responsibility on generalists and clothing them with authority, human beings will have to be found who can really divest themselves of their professional special interests. At all levels, but especially near the top, they will have to inspire in their more specialized colleagues confidence both in their devotion to the national interest broadly conceived and in their intellectual and emotional capacity to deal with the facts of military power and the facts of economic life. This is not to say that the generalist should try to be an expert in all things but that he must have a temperament which permits him to weigh all kinds of costs and benefits objectively without professional bias. With all its virtues and, notwithstanding its exceptionally brilliant members like Mr. Kennan, the old Foreign Service was not a corps of such persons, and its revival as it used to be would not solve our problems.

COMMENTARY: HAVE THERE BEEN DISCERNIBLE SHIFTS IN AMERICAN VALUES DURING THE PAST GENERATION?

by Richard Hofstadter

MR. KLUCKHOHN's essay is essentially an inquiry directed toward a matter of fact, the matter of fact being what has happened to our values, though there are in his essay some comments on value. There is an expressed anxiety about what this change in values may portend.

I will limit myself to a single constellation which I might call the "success constellation."

The shift that has been observed, and it cuts through a great many of the studies, is a shift from something that has been variously termed the Protestant or Puritan ethic to an ethic of adjustment—a shift from individualism to a socialized personality of some sort which is concerned with problems of individuality but which is not committed to individualism. It is a shift, perhaps, from a working and saving success ethic (that is, an ethic which assumes that certain qualities of behavior are organically related and lead to success) to an ethic which stresses a great deal more, the value of leisure and the pleasure of consumption. It is a shift from a concern with manipulation and production and effort in the material world, the outer world, to a concern with manipulation and adjustment to other persons. It seems, as some of the investigators Mr. Kluckhohn cites have said, to be a shift from a type of politics in which political life is an arena related to these other values of production and success in the material world to an ethic in which there is a great growth of what he and others have termed privatism—that is, to an ethic in which politics, so far as it is a part of the concern of the people, is a sphere of entertainment, a spectacle, accepted or received with relative passivity by those who display a concern with it.

353

Most of the discussion has overtones of distress and concern, anxiety about the implications of this change, and I share some of this anxiety. I also share Mr. Kluckhohn's qualified optimism about the implications of these changes, though it is an optimism so qualified that if one simply flips the coin one might just as easily call it qualified pessimism.

We are told in Mr. Kluckhohn's paper that the shift, as far as we can define it, is really not so alarming. But we are left with the feeling that the direction gives us some cause for concern. Now, here I begin to get a little autobiographical because most of my comments are going to be moralistic and reflective, rather than factual. As one whose observations of the political and social scene began in the 1930s, I can't help but reflect on a certain irony involved which has a keen edge for those of us who first saw the world as a political environment during the 1930s. The great single fact that we in that generation faced was the collapse of the bourgeois world, and our greatest impulse was the repudiation and criticism of that world. Our revolt itself we did not have to invent. The generation of the 1920s and even the generations before them had done that for us; we inherited their revolt, in a sense, but we did something to it.

The 1920s was a bad time for politics. Its revolt was largely cultural, and when the depression began, that was what we were chiefly familiar with. But our revolt was essentially a political one; the 1920s caused the businessman to become our type of villain and saw him as a boob and Philistine; we saw him as an exploiter, plunger, mismanager, and failure. We thought of what we now speak of as the inner-directed man as resembling Rockefeller or Jay Gould or the robber barons in the more predatory phases in the history of American business enterprise. It seems now, in retrospect, a little easier than it was then to realize that we were comparing a social ideal which lay typically in the back of our minds as an embodiment of a system of values. We were comparing an ideal, the ideal of some sort of socially responsible personality whose values would be adapted to a social plan or to Marxism or Socialism, depending on what our particular social or political faith was. We were thinking of this ideal and vaguely delineated type in comparison with more or less real images of the real bourgeois personality as it appeared on the stage of history. We were somewhat vague about what we meant but we had something to tie it down—the success myth of the past and all the personal traits of the enterprise and hard work that were supposed to go with it. We were intensely vague about what it was that we were positively committed to in terms of human values, though we thought we knew what certain particular programs of social reconstruction ought to be. We were not clear as to what the end product ought to be, what human values the new system should cultivate.

Our elusiveness about values was not merely an oversight. It was a philosophical myth that arose out of the assumption that the important changes were only structural and institutional changes, and that, once these were properly taken care of, human values would somehow take care of themselves—an assumption which is grimly caricatured by the very type we are worrying about today. Today, the generation that was then the young generation, the embattled generation of the wartime period and the 1930s is, at least, the middle generation, and it now has a young generation of its own to be aghast at.

Today the values of hyper-individualism which twenty years ago were identified only with evil men have tended to disappear, not because they have yielded to a frontal assault but, as is so often the case with systems of values, because they have withered away. They have not been so much refuted as they have been abandoned. The socialized, adjusted personality has become increasingly conspicuous, and his new constellation of values is a rather grim caricature or mockery of whatever notions we may have had twenty years ago about the values that would replace the competitive individualism we disliked.

Now the irony becomes complete because a transfer of values has been imposed upon us. I have noted with a great deal of interest the reaction very commonly expressed among my friends who are readers of *The Lonely Crowd*. Those who read it with care note that the approved set of values in the book are still autonomous, but much more space is given to delineating the inner-directed man and the outer-directed types. I find it significant that so many readers grow nostalgic for the characterization of the inner-directed man that they may never have known. They choose to think of him now as being cast not in the mold of Jay Gould or Rockefeller or a robber baron but in the mold of Clarence Day's rather lovable father or some such character.

We have, in short, more than made up for whatever injustices we have done in the past to the Protestant competitive individualized type.

He has become softened and idealized, while we direct our anxiety to-ward the socialized adjustable man who seems in large measure to have replaced him. When we look about at our fully employed, incredibly rich, well-adjusted, complacent, and apathetic country, we may have the humor to see in it a tacky Utopia and see the caricature of the noncompetitive socially planned world whose values we were so vague about years ago. We have the right to say, of course, that this is not what we had in mind. This is not it at all; and so it is not. But our sense of history will come to remind us that this is precisely the perennial disavowal made by designers of Utopias. The literary Utopias we read of are rather depressing. Perhaps the best example is Bellamy's *Looking Backward*, and I think William Morris was right when he called it a "cockney nightmare." But it was a prophetic book. Do not be surprised that the actual Utopias we have occasion to experience also turn out to be rather depressing when we are forced to confront them. I look upon all this not as a problem which in any satisfactory sense can be solved but as one which alludes to the very nature of our experience—if you will, to the human condition.

I have spoken thus far in very broad terms and I have implicitly exaggerated, for the sake of ironic effect, two demonstrable changes in values that have taken place simply in order to counterpose the two clear alternatives. I find it easy to believe this shift is, in fact, something of a real secular trend because it seems not surprising to me that different types of personality should flourish in a society in which large numbers of people are employed in large bureaucratic establishments where the risks, as we knew them, have been so delimited. If one desired to be tedious, one could enumerate a number of characteristics in the trends in our society which suggest that these changes in values that we think we see coming are not entirely undesirable. I am still inclined to hope this change may prove, in the end, to be somewhat self-limiting and relatively benign and that we will not all be swept away on a sea of perfectly adjusted personalities.

We are, of course, terribly worried about the possibilities for creativity and rebellion among the rising members of what might be called the "cool" generation; and our predecessors, at least since the time of de Tocqueville have worried that America might also be the country of educated masses and mediocre talents.

Culturally and anthropologically, human societies are cast in a great variety of molds, but once a society has been cast in its mold—Mr. Rostow is right that our mold as a nation was established by the early nineteenth century—the number of ways in which, short of dire calamity, it will alter its pattern are rather limited. I find it helpful also to point to another principle upon which Mr. Rostow has remarked—the frequency with which commentators find societies having certain paradox polarities in them. He refers to the polarities in French society. We may find in this something functional; that is, societies have a need to find ways of checking their own tendencies. In these polarities there may be something of a clue to social systems. If you are a Hegelian this may smack of thesis-antithesis. But, to me, a Freudian view is more suggestive. It seems to be much more analogous to what Freudians call reaction formation, and perhaps that is a part of the mechanism by which we do put limiting terms on some of the tendencies, the exaggerated tendencies in our own changes and values.

Mr. Kluckhohn's report contains some evidence that we have already passed the peak of this shift about which I have been speaking. I find some additional evidence myself in the growing revolt of middle-class parents against those practices in our education that seem to sacrifice individualism and creativity for adjustment and group values. Granted the initial polarities of the success ethic, which is one of the molds in which our society is cast, this ethic must in some way give rise, sooner or later, to a reaction. We may well wonder just how many ways there were for our "cool" generation to react to our past, granting the prosperous conditions prevailing after World War II and what might be called the exigent state of mind that was induced by the anxiety of cold war. Should there be another depression or some other kind of turn around the corner, we might find that the capacity for criticism and rebellion and for preoccupation with the success theme in a new way has not been exhausted. Failing that, we must recognize the limits of any frame of mind that we demand of others for our particular mode of self-assessment. I do not think we must be persuaded that our system of values has ceased to operate. Possibly one of the consoling consequences of the present situation may be a greater pluralism in our value systems and a greater awareness of the range in man's ways and of the possibility of diverse general value systems.

COMMENTARY: THE NATIONAL STYLE

by David Riesman

MR. ROSTOW's paper has not taken into account enough members of the American household, nor nearly enough within his own personal style, for he is at least as many people as T. S. Eliot. His paper emphasizes and reflects his important role in the policy-shaping process and in the "policy sciences"; but what is underplayed are the jokes, the irony, the poet, and the fatalistic peasant grandmother. It is uncomfortably easy for the academic person such as myself to criticize from the sidelines those who are hauling on the lifelines, and so I want to say at the outset how much I respect and admire the willingness Mr. Rostow has shown to throw himself into contemporary political developments where disinterested and perspectivistic advice might just possibly make a difference for this country of life or death, and almost certainly a difference of civility or incivility. I agree with him (as his Democratic friends have sometimes put it) in placing country above party, and I would agree with him even more if he placed planet above country.

When I got through his paper, I asked myself what kind of an America he would fashion were he suddenly made dictator with power to alter men, events, and institutions? From what he says, he would do many necessary things, civilized things and intelligent things. Many negative perils would be removed or ameliorated: rivalry in the armed services, segregation in the South, the blight of our cities, the stifling of individual initiative in large organizations, and so on. There would be more vigor in America, and less decay. Yet, I had no sense that the America he wants is radically, unmanageably, explosively different from present-day America; and I cannot believe that without a larger dream of America people would willingly make the sacrifices necessary to achieve even the minimum-decency-America that Mr. Rostow sees as viable.

358

As I read the paper there kept coming back to my mind an experience I had in 1956. During the presidential campaign Louis Harris and Stewart Alsop had come out to Chicago on one leg of their trip to take the political pulse of the country. I took Alsop's place one day and went along with Harris, polling in a suburb south of Chicago—a suburb that was being built into the wheat fields at one end while people had been living for a year or even two years in houses at the other end. It was a lower-middle-class suburb, neat, bungalow-type houses all "different," and it was a nice May day when the flowers were coming out and when the few men who weren't working were out in their incipient gardens. We asked people whom they had voted for in 1952 and they often said, "Who was running then?"—that is, who was running against Ike. They remembered they had voted for Ike. We asked them whom they would vote for in 1956 and they said Ike. Then we raised the question as to whether the heart attack might affect the matter and they told us about their Aunt Minnie or their Uncle Bill and their diseases, as if Ike were a homey figure or a neighbor for whom they had sympathy. When we asked them what the Republicans had done that they especially liked, they could say nothing other than ending the war in Korea, as a few said, and then we asked them what they disliked. They said high taxes, but that was about all. The single Stevenson support we found was an old engineer of a crusty sort who lived in the only house that had been in the area before 1955, and he came running afterward to tell us how he really felt when he saw, from our going from house to house, that we truly were taking a poll and not inquiring just about him.

Most of the people we spoke to were young housewives, often interrupted in their midday television program—as the dog used to be the hazard for the postman, so the TV has become for the interviewer. They were educated: they had been to high school and some to two years of college or secretarial school; they read a few magazines although hardly a book, and yet their complacency was such as to make Stewart Alsop feel that he had been unfair in lambasting people in Washington for being indolent, for he had not fully appreciated what their constituencies were like. As one looked over the flat Illinois prairie at all the signs of prosperity, it was not hard to see why these people were so bland politically and responded so to the same qualities in Ike. To be sure, some of them also liked violence with their political entertainment, and this was one of the attractions of both Kefauver and McCarthy. These people were not self-made men who remembered their struggles against hardship but, rather, a society-made generation who could not believe society would let them down, and, therefore, lacked not only the anxiety which often haunts but also the sense of accomplishment which sometimes enriches the self-made.

I kept thinking of these interviews not only because they were a kind of counterfoil to the responsible and devoted American whom Mr. Rostow would like to see develop but also because the quality of life these people lead is missing in something—one of the reasons indeed why they were so ready to talk to the interviewer. Many of them are bored, although still quite young and vigorous; and this boredom is one of the reasons why they could respond even to the most evident and fiercely visible crisis in only the lurching fashion Mr. Rostow describes.

While Mr. Rostow's paper is full of a sense of American errors and mistakes, tactical and strategic, and while it warns again complacency, the paper is complacent in that it has not reckoned with the social-psychological vacua in American life which would exist even if all his remedies were taken.

Let me illustrate at a few points what kinds of things in his paper gave me this reaction. Although on pages 305 and the following, he warns against ethnocentrism, I have kept asking myself how the paper would strike a sensitive reader in Indonesia or Belgium or a Hungarian refugee or a Japanese. Such a person might feel that while Mr. Rostow starts off with a very good sense of the disorderliness of America (as in his illustration of T. S. Eliot's character), he ends up in a kind of chromium-plated harmony by suppressing many things which non-Americans—and many Americans, too—would consider fundamental. Take, for instance, the comments on Latin America which are quoted from John Quincy Adams. It seems to have occurred neither to Adams nor Rostow that, with all the political turmoil and priest-ridden elements, there is in Mexico and in the Caribbean a human vigor which impresses many Americans in much the same way that Englishmen of the sensitive strata are impressed with Southern Italy. Or take, for instance, the last phrases of page 306:

We have had difficulty in understanding the complex processes at work in the underdeveloped areas and in harmonizing our efforts with those of the men and women caught up in the great nationalist revolutions now going forward in strategically decisive areas of the world. We have, to our cost, been excessively culture bound in facing this mammoth fact of the twentieth century.

Listen to the undertones of this passage—and many others of the same sort can be found. The images are power-ridden: "great nationalist," "revolutions," "strategically decisive," "to our cost," "facing this mammoth fact," "the twentieth century." What could be more culture bound than this strategic concern, this reference to *mammoth* fact—elsewhere to "hard fact" and "hard reality"—as if everything was being looked at from the American perspective alone, as it so often is regularly in our daily and periodical press. If I had to express my judgment most critically, I would say that Mr. Rostow has admirably freed himself from the parochialism of academia and its frequent snobbery of culture and topic, only to succumb to the very much larger parish of the United States of America itself. A decent version of the United States of America, to be sure—as I said, prosperous, fair-minded, intelligent; but that this America succeeds in capturing the imagination of many of the underdeveloped areas (including the USSR) is only a sign of their poverty and ours. They are becoming culture bound in our sense, and we are not becoming less so. Since this America is a going concern and since America values going concerns, I get the sense that Mr. Rostow hasn't asked himself what would seem at least a threshold question, namely, whether the American style is really worth it even with all the modifications he proposes. Or, rather, whether the kinds of rivalry within and outside the country that have given meaning and direction in the past, and still, of course, have plenty of vitality, will continue to suffice in the relatively prosperous future.

But let me return to the metaphors in Rostow's paper that illustrate the way in which strategic and "realistic" thinking has crept into our discourse—an improvement in some respects over earlier academic sentimentalities and pedantries; but, at the same time, a loss of that idealism which was more easy in a more innocent America and of that purpose which was once God-given or Destiny-given. Let me read you in this context from a sentence on page 305: "It is not the number of Soviet engineers that threatens us; it is the sharpness of Soviet priorities and their ability to concentrate their best talents around them which permit a nation with a third of our real income to close on us." The ironical thing here is that Rostow is criticizing the American emphasis on numbers and quantity in our national-Indianapolis-speedway vis-à-vis the Soviet Union and yet falls into the very same trap he is attacking by a sentence which could only have been written by an American who was interested in winning a race.

I want to make clear the perspective from which I make this criticism: It is inhuman not to be concerned with the survival of human beings no matter how "undeserving" one may think these human beings to be. We should be more concerned with the survival of all the earth, including the people of the Soviet Union, whereas, from Mr. Rostow's paper, one gets a sense of preoccupation entirely with American interests even though these are seen with generosity and tolerance toward other interests. Nationalism, which is our great peril—as we shall more fully realize when Pakistan and Israel have the atom bomb—is only assuaged and not transcended. American intellectuals have only recently escaped in a few cases from altering cycles of jingoism and defensiveness vis-à-vis European culture, but the world situation does not permit us to enjoy our new-found freedom to discover the distinctively American.

In saying this, I am commenting also on my own shortcomings. A good deal of what I am saying here in criticism of Mr. Rostow is at the same time an effort to come to terms with things I have written earlier. I am talking now out of my increasing pessimism in confronting this country's future in terms of quality of life. Whether this reflects changes in me or changes in the country I cannot say. I can at least refer to some of the changes in the country which trouble me and which make me doubt some of my own earlier convictions.

I have referred to the interviews done by Louis Harris as one example of the kind of blandness that I see as somehow inhuman. When I see a French or Italian movie the faces seem more alive and expressive than American faces in equivalent films. The very rich are perhaps unhappy in all countries. Their faces are often sour, fearful, and suspicious. In America millions are among the very rich in international terms, while the white-collar workers and many of the factory workers seem to me unhappy also—ill at ease in Zion.

I was also saddened by the attitude of many Stevenson supporters in the last campaign who felt that he had made a better campaign in 1952.

In 1952 many of his supporters were much too starry eyed; in 1956 I felt a loss of tone among them. Stevenson's courageous attacks on H-bomb tests, which at least tried to educate people to the real problem, were dismissed by many of his supporters as poor politics or poor timing. People wanted something glamorous in Stevenson—as they thought they had found in 1952—and resented his not providing this. Stevenson made a much better campaign in 1956 in his efforts at education, at groping with some of the really serious problems of this country, but he had much less emotional support from his supporters than in 1952 when they were deluded into thinking he could win and into thinking how wonderful it was to have a semi-intellectual run for President.

Much more important than any of these experiences was my confrontation during the Polish and Hungarian uprisings in 1956 with the fact that there was a more passionate feeling for freedom in the Satellite countries (and, I gathered, among the youth of Leningrad and elsewhere in the Soviet Union itself) than one found at the time in this country. When I read the articles by young Polish writers in the emancipated Polish press, or the appeals of the short-lived Petofi Club which sparked the Hungarian revolution, I wondered how many American youth and how many American writers were as clear about freedom as these people who had been radically deprived of it. I felt almost envious of people who had so clear a goal, so clear an enemy, as compared with the problems of fighting for a kind of uncontested individuality in this country. (In Mr. Murray's paper we have a confrontation with these problems which is haunting because it contains its own drama and contradiction in the very way it is presented and in the very courage not to resolve the issue or to state conclusions.) The Hungarian and Polish rebels fought, as people always do, for mixed motives, including reactionary ones; their published programs had a nineteenth century and Enlightenment flavor which at the present time, in the want of superior Utopias, remains revolutionary. It would be defeatist to conclude that one must have harsh parents in order to become strong and self-reliant children or that one must have the experience of totalitarianism in order to value freedom; nevertheless, when old oppressions have been removed, it takes a while to "discover" the new and subtle ones our better fortune presents. We have not done that in America; we have coastsed on old although still pressing and dangerous problems.

Indeed, Mr. Rostow documents the fact that our perspective on the world has not kept pace with our power in it and over it. This is so in spite of the counter-tendencies provided by anthropological and historical work which lend perspective. In fact, in some ways our perspective on the world has narrowed, perhaps since our entry into World War II and surely since our entry into the Cold War. The American posture in world affairs has recently been much more aggressive and belligerent than most decent and internationally minded Americans realize. We tend to reject all neutralist opinion as Communist inspired and, even if we ourselves do not tacitly fear being accused of Communism, fail to learn what we might learn from the more sagacious and less involved among the neutrals, thus coupling pride to power. At present, Time and the daily press—even the decent press—write about Morocco or Jordan almost entirely from the point of view of American strategic considerations whether in geopolitical or geopsychological terms. We seem no longer to be able to afford a more disinterested concern, or, when we do, we disguise it and thereby eventually fool ourselves by pretending that it is a strategic concern.

Mr. Rostow's account of the American style almost completely disregards all the transcendental and idealistic sides of American life. He has been too much swayed by the demise of Wilson's ideals and by the general shabby way in which many ideals have turned out in this period. There is a mention of the progressive movement and a dismissal of the socialists in this country, such as Debs, as a kind of no-count movement whose trendex rating was never high. Lincoln is revered as the sagacious compromiser—which was certainly one aspect of him and needs to be said against the idolatry of the merely saintly Lincoln which actually cuts down his humanity—but there is little sense of the Lincoln of the second inaugural, or of the fact that Sheldon's book, In His Steps, or Bellamy's Looking Backward, sold millions of copies during the progressive eras. Indeed, I would argue that World War I marked a sharp break with an America which was growing more and more polarized around competing ideals of the national life (just as the way in which World War II began for us ended the future debate over fascism within this country by allowing us to turn on those "yellow bastards who stabbed us in the back" and make common cause with enemies within America all too readily).

I am much more of a pacifist than Mr. Rostow, at least so far as this paper speaks for him. The isolationist position in World War II is more defensible than he thinks, and it wouldn't be the worst way to try to avoid atomic destruction for this country to disarm and to mobilize peace sentiment both at home and abroad in an almost Gandhi-like gesture toward the rest of the world.We are building an increasing iron curtain of our own about the real dilemmas of defense—an iron curtain which the Oppenheimer case itself did a good deal to help prepare.

Mr. Rostow is as liberal as I am, but I am questioning whether liberalism in its traditional American form can survive if there is no radicalism against which to be moderate. Whereas a few years ago America was more endangered by idealism than by realism, today the situation is reversed and, while we are confronted with a kind of muddy and shoddy idealism in many public pronouncements, we suffer much more from cynicism, from a lack of profound ideals which can motivate a new, or even keep going under present conditions an older, society.

I am troubled in Mr. Rostow's paper not only by an ethnocentric bias in national terms but also in terms that are applicable within America. The history of America on which he draws is a history of the self-conscious, the "we"-conscious, and perhaps the class-conscious. When he writes, for instance, "the liberty and justice for all toward which we were committed to aspire . . . ," I wonder who the "we" is, for millions of Americans have virtually no part in this, are too committed to their apathy or their bigotry to share in what Gunnar Myrdal calls "The American Dilemma." The numerous studies we have had of the prejudiced personality, whether by Allport or the Berkeley group, indicate the many psychological disquietudes beneath the surface decencies. Surely, as Rostow says on page 250, federalism has served to contain this cultural dynamite behind rather leaky bulkheads, and the uniformities imposed by the media have likewise served as a limited form of containment. Also, as he indicates, our money and wealth have saved us from problems by allowing us to pay off, save in the Civil War, many of our dissident feelings and factions—much as a university which cannot decide what it wants as an intellectual ideal can buy all the going ideals with help from the foundations. Though I am not a fan of the Civil War, I have always felt its deadly seriousness as an omen for this country—an omen of bellicosity and bigotry—and not giving enough weight to what the Civil War says about America would be like talking about France and neglecting the continuing divisive and un-liquidated role of the French Revolution. (The British liquidated their Civil War much more wholeheartedly. The containments in Britain are not federal but are internalized within each individual—so that the economist, Adolph Löwe, described the British character as an example of "spontaneous collectivism." It is this internationalization rather than such rituals as those of the monarchy which legitimizes civil peace in Britain.)

Likewise, in his emphasis on American empiricism and operational-ism, Rostow is somewhat too much captured by the rational surface of things. Surely he has his eye here on traits which are marked in America in contrast with many other cultures, and yet on an absolute scale I have never found them impressive, any more than I have felt America to be efficient rather than simply well off and able to afford such waste. How rare a thing empiricism actually is even among the followers of Justice Holmes, how often it is simply an ideology or rationalization! The American tells himself that he should be empirical, hardheaded, and sensible, and some of the "moral overstrain" to which Rostow re-fers comes from this discrepancy today rather than from the older form of hypocrisy which contrasted virtuous professions with vicious practice. And this is another way of my saying once more that he greatly under-plays the sadness of American life, the dryness of experience, and the lack of confrontation with it despite the cult of experience. Reading Rostow's account on page 256 and following of America's spirit of compromise, one would never suspect the 18th Amendment had been passed. And the appeal of McCarthy was—and here, of course, opinions differ—at least as much the result of repressed dissatisfactions even with success in America as of the rationalizations that the Cold War provided.

Rostow's account is much too rational in the sense of rationalistic. On page 264, when he talks about the southern fear of expansion to the west which led to the Civil War, he ignores the virulence created by slavery in the mind of the white southerner—the virulence so magnifi-cently described in Cash's The Mind of the South. It is the historicist view which thinks that since we survive, the motives we attribute to our past must have been manageable and containable ones. Suppose we were to blunder into war tomorrow, ignoring Rostow's kind of sobriety because of fear of the McCarthys and Knowlands from within and mis-judgment of the Soviet Union from without? Is there anything in Ros-tow's account which would really prepare us for this, or would we not have to write a new history? I think such a war quite possible, and so I gather does Rostow, but its roots would lie not only in the "mistakes" which he criticizes but also in more fundamental elements of character and style.

Even the rationalistic elements in America which Rostow describes should be attributed less to experience than to culture and character structure. Rostow says on page 258 that the Americans do not fight over a given amount of wealth but they often create new wealth. Yet this is largely not true of the Irish in America even to the fourth genera-tion. The Irish still act as if they were in a small hierarchical country where the point is to get into the bureaucracy, whether this be the priesthood or civil service as in the old country or, in addition in this country, insurance companies, utilities, and other white-collar or lace-curtain jobs. The Jansenist Catholicism of the Irish seems to me a factor here, and the trauma of the potato famine still persists, in contrast to the Protestants and the Jews who, in different ways, can focus on or perceive novelty and make something new at times, build an organiza-tion or a congregation rather than find a place in the existing one. In-deed, it is arguable that this conflict of religious cultures is one factor in the inability to take action prior to crisis that Rostow so capably describes.

Rostow is so nearly right at so many points and so very much in the right at other points that I have had to overstress somewhat our differ-ent sides to create the dialectic his paper invites. Let me give a couple of other illustrations of historicism. On page 268 he says, "The United States managed to acquire the requisite territory and to equalize the hemisphere and any increase in major power influence with remarkably little diplomatic or military cost." What would an American Indian or Mexican think if he read that? It represents the too easy grace of the winner, just as the reference on page 270, "self-evident national and re-gional interest," speaks with a retroactive voice, much like the reference on page 272 to "the nation's legitimate and abiding ideological and power interests"—this is the way that nationalists, if not wholly indecent, talk. The amount of luck and blundering, and misery that went into these

apparent destinies is understated; for instance, the point about the income tax on page 276 suggests that we got the income tax through in
order to be able to fight the First World War, while the comment on
page 277 about the lack of objection to New Deal legislation overlooks
the undistributed profits tax which really challenged the power of the
business managerial group by trying to transfer power to stockholders
in the money market—and was promptly repealed. The other acts which
are now accepted have, of course, created their own vested interests, for
instance, in the lawyers who practice before the commissions—and their
so-to-speak "vested enemies" within the commissions.

Does Mr. Rostow think that Keynesian economics is a sufficiently
accepted political strategy today, once one removes the prop of the war
economy? When millions of Americans had discovered that war "cured"
depressions, and that even a war economy did, we became war-prepara-
tion Keynesians rather than finance-leverage Keynesians and were prepared both for postwar prosperity and for postwar inflexibility in foreign
affairs.

Many of the things that I see and worry about, Mr. Rostow sees, too.
Indeed, he speaks admirably about the need for a greater scope of alternatives as the basis for making decisions, and his critique of the usual
talk about administration and decision making is very much in the spirit
of the criticisms I have presented here. I have, in fact, confined myself
to only one aspect of Rostow's paper and not even to the main themes
he raises of continuity and style, let alone to many stimulating by-the-
way observations concerning, for instance, the diminishing marginal
utility of money, and the wonderful point on page 301 that American national politics is becoming communal or small-town politics without the
forms existing for this transformation. Perhaps it would help explain the
color of my own reaction if I say that I read it just after reading Henry
Murray's paper, and the contrast between Thoreau and the National
Security Council was too much for me.

APPENDIX: SELECTIONS OF
TRANSCRIBED DISCUSSION

I. Saturday Morning
Discussion of Kluckhohn Paper

Mr. Hofstadter: Several things said before and after my comments lead me to refer again to what Mr. Wilson remarked about—the characteristic absence of the sense of tragedy in American life in the past; and I think one possible way of looking at it is to say that now for the first time perhaps we have a generation in this country in which there is a wide and deep sense of what tragedy is.

If the generalization about Americans in the past is true, as I think it is, and if this generation does have, as I believe it does, an only recently induced sense of tragedy, the realization of these facts helps to tie together many of the things that have been referred to in our discussion. I am not trying to indicate here a causal sequence but to portray a constellation of related events.

I think one of the reasons for the extraordinary panic over Korea was that the Korean war marked precisely the national moment when this sense of tragedy—or failure—was precipitated, because we had fully engaged in a world conflict and committed millions of men and then discovered that we were still confronted with the same unsolved problem. For the first time, and in an extremely dramatic way, the American feeling that problems are something you always solve—rather than that there are problems you may just have to live with—was irrefutably controverted in the Korean experience. This makes understandable a great deal of the privatization of life that has gone on since. That young Americans have the greater tolerance and humanity that have been observed, a greater passivity, and engage in the search for comfort and the kind of cultivation to which Mr. Oppenheimer referred, is our American

369

reaction to tragedy. If we cannot finally solve public problems, we cannot do it; but we are going to be comfortable and, perhaps, a little more cultivated in the process. I think it is a new kind of cultivation for us.

MR. RIESMAN: When I thought about Clyde Kluckhohn's paper and about what he said about religion and when I see figures on church membership, I think of the figures on church membership one hundred years ago. I find that it was 10 or 15 per cent in the Illinois frontier in 1850, and I feel staggered. Have the historians given us the wrong impression as to the past, the religious past? Is there something centrally wrong in the figures as not representing the state of the country? It could be that this is a way of seeing that the sense of tragedy, insofar as it came through, has been Anglican, for religion was never very strong here in spite of what we were told.

MR. OPPENHEIMER: May I make one very small comment? I agree with Dr. Hofstadter, but I am sure tragedy is not the right word—certainly not if you think not of a technical form of dramatics but, rather, of sorrow, of limited power, of being prepared for disappointment. But there is one thing that I think is important. What I intended by using the word mediaeval is that the arts in which the young people are engaged are not private. They are now typically public and communal. They differ from the art young people were engaged in in the twenties very largely in this respect. They refer to society and groups, and they are very outgoing. Calling this private may be right from the point of view of the federal government or politics generally, but not in a human way.

MR. HOFSTADTER: I had private in mind as meaning not politically concerned and—in a certain sense, when one considers the possible outlets of individual energy—as an alternative to political engagement.

MR. MORISON: I was about to take issue with you, Dick, on this sense of tragedy in connection with Korea, but I am not sure now, after you have stated your case that I will—because, in a sense, up to that time, we had almost always been able to ward off problems we could not solve. This seems to me to be why the Truman decision was so important. It defined and presented us with a problem we could not avoid.

Now on a different point. We have talked about conforming on many instances within the past few days without defining it, leaving it open and saying that we do conform. I am not really clear what we mean by this, nor am I clear whether we are conforming to a set of habits or just to each other. I would love to have a definition. What is the most striking thing we do conform to, or are we just conforming to each other?

MR. KLUCKHOHN: As I tried to say, conformity is one of the least examined words at the present. I want to make a comment on what Mr. Oppenheimer said here when he used the word mediaeval. He jelled something for me. I feel that he is right; and I want just to pass on something that Erich Fromm says in *Escape from Freedom*—that thirteenth century France, for example, was also a conformist society and that what people according to their station in life and their roles were supposed to be, as we see it, was rather rigidly laid down. But, says Fromm, precisely in proportion to their conformity there was the freeing of the psychic energy from having to ask, who am I, how do I behave toward you, and how do you behave toward me? Within the frame, there was much more genuine spontaneity than is supposed. . . . When Americans talk about spontaneity, they really mean impulsiveness, which is a fragmentation. I think that one dimension of causal conformity, at the present, is precisely mediaeval in the sense Fromm was suggesting— that within a certain limit of a certain pattern there is the possibility for genuine spontaneity and individuality.

MR. BISSELL: I agree fully with what Mr. Hofstadter said about the Korean war. I do feel that as an incident it is a major explanation of some changes in values that have occurred since that war; and I think that, unfortunately, what I call political accidents, mistakes, have both heightened the influence of that event and may render that influence far less benign than it might have been. The event itself I would interpret as the sudden and dramatic and crushing revelation that, in the larger matters of civilization, problems do not get solved; they have to be lived with. In perspective this country had been extraordinarily fortunate in that we had been shielded throughout our history from a realization, at least with respect to events external to the country, of this simple proposition that problems do not get solved. Here was the most dramatic revelation.

The first response was to meet the challenge presented by that event; and we all remember almost the day-by-day history of that time. The first response was not *just* a political act in government. It was a political act in government, but much more widely and spontaneously supported throughout the nation than the readers of today's commentary on the event would remember. Then the political accident, as I call it, occurred and somewhat altered the impact of the event. The accident was that it became fashionable—perhaps more in one party than another—to exploit the obvious discomfort, the obvious tragedy of a war, the obvious injustices inherent in a limited war that doesn't call upon all the national energy and, therefore, leaves many people free from its impact to exploit all of these dissatisfactions—to exploit, indeed, the very resistance to the concept that problems cannot be solved. However the exploitation of these aspects of the matter started, it was picked up aggressively by some of our political leadership, and the misinterpretation, or the attempt to unstate the historical effect, was apparently acquiesced in by almost all of our political leadership.

In the last six or seven years we have had the spectacle, with increasing unanimity of both leaderships, of both parties having acquiesced in our attempt as a nation to sweep this traumatic revelation, the very unpleasant facts, back underneath the carpet. I think this has produced neuroses. Now, speaking of a political problem we face again, there is a need to do it over again, a need to re-establish, to re-educate the people in the fundamental truth that problems of this kind do not get solved. I think this is a theme that should receive attention.

In 1931, when the Japanese went into Manchuria, a somewhat similar problem was presented. We did everything we could to duck it and, succeeding in ducking it, we left the thing unstated. We could go along for nine years and then lay the blame for what happened on everybody else but us. We had learned nothing. I agree with Dick that, having stated the problem in 1950, we are still, however, sweeping it under the table. The problem is there.

I don't mean to imply that we will be successful in sweeping it under the carpet. I think I made the further point that there are continuing incidents, if somewhat more trivial and less dramatic, that keep teaching the lesson.

MR. KAPLAN: What I wanted to say was along those lines. A picture began to emerge for a while in our discussions which I confess I could not recognize, in that my own experience was limited somewhat by the unfortunate disadvantage of not having access to Harvard graduates and undergraduates. Am I to understand from the scientists who look into these things that, now that Americans have recognized that their power is not as unlimited as they thought, they will have to moderate their aims; and that these aims, if they are sufficiently realistic, can be carried out, but that, having carried them out, Americans will face other problems? This sounds too good to be true, and I must admit I just do not believe it. I think, rather, that in political terms there has been the shock of realization that, no matter how unified we are, how strong we are, for some absurd reason there are recalcitrant forces elsewhere which we cannot rationalize and the hell with them—we will turn elsewhere and lead our lives in a different direction. Aren't these two different pictures? I was afraid we were blurring these pictures into one as they were being discussed. Perhaps I am only expressing a temperamental pessimism.

MR. HOFSTADTER: I think both reactions are going to exist, but the type you characterize as more mature is probably less common than the kind of privatization to which I was referring.

MR. KAPLAN: More particularly, if I may interrupt, it is not a question of the relative frequency but the relative weight.

MR. BUNDY: It does set out Arthur Schlesinger's point that the ebb and flow of political life is highly significant and that the degree of attention that is given to political problems is highly variable in our history. Even within the last six years and even within months, attention has turned to a number of circumstances in which the character of the political leadership, action by those who have the responsibility, has been very important. One way of emphasizing that is to suggest that these two classes that you have described are not classes into which individuals fall. They are classes into which parts of individuals fall. All of us here are in part pursuing busy private lives and in part accepting, we hope in a relatively grown-up fashion, the character of society and the international crises in which we find ourselves. Whether we respond to those crises will depend in part upon ourselves and in part upon the relatively atrophied character of voluntary organizations on these matters. This is a silly thing to say in a conference in which the two principal sponsors are among the most active volunteers in getting people back into political action. But I think it is true. The kind of thing that was characteristic of the 1930s, when we began to have people on both sides concerned whether to get into war, and characteristic of the 1950s during the debate over the Marshall Plan, has not been characteristic of the last three or four years.

MR. ROSTOW: I'd like to make a relatively optimistic statement whose burden is that Americans have learned to live with their international problems, if necessary on an unsolved basis, better than we seem to suppose.

There is no doubt that there have been powerful, recurrent, and vocal forces at various times over the past twenty years expressing the view that either we ought to solve our problem—whatever it then happened to be—or get out. But, in fact, neither World War II nor its subsequent major issues have really been handled in this juvenile mood. World War II was fought with a consciousness within the American people of Wilson's tragedy, the tragedy of pure crusade. There was, in 1945, relatively little cheap optimism; or, at least, there was relatively little romantic hope that war had been finally ended, that the United Nations would antiseptically solve all subsequent problems without American effort, and this view was compatible with a support for the United Nations of quite surprising strength, depth, and continuity.

Let us take a few further testing points. We had, for a while, a monopoly of the atom bomb. Arguments existed—quite rational arguments, up to a point—that we should exploit that transient monopoly, once Stalin's postwar policy was revealed. But the net weight of the political process in the United States fell powerfully on the side of sweating it out rather than for seeking a showdown which we could, quite possibly, have initiated.

Now another. The initial reaction to MacArthur's return had all the trappings of an emotional evasion of the real problems and limitations of American military policy. Then Senator Russell took over. The hearings started; and the American political process operated at very nearly its best. One forgets how much text filled the papers and how carefully it was assessed.

MR. BUNDY: It went on for three million words.

MR. ROSTOW: There was, indeed, a turning point in the MacArthur hearings. At a certain moment, perceiving no simple, gratifying solution, a lot of people turned aside. They refused, if you like, to live with the Far Eastern problem. But the nation as a whole did live with the Far Eastern problem. We went on and fought. We voted the taxes to spend a lot of money. We have never backed away from the thing. Whether we have acted wisely or unwisely, holding the line in the Far East was something we have thought we had to do.

Another case is the Hungarian revolt. Again, there was a background of much loose and self-indulgent talk. There were notions of liberation not backed by serious plans—costs unmeasured. There is no doubt that the nation was deeply torn by the spectacle of Hungary. But, as nearly as one can define a mature position, the nation behaved maturely. It accepted the fact that—for better or worse—its policy was, in fact, incompatible with liberation at American military initiative. We accepted the hard fact that we were going to live with Eastern Europe and let it evolve with only a marginal role for Americans.

And, in general, if you run our history over without a sound track, looking only at the net national performance, there has been far more capacity to live with messy, unresolved situations than our ways of talking about things would suggest.

MR. KAPLAN: What was in my mind was not chiefly, at any rate certainly not exclusively, the question of political apathy or participation, or even a question of the political attitude of large segments of the population, but the question of the presuppositions or the philosophies, locally, about the policies being made. That appears to be the kind of concrete question on which, it seems to me, alternative points of view could be formulated.

Again, I emphasize these are questions of fact about what people's attitudes are, and I'd like to know if I understand rightly what your judgment permits.

In one perspective our military assets are being thought of as directed toward the moment in which there will be a decisive revolution. They are thought of in terms of a war which is planned for, or anticipated, not at any specific date but within some kind of interval; and this is what I put in the perspective, the older one, of supposing a problem is going to arise. The problem will be settled and, if approved, we shall put ourselves into possession of the instruments which will allow us to settle it when the time comes.

In the other perspective which you say you think is emerging, which I certainly would hope, the significance of the military preparation is not directed toward a decisive moment. It is an instrument which is used

—not used, of course, in the ordinary sense but in quite another way—
as a part of the continuing and endless process of negotiation in which,
to be sure, from time to time, problems are solved, but in which it is
recognized that their solution means that some new kinds of problems
are formulated. Now it may well be there are grounds for hope. There
has been a shift more in the direction of the second perspective than
in the direction of the first, but this would seem to constitute an operational specification of the American tragedy. I want to be sure that is
what underlies American policies.

MR. HOFSTADTER: I am trying to suggest to you the type of thing to
which I think this country has been particularly prone. The only way
I can bring it home completely is to say that it has a great deal to do
with your political moralist who thinks an absolute settlement of some
moral questions can be imposed upon others within the framework of
political action. Perhaps the simplest example, which we all remember,
was Prohibition. It was going to wipe out the saloons and put an end
to drunkenness forever. That's the kind of attitude I would like to think
has been pushed very much into a corner by the last fifteen or twenty
years. I don't mean that it has disappeared altogether. It, too, is a problem which you will not wipe out.

MR. KENNAN: I am a little skeptical about that. Since World War II
and since Korea, we have progressed considerably in our thinking at the
governmental level, but it seems to me that we have done it against a
background of scorn and indifference and absence of discussion with a
great part of the population, particularly the veteran population.

What troubled me about the Korean war was the derisiveness of
the comments of the men who had to fight it about those who had to
make the policy decisions back in Washington. I must say that I often
resented it. I wanted to say to these fellows: "If you have no interest in
the thing which is at stake for us, sit in our places and decide for us
whether the entire fruits of the victory in the Pacific in 1945 should be
frivolously allowed to go by the boards. If you think they should, perhaps we are making policy under a great misunderstanding." Those chaps
came out of the war dominated by a bitter skepticism about the decisions
which put them in there.

I'd like to reinforce what Dick said. I can't think of any situation
which confused more the understanding of the Korean war than did

the MacArthur hearings. I came away from them with a complete sense of frustration, with a feeling that now the truth was really effectively buried, where nobody could get at it. This is not probably a fair sample that I have run, but a large proportion of the public seemed to me to feel that the State Department, whose motives were suspect, had prevented MacArthur from completing a thing which otherwise could have been completed.

MR. POTTER: I would like to be able to believe that we are coming to accept in a more mature way the continuing perplexities which we shall have with us, but I find it hard to believe; and some of the examples that have been offered are not entirely convincing to me.

Now, about the fact that we refrained from using the bomb. It is true, certainly, that we did refrain, but I am not sure whether we refrained because of this new maturity or because we have never been capable of taking the initiative in hostilities. If we ever did take the initiative, it was only when we were able to convince ourselves that we had been attacked and that we were not taking it. To be sure, our course in connection with the bomb was the right one, but was it the result of a wise decision or only of our inability to make a decision?

With reference to the thought that we are more aware that problems cannot be solved but have to be lived with, I feel that the Hungarian illustration kicks back very badly. We certainly encouraged the Hungarians to believe that their problem could be solved if they would just love freedom well enough, and our maturity showed up mostly in the way we stood clear of the consequences when they accepted in earnest what we had professed to believe. Have our convictions matured, or is our maturity only a matter of our knowing better than to act on our convictions?

COL. COFFEY: I realize it's theoretically impossible to add a third horn to a dilemma such as that confronting us, but I'd like to put forth a line of thought which differs somewhat from both of those advanced concerning reaction to tragedies.

It is perfectly possible to argue, for example, that our unconscious fear of destruction may have a great deal to do with the emphasis on family life and even with the increase in the birth rate. In that sense, some current social trends are, indeed, a reflection of a sense of tragedy. It is equally plausible to say that, although we have not done badly in facing up to the problems confronting us, we have retreated too much into a sense of futility concerning any ultimate solutions. I would like to point out something which I believe is a current attitude. I don't know whether it's been in existence long enough to influence values. It is a feeling of complacency.

It seems to me that part of our behavior stems from a belief that the tough problems either are solved or can be solved without any great deal of effort on our part. The former holds true particularly on the domestic scene, perhaps—as witness the political apathy of which Mr. Kaplan made mention. I would suggest that there is an even more dangerous manifestation in the international scene in terms of the thesis that the great problems can be solved even though we do not exert maximum effort.

I sense, for example—this is a purely subjective, almost a nonhistorical judgment—a trend toward neo-isolationism in many United States policies in the last four or five years, at least, and a feeling, particularly manifest since Geneva, that as long as we have a few airplanes sitting around in appropriate places and lots of things we can drop from them, there will be insured a balance of political power such that we need make only the most marginal and peripheral efforts to keep our homeland intact, our economy relatively untouched.

II. Saturday Afternoon
Discussion of Murray Paper

Mr. Morton White: What I should like to know is whether it is possible to give some estimate of the degree of individuality in American life today by reference to the principle advanced in Mill's essay, On Liberty, that one should be free to do as one chooses so long as one does not harm others. It is possible to ask the same question about the Soviet Union today. If we cannot come to any reasonable conclusion about the presence of individuality in our society as measured by the extent to which one can do as one chooses so long as one doesn't harm others, there is some doubt as to whether we can use the word individuality as an expression of what we take to be one of the virtues of our society as opposed to that of the Soviet Union. If we cannot come to such a conclusion, then a great deal of our political talk, a great deal of our argumentation before the world ceases to have any clear meaning. I believe that we can say with confidence that American life does allow more individuality in this sense, but I should like to hear the question discussed by social scientists.

MR. OPPENHEIMER: Isn't there a great danger in identifying the opportunity to act with the action? I think all three speakers were talking not about the existence of external constraints but about the frequency with which freedom is used.

MR. MORTON WHITE: I am really asking my question because it seems to me of value to get a response from a social scientist on this question. Perhaps it is not what the speakers were talking about, but I was wondering what Harry's response would be to the question I raised.

MR. MURRAY: The first thing I am going to say is about what Robert brought up—the opportunity to vary and whether one actually does vary, let's say. I would find it convenient to distinguish between what you might call, in a rough way, pre-socialized individuality and post-socialized individuality. Pre-socialized individuality could be characterized by the deviant behavior, let's say, of the teen-agers now. That's varied, in a way. The old human instincts are at work, but the current juvenile crimes being committed are rather novel. More young sons are killing their mothers in new ways than ever before and, in a sense, that is individuality. But I was limiting myself to post-socialized individuality, that is, to those who have incorporated their culture and then gone beyond that. They know what they are doing, and their responses when they go beyond their culture are varied. It was in the back of my mind that this fellow "Curt" is thinking in an evolutionary sense; he is thinking in emergents, as evolutional emergents in values of thought.

MR. WILSON: I want to suggest something about creativity. One way to describe creativity is in terms of those qualities of personality and experience which make it possible for an individual to carry developmental and deviant components in his constellation of social roles without external damage—that is John Stuart Mill's point which Mr. White quoted—or internal treachery. This second point about internal treachery is complex, simple as it might appear to some moralists.

Now, having said that, I want to go on to say that creativity, according to the definition I have just used, can only occur to the extent that a society provides an adequate degree of sanction for the developmental and deviant and creative aspects of social roles. Some comments on this were made earlier about parts of American society and about the ebb and flow of creativity in those areas where deviance is sanctioned or permitted. That ebb and flow is in part related to the depth and consistency of feeling about reality and about essential basic values. In excessively simple terms, the safer a society feels with regard to certain basic values, the more is creativity likely to be sanctioned.

To go on—I'll come back to creativity in a moment—I would like to repeat, paraphrasing it a little, a point Harry Murray raised in his statement, to the effect that some Americans are perhaps afraid of hearing from themselves. It is an open secret that none of us is awfully keen on hearing from himself all the time, and perhaps it is encouraging that we sometimes bring ourselves to do it. Now, what are the kind of things Americans don't want to hear from themselves, the things they tend to conceal from themselves? I could give you a list for the British, but that's not the topic of discussion.

One of the things Americans tend to conceal from themselves is the nature of their optimism. Earlier we were discussing a study of smiles, showing how they had broadened down the years in advertising; and it sometimes appears to the outside observer that there is a tendency in America to use a false smile which is apparently directed outward, but which the European observer feels is really aimed inward, in an attempt at cheering up, at denying less hopeful aspects of life. Earlier, I was trying to touch on contrasting European and American attitudes toward tragedy, toward the possibility of the tragic in life. Perhaps I should take a moment to elaborate on that. As Dr. Oppenheimer said, tragedy is not the right word. What I was trying to speak of was not tragedy in the sense of some external catastrophe. I had in mind a kind of experience which finally permits or forces one to recognize the inevitability of loss or failure in life, and to develop a constructive basic attitude about this. With experience of this kind—a full experience of despair—it is sometimes possible to develop a re-flowering of hope of a more realistic and creative brand, of a less anxious and defensive character, so that in the end the unconvincing and broad smile may be replaced by one which is certainly a little sadder, but perhaps more direct and genuine.

This kind of thing is related to the attitude toward tragedy in the sense I was using that idea, and it has something to do with creativity in this way: I don't think people are often capable of effectively accepting and developing their own potential creativity until they have somehow been able to assimilate enough tragic experience to provide an effective basis for development and maturation.

MR. BISSELL: What was your original definition of creativity?

MR. WILSON: I related it to those qualities of personality—and there is more than one kind—which enable a person to carry developmental and deviant role components without external damage or internal treachery. That was the rough notion. I went on to note, however, that this is a meaningless definition unless you describe also the society within which these role components are sanctioned and permitted. The third point was that the extent of such sanction is likely to vary with the balance of securely accepted and deviant values in the society as a whole.

MR. MORISON: Would you elaborate a little on the developmental and deviant role components?

MR. WILSON: The phrase "developmental and deviant role components" is meant to cover nonconforming behavior which is essential to the maturation of the individual; but, perhaps more important, the words are meant also to suggest that society can be regarded as endeavoring to assign people to such roles for its own purposes; that is, it can be said that society needs deviants of many kinds to assist in its own creative development and adaptation.

MR. BISSELL: I am bothered by the definition of creativity. It seems to have many of the elements of individuality and leaves out some of the other elements of the definition of creativity. But, it's just a matter of how one is accustomed to using the word.

MR. KAYSEN: I think there are two different extremes of usage here, corresponding roughly but not entirely to the division that I can make crudely between those of Mr. Clyde Kluckhohn and Mr. Wilson, who have gone deeply into clinical studies of individual psyches, and the rest of us who are more or less, usually less, well trained for only one thing, aggregative social science. This is what was troubling Morton, I think.

My formulation of it is something like this. To put it in colder terms, one definition, one approach, would be to talk about perceived varieties of behavior and how they would be measurable or graspable. There are problems of what behaviors you want to measure and also, having decided that problem, how you add up different kinds of varieties—how you weigh them. Once you decide that's what you are after, and if that's your definition, it may be you do look at Morton White's suggestion that the institutional constraints on the individual are produced by the external social circumstances which define his activity and condition it.

The other definition, if I have followed the ball bouncing three ways in the dialogue, and I'm not sure I have, is the definition of the potentiality of the individual psyche. There is a sense, at least a logical sense, in which that individuality Harry is looking for is compatible with a perfect uniformity of behavior as perceived by the observer. Part of the trouble which explains the temptation to oscillate from one view to the other is that we don't have a very clear view of all the Americans between these two levels of social functioning, broadly speaking. And while, ideally, we can talk in abstract terms about a working model of the whole society which incorporates both the individual psyche and how it grows and develops and the social institutions, in practice we fall so very far short of putting them together that it may be that an approach which starts out at one of these poles and an approach which starts out at the other just never do meet. There is no common discourse possible. That may be a little pessimistic, so to speak, about where we stand in our intellectual technology.

MR. OPPENHEIMER: These are complementary views of a human problem which, in the present state, can hardly be brought into correspondence.

MR. KAPLAN: I want to extend on Mr. Kaysen's last observation a line that was put into my mind. One of the things that struck me in reading the dialogue, and even more formidably in Kaysen's comment, was that when we are talking about individuality we are talking about something which is, in your words, "a matter of impressions and values" rather than fact. This seems to me to be true and important and really underlying the more limited aspect of the difficulty that Mr. Kaysen called attention to, and I will venture upon a surmise. Obviously, I can't support it, nor do I have a great deal of confidence in it. It is as follows:

You approach a problem of this kind as a social scientist. You imagine that the problem is one of identifying a certain set of facts and then making observations on them and possibly drawing certain generalities. If we find this difficult, we are then inclined to suppose either that the facts are more complex than we had credited them with being, or that our observations are not sufficiently subtle or profound, or that the generalizations are too subtle for us to uncover. But there is another alternative, which is mainly that what we have taken for granted to be a problem of describing a certain set of facts is not altogether a problem of this kind. In discussing individuality, even when we purport to be giving a description of the state of society and a generalization of changes, what in fact we are doing is engaging in an appraisal of values in which our own values are operative.

That is, I am suggesting that this kind of discourse may have more similarity than we are inclined to suspect to the discourse of the art critic who is not merely giving a technical analysis of a structure but is also trying to contribute to an appreciative response for values that he himself has experienced. Now, I don't mean to get us involved in the rat race of general social science methodology and objectivity. But, in a much more specific way, you indicated that you wanted to talk about individuality rather than individualism. And so I would say that, if what I have been saying up to this point has application, we ought to recognize that in every case where we are speaking of individuality there is implicit in our speaking a tacit individualism, a tacit set of values which defines for us our particular problem, which delineates the range of what we call the individual. I mean the person, not how much individuality he has. If one approaches a problem as a theorist, he will assess it in one way. If he approaches it as a teacher or educator, he will assess it in another way, and if he approaches it as a man in government service he will assess it in still another.

In short, I don't think we can escape involvement with many other questions if we are to give meaning to the question that we are raising—has individuality increased or decreased? While I was aware of the sense of uneasiness in your dialogue, I felt that, rather than being a stylistic shortcoming, it was the mental impression of something that is very basic in the situation. There is no other way you can adequately discuss something of this kind and be able to exploit a whole range of possibilities. Not that the truth lies somewhere between or is a compromise but, rather, that the question being asked is a congress of questions and, therefore, requires a multiplicity of answers.

MR. NORTON-TAYLOR: If I follow this conversation, we are trying to determine what individuality is by what individuality does, and I would like to venture a definition of the individualist. It may be too cryptic. On the other hand, it may be quite simple when applied to the problem. In the first place, we are talking about an individualist. I gather we are talking about a person. I would venture this definition. The individualist is a person in a state of not being aware either through his own actions or his own thoughts that he is an individualist.

MR. MURRAY: I thought that it was perfectly obvious from this dialogue what my partialities were, and you're getting hot on it, as it were. Individuality is something to strive for and to approach during certain periods of one's life, particularly as a young man pointing his way to finding his own place in the world, his own function, getting a sense of his identity and his role. When that has been accomplished, he has become individualized. That's the time to forget his individuality and/or put it at the disposal of a larger issue; most individuals don't talk about individuality except during this period where they have to hold themselves against pressures all around.

MR. NORTON-TAYLOR: Apprentice individualist.

MR. MURRAY: Apprentice individualist, yes. In regard to your question, we had about seventy subjects who volunteered for experiments in research, and these subjects were scored or rated on thirty variables having to do with values. I go into the realm of assumption now, but when such scores are collated, we can correlate every individual with every other individual and on all these bases. This means thousands of correlations, and we can find out which individuals are more like every other individual and which individual is less like all the others in the realm of behavior values. But this result, when you examine it, turns out as a rather mechanical and not at all reassuring value. You know the person and then the result of the correlation is that he is the most individual person, and it doesn't necessarily follow.

MR. BUNDY: That's really the point. That's greatly encouraging. That's what I thought we were talking about earlier when you seemed to be suggesting what made an individual different. From your conclusions, we are making progress.

MR. MILLIKAN: There's another point I'd like to raise. It is a simple-minded one, designed to pose a question for the two representatives of the arts here. My simple-minded point is that the size of our population makes a great deal of difference, even the size of that fraction of our population on whom we are concentrating our attention. I would have guessed that one of the things that has certainly happened in art is that the proportion of our population that has possibilities of artistic experience and artistic creativity has vastly expanded. The question that I would like to direct to Messrs. Barr and Jonas is whether, in the process of expanding the proportion of the population exposed to aesthetic experiences, we have increased the inhibitions on the creativity of the small constant fraction that is at the top of the heap? Are they any more inhibited or is their individuality any less than it would have been before because of the mass audience for art we have been developing? That's really an empirical question.

Mr. Jonas: My own feeling is that the increase in the number of people doing creative work has largely expanded the second rate, and that has made the first rate very much less visible. I don't know whether it has placed any more inhibitions on the first rate. I think those are fairly constant. In some periods it is easier for talent to perceive the problems that have to be dealt with than in other periods. I think in recent periods it's been particularly hard to find the problems which have to be dealt with, at least in novels.

In the case of the novelist, in the 1920s, if he wanted to make a protest, he had so much to protest about that he found his objective easy to define. A great many novelists in our period are afraid that if they try to strike a blow they won't hit anything.

Mr. Millikan: You added something, another dimension to it, which I had not thought of.

Mr. Murray: One thing that has been running in and out of this conversation—Morton brought it out very clearly and Mr. Oppenheimer made the distinction also—is the distinction between freedom to do things and the capacity to do them. My hunch is that if there is too much freedom too early, there is an outlet for a kind of juvenile individuality, if you will. If there's too much repression, then you stifle individuality. But somewhere along the line, somewhere between those extremes, there is quite a lot of resistance. You have to get through partly in the way of discipline and partly in the way of standards.

Mr. Bundy: You sound like a Groton boy.

Mr. Murray: I'm talking about standards in the scientific field or ethics. I think that at the present time we have a tremendous amount of variation everywhere in a rather superficial behavioristic way. Do this and do that. It does not amount to much, I think, and it dissipates a certain amount of generated energy which, if it were put up against a resistance, would come through in a more encouraging form.

Mr. Millikan: I take it that very closely follows Mr. Jonas' remarks that if your problem is more clearly defined, you can be more creative.

Mr. Barr: It is indeed a fact that the number of amateur painters has increased to an unforeseen degree but, rather than handicapping the professional artist, the amateurs have increased the general interest in art. It is perfectly true that I am sometimes cornered by an amateur who feels our museum ought to buy or accept one of his pictures. But, if he is kept in his place, he does not seriously compete with the professional artist so much as enhance the background against which he may shine.

I should like now to refer to Mr. Murray's "Dy," who seems to me a most sympathetic character. [Laughter.] I am not sure that it is right to read something Dy said in order to contradict it, but there is a passage in Mr. Murray's dialogue which leads to an important question of a nonphilosophical character. Dy remarks: "Destiny has brought us to the position of top power among the free nations of the world, and, hereto-fore, top power has consisted not only of the greatest military strength and material resources but also of a high level of civilization, a center of humanistic and artistic excellence to which people were drawn for re-freshment, enchantment, and invigoration." This seems to be rather doubtful in that often the very top economic or military power has not been a good host to the artist or to the humanistic life. He then goes on to ask the question, "Where do we stand in these respects in the eyes of those nations of whose friendship and respect we are not unrea-sonably desirous?" And he answers it sadly: "Way below normal expec-tations."

I cannot agree with Dy. The artists of this country, as well as its writers, now stand in a position of international prestige and, to use that nasty, competitive word, success, that is quite unprecedented. In spite of traditional indifference and even active official censorship our most radical painters and, less conspicuously, our sculptors, have flour-ished to an extraordinary degree. They are now respected and, what is even more surprising, imitated and bought in Western Europe, Latin America, and Japan.

In other words, our best artists, or the men we think are the best at the moment, have, in spite of a good deal of suffocation, won through to an international eminence which ought to make us very proud and should be more widely known in this country. All too frequently, as in the case of Dy, we accept the myth that with all our success and power, military and technological, we have not gone very far in the arts.

There is another question here to which I'd like to refer. Dy also says, "As always, it is the artists and the poets who set forth most accurately the inner human situation, a condition of which the rest of us may not become aware for two or three decades."

Since the mid-nineteenth century, the artist has, from time to time, been burdened with the challenge of serving as both a thermometer and a symptom and also as a prophet or even a savior of civilization, and he has been plagued because he has not fulfilled these obligations. The chief argument used to attack our painters who at the moment seem to be most active and most admired throughout the rest of the world is that they are not sufficiently humanistic. Their paintings are called evasive or irresponsible because they are abstract, although, if such artists had written symphonies instead of painting pictures, they wouldn't have been criticized for being abstract. That these painters are now so esteemed throughout the rest of the world has troubled our Soviet opponents (whose painters are internationally despised). Communist critics charge our painters with antihumanism symptomatic of the technological desert which has created this country. This is a plausible though specious charge. But I think I shouldn't take your time by defending our artists.

MR. RIESMAN: You don't need to in this circle.

MR. BARR: Perhaps I had better stop talking.

MR. RIESMAN: I don't mean that.

MR. BARR: I'd like to end by noting a curious plea from Francis Henry Taylor, which appeared in a periodical in connection with the interchange of art exhibitions between ourselves and the rest of the world. He said, in effect, that we ought not to send exhibitions of American art abroad, especially when they show some quality and importance, because this will discourage and further humiliate our European friends, who, having lost their other instruments of self-esteem, should be left to

glory in the relics of their past and present culture without our competition. [Laughter.]

MR. OPPENHEIMER: If anyone has further talk on this wonderful
theme, what I have to say is not relevant to it—

MR. BUNDY: I would like to have Harry's reaction to the comments
just made.

MR. MURRAY: In part of that paragraph I tried to point out that I
was using the word artist only in a general sense, and that I had poets,
playwrights, and novelists more in mind. I could mention quite a few
who have not only suppressed this general alienation in their works but
also actually avoided it. Poe, in poetry, and in the theatre, Eugene
O'Neill. I, too, think of the artist as the unconscious prophet of what is
going to happen. If people had been clever enough they could have seen
it in the romantic hero of Byron and in certain heroes of Dostoievsky
who are going right toward fascism; and the whole superman idea is, in a
sense, showing what is down below and has not come out yet.

I am in favor of all of these people who are painting and writing and
doing things that don't belong to this time at all. I am all in favor of
them, but that what they are expressing is not serenity but, in a vision-
ary note, hope. To quote—I think from Ruskin—"There was a time
when artists used their talents to exhibit sacred objects and then they
used sacred objects to exhibit their talents." Then they used their talents
to exhibit the best in man. That's going beyond Ruskin. Now they are
exhibiting very great talents and showing some of the worst in man and
I am wondering if they can do anything else. But I won't say that they
aren't exhibiting something that has real human values in the sense of
a vision.

MR. JONAS: The visual arts in which we are doing some of the best
jobs are what we might call arts and crafts, a matter, fundamentally, of
design.

MR. MURRAY: When I made that statement about civilization, I
wasn't thinking just of our product as such. I was thinking of the whole
temper of people toward music, for example—the quality of their real
appreciation; not just that they may be buying records but whether they
are making music a part of their lives, living it in a way that people did
when they went to London, to Paris, to Renaissance Italy, and to Athens.
There they found refreshment. Do people come here for that kind of

refreshment? They come here for technical training and courses in science and medicine, and so on; but I don't believe I have ever met one who came here for spiritual refreshment—for invigoration and peace.

MR. BARR: Obviously a sense of peace is not something that visitors come for. But they do come for a sense of—I'm speaking now of visual art—vitality, original inventiveness, and quality such as visitors of the past never expected, certainly not the visitors of the thirties or even the forties. In the 1950s, for the first time, this country has become a place for the foreigner to study art. I refer not only to the distribution and consumption of art but also its production, especially by American painters.

MR. OPPENHEIMER: Certainly foreigners come here to study music on all levels.

MR. BUNDY: They come to concern themselves with the theater. Whatever the implication or the character of playwriting may be, it is less apparently depressing than the playwriting of Western Europe.

MR. WILSON: That's the point I want to temper a little bit. There are different areas of development here as against Europe. There would be something wrong somewhere in a society such as yours—evolving and trying to develop so rapidly—which had painters who weren't as Harry Murray described them. It would be out of key.

MR. MURRAY: I agree.

MR. OPPENHEIMER: This, of course, goes quite a way back to the relation of liberty and individuality, and something has happened to our understanding of sensibility since Mill put his question. We would, I think, all agree that in that sense we have identified individuality. An important judgment of our society was that a lot of individuality was a good thing. We welcomed it for a while, our concern being with the way society would interfere with individuality. Today we understand that one of the things society does is to make people, to alter them and enrich them, as well as to inhibit them. Therefore, the judgment which Harry is trying to make is a judgment with regard to the effect on a much broader class of society than Mill was contemplating, and the answer to Mill's question would still not answer the question we are concerned about. Is this America, is the world we are trying to live in, worthy of the men?

The platonic method of dealing with it is supremely right, as everyone has said and felt. In terms of the magnitude of creativity and variety and the curvy specific figure of a man's life, there's hardly any question but that the 180 million Americans have a lot more, both absolutely and relatively, than any society has had before.

This does not mean that they produce the best art. I don't see how we could hope to agree on that; and my affirmative is a qualified and modest and anxious affirmative. But it is appropriate both with regard to the limitation on what constrains opinions and on the question of whether people are creating and individuating on a vast scale.

Col. Coffey: I thought I was going to have to use the "ship with the infinite number of sails" to set this discussion on a different tack, but Mr. Oppenheimer has set me on the course.

I would like to raise the question of whether the problem we should be concerned with is not an entirely different one from the problem we have been talking about. Let me lead into this a bit. It seems to me, on the basis of a purely subjective personal judgment, that in many respects there are fewer pressures to conform existing in the United States today than there were in—you pick your time—the twenties or the thirties. To give just one illustration, I am sure that if you hauled out your grade-school pictures, as I do mine once every five or six years, and looked at them, you'd be amazed at the conformity in dress. All the boys are in knickers, long stockings, and white shirts, and all the fathers in black suits and high collars, just to take a very superficial example.

We no longer, in a given period, generally construct all of our houses in a single style. Architecturally, the "colonial rambler" may be monstrous, but it is different—at least, it is different where I live in Washington. What I am trying to suggest is that the social pressures to conformity, even in this country, have lessened materially in a relatively short period of time as compared to other eras in other countries. We are, in the broader sense, freer than perhaps any other people at any other time.

I am aware there are more subtle pressures in other terms of reference, in terms of functions and common methods of thought and common viewpoints which inhibit creativity. I would suggest that these have always been present in every society—in Athens as in mediaeval France. The problem which I would raise is whether the degree of individuality, or creativity or whatever you wish to call it, is sufficient to meet the needs of our times. The tremendous range and complexity of the problems with which we are confronted demand more genius, if you will, more originality of thinking, more freshness of perception as well as approach, than perhaps in any other period in history. I wonder if we are not, perhaps, taking the shadow for the substance when we talk about individuality per se and not in relation to the specific thing that concerns us.

MR. MURRAY: I'm glad you said that because I have a feeling that most speakers are using the word pessimistic and looking strongly at me. I won't admit to pessimism. But since the war, since 1945, my standards have been upped quite a lot, and I have become critical for the first time, not in terms of other countries or other nations, but in terms of what is required in this particular crisis. Also, looking at it from a historical perspective, what are we going to look like 300 years from now? This is our opportunity to do something, and I want America to put on a really good performance. I am terribly concerned that we put on a good performance, and I think the exigencies have never been so great. I am rather inclined to the view that there is not enough genius in the arts and sciences and human nature to deal with this situation, and I don't want to lower the standards. If we do, I'm afraid that we are going to get complacent, that we are going to think of comfort as civilization and not be equal to our situation. I think we have grown extraordinarily well, and I am proud, and I will go all the way on the positive things.

COL. COFFEY: I was not beating my chest or the American drum; I was wondering if this was not the question under debate.

MR. MURRAY: Exactly.

MR. RIESMAN: There's one question that I'd like to look at, not taking the view of the particular society but the expectations held by human beings at a particular stage of history. I have been thinking about the French Revolution and recalling that the expectations the society was living under then were rising even faster than the rising standard of living prior to the Revolution, so that the growing discrepancy produced an explosion. I was thinking of Mill also when Mr. White spoke of him and of his tragedy. He came, as you know, out of a home with an authoritarian father, and he found himself a freer, unaffected way of life. His expectations had grown as his life blossomed, with his marriage and his coming out from under the shadow of his father. I think we all here have been coming out from under the shadow, as others have indicated. Our expectations have prefigured what life ought to be, but is not, like. I think the very fact that we have met here, as Mr. Wilson pointed out, and that there are probably forty conferences going on at this moment, including many in corporate offices, shows disquietude.

I was talking with Mr. Oppenheimer about "The Man in the Gray Flannel Suit," the movie, and about how irrelevant is the notion which has been given to the gray flannel suit. Sometimes we displace the problem of conformity to trivial areas such as dress—and then prove we are nonconformists by marginal differentiations through which we don't quite succeed in kidding ourselves. Or we allow ourselves to be criticized because we have similarities in dress or other external things. In the movie, what is more important is that the great current conformity of attitudes toward family life—the conformity in styles in domesticity— is accepted as normal; and here the movie shows the hero making two significant choices.

The hero prefers for some reason, which is not fully made clear, his standard suburban American girl to an Italian. So we are through with the D. H. Lawrence or Henry Adams era. But he also chooses family life (though with a rather limited, uninformed woman) instead of an exciting business life and, in this choice, he speaks for his generation. This choice is nearly but not quite right; the youngsters are superior to their more frenetic elders—even though they worry Col. Coffey and others in this room concerned with the country's survival. But the young people are sometimes, when they are sensitive, worried, too, not for the reasons their elders give but because they fear that they have left something out. They are worried less in terms of man's survival or civic dutifulness, let alone defense, but, rather, because some of man's possibilities seem to have been curbed. It is their feeling that life in some way, because of or perhaps in spite of all the good things the young have done and chosen (to which we have subscribed here), does not come up to their dreams. They cannot, Mr. Bundy, find models very often, either in the pals who pretend to be pals although they are older and wiser, or, let alone, find many models of how life might be lived with what, I suppose, is more freshness of perception.

Here I want to go to what did not get discussed this morning in Mr.

Kluckhohn's paper—how our language, which we now see as prohibiting constraints, is a way of freezing our perceptions, and where the sound barrier takes another form. So I don't agree with you that we have freshness of perception. I am not sure you agree that we do either. We have ease of categorization and facility of discipline, but whether we have freshness of perception and its life-giving qualities, I don't know.

MR. FREUND: May I suggest that the business of individuality, it seems to me, has a double aspect—not merely freedom or capacity but also responsibility. "Every man his own priest" I think is taken to mean, as in Mr. Kluckhohn's paper, individual freedom of interpretation and belief. But I heard a Protestant theologian say not long ago that that is a vulgarization of the idea; that basically it means that every man has the responsibility of a priest. He said it in the context of a moral problem of disclosure to an investigator of what had been told in confidence, in a private confessional as it were. If you look at individuality in the aspect of individual responsibility—every man a priest, in that sense—there is a very complex question of the relation of our society to the development of this as an aspect of character.

I'd like to refer to one concrete institution which points up the dilemma, and that is the principle of insurance which has taken over so much of our life and has, in a sense, relieved us of a measure of responsibility for our failures and irresponsibilities. Justice Brandeis used to say that fidelity insurance, by which management cushions itself against the default of trusted employees, is an abomination because it relieves management of the responsibility of knowing its employees and standing by the consequences of its own misjudgment. By coincidence, I recently ran across a passage extolling fidelity insurance on the ground that it opened up careers to young men relatively unknown who would otherwise not have been taken into positions of trust and confidence. [Laughter.] I just put it to you, which is the more deeply philosophical approach to the issue of individuality?

MR. BUNDY: What do you say, Paul?

MR. FREUND: Well, of course, I'm prejudiced.

MR. WILSON: I wanted to ask if there were any comments on the difference between what we call libel and slander, as there is a very central legal comparison which has repercussions in freedom of speech.

MR. FREUND: That's quite true, but the English, if you want to generalize, value privacy a good deal more than we, and we value talk—talk is cheap. There is a comparable contrast in the method of conducting trials and the problems of the press reporting trials. Some papers are getting into trouble in England because of what they said about the Dr. Adams' trial. Even in the matter of the advocate's manner in court, the British are much more disciplined; if the judge raises his eyebrow at a line of questioning, the barrister is expected to announce, "My Lord, I was about to desist." In the American court, of course, he says "I object," and reserves his objection for the sake of appeal. He may even argue with the judge. I am not sure, on balance, which is socially more useful; that is, whether the relative freedom and rudeness may not have a value over and against privacy and sensitivity in areas of public concern. I am not now speaking of private libel but of something of more general concern.

MR. MORISON: The interesting thing is that as a result of the English treatment of libel, although it may be a device for protecting privacy in general, in particular cases, you get far greater notoriety.

MR. JONAS: In publishing books, it is confining. The writers are much more concerned about what the law says inasmuch as the publisher doesn't want to be involved in a suit. He knows that the suit can't be won by the person bringing the suit but, at the same time, if an injunction is brought on the books, the books can be tied up for a considerable period of time and the publisher loses his investment. So, as it works on the writer, the publisher puts pressure on him to cut out libel possibilities.

MR. MILLIKAN: Gentlemen, we have gone a good deal past our closing time. I think we ought to terminate this discussion after any final remarks anyone wants to make.

[No further remarks.]

MR. MILLIKAN: Very good. I have been asked to announce to those who might be tempted to wander into the woods for an hour or so, that something of a novelty in the form of an oyster bar will be set up out on the terrace.

MR. BUNDY: Creativity has not failed in this conference. [Laughter.]

THE COURSE OF DISCUSSION

by Elting E. Morison

THESE papers served as a basis for discussion by the men who met in conference at Endicott House in May 1957. There was, at first, some thought that the record of the discussion itself might also be included. A sample of the flow of talk, somewhat edited, is included, but a complete record of the remarks would prove both impractical and, on the whole, unrewarding. The transcriptions of the conversation of twenty-five talkative men talking together for four days were long, and they were also, not unnaturally in the conditions, imperfect. The conversation itself was not, at all times, perfect. There were occasions when speakers confessed that what they were about to say was "not responsive to the previous comment"; there were moments when a man, "not sure that this is really in answer to the last question," proceeded to the formulation of a question of particular interest to himself; there were times when one or another was moved to raise "the question of whether the problem we should be concerned with is not an entirely different one from the problem we have been talking about." Still, there was sensible conversation going forward, on the whole, in good order; there were few diversionary pursuits of the irrelevant or private quarry; and, as someone said, few, if any, interrupted the program in progress merely to give station identifications. There were, out of these deliberations, enough things of substance, enough matters worth further thought, enough engaging collisions of personal attitude or spirit to make those who planned the conference wish for some summary view of these spontaneous proceedings. There was even a wistful feeling that in such a summary the atmosphere within which the deliberation took place could be recaptured.

Within strict meteorological limits, at least, this is possible. The days from May 23rd to May 26th, 1957 were, in Dedham, Massachusetts, clear, blue, and bright. This kind of weather enabled the members of the conference, in between sessions, to walk in sunshine across the long lawns, around the borders of gardens in spring flower, and under the trees of the considerable arboretum of Endicott House down to an isolated pond. It enabled them to drink sherry before lunch and martinis before dinner together on a stone terrace in the sunshine. It enabled them to sit at small tables drinking beer or gin fizzes in the twilight talking together as they watched an evening fall on four of their number playing bridge under an umbrella at one end of the terrace. Everyone talked a good deal about the food at the time because the food was, in fact, worth talking about. Some adroit administrative intelligence had arranged light but interesting lunches and less light but interesting dinners. The weather, the things to eat and drink, the way people were taken care of, the sense of momentary protection from the world under discussion produced a set of favoring atmospheres.

A review of the transcript suggests some interesting things. In the final stages of the conference the incidence of the first name sharply increased. By the last day, also, conversations proceeded in the clear, brought almost completely out of professional codings. The record further indicates that the input of words was a function of the calling. The amount of conversation contributed appeared to vary almost in direct proportion to the level of abstraction presumably maintained in a speaker's intellectual field. As McGeorge Bundy observed—historians never say anything, and it went on up from there.

Some other generalizations may also be permitted. There were, in the four days, some recurring themes. These will not be unfamiliar or, perhaps, especially illuminating. But they may have their use in suggesting some of the primary characteristics Americans think they find in themselves when they think about themselves as a society or a nation. There was, first, a prevailing sense that in spite of all the talk of gray flannel suits, organization men, and conformity ("about which there is in fact a tremendous amount of semantic confusion"), there remained a society pluralistic, fragmented into numberless small communities organized on varying social, geographical, professional, or intellectual principles; a society infinitely diverse. There was, second, the reiterated observation that the nineteenth century was at last really over, and that with it had departed the Puritan imperative to do and to bear oneself the responsibility for oneself. Third, it was continuously insisted that America was the land of antithesis and paradox (ideals versus materials; determinism versus responsibility; spending versus saving; awe for the huge versus attraction toward the Little Man). Nowhere was this sense of antithesis more apparent than in the collision between theory and practice. As Rostow said, "We are given simultaneously to extreme empiricism in dealing with reality and to applying peculiarly spacious abstractions to particular circumstances." Finally, in many different ways it was said that, "we stand in the midst of a deep, refractory, and quite unprecedented cultural crisis."

What twenty-five men said about these and related subjects in the course of four days cannot be placed in any very symmetrical arrangement. One can perhaps look for a kind of organizing principle in the general intent of the conference as stated by Mr. Rostow: the participants were to try to find out what Americans are, not what they ought to do about it. The most natural way to organize the details of such a search appears to be in the principle of chronology—The Chase, First Day, and so following. And on the first day when the topic was American Ethics (or, more specifically, good and evil) and Public Policy, there were the troubles of first days. Members no doubt were somewhat concerned about how they might fare with such a topic and in such a company. Also they were confronted, in Mr. Kaplan's paper, with an extended line of argument so finely wrought and nicely formed that it offered few rough places at which to grasp and fewer fissures in which to insert a wrecking bar. Furthermore, the beautifully sustained argument encased an attitude of mind and spirit about which there was little to quarrel and much to respect. Nor did the opening comment offer much opportunity for debate by setting up issues between Mr. Kaplan and the commentator. The comment was more, as someone said, an oblique reflection in the manner of Robert Frost than an agenda for discussion. By offering a definition of evil it did provide a point of departure for a conversation which took the form of a search for a more satisfying definition.

There was, in the next few hours, much said in the familiar idiom: "If all people were the same and had the same tastes and started out in life with the same initial endowments, etc." This was a little like pitchers in a bull pen—the ball was kept with a professional grace almost unconscious, in gentle, controlled, constant motion; but nobody was ready to come through with the high hard one. In part, this was probably because there was no one to throw it at. The definitions offered, while they often served to set some limits for the good and more particularly the evil, rarely seemed to have much bearing on American life. This may well have been because the sense of good and evil has since the days of the Great Awakening been gradually replaced, at the conscious level, by considerations of operational performance—it works or it doesn't work; it succeeds or it fails. For instance, the trouble with the house divided, it had been said in our moment of greatest moral peril by the man who most clearly perceived the nature of the peril, was not that it gave room to evil solutions for some of the problems of human experience, but more simply that a divided house would not stand. So for much of the evening we all sounded like men trying to translate the works of John Dewey into the idiom of Jonathan Edwards. Though it was never an enterprise that carried with it much promise of success and though it was attended by some frustration, it nevertheless suggested a disjointedness in the structure of the American character that was to come up for discussion again and again in the ensuing debates.

On the following morning, May 24th, the investigation of the deep, refractory, and quite unprecedented cultural crisis was begun. The nature of that crisis was at first explored in the paper prepared by Robert Oppenheimer and in the comment by David Potter on that paper. Mr. Oppenheimer opened the general discussion by saying he was "enough of an eighteenth century man to be interested not only in whether the government works but also in what the quality of life is that the government is sustained by." The quality of life in America had been placed in jeopardy by "the very grave cognitive difficulties" presented to the society in a time of "unprecedented, rapid change and unprecedented, complex, intellectual specialization." Between the accumulations of intricably related, infinitely refined, immediately useful special knowledge piled up by highly trained minds and the stated affirmations and desires of the generality of American citizens there existed a void. The question, for instance, of "how to deal with nuclear warfare, the question of how to deal with the Communist adversary—these questions cannot be easily answered [by] the consensus the American people have of the value of the individual, the value of liberty. Between these generalities and the wisdom or unwisdom of decisions on policy or causes of action, a lot of knowledge, a lot of detail, of technical knowledge, and a lot of reasoning have to intervene, and, it is in this area that we all have a sense that we are not doing things."

The nature of the difficulty was taken to be that between what Oppenheimer called "the learned folk and the common folk" there were not proper channels of communications along which the meaning or even the implications of special knowledge could be transmitted. This did not mean that the United States had to turn itself into a nation of 162,000,000 highbrows—but it did imply that between highbrows and everybody else there had to be "a different kind of motion" if we are "to bring to bear the resources of understanding, prediction, and analysis which we need in those issues which cannot be decided as between interested groups struggling with each other, but which might be or must be decided in terms of the wisest assessment of what will come of what we are doing."

That the problem thus stated actually existed no one appeared to doubt. A discussion immediately developed about the best ways and means to introduce a different and more satisfying motion between those who knew and those who had to know. Although the problem had originally been stated as something which had to do with the quality of life, it turned out in the course of the talk that people were much more concerned by its immediate effect on the determination of public policy— especially with its effect on our relations with Russia and on the question of nuclear energy.

The most optimistic view was taken, at the outset, by Lyman Bryson. The essential idea of democracy, he began, was that the lives of people who are involved in their own decisions are better lives than the lives of people for whom the decisions are made. Democracy, therefore, was in itself an educating process in which people learned as much from their mistakes as from their correct decisions. This was not an idea, he recognized, that usually commended itself to professional intellectuals since they tended, properly, "to be primarily concerned with the rightness or wisdom of the decision." Furthermore, in this process, in this loose, free, and erratic system of trial and error by which people learn in a democracy, "the things of the mind make their own way slowly no matter how much people stop them."

These assumptions would, no doubt, have been accepted by all members of the conference as holding in the best of all possible worlds. But two things made some doubt that the assumptions would satisfy the requirements of the existing world. First, people in general tended to think most and learn most about what were frequently called their "immediately felt needs." In the old and simple days of the Republic such needs may have served as sufficient prods to the learning process. As David Potter said, in the unmolested times "the chief business of the government was to referee a distribution by the people themselves of the plentiful supply of loaves and fishes." But today the real necessities did not reveal themselves in the immediate feelings; they lay somewhat removed—as in the need for teachers ten years hence, as in the possibility of a nuclear war sometime. Thus, said Mr. Potter, "we may have arrived at a point where the immediately felt needs of consumers no longer coincide with the ultimate, long-range needs of the national economy, and the immediately felt needs of the voter no longer serve as sound controls upon the process of decision because they no longer coincide with the ultimate long-range needs of public policy." With this David Riesman agreed. What we really needed, he felt, "was teachers to teach us how to feel what our feelings are."

Beyond this concern that immediately felt needs were no longer a sufficient guide to our real, ultimate necessities was the concern over time. Things were moving so fast in this period of unprecedented change that in the interests of survival people had to learn more, faster than they ever had before. The learning process could not be left to work with its classic randomness and waste. It had to be cleaned up. How this could be done was a topic of much discussion. The first proposal was to increase the amount of public debate on critical current issues. Rostow pointed out that schools and colleges had already made great advances in this pursuit through the kind of courses they were developing. As one instance he cited the fact that M.I.T. students as a matter of routine read and discussed George Kennan's views on foreign policy and scrutinized the problems proposed by Kaplan and Oppenheimer in their conference papers. The bibliography with which students were confronted seemed less important to David Riesman than the fact that he wanted undergraduates "to understand in their bones what it was to do a hard job of work, what it took."

Others had views on public debate. Bryson felt that, while such de-

bate on radio and TV did not perhaps give much information, it established "the general atmosphere, the habit of mind, almost the moral
effect" which, rather than the retention of exact information, "was the
purpose of an education." The mass media, he believed, had in fact
greatly raised the level of public understanding. Oppenheimer was not so
sure; the radio and TV left out the "athletic quality" involved in learning anything. Paul Freund, while agreeing with Bryson that the mass
media could have a civilizing effect, nevertheless believed that they
avoided "the fundamental need of modern education." That need was a
training in judgment. Taking for granted that the average citizen could
never know all the special and appropriate information in a given situation, nevertheless "we at least ought to know what the experts ought to
know and ask whether they have satisfied themselves about the fact."
What was needed was not the program that made a recollection of the
location of Death Valley worth $64,000 but "some kind of instruction
on the process of judgment." When debates were held on the radio the
need to select the proper criteria for choice as well as the opportunity
simply to choose between debaters should be imposed upon the audience.

Still on the question of the value of public debate as an educational
device, William White suggested that the principle of bipartisan foreign
policy for all its virtues deprived the citizen of some opportunity to
learn. Since it "foreclosed areas of discussion," supplied "no angles of
discord," produced no "spark," it supplied no real basis for developing
sufficient information. The results of this process were further exaggerated, Kaplan believed, by the tendency of politicians to justify new policies in terms of existing felt needs rather than in terms of larger, less
easily distinguished, but more vital considerations.

Out of these discussions three specific, quite different, suggestions for
dealing with the cognitive crisis emerged. The first was most clearly
stated by George Kennan. "Our responses," he began, "are so far behind
the questions to which we are trying to respond that actually reality is
overtaking us quite regularly." In this situation the traditional means
by which we used to arrive at understandings and judgments of public
affairs would not serve. The solution was to introduce institutional
changes, exactly the kind of solution "Americans most dislike to examine, and institutional changes take years." As an example—only as an

illustration of what he had in mind—he said he sometimes felt he "would gladly sacrifice the last two years of the undergraduate training of 85 per cent of those who are now being subjected to it in exchange for 500 really well-educated and thoughtful and courageous men. That," he concluded, "is what is involved and seems to me an institutional question."

Mr. Oppenheimer agreed that the institutional arrangements needed re-examination and he was, no doubt, prepared to accept the value of 500 brave, intelligent well-educated men anywhere, but he preferred what he took to be a more powerful educational influence, one that could act rapidly and on a large scale, "the influence of a persuasive example." "It doesn't take a great deal," he went on, "to make people recognize that they have needs, duties, hopes, and opportunities of which they had been unaware." If changes were to occur in the next decade, he felt, "they would be the result of what one man or two men did and said that touched the spirits of many people."

Richard Bissell believed that the attitudes implied in these recommendations were unnecessarily pessimistic. With proper executive leadership a democracy could educate itself quite successfully in the things it needed to know about and could go on to sensible decisions. He cited the debate conducted throughout the country upon the Marshall Plan as "an amazingly careful investigation of an issue that had nothing to do with immediately felt needs"; he cited the original proposals for the international control of atomic energy as "an unparalleled achievement"; he cited the origins of NATO—all these as examples of what leadership can do to define the needs not immediately felt by the constituency, to lift debate above mere partisan discussion, and to mobilize public support for wise policies.

In the afternoon of May 24th the morning theme was supplied with a new set of variations. The American was having difficulty in managing his environment, in part because of the cognitive crisis, but, at least in equal part, because the existing administrative machinery was not much good. There was little dissent from Mr. Kennan's proposition that the American government had become both complicated and inefficient, that it had produced administratively, as Richard Bissell said, "a monstrous state of affairs." The causes of this unsatisfactory condition were investigated at some length. In Mr. Kennan's opinion the apparatus was simply too big. He wondered if "it was really possible to govern people intelligently on so broad a scale as we were trying to do." He had noticed that in the international field the most remarkable contributions rarely came from countries with the biggest bureaucracies but from men like Lester Pearson or Charles Malik who did not appear at conferences supported by numerous cohorts. David Riesman offered measured support to this position by saying that he "wished we had lost the Civil War and would give California and Texas back to Mexico, and maybe that at least would be a beginning." Though it was generally accepted that the presumed inefficiencies of the government were in considerable part a function of size, there was not much confidence expressed that much could be done to make the government small again.

The commitments at home and abroad were extensive; the expansion and subdivision of knowledge had necessarily produced an expansion and subdivision of the bureaucracy which existed to fit related pieces of information together. Most decisions involved due consideration of many diverse influences: military, political, economic, social, and scientific. The accumulation and digestion of all the steadily increasing, appropriate data inevitably forced the creation of agencies more various, more specialized, more new. "Now how," asked Carl Kaysen, "do you [as a government official] deal with conflicting specialisms when you yourself are ignorant of the specialty, when there is no well-defined common unit in which you can measure the outcome? You compromise? This is not a foolish or a lazy or a weak-kneed way to do it. It is in some sense the right way to do it." The essence, it was said several times by several different people, of the democratic process was negotiation of difference, compromise between opposing points of view; in the changing, intricate world of interacting specialties, accommodation of differing interests was the obvious way to reach decisions. And yet, it was not a good way to run a government.

For one thing, as Mr. Wilson pointed out, compromises taken to accommodate the local or domestic conflicts of interest were often confusing to those unfamiliar with the local situation. If, as an Englishman, he asked himself whether he would rather be confronted by a comprehensible American decision or an uncomprehensible compromise, he believed he would rather face the comprehensible even if it were "a bit wrong." Then, too, as Kennan said, compromise gave no sense of per-

sonal style, and, ironically, compromise solutions gave no flexibility to
policy. An individual making a decision could go and discuss it with a
foreign government; there was thus a possibility of modification, of rapid,
sensible adjustment by responsible individuals. But when a decision came
out of the Joint Chiefs of Staff, pummelled into shape by opposing interests, "there wasn't anybody helpful to talk to." "If you try to persuade
him that the decision was wrong it would break his heart because there
isn't anything to do about it now." And Rostow pointed out that the
forms of compromise were often verbal forms so vague as to leave a man
in business for himself covered by a phony shield of apparent policy.

Most serious of all, in Richard Bissell's opinion, was that the existing
procedures of negotiation, lateral clearance, and compromise produced
an attenuation of authority and a diffusion of responsibility. One could
look far in the corridors before he could find someone and say with any
confidence, "This is the man who knows he must and can." He proposed, as a single example, that in the State Department there should
be allocations of authority and responsibility "at least to the point
where the Assistant Secretary in charge of, for instance, European Affairs
is made, as an individual, clearly responsible for and given clearly the
responsibility to make decisions on many, many issues of the most important matters of policy even though they involved the whole variety
of interests—political, military, economic—of the United States government." This required, he understood, not only a new kind of organization chart but also a new kind of man in government.

No one disagreed with this line of argument. It appeared as given
that, at the moment, nowhere save at the very top of the administrative
pyramid was there either a sufficiently defined sense of responsibility or
a clearly specified grant of authority adequate to get things done. But
there was a qualification of the argument. The need to take effective
decisions always arises, Carl Kaysen proposed, out of ignorance, uncertainty, and a conflict of values. For business organizations the reduction
of ignorance and uncertainty is important, but, he went on:

It is interesting and I think correct to say that from their point of view conflicts of value are rather unimportant. Therefore, delegations of power and
delineations of responsibility can work because you can give to each sub-
unit its own balance sheet and income account and say, "You operate that
and let the other fellow operate this and we will judge whether you are doing

the things right." The problems of government, involved as they always are with questions of value, are infinitely more complex, and the difficulties in the delegation of responsibility or authority in matters of value are not an order of magnitude but a cardinal domain away from the difficulties of delegation in matters of ignorance and uncertainty.

Beside size, the spirit of compromise, and the diffusion of authority as sources of governmental inadequacy was laid a fourth and interesting influence. "The locus of the problem was not organizational structure," Carl Kaysen suggested, "but simply that in ordinary affairs we are trying to be more rational than we know how to be, and than the probability of our knowledge and understanding support our being." In exaggerated form his proposition could be well illustrated by the military. With all its new postures of self-conscious rationality and subtle negotiation the Army still acts on orders. In the Army more than in the State Department the tendency is still to say, "Let's not have a committee which will give us a profound report on the economics, government, and culture of Vietnam; let's just have in a fellow who was there once, and without reading a profound report we will decide something." This idea, which suggests some of the paralyzing side effects of the cognitive crisis, appealed to Robert Oppenheimer. He was pleased with the notion that there were still some men prepared to recognize that some problems existed containing so many variables and hidden intricacies that it was better to make even a bad guess about them than to subject them to extended, systematic critical analyses. But he believed that such an attitude required degrees of courage and of sophistication that in the present or in any circumstances were rarely found.

There was much mulling over of "this monstrous state of affairs," much elaboration offered from the personal experience of those present, and some inevitable mention of Parkinson's Law, to which Clyde Kluckhohn added an interesting amendment. The redistribution of the national income in recent years, he believed, had produced a sharp rise in the proportion of the private income that families devoted to services as opposed to goods. This effect had extended to institutions. The Dean of a college thirty years ago did or left undone what today a Dean, a Director of Administration, a group of statisticians, six psychiatrists, and four clinical psychologists now do. So with the government—the number engaged in research, education, statistical endeavors, all sorts of extras and services has fantastically increased. But the longer the arguments and reminiscences continued, the more refined and grave the problem of sound government administration became and the less probable did any satisfying solution appear to be. At the very end of the afternoon Mr. Kennan restated his previous position:

I would like to say one word on the results of this: I am very grateful for this discussion this afternoon because it has made me much clearer in my mind as to the nature of my own prejudices. I am brought to realize by what has been said about administration in other fields that my prejudices here are against bigness and for littleness in any field of human cooperation which puts a task of intellectual analysis on us in matters affecting the human being himself. I distrust anything that gets beyond the realm of community in this field, whether it is the educational process or the process of policy formulation or even the determination of the policies of a great business company. In all these things we have to keep numbers down to the point in any human community where communication can be a reality; that is, where we are dealing with human personalities whom we know and have some intimacies with and understanding. I fear anything that gets beyond that in any of these fields. This is instinctive; I cannot argue it. I really think that I would hold a brief again for the college small enough so that the person in it, the student, knows practically everybody in it. If today I should have to take the responsibility for an organization like the Department of State with its 17 or 18 thousand people, the only thing I could do would be to scratch around and try to find the 300 who could really make it work and take them away to another building and tell the other sixteen thousand, "You go on cooking your coffee in your offices and do whatever you are doing."
There are certain types of human activity which cannot exceed this limit. They cannot exceed the limit in which people can look other people in the eye as friends, as people to whom they have a human relationship and talk to them in that capacity.

On the following day, May 25th, the conversations took quite a different turn. In the morning the conference considered the remarkable paper of Clyde Kluckhohn on the shift of American values in the past generation. The mood of the discussion was set by something Richard Hofstadter said in his opening remarks about our "fully employed, incredibly rich, well-adjusted, complacent, and apathetic country." What good thing could come out of such a community was, as Hofstadter said, "a source of distress, of concern, of anxiety." But, as he also said, "a source of possible optimism, and yet an optimism so qualified that if one simply flips the coin one might call it qualified pessimism." In something of this uncertain spirit the members of the conference attempted to assess the extent and nature of the changing schemes of value in America.

Mr. Arthur Schlesinger, Sr. began the general discussion by saying that Mr. Kluckhohn had failed to mention a value which in many ways differentiated us from other societies, a value he called "voluntarism" or the way in which we sought to achieve by voluntary private endeavor ends which in other countries were ordinarily brought to pass by government action. The influence of this voluntarism persisted he believed. He also could offer comfort in the thought that we have proceeded throughout our history by movements forward and backward, by a freezing and a thawing, by the washings of recurring waves of liberalism and conservatism. Possibly, in view of these cyclical alternations, we all might be taking too seriously the possibility of permanent changes in value. Indeed, if his projection of a line that reached back to 1765 was correct, he believed he could say that the present period of political complacency and conservatism would reach its end around 1962.

Clyde Kluckhohn, while accepting much of this, went on to say:

Really, for the first time in American history, and I mean that quite seriously, for the first time there has been a genuine change in one particular as opposed to these significant ebbings and flowings. While I am entirely prepared to believe and indeed I would also anticipate, although I couldn't give an exact date for it, but I would anticipate on matters such as political complacency, etc. that these things will go back and forth as they have previously in American history; I do not think that Americans again in the foreseeable future are going to have the achievement motive and other aspects of the Puritan ethic at the very center of their values system.

This was said without the use of words like "home" or "optimism" or "despair" and simply as a judgment of what had happened.

No one dissented from this judgment. It was taken as a fact that the Puritan ethic of "doing and of personal responsibility" which had come down through so many previous generations, almost like the Hapsburg lip, as something in the gene—this ethic it seemed had simply disappeared. The question was, "What was being put in its place?" Hofstadter had spoken of privatism or, as Kennan said, "of people who tried to get what they could out of the present, who excluded themselves from feelings of public responsibility." Would, it was asked, the cultivation of purely private and personal concerns—hi fi, the children's reading disabilities, the woodworking shop in the basement, the do-it-yourself for yourself and all the rest of it—would it create a public vacuum? More dangerous—if there was something to all this dedication to leisure and personal cultivation, "then it may indeed be," Kluckhohn observed, "that, in the not so long run, this kind of abdication will throw to the uncivilized the chance to make for people who are cultivating their own garden political decisions and institutions, educational as well as political, and that is not a very pleasant fantasy."

To the great majority this possible future was a source of concern, but Mr. Oppenheimer spoke up with a note of qualified hope. In the small and selected samples of American youth that he saw, he had discovered "a little different quality to the loss of the Puritan zeal." To be sure he discerned among those he knew "less optimism, less pioneering, a less Puritan, a less Protestant feeling." Instead there was

almost a mediaeval touch to the quality of these people's lives and this comes out, I believe, not really in the lack of inner responsibility but in a much more sophisticated and truer evaluation of what they are likely to be able to accomplish; and it does mean that their zeal and activity, which are great, go into the arts and, you might say, hobbies. Many of them look forward to a life which will not be very exciting, but the way in which painting, music, writing, the creation of things is flourishing in this country today is not a bad thing. It is a sign of a civilization that is enjoying the present, partly because of the limited notion of others to shape the future and partly because of the overhanging doubt of what the future may be of a civilization that takes it out in really improving the quality of life in the present.

By using the word mediaeval he intended to suggest that the arts in which the young people were engaged were not privately pursued—did not represent withdrawals into private gardens. They were "typically public and communal, differing from the art young people were engaged in in the twenties; they referred to society and groups and were very outgoing, though they did not necessarily relate to the federal government."

This was not a view that gave much comfort. The fear was frequently expressed that the tendency to exploit the private resources for private purposes might well place in jeopardy the resources and purposes of the whole society. The origin of this shift from the Puritan ethic was canvassed at great length and from many different positions. In the course of the canvass, Mr. Wilson remarked—in the form of an exceedingly cautious inquiry—that many Europeans feel that the possibility of tragedy is not fully accepted by Americans.

In reply, Hofstadter offered Korea as the first time we had been introduced to a sense of tragic possibilities—the first time "the American feeling that problems are something you solve rather than things you have to live with unsolved was irrefutably controverted." Confronted with this situation, Americans had been shocked not only into greater tolerance and humanity but also into a search for shielding diversions—comfort and cultivation. This, he concluded, is our response to tragedy: if we can't solve it all, we are going to be comfortable and perhaps a little cultivated in the process.

From this line of argument the conference speedily departed, at the mention of Korea, into an extended consideration of the Truman decision, "the MacArthur thing," "the brink Dulles is talking about," Radford, the Executive Branch, the Joint Chiefs of Staff, and the possibilities, in the time of the atom and in an age of technology, of fighting a "sensible" war.

The argument went on until the chairman, disturbed that "we had not pursued some of the aspects of Mr. Kluckhohn's paper as far as we might have," adjourned the meeting for lunch with the thought that the afternoon paper would give the opportunity to talk further about the untouched aspects of the Kluckhohn essay.

The paper of the afternoon was Harry Murray's delightful reflection upon individuality. The subject, as McGeorge Bundy observed in his opening comment, is "very ticklish," "very slippery." Entertaining things were said in the course of the afternoon conversation. It was remarked that over the last thirty years the width of American smiles had increased; it was noticed that on the most terrible occasions—the eve of a close election, on greeting one's bitterest enemy, at the prison steps, before the grave—the smile was at its largest. Carl Jonas said that modern novelists were having trouble deciding what problems to deal with; they were increasingly unwilling to strike a blow because they were afraid they would not hit anybody and would just throw their arms out. It was asked which view of individual development was more philosophical: that of the lawyer, Justice Brandeis, who opposed fidelity insurance because it relieved employers of the responsibility for their misjudgments of defaulting employees, or that of the philosopher, Josiah Royce, who approved such insurance because it opened up careers for unknown young men who would not otherwise be given positions of trust.

For the first time, Alfred Barr observed, the country had become an almost necessary place for Europeans and Far Easterners to study art. These visitors were drawn by a vitality, an original inventiveness, a quality such as visitors in the past, even ten or twenty years in the past, never had found before. The opinion was offered that the United States was not, in the sense that everybody thinks the same thing, a united country. It was full of different communities composed of different professional, social, political, and intellectual interests. These differentials were intensified by constant geographical and technological changes. On surface matters—dress, bourbon, the importance of automobiles—there was perhaps a good deal of agreement, but on things of any degree of subtlety or depth there was a diversity of opinion produced by the different communities into which we were subdivided. It was one of our hedges against conscious or unconscious tyranny.

Entertaining or interesting these observations may have been, but few of them bore very directly on the subject of individuality. Such efforts as were made to come to grips with the topic turned usually into efforts to be clearheaded and systematic in the matter of definition. When the definitions were left indefinite, as they were, the talk drifted toward related subjects like creativity about which nothing very instructive was offered. Colonel Coffey conducted a rear-guard action to bring the talk back to the subject, which he stated was not individuality per se but the American sense of individuality in relation to the present circumstances. But his effort was unsuccessful. By the end of the day, after all the exercises in definition, the gossamer of Harry Murray had been severely damaged in the handling of those seeking to classify the web he had spun.

Three days had gone by and the conference had gone some way toward proving what some of the authors of the original papers had contended. The United States was skilled in operations, in practice, in procedures; restless in the realms of theory, value, superior meaning. Once George Kennan had said, "For the future, I think we are really in the lap of the Gods, if you can take our international situation as an example. I don't believe that we have any great measure of control today over our fortunes at all in the world. I think we pretend that we do, but I think actually this is very, very far out of hand." When he said this no one took issue with the idea, but the better part of one day was spent in investigating the kind of machinery that might be concocted to bring the future under administrative control. When Oppenheimer suggested that the quality of life was at least as important as the government of a country, no one disagreed, but the discussion turned on the problem of how to distribute information so that the decisions of the government rather than the quality of life could be improved. In other matters also the conference had concentrated on things you could do something about. Confronted on the first night with the question of good and evil, it sought refuge in definition; asked twice by the visiting Englishman about "this question of tragedy" it examined something else; confronted by a paper on values it took interesting evasive action; offered a chance to talk about individuality it slid once again into definition and diversionary tactics. What had happened, in Rostow's words, was that "we have vacillated between a contemplation as honest as we could bring ourselves to make of our inadequacies and a review of our widely shared and often unexpressed values," which were left almost always unexpressed.

The last day was different. Riesman's opening comment, both witty and penetrating, on Rostow's paper was, in effect, a restatement of Oppenheimer's earlier concern for the quality of American life. These two essays—Rostow's and Riesman's—as Harry Murray said, if put together are a remarkable single document. Taken together they put the two halves of the conference—the honest contemplation and the hitherto unexpressed concerns—together. And they provided the means for a sustained and relaxed conversation on Sunday morning. Harry Murray began by urging the necessity of putting operational efficiency within some larger vision of American life. He asked for a new exciting view of ourselves that might serve as this vision. Clyde Kluckhohn agreed by saying that any life with meaning had to be engaged not only with perpetuating itself but also in surpassing itself.

George Kennan admitted that he was taken aback by any suggestion that we might or ought to have a vision of American civilization. But he confessed that he had one of sorts, not an adequate one, unquestionably a crude one—but, nevertheless, a view. It consisted first of the cultivation of the small beauties—the disappearance of the automobile dumps, the piggeries at the exit from the Lincoln Tunnel—of the development of sensible attractive arrangements in all our physical properties. It consisted also of the development of the community by unclogging the lines of communication along which simple messages passed. He saw the whole process of communication gummed up by the proliferation of meaningless material—mostly advertising. For revealing even so small a vision he had, he said, been accused at times of trying to play the part of Plato.

To Robert Oppenheimer part of our mission was to see that the concept of "the nation" as the dominant source of energy should lose its power. America had done much with the word fraternity—it had a persistent and real bearing on American life and style. There were grounds to hope that in time to come the influence of the sense of fraternity would act to limit other purely national energies. If one were to ask how the overriding, obsolete, dangerous power of the nation could be moderated, "I think one must look," he said,

to the growth of functioning international groups who work together many times on rather narrow problems—often torn apart by the governments' pulling back. Though we are not unique, we are well equipped to give meaning to the uses of fraternity and to look ahead in hope that the quality of our own life will be refreshed from foreign sources as well as by our own genius.

Mr. Wilson urged that our achievements should not be assessed by us too modestly. Viewing the United States from a distance he felt that the "really quite remarkable" thing about the country was how rapidly it was learning to handle the power at its disposal in the world. In the same vein McGeorge Bundy offered the opinion that "nothing in the nineteenth or eighteenth centuries except the formation of the union itself stands on a larger platform and is more entitled to respect than the developments which occurred between 1947 and 1950 in the behavior of the United States on the international scene."

Other elements of comfort and hope were also noted in the quality of our national life. It was said that the role of the intelligence appeared to be growing; that the relationship between learning and action was increasing, and that the people in universities have more and not less to do in society than they did fifty years ago. Other elements of challenge and opportunity were also noted. The most arresting was raised at the last moment when, for almost the first time, the subject of American industry was taken up at the suggestion of Mr. Norton-Taylor. He had admitted his legitimate surprise that a four-day conversation on America could omit any but the most casual references to American industrial energies and American industrialists.

Carl Kaysen, in response, suggested that the universal problem of any industrial society, which goes a great deal deeper than the intellectual presentation of the problem of socialism, lay in the relation of the worker to his work. This is a problem, he continued, that insofar as one could hear these things, was troubling the Russians too. The problem was:

How do you give somebody who is going to work in a big, impersonal, fragmented organization in which everything is characterized by the extreme division of labor—how do you give him some sense that this is real life? The romantic primitives are wrong in thinking that there is any alternative to the division of labor. We have an opportunity which is peculiar, for reasons of luck and also for reasons of what American values are, to grapple with this problem.

The efforts to grapple thus far did not impress Kaysen. They were in fact often pointed 160 degrees in the wrong direction; human relations and industrial sociology were frequently worse than anything Karl Marx ever had nightmares about. But the grapplings did show a concern. And if we wished to make other people see and understand what our values were—it seemed to Kaysen there was "within our tradition the material for dealing with this problem successfully, for contributing some great new social solution that would be peculiarly and characteristically an American invention."

On this note the discussions were brought to a close. An hour or two later, after lunch, people began to leave. Standing at the door of Endicott House, waiting for a cab to take him to Logan Airport a man said, "This was the best thing of its kind. We laid our lives on the table." It was true that on the last morning people had spoken freely of opportunities, challenges, fraternity, the possibility of even a crude vision, and the desire to surpass oneself. It was also true that in so speaking the conference appeared to achieve a kind of unity it had not before possessed. Four days and twenty miles from anywhere, with sun and conversation, had produced if not a band of brothers or a company of scholars at least a sense of fellowship among diversely educated men. Within this sense of fellowship it appeared on that Sunday as if the members of the conference might even have made some headway in resolving what Riesman had called the conflict between Thoreau and the

National Security Council. But maybe, as F. Scott Fitzgerald used to say, "it was merely personal" and, therefore, only momentary.

This conflict, noticed so many times in so many different ways by the men at the conference—as the ideal versus the material; the theory versus the practice; the true versus the possible—is, of course, the ancient counterpoint that works through the whole heritage. It was a subject of special concern at this conference, perhaps, because it had been at work in the actual lives of so many of those around the table. Most of the men present had made careers in the secluded freedom, the privatism of the library stall or the laboratory; but they had also, most of them, proceeded by government travel orders to give some service to the state. They had, some of the time, written their books and thought their own thoughts. But they had also, some of the time, sought lateral clearances, composed policy papers, and argued with men from other agencies. They in their time had at least thought about what might be true, and they had also tried to do what might be possible. So, in a sense, the gap between Walden and the Pentagon which they all talked about had been by their acts at least reduced if not wholly closed. Perhaps what they had been describing in their discussions was the pain and not the impossibility of doing what they said it was necessary to do.

And, what, more specifically, was it necessary to do? In the four days of discussion the conference had put together an agenda that may be summarized as follows: As for Americans:

Their fate is still in their own hands, but very soon they may lose control. The first of the duties that are at this time imposed upon those who direct our affairs is to educate democracy—to purify its morals, to mold its action, to substitute a knowledge of statecraft for its inexperience and an awareness of its true interest for its blind instincts, to adapt its government to time and place, and to modify it according to men and conditions. A new science of politics is needed for a new world.

This was the way Alexis de Tocqueville felt about it.

No doubt it is a little depressing that twenty-five learned Americans could find so little more to say about ourselves in 1957 than a single visiting Frenchman had said in 1835. It is also no doubt of some comfort to discover that as things have been they remain. But beyond small depression and somewhat less comfort, the similar views of de Tocqueville and the twenty-five suggest another thing. The given condition of people in a democracy is perpetual danger. At any moment of time, since things change, "they may very soon lose control." As long as this source of anxiety is recognized and lived with and used, the opportunity to educate, to purify, to substitute awareness of true interest for blind instinct, to adapt government to time and place—in a word, to retain fate, to some degree still in our own hands—remains. All this and a good deal more was said by Walt Rostow in the concluding comment he made at the request of the Chairman, Max Millikan, on Sunday morning:

One way the central question can be put is this: What is the relation be-tween the good life for the individual at home in modern America and the success of the national community on a dangerous and turbulent world scene? At the margin, of course, the question can be simplified by the obser-vation that there can be no good life at home unless the nation survives; and while this observation is not wholly irrelevant, it is distinctively evasive, and we should press beyond.

There are vast private areas in human life the reality and urgency of which make the affairs of foreign policy and the world around us seem often to be marginal and remote. There was a poll recently asking what people were most worried about in America; and it turned out to be money, children, and health—the worries of anybody, anytime, anywhere. And those concerned to apply science to human affairs should not forget that their task is to im-prove the quality of life in its broadest sense.

Nevertheless, in the United States and in most all other communities of the world, the quality of private life is not wholly independent of the commu-nity's vicissitudes and of its public policy. The world intrudes on our homes and families, in taxes, conscription, and the pervasive news of trouble. It creates an aura of uncertainty, ignorance, worry—a sense of common inade-quacy in dealing with the problems on which our common fate depends.

The weight with which this external dimension of experience is privately felt clearly varies; and I would take instruction on this point from those whose professional lives are devoted to the study of social life at all its levels. But, from what I can detect, the problems of America in the contemporary world significantly affect the quality of life for a high proportion of the national community.

In trying to understand the nation's external problems, to prescribe for them, and to act on this understanding and prescription it would be an illusion to think that the great issues of the second half of this century—to look no further ahead—are to be defined—let alone solved—once and for all. If any-thing is certain it is that, in one way or another, history is going to play on the wisest of us the kind of joke that Richard Hofstadter laid before us yes-terday with such precision and charm; that is, the emergence of situations and problems never anticipated, contrary to proudly developed analyses and passionately held convictions. Nevertheless, there is something to strive for;

and I would describe it simply this way—a public policy which permits a setting of good morale for our private lives.

Now in what does such a public policy consist? It consists first in leadership that uses the best minds and spirits of the nation to try to establish what our problems are and what alternative ways there are to deal with them which, if possible, strengthen and extend the expression of our basic moral and ethical values; and if that is impossible, ways which damage these values to the minimum.

Second, a leadership that clearly tells us what the choices are and, broadly, which is proposed for the common salvation.

Finally, a leadership which creates a sense and setting of participation—participation in both the final choice among alternatives and in the common efforts that follow from that process of decision.

This concept of morale holds for the smallest as well as the largest units I have ever been able to observe: for the children in my cabin when I was a counselor at camp; for military units, a university, a business firm. In the end, good morale, under circumstances of difficulty and pressure, is simply a facing up to the probable nature of dangers, combined with a sense of participation in whatever it is that can be done to limit those dangers and with a sense of confidence that the best conceivable measures have been chosen.

If this view of morale is correct the public and private sectors of our lives cannot be cleanly separated. If a sharp separation exists, it is between the view of men and women. We are saved by the fact that women screen out a great deal of the nonsense with which their ardent men of affairs concern themselves. More generally and more positively, the two realms—public and private life—converge in Harry Murray's vision of how a unique personality matures and finds fulfillment, emerging from a period of test and exploration and defiance into a partial but substantial dedication to goals beyond himself. These transcendent goals and commitments need not concern national policy; and they will concern national policy for, relatively, only a few. But a widely shared sense of where we are in the world and a sense of participation in what we seek to do as a community to save ourselves is essential.

Now, a final impression. Especially this morning—but also in general over the past three days—we have vacillated between a contemplation of American inadequacies—many of which are part of the human condition, some of which are special products of our society at this phase of its history—and an assertion of the will to see our hopes and ideals take on increased vitality.

The shifting dialectic is an invaluable method; but it requires a synthesis. To act wisely at the highest level requires that a sense of hope and tragedy be held firmly in suspension and, when tempered with irony and humor, that this suspension serve somehow as a basis for day-to-day action. I take something like this to be the implication of our happy contrapuntal exercise.

INDEX

Abegglen, James C., 155–56
Absolutism, 6–7, 15, 106
  moral, 42–51, 97–98
Abstraction, 44–45
Acheson, Dean G., 345
Adams, Dr., trial of, 394
Adams, Henry, 392
Adams, John Quincy, 270, 306, 360
Administration, 124–25
  anxious view of, 128–32
  basic faults in, 132–44
  commentary on, 334–52
  and national style, 278–86, 287–88,
    300, 308, 309
  problem of, 125
  reassuring view of, 126–28
Adorno, T. W., 198
Advertising, 104, 147, 171, 186
Advertising Council, 198
Aggression, 59, 78
Agrarianism, 32
Agriculture, Department of, 338, 344,
  350
Air Force, 304
Alaska, 269, 270
Albany Plan, 262
Aldridge, John W., 195
Alien and Sedition Acts, 267, 295
Allen, Frederick Lewis, 149, 156, 189,
  194, 206
Allport, Gordon W., 157, 167–68, 179,
  185, 244, 365
Almond, G. A., 166–67
Alsop, Stewart, 359
Alva, Duke of, 320
Americanism, 53, 62, 63–65, 68–69,
  104–5, 106, 197–98, 252
Amiens, Peace of, 270
Ananke, 14
Anglo-Chinese War, 270

Anti-intellectualism, 31–32
Aquinas, St. Thomas, 8, 15, 71
Aristotle, 20, 29, 46, 68, 71, 85, 88, 91,
  93, 100
Armed forces, faults in, 304–5
Army, 283–84, 304, 405
Articles of Confederation, 262, 263
Arts, 29, 30, 193–94, 241–43, 385–90
Atom bomb, 40, 142, 374, 377
Atomic Energy Commission, 344
Atomic radiation, 120, 121
Auden, W. H., 248
Augustus, 29
Authoritarianism, 81, 82, 97
Authority, concentration of, 136

Barr, Alfred H., Jr., 385, 386–88, 389,
  410
Barzun, Jacques, 193
Beck, Dave, 294
Beerbohm, Max, 43
Bellamy, Edward, 356, 364
Bentham, Jeremy, 16
Best sellers, value shifts in, 168, 169–71
Bigotry, 87
Bird, Caroline, 179, 182, 183, 189, 191
Bissell, Richard M., Jr., 371–72, 381,
  402, 404
Blaine, James G., 270
Blondie, 52–53
Bourgeois morality, 72
Brandeis, Louis D., 104, 393, 409
Braverman, Harry, 198
Brogan, D. W., 156, 181–82, 185, 193
Brown, John, 232
Bryan, William Jennings, 57
Bryce, James, 12, 32, 47, 58, 61, 70, 86,
  150, 151–52, 153, 276
Bryson, Lyman, 202, 205, 399, 400–401
Buber, Martin, 53

Buddha, 57
Bundy, McGeorge, 373–74, 384, 385, 388, 389, 392 ff., 396, 409, 412
Burdick, Eugene, 206
Bureaucracy, 131, 138, 143, 223, 278–79, 280, 285, 286, 287–88, 299–300, 303, 305, 308, 309, 356, 367, 403
Burke, Edmund, 105
Burma, 338
Business cycle, 277
Butler, Samuel, 233
Byron, George Gordon, 388

Calhoun, Arthur W., 178
Calhoun, John C., 270
California, 98, 146, 197, 233
Calvinism, 250
Canada, 269, 270
Canning, George, 269
Capitalism, and national style, 274, 276, 289, 294, 296, 328
Case, Clifford, 150, 194
Cash, Wilbur J., 366
Center for International Studies, 205
Chambers, Clark A., 168
Chaplin, Charles S., 39, 190
Character, 43, 46–47
Chase, Mary Ellen, 200
Cheevy, Miniver, 230
Chicago, 359
China, 270–71, 297, 306, 338
Christianity, 9, 10, 30
City College of New York, 63
Civil service, 142, 288
Civil War, 258, 264–67, 268 ff., 275, 283, 296, 365–66, 403
Claire, René, 39
Clay, Henry, 270
Clayton Act, 322
Coffey, Joseph I., 377–78, 390–91, 392, 410
Cognitivism, 22–23
Coignard, Abbé, 221
Cold War, 40, 121, 125, 126, 291, 292–93, 295–99, 357, 364, 366
Coleman, Lee, 149
Collective judgment, 130
Collectivism, 89
College students, values of, 163–68, 175–77
Collins, Jerome, 157, 169–70
Colorado, 168
Comic strips, value changes in, 199

Commerce Department, 344
Committee for Economic Development, 162
Committees, and administration, 135–36, 294, 342
Communism, 7, 37, 47, 64, 71, 75, 76, 80, 81, 82, 85, 97, 103, 104, 146, 162, 185, 244, 324, 364, 387, 398
    and American idealism, 296–98, 306, 309
    power, conflict with, 111–14, 117, 122
Compromise, 50–51, 285, 366, 403
Conformity, 61–70, 104–5, 179, 187–89, 194, 196, 202–4, 223, 325–26, 370–71
Confucius, 103
Congress, 33, 79, 94, 130, 142, 344, 348
Conscience, 50, 62
Consent, 76
Conservatism, 15, 204
Constitution, 97, 136
    and national style, 251, 261–64, 268, 274, 295, 307
Constitutional Convention, 261, 262, 265, 266
Constitutionalism, 52, 82–83
Contextualism, 94
Control, governmental, 194
Controversy, 64
Coolidge, Calvin, 294
Coordination, method of, 22
Corning Glass Works, 198
Couch and Keniston, research of, 221
Cowley, Malcolm, 179
Cozzens, James Gould, 246
Crimean War, 270
Crisis mentality, 103–4
Croce, Benedetto, 8, 100
Croly, Herbert, 276
cummings, e. e., 3
Cushing, Caleb, 270

Dante Alighieri, 106
Darwinian theory, 228
Day, Clarence, 355
Debs, Eugene V., 276, 364
Declaration of Independence, 15, 20, 21, 263, 265
Dedham, Mass., 395
Defense Department, 304
Deism, 250
Democracy, 6, 7, 9, 13, 21, 50, 67, 71–72, 73, 75, 77, 81, 83–84, 86, 88–89,

91–93, 96, 97, 101, 105, 251, 330–33, 399
Depression, 155, 276–78, 287, 354, 357, 368
Depth psychology, 81
Descartes, René, 30
Desegregation, 41, 105
Determinism, 80
Dewey, John, 8–9, 18, 22, 25, 30, 31, 36, 40, 50, 51, 81, 103, 255, 308, 398
Dickinson, Emily, 233
Dictatorships, 70, 92
Diplomacy, 74, 75–76, 102
    and administration, 126, 138–40
    and national interest, 269–72
    See also Foreign affairs
Disagreement, 26–27
Discrimination, 88, 99
Distributive justice, 85
Diversity, 63, 114, 117–18, 197
Dogmatism, 49
Donne, John, 119
Doolittle, Liza, 58
Dornbusch, Sanford M., 157, 168–69, 171, 177–78, 183, 184
Dostoevski, Feodor, 9, 77, 388
Drucker, Peter F., 186
Dualistic code, 27–35, 81
DuBois, Cora, 204
Dulles, John Foster, 345, 409
Duveen, Joseph, 28

Eastman, George, 280
Ecclesiastes, 319
Economic royalists, 52
Economics, 274
Education, 111–14, 116–17, 122, 255, 308–9
    increase in, 289–90
Edwards, Jonathan, 398
Efficiency, 37–38
Egalitarianism, 114, 131
Egypt, 67, 121
Einstein, Albert, 98
Eisenhower, Dwight D., 272, 359
Eisenhower Doctrine, 297
Eliot, T. S., 242, 248, 319, 358, 360
Elite, 71–72, 76
Elizabeth I, Queen, 29
Elkins Act, 322
Embargo, 267
Emerson, Ralph Waldo, 63, 106, 232
Emerson Hall, Harvard University, 12

Emotivism, 22
Empiricism, 9, 76, 115
    as foundation of values, 18–27
Endicott House, 395–96, 413
England, 24, 52, 53, 59, 68, 73, 99, 114, 117, 136, 206, 247, 253, 261, 267, 269–70, 271–72, 274, 324, 366, 380, 393–94
Enlightenment, 21, 24, 250, 298
Entrepreneurship, 156
Epictetus, 20
Equality, 12–13, 14, 84–86, 88, 90, 99, 105
Erikson, Erik H., 190, 198, 236
Eros, 59
Ethics and public policy:
    commentary on, 319–26
    conclusion, 101–7
    conformity, code of, 61–70
    dualistic code, 27–35
    empirical foundations of values, 18–27
    introduction, 3–8
    metaphysical foundations of values, 8–18
    methodology of morals, 90–101
    moral absolutism, 42–51
    morality and power, 70–80
    moralization, 52–61
    political ideals, 80–90
    vulgar pragmatism, 35–42
Eudaemonian fallacy, 68, 71
Eurasia, 271–72, 296–97
Experience, 21, 24, 25
Experts, team of, 118
Exploitation, 72
Export-Import Bank, 347, 351

Far East, 270–71, 374–75
Far West, 197
Farber, Maurice L., 191
Fascism, 37, 52, 73, 74, 364, 388
Faulkner, William, 242
Faust, 59
Fava, F. F., 157
Federal Reserve Bank of New York, 345
Federal Reserve System, 276
Federalist Papers, 21, 61, 91, 262
Fiddle, Seymour, 188
Fidelity insurance, 393
Films, plots of, 160–62
Fish, Hamilton, 270
Fitzgerald, F. Scott, 414
Ford, Henry, 280, 320–21

Ford Motor Company, 304
Foreign Affairs, 112
Foreign affairs, 33, 48, 54, 69, 71, 95
  and administration, 126–27, 129–31,
    134–35, 138–42, 285–86, 346–52
  and national style, 267–72, 296–98,
    305–7
  policy in, 112, 121
  and pragmatism, 115
  See also Diplomacy
Formosa, 324, 338
Fort Sumter, 265
Fortune magazine, 146, 223
Foster, Margaret P., 171–72
France, 24, 53, 68, 114, 187, 267, 269
  ff., 338, 350, 357, 366, 371
Franklin, Benjamin, 96–97, 247
Fraternity, 12–13, 86–88, 90, 105
Freedom, 81, 98, 136, 295, 328
Freud, Sigmund, 36, 50, 196, 231, 243,
  357
Freund, Paul A., 393–94, 401
Friedmann, F. G., 184, 192
Fromm, Erich, 50, 183, 186, 202, 203,
  371
Frontier, 118, 119, 257, 290
Frost, Robert, 397

Galantiere, Lewis, 156, 194, 206
Gambling, 58
Gandhi, Mohandas K., 221
Gardner, Trevor, 304–5
Garrison, William Lloyd, 221
General Motors Corporation, 105, 304
Genêt, Citizen, 267
George, Henry, 274
Germany, 40, 53, 128, 255, 269, 271,
  322
G.I. culture, 234
Gibbs, Josiah W., 116
Gillespie, James, 166, 179, 185
Gimmick society, 188
Glazer, Nathan, 184–85
Goldman, Eric, 149
Good neighbor policy, 61
Gould, Jay, 354, 355
Government, administration of, *see* Ad-
  ministration
Greenwalt, C. H., 187
Groupism, 232, 234, 235
Guided-missiles program, 304–5

Hale, William H., 193

Hamilton, Alexander, 21, 274, 294
Harris, Kenneth, 194
Harris, Louis, 359, 362
Harris, Townsend, 271
Hartz, Louis, 305
Harvard University, 12, 148, 223, 235,
  372
Hebrew University, 53
Hedonism, 192–94
Hegel, G. W. F., 5, 9, 37, 72, 73, 97,
  357
Heresy, 65, 104
Heterodoxy, 97
Heterogeneity, as value, 196–98, 204
Hickman, Lauren, 171
Hicks, Granville, 203
Himmelhoch, J., 157
Hiroshima, 65
History, 73, 75, 148, 155, 193
Hitler, Adolf, 74–75, 76
Hobbes, Thomas, 7, 15, 19, 65, 72
Hofstadter, Richard, 369 ff., 376, 406,
  407, 409, 415
Hollingshead, 153
Holmes, Oliver Wendell, 48, 82, 257,
  366
Homans, George C., 202
Homogeneity, social, 290, 295
Hook, Sidney, 10, 191
Hoover, Herbert C., 278
Hopson, A. L. B., 157, 168, 183
Horkheimer, 189
Household, national, 248–49, 293–94
Howard, Leon, 199
Hubris, 15
Huckleberry Finn, 179
Hughes, H. Stuart, 154, 197
Human rights, 86
Hume, David, 17, 23, 243
Humphrey, George M., 296
Hungary, 60, 363, 375, 377
Huxley, Aldous, 39
Hydrogen bomb, 363
Hypocrisy, 58

ICBM project, 304
Ickes, Harold L., 79
Idea of the Good, 46
Idealism, 8, 12, 33–35, 73, 77, 365
  contemporary role of, 294–99
Ideals, political, 80
  unifying function of, 249–52
Ideas, operator's way with, 252–56

Ideological offensive, 7
Ideology, 31
Immigration, 84, 106–7, 253, 290
Incentive system, 329–30, 332
Income, real, increase and stability of, 288, 299
Income tax, 86, 98, 276, 368
India, 117, 338
Indian wars, 270
Individualism, 88–90, 151, 162–63, 185–87, 191, 273–74, 307–8, 353, 355
Individuality, 88, 187, 190, 353
   discussion of, 218–45, 378–94
Indonesia, 121, 338
Industrialization, 272–78, 299
Industry, and national style, 302–3
Infant Care Bulletin, 184
Initialing system, State Department, 135
Inkeles, Alex, 180, 195
Inner-directedness, 157, 166, 171, 325, 354, 355
Integration, 12
Intellectual level, rise in, 289–90
Intellectual values, 30–32
International Cooperation Administration, 347, 351
Intuition, moral, 17, 62
Irish-Americans, 367
Israel, 67
Italy, 73, 88

Jackson, Andrew, 294
Jacob, Philip E., 163–65, 167, 185, 205
James, William, 12, 36, 59, 115, 116, 119, 308
Japan, 271, 306
Japanese-Americans, 40, 295
Jay, John, 270
Jay's Treaty, 269
Jefferson, Thomas, 13, 21, 31, 63, 64, 82
   and national style, 247, 267, 268–69, 274–75, 277, 294
Job, Book of, 13, 40–41, 321
Joint Chiefs of Staff, 112, 285, 303, 404, 409
Jonas, Carl, 385, 388, 394, 409
Jordan, 364
Jung, C. G., 231, 243
Juvenile delinquency, 178–79

Kafka, Franz, 145, 151, 243
Kangieser, Helen G., 170–71, 189

Kant, Immanuel, 5, 22, 42–43, 44, 72, 90, 96, 97
Kaplan, Abraham, 247, 319, 322 ff., 327, 372–73, 375–76, 378, 382–83, 397, 400
Kardiner, Abram, 157, 202
Kaysen, Carl, 381–82, 403, 404–5, 413
Keats, John, 239
Kefauver, Estes, 360
Kennan, George F., 247, 334, 335, 341, 352, 376–77, 400, 401–3, 406, 407, 410–12
Keynes, John Maynard, 278, 368
Kimbrough, Emily, 200–201
Kindliness, 60–61
Kinsey, Alfred C., 38
Kinship system, American, 202
Kissinger, 112
Kluckhohn, Clyde, 145, 148, 151, 219, 247, 299, 319, 353–54, 357, 370, 371, 381, 393, 405 ff., 411
Kluckhohn, Florence, 148, 157, 202
Knowland, William F., 367
Komarovsky, 154
Korean War, 60, 292, 293, 297, 359, 369, 370–71, 376, 409
Kouwenhoven, John A., 190, 194

La Barre, Weston, 199
Labor Department, 344
Ladies Home Journal, 171
Laski, Harold J., 33, 44, 54, 63, 71, 106
Lasswell, H. D., 55, 56, 73
Law, 43, 52, 71, 257, 258
Lawrence, D. H., 243, 251, 392
Leadership, 70, 105, 162, 284, 416
Lecky, W. E., 29
Lee, Dorothy, 157, 172–74
Leisure-time activities, 192–94
Leites, Nathan, 160–62, 175
Lenin, Nikolai, 72
Lewis, C. I., 24
Libel and slander, 393–94
Liberalism, 106, 365
Liberty, 12–13, 80–84, 88, 90, 105, 328
Liberty League, 52
Libido, 59
Life magazine, 200–202
Lincoln, Abraham, 57, 58, 63
   and national style, 264–67, 268, 297, 364
Lindner, Robert, 183
Lippmann, Walter, 8, 101–2

Locke, John, 15, 19, 23, 71, 75, 76, 85
London *Economist*, 128
London *Times*, 324
Louisiana Territory, 270
Löwe, Adolph, 366
Lowell, Francis Cabot, 279–80
Loyalty, morality of, 47–48
Luce publications, 187–88
Lynd, Robert, 152
Lynes, Russell, 204, 233

MacArthur, Douglas, 374, 377, 409
McCarthyism, 147, 179–80, 187, 295, 296, 360, 366, 367
McDonald, David J., 294
McGinley, Phyllis, 201
Machiavelli, Niccolò, 73–74
Machines, and values, 189–91
McKinley, William, 294
McLuhan, H. M., 186, 188, 189
Madison, James, 21, 61
Magic, verbal, 53–54
Mahan, Alfred Thayer, 272, 298
Majority rule, 98–99, 121
Malik, Charles, 403
Manchuria, 372
Mann, Thomas, 242
Mannheim, Karl, 55
Marcus Aurelius, 51
Maritain, Jacques, 9, 10
Marquand, John P., 227
Marshall, George C., 345
Marshall, John, 264, 274
Marshall Plan, 297, 374, 403
Marx, Karl, 71, 73, 243, 413
Mass production, 190, 279
Massachusetts Institute of Technology, 400
Materialism, 27–31, 71, 101–2, 105, 162–63, 225, 299
Mather, Cotton, 5, 294
Maupassant, Guy de, 105
Mead, Margaret, 156, 157, 179, 195–96, 200
Melville, Herman, 221, 232
Men, changing role of, 199–202
Merriam, Charles E., 11, 55
Merton, Robert, 223
Metaphysics, as foundation of values, 8–18, 53
Mexican War, 270
Meyer, Agnes E., 203
Miami University, 167

Michels, Robert, 74, 83
Middle class, 146–47
Middle East, 33–34, 60, 67, 306
Military services, faults in, 304–5
Mill, John Stuart, 29, 82, 378, 379, 389, 391
Miller, William, 155
Millikan, M. F., 115, 116, 321, 384–85, 386, 394, 415
Mills, C. Wright, 158, 189
Milton, John, 82
"Miranda" of politics, 11
Missiles program, 304–5
Missouri Compromise, 265
Mobility, occupational, 155–56
Modern Republicanism, 52
Monopoly, 275
Monroe Doctrine, 269–70
Moore, G. E., 21
Morality, methodology of, 90–101
    and morale, 41
    and power, 70–80
Moralization, 52–61
Morgan, J. P., 325
Morison, Elting E., 370–71, 394
Morocco, 364
Morrill Act, 255
Morris, Charles, 149, 156, 165–66, 167, 183, 185, 197, 229
Morris, William, 356
Morrison, Theodore, 145
Mosca, Gaetano, 74
Moscow Embassy, 128–29
Moses, 45
Motion pictures, plots of, 160–62
Muckraking, 276
Muller, H. J., 188
Municipal reform, 33
Murray, H. A., 147, 247, 319, 363, 368, 379, 380, 384, 385–86, 388–89, 391, 409 ff., 416
Mussolini, Benito, 74, 75
Myrdal, Gunnar, 12, 147, 153, 252, 365

Naegele, Kaspar, 152–55
Napoleon Bonaparte, 269
Napoleonic Wars, 267
National Academy of Sciences, 120, 121
National Association of Manufacturers, 162
National Bank, 274
National Science Foundation, 31

National Security Council, 112, 134–35, 285, 303, 368, 414
Nationalism, 249–50, 258, 293–94
NATO, 297, 306, 402
Natural law, 8, 14–21, 48, 250
Natural rights, 6, 14–21, 71, 76
Naturalism, 25–26, 65
Naval War College, 112
Navy, 283–84, 304
Nazism, 81, 117, 122
Negativism, 221
Negro, status of, 265–66, 290
Neo-Freudianism, 175
Neo-Kantianism, 9
New Deal, 32, 52, 277–78, 368
New England, 118, 146, 250, 252, 279–80
New Freedom, 276
New Orleans, 266
New Testament, 321
Newcomer, Mabel, 155–56
Niebuhr, Reinhold, 205, 250
Nietzsche, F. W., 68, 73
Noah, 91
Nonconformism, 63, 162
North, and slavery, 264–65
Northrop, F. S. C., 145
Norton-Taylor, Duncan, 383–84, 412–13
Novels, value shifts in, 195
    See also Best sellers
NRA, 277–78
Nuclear energy, 102–3, 155, 399, 402

Occupational mobility, 155
Office of International Security Affairs, 349
Oligarchy, 83
O'Neill, Eugene, 242, 388
Operationism, 94
Oppenheimer, J. Robert, 247, 321, 327, 328, 331, 332, 365, 369 ff., 379, 380, 382, 385, 388, 389–90, 392, 398–99, 400 ff., 405, 408, 411, 412
Ortega y Gasset, José, 28
Orthodoxy, 65, 104
Orwell, George, 39, 46
Other-directedness, 157, 166, 171, 183, 186, 191–92, 218, 326, 355
Ownership, 85–86
Oxford University, 194

Palmer raids, 295
Pareto, Vilfredo, 55, 74

Parkinson's Law, 128, 341, 405
Parrington, V. L., 156
Parsons, Talcott, 179–80
Partisan Review, 225
Paternalism, 131–32
Pearson, Lester, 403
Peerism, 226, 234, 237
Peirce, Charles, 5, 36, 115, 116, 223
Pentagon Building, 125, 129, 304, 338, 347 ff., 414
People, and morality, 76–77, 91–92
Pericles, 29, 81
Perry, Matthew C., 271
Perry, Ralph Barton, 150 ff., 185, 186
Personality, defined, 147
    and politics, 81–82
Personnel, and administration, 127–28, 132–34, 141–42, 293
Petofi Club, 363
Philippine Islands, 323
Phillips, H. P., 159–60
Plato, 8, 30, 46, 51, 59, 75, 76, 88, 96, 412
Platonism, 42
Plays, value shifts in, 172–74
Pluralism, 83, 117–18
Plymouth colony, 250
PM (newspaper), 331
Poe, Edgar Allan, 388
Poland, 363
Policy Planning Staff, State Department, 112
Poor, Henry Varnum, 281, 283
Potter, David M., 155, 377, 398, 400
Power, and morality, 70–80
Pragmatism, 12
    and foreign policy, 115–16
    vulgar, 35–42, 74, 77, 102
Prejudice, 87
President, and administration, 131, 135 ff., 139 ff., 143, 283, 286, 337, 341, 348
Press, free, 79
Principles, 43–44, 47
Privacy, right of, 104
Probability, 96
Profit motive, 68
Progressive movement, 276, 288
Prometheus, 59
Propaganda, 52, 55–56, 71, 78–79, 102
Property, 85–86, 263
Prophets, 43
Protestant Ethic, 183–85, 225, 353

Protestantism, 12, 13, 146, 250, 251
Psychiatry, 50
Psychological health, value upon, 194–96
Psychology, depth, 81
Puritanism, 59, 156, 179, 184–85, 187, 192, 198, 199, 353, 396, 407–8

Quotas, 99

Ranke, Leopold von, 308
Rationalism, 77
Reaction formation, 357
Readers, third grade, value shifts in, 171–72
Realism, 77, 92–94, 163, 365
Realpolitik, 74, 92
Reconstruction, 266
Relativism, 25–26, 51, 66
Radar-orientation, 186, 192
Radcliffe College, 167
Radford, Arthur W., 409
Radhakrishnan, Sri, 32
Railways, and administration, 281, 283
Religion, 370
    and American ideals, 250
    college students, value shifts of, 167–68
    literature, value shifts in, 168–69, 180
    social, 11–14
    value shifts in, 198–99
Representation, doctrine of, 75–76
Republican party, 359
Resources, national, 113, 252
Revolutions, American, 50, 267, 269, 271
    French, 267, 366, 391
Rieff, Philip, 225
Riesman, David, 35, 157, 166, 171, 175–77, 182–83, 184–85, 186, 191–92, 218, 223, 227, 307, 325, 370, 387, 391–93, 400, 403, 411, 413
Ritualism, 53–54, 56
Robinson, G. T., 199
Rockefeller, John D., 280, 354, 355
Roosevelt, Franklin D., 52, 272, 277, 278, 294
Roosevelt, Theodore, 59, 68, 322
Root, Elihu, 322
Roseborough, H. E., 159–60
Rossi, Peter, 180
Rostow, W. W., 112, 149, 319, 321, 357, 358, 360–62, 364 ff., 374–75, 397, 404, 411, 415–16
Rousseau, Jean-Jacques, 5, 20, 75, 243
Royce, Josiah, 12, 410

Ruskin, John, 388
Russell, Bertrand, 14, 23, 36, 63, 93
Russell, Richard B., 374
Russia, 25, 54, 56, 67, 78, 94, 102, 107, 128–29, 240, 270, 271, 304, 305, 324, 329–30, 348, 361–62, 363, 367, 378, 387, 399, 413
    and education, 111–12, 117
Russian Research Center, 159

Sado-masochism, 198
Santayana, George, 5–6, 32, 49, 61, 64, 205, 246
Schlesinger, Arthur, Jr., 204
Schlesinger, Arthur, Sr., 150, 151, 373, 407
Schneider, David M., 202
Schneider, Louis, 157, 168–69, 184
Schopenhauer, Arthur, 105–6
Science, 24, 43, 90, 93, 102–3
    and education, 111–12, 115, 116–18, 290
    and government, 120
Scientism, 38–39, 51
Scodel, Alvin, 157, 174–75
Sears, Roebuck & Company, 280
Security, 76, 77, 79, 114, 132–33, 138, 141, 285, 293, 295, 303
Segregation, 99, 295
Selective Service, 293
Self-righteousness, 60
Separate but equal facilities, 84
Sermon on the Mount, 56
Seward, William H., 270
Sex, value shifts relating to, 157
Sexualization, 58
Shakespeare, William, 239
Shaw, George Bernard, 15, 33, 59, 65, 99, 243
Sheldon, Charles M., 364
Sherman Antitrust Act, 322
Siberia, 270
Silone, Ignazio, 88
Simon, Herbert, 281, 282
Sirjamaki, John, 152
Skinner, Cornelia Otis, 201
Slavery, 12, 264–66, 366
Smith, Adam, 279
Smith, M. B., 197
Social Darwinism, 36, 73
Socialism, 52, 75, 276, 329, 364
Socrates, 29, 31, 42, 57, 95, 116
Solon, 45

Songs, popular, value shifts in, 174–75
Sophists, 116
Sophocles, 15
South, 118, 146, 258–59, 264–66, 290, 305
South Africa, 121
South Carolina, 275
Spanish-American War, 284
Specialization, 3, 120, 284
Speech, free, 82
Spengler, Oswald, 73
Spindler, George D., 167, 180–81
Spinoza, Baruch, 15, 20, 57, 65, 70, 76
Square Deal, 276
Stalin, Joseph, 272, 374
Standardization, 66
Stanford University, 167
State, and morality, 71–73
State Department, 95, 112, 377
    and administration, 124, 127, 129–30, 135, 283, 338, 344–45, 347–49, 404–5, 406
    Foreign Service, 127, 128, 131, 350–52
    Secretary of State, 137, 139, 141, 143, 270, 283, 345, 347, 348
Statesmanship, 91, 103
    and administration, 126
Statism, 72
Statue of Liberty, 106
Stevenson, Adlai E., 359, 362–63
Stevenson, Charles, 9
Stoics, 15, 20
Stouffer, S. A., 157, 162, 167, 179, 184, 185, 197, 198, 205
Strategy, policy in, 112, 120, 122
Strunsky, Robert, 195, 203
Style, national, 247–48
    assessment of, 307–10
    changes and problems, 286–310
        domestic society, 287–91
        idealism, role of, 294–99
        and national household, 293–94
        incentives and alternatives, 299–300
        problems, solution of, 300–307
        world power status, impact of, 291–93
    classic style, 248–61
        American household, 248–49
        continuity, success, and ad hoc formula, 256–61
        operator's way with ideas, 252–56
        unifying function of American ideals, 249–52
    classic style in action, 261–86
        Constitution, 261–64
        concept of national interest to 1898, 267–72
        industrialization and individualist society, 272–78
        large-scale administration, 278–86
        Lincoln and Civil War, 264–67
    commentary on, 358–68
Subjectivism, 26, 66, 100
Suburbanization, 287
Suez Canal crisis, 306
Supreme Court, 258, 262, 264, 278
Sutton, Francis X., 156, 162–63, 184, 189, 195
Symbol specialists, 32
Symbolism, 11–12, 52, 53, 54–56, 78–79
Syracuse, University of, 167–68

Taiwan, see Formosa
Tao, 14
Tariff, 274–75, 345, 349
Taste, popular, 193
Taussig and Joslyn, study of executives, 155
Taylor, Francis Henry, 387
Taylorism, 279, 283
Tawney, R. H., 105
Teaching, 111–12, 117, 122
Technology, 29, 66, 102–3, 111, 122, 279
Theocracy, 252
Thermonuclear weapons, 155
Thoreau, Henry David, 221, 232, 233, 368, 413
Thrasymachus, 72
Thurber, James, 199
Time magazine, 175, 364
Tocqueville, Alexis de, 41, 84, 90, 150, 186, 203, 247, 251–52, 253–54, 305, 356, 414
Tolerance, 87, 198
Torah, 14
Tradition, 61–62
Tragedy, sense of, 369–70
Treasury Department, 344, 345, 347, 349, 351
Trilling, Lionel, 196
Truman, Harry S., 272, 296, 409
Truman Doctrine, 115, 297, 298
Truths, old and new, 119–20
Turner, Frederick Jackson, 247

Two-party system, 262, 264
Tyranny, 58, 72

Undershaft, Stephen, 99
Unemployment, 276–78
United Nations, 205, 297, 298, 337, 374
    Universal Declaration of Human Rights, 9–10, 15–16
United States Chamber of Commerce, 162
United States Information Agency, 338, 348
Unity, national, 265–66, 275
Upper Bohemians, 233
Urbanization, 287, 299
Utilitarian fallacy, 40
Utilitarianism, 37, 273–74
Utopias, 356

Valentine, Alan, 149, 156, 194
Values, shifts in:
    applications to politics and international affairs, 205–6
    background, 148–58
    commentary on, 353–57
    discussion, 202–4, 369–78
    introduction, 145–48
    reconstruction, 178–202
    research results, 158–78
    theory vs. practice in, 111–23
    commentary on, 327–33
Van Buren, Martin, 270
Veblen, Thorstein, 68, 116
Venezuela Boundary Dispute, 269
Verbalism, 53–55, 93, 94
Vernacular tradition, 194
Viet Minh, 297
Violence, 78
Virginia, University of, 31
Vogt, E. Z., 158
Voltaire, 243
Voluntarism, 407

Vulgar pragmatism, 35–42, 74, 77, 102

Wagner Act, 278
Wanghia, treaty of, 270
War Industries Board, 277
War of 1812, 264, 267
Warner, W. Lloyd, 155–56
Washington, George, 267–68, 271, 306
Washington, D.C., 107
Weber, Max, 5, 44, 60, 94, 101, 223, 225–26
Webster, Daniel, 270
Weimar Constitution, 76
Welfare state, acceptance of, 288–89
West, and national unity, 266
Whatmough, 189
White, Morton, 378–79, 382, 385, 391
White, William S., 401
Whitman, Walt, 232
Whitney, Eli, 247, 279
Whyte, William H., Jr., 154, 184, 187, 189, 192, 226
Williams, Roger, 294
Wilson, A. T. M., 369, 379–81, 389, 392, 393, 403, 408–9, 412
Wilson, Woodrow, 272, 275, 294, 364, 374
Wisconsin, University of, 168
Wolfenstein, Martha, 160–62, 175, 184
Women, value shifts relating to, 157, 177–78, 199–202, 204
Workmanship, instinct of, 68
World power status, impact of, 291–93
World War I, 7, 40, 63, 117, 121, 122, 125, 155, 275, 277, 287, 289, 298, 364, 368
World War II, 40, 117, 121, 122, 125, 136, 155, 234, 272, 278, 287 ff., 293, 295, 298, 303, 364–65, 374

Yeats, William Butler, 241
Youth, lawlessness of, 178–79

Set in Electra
Format by Seamus Byrne
Manufactured by The Haddon Craftsmen, Inc.
Published by HARPER & BROTHERS, *New York*